KING HENRY VIII's MARY ROSE

KING HENRY VIII's
MARY ROSE

ALEXANDER McKEE

STEIN AND DAY / *Publishers* / New York

First published in the United States of America
    by Stein and Day/*Publishers*/in 1974.
Copyright © 1973 by Alexander McKee
Library of Congress Catalog Card No. 73-93035
All rights reserved
Printed in the United States of America
Stein and Day/*Publishers*/Scarborough House, Briarcliff Manor, N.Y. 10510
ISBN 0-8128-1656-0

CONTENTS

LIST OF ILLUSTRATIONS

FOREWORD

I cannot remember when I first heard about the fate of the *Mary Rose*. Probably it was as a boy, playing in the pools of the rocky foreshores at Bembridge in the Isle of Wight. The story of how the French had stormed ashore across those beaches was a well-worn item of local history (although everyone else in England always assumed that the last foreign invasion had been in 1066). The passing close inshore of the Spanish Armada under heavy English attack in 1588 had left no mark on the island, whereas some of the villages and havens wiped out by the French troops in 1545 had disappeared literally from the face of the earth and in modern times there was no trace of them. Much later, I was to comprehend exactly what it felt like to see an enemy commanding the waters immediately offshore of Portsmouth and the Wight and to watch the smoke of fires rising from the downs above Bonchurch, 405 years, almost to the day, after actual invaders had scaled those heights. The fact that the 1940 target was a radar station dive-bombed by German stukas, instead of a village and its surrounding farms fired by French soldiers in armour, made no difference to me; the experience was essentially the same and anyway both are "history" now. That is, we know how the story ended.

The oddest thing, I find, is that as a boy I must have passed many times directly over the remains of the *Mary Rose* when crossing between Portsmouth and the Wight in ferry steamers. But I did not know and nor did anyone else, for the precise site of that Tudor tragedy had long been lost when I began my search in 1965. Nor, at the start, did I suspect that the remains were buried entirely and that I was looking for an invisible wreck. But it was so, and consequently the later stages of my enquiry consisted of that rare process in what is sometimes grandly called "underwater archaeology" and is often merely the random collection of material from the seabed, a genuine excavation, complete with deep, straight-sided and properly tagged trenches.

Although my object is to raise the ship and the remains of

that Tudor naval and military society which went down with her, I have only once, when underwater, been conscious of their nearness to me. That was when we had just begun our first cautious examination of the buried hull and I had gone down at the end of the day, when it was night on the seabed, to check on the progress of the dig along with a score or so of ghostly fish seeking fresh morsels from the excavated clay. Then indeed I thought of the dead men lying perhaps only a few feet away and remembered that I knew only two of them by name and reputation, Sir George Carew and Roger Grenville. Even more strangely, when further progress had exposed a dead man trapped in the upper levels of the wreckage, my attitude was entirely clinical—I examined his remains carefully to see if it really was one man and not just a collection of bones.

To the layman, more accustomed to reading about wrecks accidentally discovered, it may seem surprising, although to the archaeologist it is the rule, that thorough research precedes the search which precedes the excavation which in turn determines what is to be done with the site. But a structure without its context means nothing at all. As a professional historian, although only an amateur archaeologist, I knew from the first that I needed to know as much as possible about the ship itself, the sort of battle for which it was designed, the people who manned it and much general background besides, and not merely where, how and why she sank (although these questions were vital during the search phase). The *Mary Rose* was particularly interesting because so little was in fact known and long hours spent sitting in musty, old-fashioned libraries were just as important as swimming 50 to 90 feet down over the sordid and depressing clay plains which somehow, somewhere, concealed Henry VIII's revolutionary battleship, the direct ancestor of H.M.S. *Victory*.

They proved equally rewarding in the end and it was sometimes a curious sensation to take up a bundle of old parchments with faded pink seals and, while trying to transcribe the phonetic Tudor penmanship, realise suddenly that almost the last man before me to so closely study that document was Henry VIII himself. The man who gradually revealed himself to me in his decisions and actions was statesman, general and

admiral combined. As such, he plays a large part in my opening pages, a most unusual character—King Henry VIII without the wives! And perhaps I may be forgiven if I say that in
my humble opinion this is the real Henry VIII.

ALEXANDER McKEE

Pine Beach, Hayling Island, October, 1972

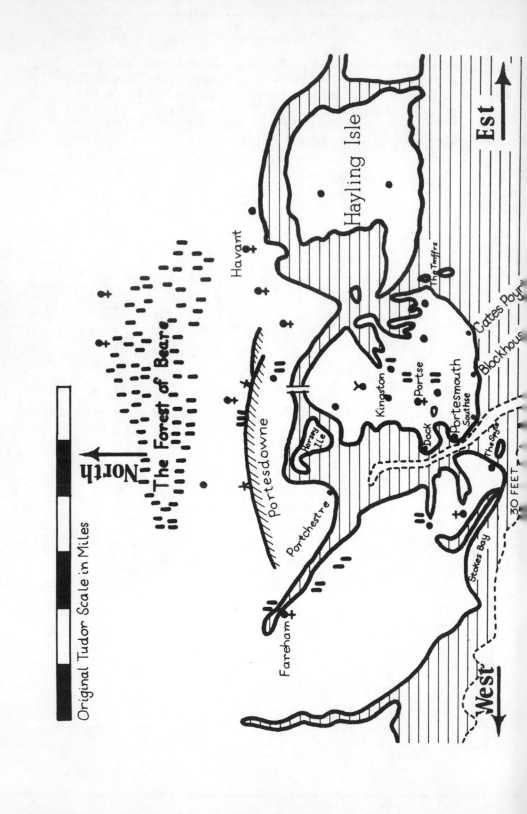

Original Tudor Scale in Miles

North

The Forest of Beare

Havant

Portesdowne

Portchestre

Horsey Isle

Kingston

Dock

Portse

Portsmouth

Southse

The Toffrs

Cates Poynt

Blockhous

The Seyle

30 FEET

Stokes Bay

Fareham

Hayling Isle

Est

West

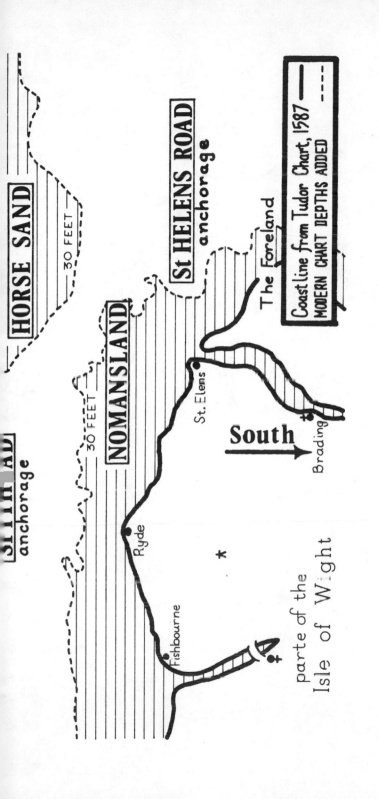

HORSE SAND

30 FEET

St HELENS ROAD anchorage

NOMANSLAND

30 FEET

anchorage

The Foreland

Coastline from Tudor Chart, 1587
MODERN CHART DEPTHS ADDED

St. Elens

South

Brading

Ryde

Fishbourne

parte of the
Isle of Wight

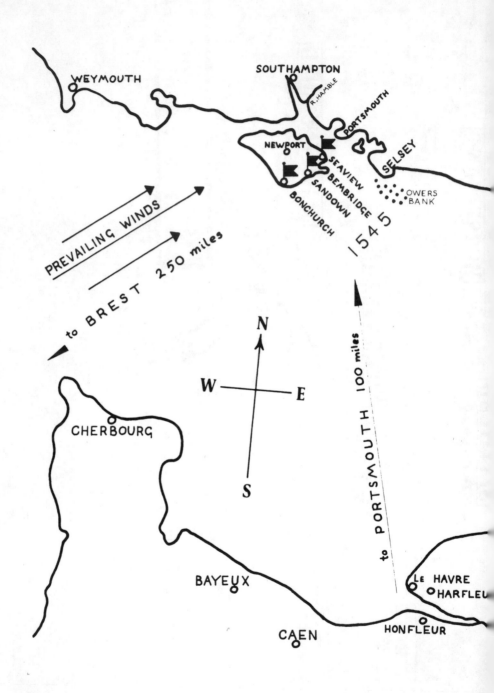

WEYMOUTH

SOUTHAMPTON

R. HAMBLE

PORTSMOUTH

NEWPORT

SEAVIEW

SELSEY

BEMBRIDGE

OWERS
BANK

SANDOWN

BONCHURCH

1545

PREVAILING WINDS

to BREST 250 miles

N

W   E

S

CHERBOURG

to PORTSMOUTH 100 miles

BAYEUX

Le HAVRE

HARFLEU

CAEN

HONFLEUR

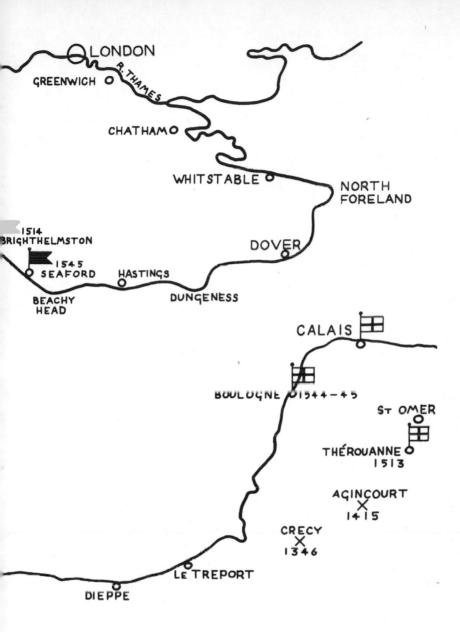

LONDON

GREENWICH o

R. THAMES

CHATHAM o

WHITSTABLE o

NORTH FORELAND

DOVER o

1514
BRIGHTHELMSTON

1545
SEAFORD

HASTINGS o

DUNGENESS

BEACHY HEAD

CALAIS o

BOULOGNE o 1544 – 45

St OMER o

THÉROUANNE o
1513

AGINCOURT
X
1415

CRECY
X
1346

LE TREPORT o

DIEPPE o

o ROUEN

Part I

FROM HENRY V TO HENRY VIII

CHAPTER ONE

"A HARD BEGINNING"

Of course, the end of the *Mary Rose* was pure cinema, even if a scene here and there was out of focus and some sequences had been cut altogether. Centre, foreground, was occupied by the main character, Henry VIII of England, playing his favourite role of Monarch and Minister for War. And in a particularly demanding scene, where the organisation of his fleet, his ideas on the design and armament of his warships, his decisions regarding the latest developments in land forti-fication, his arrangements for the call-up and concentration of the militia, were put at last to the final arbitration of battle in supremely unfavourable circumstances. And with not merely the future of the Tudors, but the very existence of England as an independent sovereign nation, at risk.

A peculiarly delicate touch was the inclusion in this scene, standing actually beside the king, of Lady Mary Carew. Her husband, Sir George Carew, Lieutenant-General of the Horse, had only yesterday been appointed by the monarch to be Vice-Admiral of the English fleet, with the *Mary Rose* as his flag-ship. In a few moments he was to go down with his great battleship a little over a mile from where she was watching, so that the long, wailing cry of the men trapped inside the reeling hull carried distinctly over the sounding board of that calm, summer sea. Many other women were widowed at that moment and hundreds of children made fatherless. Among them was the captain's son, little Richard Grenville, only three years old. Growing up without a father, headstrong and self-willed, he was to help found the new colony of Virginia and, as Sir Richard Grenville, in his turn to die violently at sea, in the last fight of Drake's *Revenge* off the Azores.

The poignancy of the tragedy was heightened for the main characters in this scene, because of their personal involvement not only with the doomed men but with the ship itself. Henry had signed the warrants for her building soon after he had ascended the throne in 1509, thirty-five years before, when he had been a handsome youth of eighteen, fond equally of hunting and music,* with a lay interest in theology, and about to be betrothed to a Spanish princess. The new fleet flagship, revolutionary both in design and armament, had been his first direct involvement with the changing techniques of war in which he was to become expert, as befitted a king, and he had named her the *Mary Rose* after his sister, Mary Tudor. Years of victory over the French and the Scots had followed her building, while her rebuilding in 1536 had marked the great crisis of his reign, when it seemed as if his policies had resulted in a league of all Europe against his tiny kingdom. She was still a major card in his hand for this year of 1545 and now, with the vast invasion fleet in full view five miles ahead, suddenly and shockingly, she had been swept from the board. It was, as he exclaimed then, such a hard beginning to the battle that better fortune must surely follow.

Among the high officers of state accompanying the king was Sir Charles Brandon, Duke of Suffolk, the commander of the field army assembled in front of the king's new fortress of Southsea Castle, and a dying man, with a little more than a month of life left to him. He had also married and outlived that Mary Tudor for whom long ago the formidable battleship had been named. His equal in rank, appointed Lord Admiral in 1543, was Sir John Dudley, Viscount Lisle. He was out there on the blue arena of Spithead, between fortified Portsmouth and the green hills of the Isle of Wight, leading the English counter-attack in the *Great Harry*, a larger version of the revolutionary *Mary Rose*.

Two of the battleship captains following him into action were even more personally involved. Sir Gawen Carew, commanding the 600-ton *Matthew Gonson*, was the uncle of Sir George Carew and had been following in the wake of the *Mary Rose*. As he passed the stricken vice-flagship, he had called out across the water to know what had happened and had heard Sir George's shouted reply, "I have the sort of knaves I cannot rule." These must have been almost his last words. No one recorded the feelings of Sir Peter Carew, the younger brother of Sir George, as the great, gaily painted ship, gunports open and guns run out, reeled right over and sank

* It has been suggested that he may have been the composer of "Greensleeves".

almost instantly, flags and pennants flying, hardly a man escaping. At 31, he was now the senior member of the family and would succeed to the Carew estates in the West Country. That is, if he survived a battle which must be fought against odds of four to one.

What Henry felt, as distinct from what he said in order to encourage others and so as not to appear downcast in front of the foreign ambassadors who were also present, we cannot know. But we can guess, from the tone of official correspondence afterwards. Rage. For it was the king who really commanded here, notwithstanding Suffolk and Lisle. It was Henry who had devised the difficult, subtle battle plan, who was present in person to see it carried out to the last detail, who would be responsible if it failed, even through the faults of underlings. That damned Francis was boasting that he would invade England with his great force of ships and soldiers, and clearly nothing could stop them now. Well, let them land! The King of France would be surprised to find how few escaped. . .

After she went down, the topmasts of the *Mary Rose* still reared out of the water to mark her shallow resting place. King Henry's council thought she might be recovered, with her great and costly armament and her ghastly cargo of drowned dead. Then, inexplicably, she resisted the efforts of the well-equipped Venetians who were appointed to salvage her. It seems they failed even in their first task, to bring her upright prior to lifting and beaching. Something was holding her down and I can guess now what it was and understand why they failed.

When I set out to find her in 1965, the *Mary Rose* had been built 455 years before and had been on the bottom of the sea for 420 years. She was a famous but virtually unknown ship from an almost unknown period, sunk somewhere between Portsmouth and the Isle of Wight in the course of a battle which had received little attention from scholars. This great gap in historical knowledge was of course the whole point of organising such a difficult search in the first place. It was a severely practical form of research: to note where documentary information was missing and to fill the gap in the knowledge with an appropriate vessel from the required period. In effect, it was to state that specified historical wrecks could be found on demand.

I was not the first to say this, still less the first to prove that it could be done, but the idea of systematic search for historically valuable wrecks—as opposed to "treasure" ships— was still fairly new and, I suppose, to some scholars must have smacked of non-academic effrontery, if not downright wishful thinking. But I was an historian of a different sort, professional rather than academic, and my hobby was underwater exploration; I saw no reason at all why I should not succeed. Even if I failed, the task was well worth attempting and no one had made that clearer than the nautical historians themselves.

They were brief and studiously vague whenever they had to narrate the early development of the sailing warship and the place occupied in that story by the *Mary Rose*, the franker scholars admitting that nothing whatsoever was known about the construction of Henry VIII's ships. The military historians were similarly crippled in their attempts to describe the revolutionary developments in artillery which occurred during the reigns of Henry VIII and his father, Henry VII. They openly lamented the lack of evidence. What there was of it consisted of scraps of information, mostly accounts and inventories, with plenty of gun names but few clues as to what those guns actually were. All that everyone was agreed on, was that the *Mary Rose* had been a "key" vessel in the startlingly rapid evolution of the wooden battleship as a floating gun platform.

In this one ship, the studies and the interests of both naval and military historians coincided. They were important, because the effect of what are now virtually unknown technological changes was so great as to result very shortly in European dominance of half the world for many centuries. No doubt the character and restless nature of those Europeans had much to do with this startling expansion across the globe, but it is chastening to realise that we know little for certain about the means with which it was carried out.

The detail of their daily life also was less well known than one might expect. Some of Henry VIII's personal armour has been preserved, but what armour did his shipboard archers wear? What was the working clothing of the sailors? What uniforms did the officers wear? What domestic utensils did they bring on board with them? While the family plate, the silver and gold of the rich, tends to be kept for centuries and thus have an obscure dating, the mugs and plates used by the common people were usually thrown away when broken and on a Tudor land site all that would be left might be merely sherds. Inside the hull of a great ship many of these personal possessions might be preserved intact, evidence of how naval and military communities of the time actually lived, giving revealing glimpses of the differences between the naval and the military, the officers and the men.

At least 400 men went down with the *Mary Rose* (one contemporary account put the number as high as 700) and most of them should still be there. On land, one could not purchase such an insight into life in Tudor times, not for the worth of the Crown Jewels or all the gold in Fort Knox, for it does not exist. Only in the sea is such complete preservation possible and then only in extremely favourable circumstances, where the nature of the seabed, the chemical constituents and temperature of the water itself, together with the reasons for the ship sinking there in the first place, all combine to preserve rather than destroy the hull and its contents. As an amateur but increasingly experienced explorer of the underwater scene off Portsmouth since 1958, I judged that all circumstances known to me were broadly favourable and that a search should be organised when our own resources, state of training, and archaeological experience justified it. That time was to come in 1965.

As a professional historian, however, there was nothing to stop me from putting in some spare-time research occasionally, as I could do this single-handed in libraries and at home. Had I followed my normal research practice, most of my books being concerned with twentieth-century wars, I should have asked at once for the honour of an interview with Henry VIII, clearly one of the world's leading authorities on the subject, and followed this by obtaining eye-witness accounts from the English fleet, being careful to cover all ranks from Lord Admiral to cabin boy and to balance the narratives between the navy and the military and between the various types of English ships involved. Then I should have done the same for the French, starting with their commander-in-chief. A round of interviews in the Isle of Wight and Sussex to obtain vivid recollections of the horrors of burning villages and hand-to-hand fighting in the lanes and woods would have brought the invasion into sharp focus. Undoubtedly, I should have had to visit English dockyards, gun foundries and armouries for explanations of technical matters, but I suspect that to obtain definitive results, journeys to Italian and French ship-building centres, and to Flemish, German and Italian gun foundries would have been necessary.

Of course, this was now impossible; the only exploratory journey I could make would be to the bottom of the sea, to the actual wreck site of the *Mary Rose*. I hoped, by documen-tary research, to obtain at best some clues to the most likely area for search; to expect a pin-point position would have been optimistic. However, if I were to evaluate the wreck when I found it I should have to undertake study of the published sources for the ship and the period before looking for un-published material. In spite of her importance, the *Mary Rose* had not been researched previously with the intensity I was to bring to it in due course and now, although there is still a large gap between what I want to know and what I actually do know, I can give a more detailed and accurate account of her than is to be found elsewhere. This is not saying very much, for the ship itself is still the great research prize. Only in one field of research, a study of the early divers who worked on the wreck, did I achieve a tremendous haul of fresh, un-published, unsuspected information—a complete break-through overturning all previous ideas, including my own. All this was the result of odd afternoons spent in the Ports-mouth Central Library and a few one-day visits to London and Chatham. These were in the nature of indulgencies in my spare time, for the subjects I was then researching pro-fessionally for commissioned books were the Canadian battle for Vimy Ridge, 1917, and the British–Canadian battle for Caen, 1944. From these I would switch for a few hours to the naval battle off Brest in 1512, and the invasion battle off Portsmouth in 1545.

One of my most important assistants was Sir Anthony Browne, in his lifetime King Henry VIII's Master of the Horse, a vain little man disliked by other members of the court for his habit of over-selling his own achievements and always criticising others for faults which he possessed more abundantly himself. It was his vanity which made him valuable to me. In modern times, Sir Anthony would have made sure that press and television were present to record him riding into camp on Southsea Common beside Suffolk and the king on the day of battle in 1545. Instead, he was forced to employ the less ephemeral media of paint and canvas, commissioning an artist to depict the historic encounter of the two fleets in a great panoramic picture, with Sir Anthony prominent in the foreground.

The picture contained the only real clue to the wreck site of the *Mary Rose*, as it showed two of her masts sticking out of the water. When in 1965 I set myself to solve the problem of her exact location, it was to be vital. The picture was also to be important in helping me to reconstruct the course of the battle and this in turn was to have a later application in narrowing the search area for the *Mary Rose*. The third factor supplied by the picture was an extremely detailed representation of all the different ship types of both sides, shown together, at a time when very rapid and important changes in design were taking place. And here the vicissitudes which that painting had undergone in 400 years were less vital than they were when at length I came to consider it as a practical key to actually finding the *Mary Rose*.

The Society of Antiquaries, much maligned by modern archaeologists, had had the foresight to pay for an engraving of the painting to be made in 1778 and one of them, Sir Joseph Ayloffe, had taken the trouble then to write down a detailed description. For this reason, we know that Suffolk's beard was quite white, that Henry was wearing a black bonnet with a white feather, a jacket of cloth-of-gold and a surcoat of brown velvet. For the engraving and this description survived the destruction of the original art work by a fire at Cowdray House shortly afterwards. As a result, although the last moments of the *Mary Rose* are not at all clear, either from the picture or the documents, sharp colour detail can be given to parts of the scene. This is typical of the research problem as a whole, a few facts have survived to give crisp focus to this or that sequence, whereas other elements are either blurred or absent altogether. If anyone wants to know the cost of food and stores delivered to the *Mary Rose* between certain dates, he is a happy man—the accounts have been preserved (although not transcribed, let alone published). But if he should ask the large question—What elements of design and armament made the *Mary Rose* such a revolutionary ship?—then he will get only a wet answer: go down into the sea and find her.

The second-hand nature of the engraving brings the first element of uncertainty, in that the copier may have been faced with a deterioration of the original and been forced to imagine parts of his picture rather than repeat them. For instance, the tower of Southsea Castle is shown as being round when it is in fact square. We know this, because that tower still exists. The *Great Harry* has a much reduced bow castle and a notably overhanging stern castle, when compared to another contemporary likeness of her made officially for Henry VIII. But here we do not know who is right, because the *Great Harry*, unlike the *Mary Rose* and Southsea Castle, no longer exists. And to all this we must add the fact that any picture, let alone photograph, is unreliable because it is a two-dimensional representation of a three-dimensional object.

And just to make matters more difficult, the inaccurate modern convention of indicating space by perspective was not used by medieval or Tudor artists, who employed a quite different set of artistic conventions which are hard for us to understand and interpret. They would have been equally astounded to see a wall, which in fact is of regular height, portrayed as a kind of ramp, much higher at one end than at the other. But this was to present really severe problems only when it was time to find the *Mary Rose,* which meant comparing an engraving of a painting drawn with inaccuracies due to Tudor artistic conventions with a modern naval chart which, like all charts and maps, contained specific errors resulting from the method of projection employed.

A preliminary study of the ships shown in the engraving was a far less tricky business, mere scholar's work where errors could have no practical consequences, although this made them harder to detect. A few scraps of contemporary evidence concerning the warships built by Henry VII still existed and Henry VIII had fought a number of sea wars with these ships and others he had built himself, the surviving documents giving hints as to how the different types of ship were actually used. As I saw it, the development of ships was not an organic, evolutionary process. There was technical progress of course, and in the Tudor period that progress was unusually rapid, but the main factor was demand. A particular type of ship was designed and built because a government, an industry or even a few individuals wished to do this or that and laid down a specification which contemporary technology could be expected to meet. Often, a ship would have to do double duty as a cargo carrier in peace and as a warship when required. But as the overriding demand of governments was for control of the English Channel and its trade, and as this often required the carrying out of amphibious operations on the opposing coast, and occasionally full-scale invasions, large cargo ships were always useful and, up to a point, could be converted into warships of a sort. A large body of armed men placed in a stoutly built high-sided ship made it a kind of fortress as well as a troop transport. But by the time of Henry VIII this kind of vessel could be considered only as a second-class battleship in an actual engagement at sea. The new type of battleship, of which the *Mary Rose* was the first English example, packed so much artillery of so greatly improved a nature that it dominated any sea battle and dictated the tactics to be used.

But it could do this only when there was sufficient wind to move and manœuvre such large, heavy and clumsy ships. When the wind was light or there was, worse still, no wind at all then the floating castle, whether gun-armed or not, was at a disadvantage against oared vessels; and by Tudor times large, oared vessels were mounting a few heavy guns which could do considerable damage to the weak points of large sailing ships. The engraving shows this very clearly. The French fleet is made up of three distinctive types of ships: large, gun-armed battleships, flat-bottomed transports, also large, and a group of Mediterranean galleys. Although the latter have masts and sails their strong point is the powerful rowing machinery packed into a lightly built vessel which serves to point three heavy guns firing ahead. Like a submarine, the bulk of their armament is forward and there is no broadside firing capacity. The whole ship has to be aimed at the target. On a calm sea they could be deadly; in a heavy sea quite useless.

The English fleet represents Harry VIII's own ideas on naval warfare in the English Channel and includes brand-new types of ship. The key vessel is still the floating siege-battery with its supporting infantry component of archers and pike-men, not unlike the French; but there are no Mediterranean galleys. Instead there are hybrid vessels, just launched, which have auxiliary oar-propulsion but are basically lightly built sailing ships mounting broadside gun batteries. The guns must have been small and the speed under oars not so high as that of a galley, but in a calm they could have manœuvred to protect the big ships from the galleys and they could have kept the seas in conditions which would have forced a galley into port. There are also some long, narrow vessels which are almost scaled-down galleys and obviously very fast. What Henry has built is a fleet to meet the French balance of com-bined Atlantic and Mediterranean types. This is quite a modern conception, alien to the better-known times of Horatio Nelson, when the battle fleet consisted of battleships only, the smaller vessels being used for scouting or convoy.

By the end of the reign of Elizabeth the galley was obsolete outside the Mediterranean, presumably because of the development of a new type of sailing warship called the gal-leon which was in effect a fast and handy "pocket battleship". However, oared warships outwardly similar to those of Harry VIII were employed in the Baltic for several centuries after that, although the English navy no longer used them. But we do not know if they really were the same, or even how the galleon developed from the floating fortresses of the early Tudors. And we know even less about those fortresses and their development.

The generic name for the type is carrack, although the etymology is doubtful, supposedly derived from an Italian word meaning "the face of a citadel". The *Mary Rose* was probably a "stretched" carrack, almost the ultimate version of a type of ship which was capable of very great development between the fourteenth and sixteenth centuries. Old pictures show them as looking rather like huge celluloid ducks, float-ing high on the water, with an exaggerated bow castle carried up and forward exactly like a neck and head, and higher than the stern castle. This characteristic, because it was a definite fighting feature, marks all carracks; but the method of building the hulls was altered decisively at some time unknown from clinker to carvel and the rig—the propulsive mechanism —was multiplied and improved.

Clinker construction is the method used by both the Vikings and some modern builders of small boats: the planks of the hull overlap. Carvel building is where the planks butt on to each other, edge to edge. Normally, these two types also imply a different order of building. With a carvel-built hull, the skeleton of the ship is constructed first and then the planks are laid on the ribs, but with clinker building the planks —the "skin" of the vessel—are erected first, and then the supporting skeleton is built inside them. It is an important distinction, and as carvel is potentially much the stronger construction possibly the change took place when it was decided to mount an increased number of heavy guns. But such a strengthening would also facilitate ramming and boarding for the final phase of a battle which had been begun by gunfire.

The improvements in rig are much easier to understand. The early carracks had two masts—the great main mast having a square sail and the small mizzenmast having a fore-and-aft lateen sail. This was to combine the advantages of both types of sail. The later carracks have four masts but the general plan is the same. The first two masts are tall and stout and carry square sails while the last two masts are small and carry fore-and-aft sails. The driving power of the square sail with a following wind is combined with the lateen sail which allows a ship to sail more nearly into wind. This scaling up has been accompanied by a detail improvement. Instead of the heavy masts carrying just one enormous square sail, hard to handle, there are now superimposed topmasts. Two or even three smaller sails take the place of the single brute sheet of canvas. The true battleship has emerged, somehow, out of the mists of the Middle Ages.

There are no builder's plans or models of these ships at the various stages of their development and when I began my search for the *Mary Rose* in 1965 the only hard evidence consisted of the meagre, burnt-out remains of a much earlier English carrack, the *Grace Dieu*, built by Henry V, the victor of Agincourt, in 1416–18. Although the type originated in the Mediterranean and was used for many of the long, early voyages round Africa and across the Atlantic, no other carrack wreck had ever been found anywhere in the world. And this one also, like the *Mary Rose*, was almost on my doorstep. It did not even have to be discovered, but had always been visible on the mud flats of the Hamble River, although only for an hour or less at a time during the largest tides which occur for a few days only during the spring and autumn. Because the wreck lay far out across the soft and evil-smelling mud, few cared to venture out and examine it properly and it was not until 1933 that a group of nautical historians carried out a survey and identified the remains.

Up to this time, the wreck was locally supposed to be that of a Viking longship, but the peculiar double-ended shape of the hull was explained by the fact that what remained was really only the bottom timbers. Another feature which vaguely suggested a Viking origin was the clinker construction of the planking, but a close examination showed that each plank really consisted of three planks fastened together, a massive and altogether unheard of method of building. Even more surprising were the dimensions of the remains, which were 135 feet long with a maximum beam of $37\frac{1}{2}$ feet. Remembering that this was only the bottom of the hull and not all of that even—for the stern lay somewhere out in the deeper water—the historians concluded that her original length overall could have been as much as 200 feet and her maximum beam perhaps 50 feet.

But these dimensions would have been attained at points higher up the hull in areas totally destroyed by the great fire which consumed her in 1439. What was left was re-examined in 1967 and 1968, from the air, from the mud, and underwater when the wreck was submerged, by some of the *Mary Rose* search team, including myself. Apart from discovering that underwater excavation is infinitely easier, more pleasant and less potentially destructive than floundering to the knees in pungent slime, the results were depressing. The remains appeared to represent the hull at a point well below its loaded waterline. As the *Grace Dieu* had been out of commission with only a maintenance crew of eight men aboard at the time of the thunderstorm which set her on fire, this was not surprising. Although she was a direct ancestor of the *Mary Rose* we were not going to learn much from her blackened oak timbers.

However, we came away with the distinct impression of a ship of very great size, probably the largest ship in the world at the time she was built, although documents showed that carracks nearly as large were the principal warships of the age. They required a retinue of smaller ships to manœuvre them in and out of harbour and it is unlikely that any dry docks large enough to take them existed. Why, then, were such unwieldy monsters constructed?

Probably the carrack was first developed as a capacious cargo carrier, capable of making long voyages without having to put into port too often. They were always large, in comparison with other types, but those used primarily as warships were greater still. By the measurements of her time, the *Grace Dieu* was of 1,400 tons, but other ships in the English fleet were listed up to 1,000 tons and the carracks of other nations can hardly have been less. It seems that for war purposes there was at that time a premium on size, because the greater the ship, the higher could its castles and bulwarks be, and, other factors being equal, the soldier on the highest fighting platform was most likely to win the battle. One really great ship would be more than a match for two or even three opponents of half her size, as long as the main armament of a warship consisted of infantry.

Nothing so crude as hand-to-hand fighting was intended, because this would give all the advantage to the defenders. Since the time of the Normans land warfare had involved the sophisticated use of all arms in a scientific way, rather than a rugger scrum in armour, and it was the available weapons-system which was put into the ships and which indeed dictated their design and development. This is still the case. In the late nineteenth century the "capital" ship was a heavily armoured, floating gun platform, which gave way to the floating aerodrome which has now yielded place to the nuclear-powered submarine designed to launch nuclear tipped rockets. A certain aura of romance now surrounds the time of the big-gun battleship and plain sentimentality distorts everything to do with anything which floats and has masts and sails. The truth is, that a ship is a means of transport, like a train or a truck; there is nothing holy or romantic about it.

Looked at in this way, the approach of an enemy carrack would be a terrible sight. Its commander would intend, if he could, to strike one's own ship bodily, thrusting the great, overhanging bow castle over the low waist of the vessel. That bow castle could be many storeys high, looming larger and more formidable for every long minute of its approach. There would be the noise of the wind and sea, the creaking of the ropes, the last-minute shouted orders to try to avoid the collision, the rolling and pitching of the deck and then, just before the shock, as the enemy's fore castle reared up above like a wall, from it would come the howl and whip of loosed arrows and the whispering sigh as hundreds of shafts shot to their target, turning the deck into a bloody shambles of screaming, groaning, writhing men. Volley after volley would search out the living from the dead and when the deck was a slaughterhouse, then, and only then, would the armoured infantry leap down on to it to attempt the physical conquest of the ship. This was always how it had been in war, since the battle of Crecy in 1346 had opened, not with a charge but with a fire-fight between opposing bowmen. There was one crucial difference when the fight took place at sea. Fighting instructions to commanders stressed as late as the seventeenth century the inadvisability of giving quarter because any large body of prisoners might retake the captured ship. So, if you lost, death on the glittering steel of the cruel pike-points was nearly certain.

It was with dread in their hearts that men would begin a battle.

Crecy had added to this, if only potentially, the shattering mental and nervous shock of a bombardment by gunfire, for the English army had there brought into action three primitive guns. All they did at their debut was to, "with fire throw little balls to frighten and destroy horses". By the time of Henry VIII all that was changed. The old-style fortifications were becoming obsolete and even the greatest ship was of little account in war unless she mounted heavy guns in numbers. It was Henry above all who saw this clearly, at the very start of his reign, and demanded that his navy be brought up to date, and, this being done, shortly after committed his new ships to battle against the traditional enemy. It was to be the Hundred Years War all over again, but with new weapons and with new methods.

CHAPTER TWO

"THE CHANGE OF WEAPONS AND FIGHT"

'. . . but since the change of *weapons* and *fight*, Henry the Eighth, making use of *Italian Ship-wrights,* and encouraging his own people to build strong ships of war to carry great ordnance, by that means established a puissant Navy. . . .'
Report of Royal Commission on the Navy, 1618

What puzzles me still is how much Henry knew when he came to the throne in June 1509. For the campaign of 1545 there was soon no doubt in my mind. The king knew exactly what he was doing and was in absolute control of his armed forces, with admirals and generals unwilling to make any move unless he sanctioned it. But he was then in middle age, whereas in 1509 he had been eighteen. Had there been a board of advisers, anonymous now? Or did he learn from his father, Henry VII? He was skilled in actual combat, in the use of horses and weapons, because this was part of the training of a prince. Indeed, he was said to be one of the best archers in England and a formidable horseman. A king was then a military leader or he was not a king. His very throne depended on it, often enough.

In the first year of his reign he signed warrants for the building of two warships of new design at home and for the casting abroad of bronze muzzle-loading guns of the latest type with which to arm his sea and land forces. Both acts implied decisions as to the future nature of war, based on an appraisal of the most modern developments. At the same time he signed a statute forbidding the use of the new hand-guns and crossbows, except under special licence, in order to encourage the traditional skills of his people with the long-bow. That also implied a conscious decision, that the older weapon in this case was still the best one. It was a conclusion he could have reached from a personal, practical test, but the

three decisions taken together imply an understanding of the
changing nature of war and of the technological developments
behind this, plus a grasp of the organisation and infrastructure
necessary to make his new fleet a permanent force. Indeed,
this is what is astonishing when one considers the consequences of his acts. That the results were almost always permanent, in small matters as in great, which argues for a
soundness of decision most modern statesmen would envy.

His talent he may have inherited from his father and from
him also he may have learnt much of naval affairs. There is
a curious parallel between the openings of the two reigns
which strongly suggests it. Both kings began by building two
formidable battleships of modern design copied from foreign
models but which beat their opponents in battle. The ships
built by the son were more of a leap into the future than those
built by the father, and Henry VIII was to go further and
found the first permanent English navy, but this may have
been because his reign coincided with a period of continental
wars between what were in effect super powers, France and
the German Empire. And because of these wars, the four
battleships went into their first action together, as part of
Henry VIII's fleet.

Although the ships were normally laid up in the Thames
near Henry VIII's waterside palace at Greenwich, their main
battle base—and the place where two of them were built
—was Portsmouth. Portsmouth is opposite Cherbourg and
upwind of Le Havre and offers much better harbour and
anchorage than either. This was the town's sole importance
in Tudor times, for it came to life only in time of war. Its
neighbour, Southampton, then as now, was the great commercial port of the south coast. John Leland, Henry VIII's
court antiquary, wrote a description of Portsmouth, its harbour and its defences, in his *Itinerary*. The principal features
are still there, although surrounded and overtopped by the
present naval base and modern tower blocks, and made very
much noisier by continual hovercraft and helicopter traffic.

For the benefit of newcomers to our diving team, I have
my own well-worn "itinerary" to give. This comes naturally,
because we load our boats at a quay just north of the naval
dockyard and proceed to Spithead along the path the *Mary
Rose* took so many times, until the last time. But perhaps not

quite, for the first item of interest is a small floating dock holding a 1,500-ton submarine. "Two of those to raise the *Mary Rose*." Then, opposite, a small yacht; tiny, really. "That's *Lively Lady*, Sir Alec Rose's boat." A moment of silence, while they think, "Did he really go round the world in that?" And just beyond, a much more sumptuous vessel, with a hull of royal blue. "Wouldn't mind that for a diving boat, when *they*'re not using it." Then across to our own moorings to pick up our compressor barge. "Harry moored his big ships just beyond ours, off Elson—with iron mooring chains, too, just as we do."

What we are doing would seem quite crazy but for the continual reminders that the long ago past is really very recent, with specific examples. Two miles to the north rise the massive grey walls of a vast fortified barracks, the "Saxon Shore" fort of Portchester built to command the anchorage of the Roman Navy some 1,700 years ago and still formidably intact; and so large that the Normans built both a castle and a church inside it, although the Norman castle is more ruinous than the Roman. And all along the crest of Portsdown looming behind that again are the space age arrays of radar, scanning rather further, but in principle no different to the Roman lookout and the Norman keep.

The first of the historic ships comes up on our right, at bow and stern moorings off the Gosport shore. Although she is a frigate, she looks odd because of the extra superstructure added to turn her into a training ship long ago. Now named the *Foudroyant*, she was built as the *Trincomalee* at Bombay in 1817, two years after the battle of Waterloo, and is still afloat. While the new divers ask how did the *Mary Rose* compare to her in size—"larger, probably much larger"—the experienced members of the team are once again considering her lines, perhaps mentally comparing the width of the stern and its precise curves with certain features, buried below the seabed, which they will be working on one hour from now.

The opposite side of the harbour is a wall of grey steel. First of all the aircraft carriers and commando carriers and helicopter cruisers and assault ships, mostly British, but often with a United States or French ship among them to afford variety in the types of aircraft parked on deck or flying overhead. The ships themselves are all very much the same, par-

ticularly the British and American; the purpose for which
the ship was built is obvious a long way away, its nationality
becomes clear only later.

It is true that the French vessels have a certain air about
them, as if they had just come out of a Paris fashion house,
although it is hard to pin down the precise curve or elegant
dash of black paint which produces this effect. A Gallic radar
dome, particularly in the soft, golden sunlight of early morning or late afternoon, for sheer beauty beats all modern
sculpture hollow.

Perhaps it is a sense of irony among a succession of
Captains of the Port, but the French ships seem always to be
berthed opposite the *Victory*, with the tricolour floating in
front of the buff-coloured masts of Nelson's flagship. (It makes
an intriguing photograph, although my greatest scoop was to
get into the one shot a space capsule on the foredeck of an
American Coastguard ship and the hull of the three-decker
ship-of-the-line.) The *Victory* was laid down at Chatham in
1759 and sustained her last battle damage in 1941 from a
500-pound bomb which landed in the dry dock where she is
displayed to something like half a million visitors a year. The
damage was much more local than one would expect. This is
a ship we have made it our business to go over in great detail,
including grateful access to all those awkward places not open
to tourists, but which best show the methods of construction.
However, from the general itinerary given on the deck of
the H.Q. boat of the diving fleet, it is the dock and not the
ship inside it which matters, once the usual question of size
is roughly answered. "I don't think the *Mary Rose* was as
big as the *Victory*, although no one knows for sure. But for
the moment we're assuming she was somewhere between the
Foudroyant on the one hand and the *Victory* on the other.
And we could be quite wrong. There'll be many surprises
before we're through, that's why we're here."

Then the key question often follows. Where was the *Mary
Rose* built? "There." I point a finger straight at the *Victory*.
"Not actually in that dock, but somewhere close. You see
Semaphore Tower—that's where the Captain of the Port is;
it's his job to help police the *Mary Rose* site against plunderers
and trespassers. Well, just in front is King's Stairs. About
there, probably, Henry VII built the dock, the first dry dock

ever in England, to service his two big battleships. And Henry VIII used it, too, for his father's ships and the new ones he had built. The land was all open then; the modern Portsmouth didn't exist. The rope lofts, sail lofts and brew houses Henry VIII built are all underneath it now, just about where the power station is, by the harbour entrance. Between them, that's *Vernon*, of course, the navy diving school, but one end of it is still called the Gunwharf. That's where guns were issued to the navy by a central organisation at the Tower of London originally set up by Harry to streamline his armaments industry. It was called the Board of Ordnance and as a kind of Ministry of Munitions, lasted until halfway through the nineteenth century. It was there at the Portsmouth Gunwharf that John Deane landed the guns he recovered from the *Mary Rose* in 1836 and 1840."

Straight out through the harbour entrance, still flanked by some of Henry VIII's defences, was the battleground of 1545; the end of the story of the *Mary Rose* as a fighting ship. The way to it was marked by black conical buoys on the left and red rectangular buoys on the right. These also were the result of Harry's work, for it was he who first had the main channels buoyed for his great ships in time of war. His temporary measure turned into a permanent organisation, now known as Trinity House. But it was the Board of Ordnance, firmly controlling gun development for both land and sea use, which was his major contribution to the technological power of England. The unity of the state was of course his major political contribution, leading eventually to England breaking off from the Common Market. That could not have been achieved without a modicum of brute force to stop the foreigners. And the power to do that grew out of the barrels of his new-fashioned guns.

The process had begun with Henry VII, who had two battleships built for him between 1486 and 1488. They were the *Regent* and the *Sovereign*, both four-masted ships, probably of 1,000 and 800 tons respectively. There are no identifiable pictures of them, except for a battle scene in which the French artist has shown the *Regent* largely obscured by her French opponent. Apart from an inventory which gives the numbers of her masts and yards, there are only two clues to the *Regent's* design, a building warrant which states that she is to be made "like unto a ship called the *Columbe* of France" (of which nothing is known either) and a note that she was made by a "novel construction . . . with ordnance and fittings". For the *Sovereign* we know even less. Apart from an inventory which lists the number of masts and yards,* there is only a mention in 1525 that she is in bad condition but worth repair because "the form of which ship is so marvellously goodly that great pity it were that she should die".

The "novel construction" of the *Regent* could refer to a change from clinker building to carvel or to the introduction of the square stern which occurred generally about this time. Perhaps it was the answer to the mounting of high-velocity, long-range guns in the bows of galleys, which in a calm could manœuvre to fire into the weak and unprotected sterns of the great sailing ships. The obvious defensive answer was to mount heavy guns in the sterns of the carracks, and more of them; and the only way to provide space for a rearward-firing battery was to make the stern square.

Pictures of early carracks often show them fitted with guns, usually three-a-side in the waist, firing through the deck rails. The inventories of the *Regent* and the *Sovereign*, taken in 1495, appear to show a greatly increased gun armament to support their infantry battalions. The *Regent* had 225 serpentines, 30 being brass, the rest iron. These were probably "long guns" firing iron shot. The *Sovereign* had a more mixed armament of 110 serpentines (one only being brass) and 31 "stone guns". The latter were probably large but lightly built guns, certainly firing stone shot. Her inventory records that these 141 guns were mounted in the waist and in the castles; that is, all were at upper deck level or above. The lower deck was probably too near the water to mount any guns at all at this time.

"Serpentine" was a picture-name for a long, thin-barrelled gun firing a small iron shot for a good distance, but there were at least four sizes of gun in this general class. Fortunately,

* Published in 1896 in *Naval Accounts and Inventories of the Reign of Henry VII: 1485–8 & 1495–7*, Ed. M. Oppenheim (Navy Records Society). These documents prove that both ships were four-masters, and it is difficult to understand why so many naval historians continue to describe the *Sovereign* as a three-masted ship.

Henry VII had a small war in Scotland during 1497 and he sent his siege guns round by sea from the Thames. A list was made of all these guns, their ammunition and the number of horse harnesses which accompanied each one; and that list has survived. The two brass serpentines were obviously heavy, requiring 20 horses to drag them. Equally heavy were the 13 brass curtows, but the heaviest guns were a bumbard and a bumbardell, each needing 26 horses to draw it. Therefore, although some of the serpentines put into the ships could have been large, the absence of definitely heavy curtows and bombards from the ship inventories indicates that most of the serpentines were probably of less than the largest size. Many may have been quite small. What is certain is that the ships still lacked the heavy brass "battery" guns of the types which were now being used in numbers to smash down castle and town walls before the infantry were sent in to storm the breaches they made in the fortifications. The reason why the ships could not mount such deadly effective batteries can only have been because they had to carry all their armament high up, well clear of the water that might otherwise swamp them through the ports, either in a heavy sea or when the ship heeled over in a strong wind.

As long as this situation existed there must have been a severe weight limitation on the armament. The ships were doubtless top-heavy anyway, from the height of the castles, and particularly so in battle when the castles filled up with armoured fighting men in their hundreds. The loading of a warship was dangerously different to that of a merchant ship, in which the bulk of the heavy cargo would be stowed low down, thus making for stability. The problem of how to mount large numbers of heavy siege guns in such a ship was solved in about 1501 by a French shipwright of Brest called Descharges. Traditionally, his solution had something to do with gunports, but he cannot have invented them, for side-loading ports in merchant carracks had been known for some time. What he may well have done was to construct a solid, watertight lid for a gunport which would remain watertight even when temporarily submerged by the heeling over of the ship before the wind. If that was what he did, then the larger carracks could at once mount guns on the main deck, and because this was much lower down they could be really heavy pieces which would actually improve the stability of the ship. They could not at once mount guns along the whole length of the main deck, but only at bow and stern where that deck rose in a gentle curve upwards from the water. Amidships, the main deck curved downwards to a position almost flush with the water and in some cases perhaps below it.

Therefore, to make full use of the new invention, a fundamental redesign of the carrack would be needed. The main deck would have to be raised several feet at least, the slightly increased height being offset by the very heavy weights of the complete gun batteries now to be placed upon it. Superficially, above water at any rate, the ship would look not unlike her predecessors; but she would in fact be very different. Probably an altered hull shape below the water-line, stronger, certainly more stable, and incomparably more formidable in the weight of shot she could throw. This would be a true bombardment ship, altering all the established tactics of sea fighting, able to give much greater support to the assault troops in a seaborne landing.

This is guesswork, but if it is in any way true it most certainly explains the naval rearmament programme which Henry VIII at once began on inheriting the throne and which turned the tiny harbour town of Portsmouth into a bustling encampment of shipwrights, sawyers, caulkers, pump-makers, smiths and general labourers. One old battleship, the *Sovereign*, was being completely rebuilt in a dock just vacated by the *Regent* and two new battleships were being laid down nearby. These were to be named the *Mary Rose* and the *Peter Pomegranate*, the latter in honour of his wife, Katherine of Aragon, the pomegranate being part of the arms of Granada, then an heroic battlename in the recent history of Europe.* At the same time as the young king was signing the warrants for the building of the ships, he began ordering batches of

* Many of Henry VIII's ships were named after people, but the spellings vary, probably reflecting actual pronunciations in different dialects. *Mary Rose* appears in documents also as *Mare Rose, Marye Rose, Marye Rosse, Marie Roos, Mary Roos, Mary Roose, Mary Roase*. The *Peter Pomegranate* is usually called the *Petyr Pomie Garnade* or the *Petar Pome Garnett*. In Henry VII's time the *Sovereign* (also the name of a coin of the realm this monarch introduced) is usually spelled *Souvraigne*, while in Henry VIII's lists she often appears as the *Trynitie Souvryan*.

the latest siege guns from abroad. In January 1510, the same
month as he signed a warrant to pay for wages, timber, ironwork, fittings and "necessaries" such as "tankerds, bolles,
disshes" for the *Mary* and the *Peter*, he ordered from a famous
Flemish gunfounder, Hans Poppenreuter of Malines, a dozen
heavy brass curtows of 40 cwt., a dozen lesser brass curtows of
28 cwt., and two dozen brass serpentines of 11 cwt. The iron
guns were probably made in England, mainly at the Tower
perhaps, by an earlier and more primitive technique than the
latest muzzle-loaders of cast bronze, which were the product
of continental foundries.

When the work at Portsmouth was completed, the ships
went round to the Thames to take on their armament. By
then, it was the late summer of 1511. Almost certainly, some
of Poppenreuter's guns were issued to the *Mary Rose* and the
rebuilt *Sovereign*, for curtows (or curtalles) headed their lists
of heavy guns. The inventories for these ships have not been
published, and to judge by the writings of the nautical historians few people have looked at them since Tudor times.
But they exist, fair copies in Tudor copperplate for the permanent records of the state, plus a few extra gun lists made
at various times in the *Mary Rose*; literally in the *Mary Rose*,
for they are jotted down on odd scraps of paper, probably as
the clerk walked from gun to gun, perhaps asking the master
gunner by what name he would describe the piece, and
lingering at the iron guns to list their more complicated gear
and fittings; sometimes he put down what sort of a carriage
the gun had. Only the most conscientious clerk, such as the
man who did the *Peter Pomegranate*, bothered to write
down whereabouts in the ship each gun actually was. The
documents had sustained rough usage since they had been
extracted from Cardinal Wolsey's files, and some had been
badly stained by water, but it was interesting to reflect that
the last man to scrutinise them—bar perhaps two or three
people in 450 years—was Henry VIII. The navy was his own
personal possession and he probably paid more attention to
his ships than he did to his women—and he certainly chose
more wisely.

The main inventories were dated July 1514 and were a
record of the actual armament which was in the ships when
they were put into reserve at the end of Henry's first war

with France. The figures are not theoretical. Those for the rebuilt *Sovereign* are the most interesting as they can be compared directly with the inventory of her original armament taken under Henry VII in 1495. There has indeed been a revolution. The number of her guns has been reduced from 141 to 83, of which 62 are still iron serpentines, perhaps some of the original 109. But now, for the first time, the names of the really heavy battery pieces (the brass curtalles or curtows) appear at the top of the list, followed by the names of new guns of the long-range class, brass culverins and iron slings.

The inventories for the *Mary Rose* tell the same story but with greater emphasis, as might be expected from a ship which, although slightly smaller than the *Sovereign*, was designed from the first to mount formidable siege artillery. There are seven heavy brass battery pieces, curtalles and murderers, and all the curtalles are heavier than those given to the *Sovereign*. There is also a battery of 6 heavy iron guns matching a 7-gun battery in the *Sovereign*, plus 26 stone guns she did not have, as well as some of the new long-range guns, brass falcons and iron slings. There are only 28 iron serpentines, compared to the *Sovereign*'s 62. It is also a very expensive armament, as at this time bronze guns cost three times as much as iron guns, except for those of the sling class which were almost as costly, indicating something special in their manufacture. What that might be, we were to find out in due course. The smaller *Peter Pomegranate* was armed mainly with the cheaper iron guns, although these included numerous sizable pieces such as 25 double-serpentines and 6 "grete murderers". For those interested in detailed comparisons, I have tabulated the gun lists for the key ships between 1495 and 1545 (Tables 1 and 2), but it is clear that Henry VIII's rearmament programme of 1509–11 represented the most rapid and revolutionary advance in English naval history which had ever taken place up to that time and was not to be matched, comparatively, until the advent of the nuclear age at sea in the 1960s. The siege gun, which was dominating the land fighting in Europe, had now appeared at sea in a ship designed expressly to deploy it to killing effect.

A gun is a tube to control and direct the expansion of gases. The first primitive tubes were made in Germany shortly after 1300, as far as we know, with the aid of a technology little above that of the village smithy. They looked as funny and about as formidable as the first aeroplanes, but in neither case did the laughter last very long. The design was basically sound, however. Like modern guns, they were breech-loaders; and, as with the larger modern guns, the shot was separate from the powder charge which was held in a "chamber" similar in shape and purpose to a modern cartridge case. Each gun had two or more chambers, so that when one was fired, it could be extracted immediately and the next quickly wedged home. Anticipating a Mary Rose discovery, I can now show that the "open" ends of the chambers of such guns were lightly sealed by a thin wafer of wood cut from a tree trunk of the appropriate size. The chance of an accidental explosion would be less than with the muzzle-loaders which were to succeed these early breech-loaders, and indeed a modern soldier would be much more at home with the medieval breech-loaders than he would be with the cannon of Napoleonic times. In less than five minutes he would be getting rapid fire out of them, whereas with the muzzle-loaders he would be scratching his head and referring to the book of instructions.

The only substantial difference between then and now lies in the method of manufacture of the tube, now called the "barrel". (We call it the barrel because the tubes of most early guns were made in the same way as a wooden cask, but entirely in wrought-iron.) The makers called it the "pece", a word we still use, as in a "piece of artillery". The first stage in making a "built-up" gun was to hammer out long flat strips of iron about the width of barrel staves and then assemble them round a core. The next major stage was to hammer out iron bands or hoops and then slip them on over the staves so that when they cooled the inner tube of horizontal staves was held tightly together by an outer tube of vertical hoops. Re-inforcing bands were shrunk on at intervals on top of these again, so that the typical "built-up" gun has a knobbly, ribbed look. Both ends of the tube were open, but they were not the same, the breech end being constructed so as to ensure a tight fit with the "chamber". The tube was mounted in a wooden slide with space for the loading of the chambers and a wooden back-stop to prevent the chamber moving when the black powder was ignited through the touch-hole. This was the

weak point of the design at that time. Not until the late
nineteenth century was it possible to manufacture a truly
efficient, fully sealed breech to completely contain all the
expanding gases.

But such built-up guns formed the bulk of the armament
of the *Mary Rose* throughout her long career as an effective
fighting ship, and indeed did not go out of use until some time
in the seventeenth century, so they had a rather longer run on
shipboard than did the cast muzzle-loaders which eventually
replaced them completely. There must have been very good
reasons for this. Perhaps it was because they were cheap, light,
and using only weak charges had fewer recoil problems; certainly they would be easier to load and their rate of fire would
be higher. No doubt they had a specified place in the battle,
probably at close range in the final phase of the fire-fight, as
rapid-fire man-killers.

The really heavy punch of the *Mary Rose* lay in her big
bronze muzzle-loaders, cast in one piece, so that there were
no gas-escape problems; and probably they were capable of
utilising the finer and more powerful types of gunpowder
which were becoming available. They were not man-killers
and they would be useless on a battlefield even if they could
reach it. They had been developed as the answer to a specific
military demand, as castle-crackers. The early wrought-iron
guns had not been much better than the traditional giant
catapults, although they could probably get a closer grouping
of shots, which was a great advantage when you were trying
to blow a breach in a city wall. But the new cast-bronze guns,
with their finer powders, throwing heavy iron shot, almost at
a stroke made the old fortifications obsolete. They could blow
a way through for the infantry in a day or so, even when faced
by stout masonry, let alone earth-and-timber walls. And they
could do this better than most modern guns, which are
designed as man-killers. The only answer to them was another
cast-iron gun with a greater range, so that the unwieldy
battery pieces could be harassed even before they were em-
placed. This meant a longer gun, but with a much smaller
bore; the basic difference today between the rifle and the
revolver which everyone knows (except, apparently, the pro-
ducers of Western films). So there were two main types of
artillery—the short battery gun and the long counter-battery

gun. Both types were put into the ships and possibly the long guns were mounted for bow or stern chase; the galleys certainly used long guns only. One thing is certain, their rate of fire would have been very slow, from the muzzles being outboard, and there would have been recoil problems. They were immensely heavy and they would have to be manhandled back-and-forth during the reloading process. But if the fire of the first, carefully loaded salvo could be well judged, the sides of the enemy ship would be a sorry sight, her crew shaken, dazed and confused by the hellish noise as well as by the reeking smoke.

Now would be the time, during the long pause for reloading, for the rapid-fire iron guns to maintain the bombardment, probably with stone shot which would splinter into scores of jagged, hissing fragments. Then, when the ships grappled, the bowmen would sweep the ruined decks, the shattered castles, the riven bulwarks in a hail of deadly, precisely aimed death. And then, and only then, with the defenders decimated, defences blown down, boarding netting ripped open, would the armoured infantry storm to the assault, just as they did to the breach of a city wall. It was carefully orchestrated, "scripted" almost. It had to be. What was being put into the ships was not just bigger guns, but the complete weapons-system that went with them, that made them effective by following up the blast of the bombardment.

That they did not expect to sink their enemy by gunfire but would be forced to obtain a decision only by boarding and capturing him, is shown by the retention of infantry in the ships.* But the effect they expected from the bombardment is shown by the reduction in their numbers, effectively from an infantry battalion to two companies. In the two vessels built from the first as siege-gun platforms, instead of the soldiers outnumbering the sailors, their numbers are now exactly equal. The *Mary Rose* has 200 sailors and 200 soldiers, the *Peter Pomegranate* has 150 of each. On the other hand the larger *Sovereign*, although rebuilt, still basically an old-

---

* Many "returns" from the fleet have survived to be published in *Letters and Papers relating to the War with France, 1512–1513*, edited by Alfred Spont for the Navy Records Society, 1897. See also M. Oppenheim's *A History of the Administration of the Royal Navy*, 1896.

fashioned ship, has to rely more on her infantry; she has a crew of 300 sailors and 400 soldiers.

Among the warlike stores of the *Mary Rose* are all the infantry weapons: 300 bills, 300 Morris pikes, and 220 sets of armour. For the archers, 350 bows, 700 bowstrings, 700 sheaves of arrows, and 200 "stakes for the field". The latter, first used at Agincourt a century before, were about six feet long and had sharp, iron-tipped points at both ends, so that by thrusting one end into the ground at an angle a body of archers could in minutes surround itself with a hedge lethal to cavalry; the medieval equivalent of barbed-wire. This is a sharp reminder that battleships were not designed purely for fighting at sea, as they were to be later, but to provide both the bombardment and assault force in amphibious operations. The men would be ferried ashore in her great boat, or tender, a large, decked craft with a mast and sail and 20 oars.

It would be very interesting to know what the old-fashioned *Regent* carried now in the way of guns and men, but the last surviving inventory is from the reign of Henry VII. For a very good reason, there were to be few returns from the *Regent* during the coming war.

CHAPTER THREE

BATTLE OFF BREST

In September 1511 the Pope and the King of Aragon were planning to strike against Louis XII of France. In December Henry VIII of England joined this alliance and on 25 January 1512 the English Parliament decided on war. A Spanish fleet and army were to co-operate with the English forces and the main operation was to be an invasion of France, for which control of the Channel was an essential preliminary. The campaign was to open in April and Sir Edward Howard was appointed "chieff capteyn and admyrall of the flete" with the *Mary Rose* as his flagship. He was to dominate the Channel by cruising from the "Trade" (Brest) to Calais and London, revictualling every three months at Southampton. His force was to consist of eighteen warships plus two crayers as waterboats and supply vessels. A Spanish fleet was to assist him.

It has been said that the mutual ancestor of modern England and America is Ethelred the Unready, but this tradition did not apply to Henry VIII. His war preparations were made with such "wonderful speed" that he took the first trick without firing a shot. Neither his enemies nor his allies had mobilised at his pace and the new English fleet had the Channel to itself, with war declared. They made the most of this opportunity by sweeping it clean of all foreign shipping; French fishing boats or Flemish and even Spanish merchantmen, it was all the same to them.

The performance is the more remarkable considering the sparse population of the country, probably less than 4,000,000, and the large distances to be covered on foot. Thomas Spert, the master of the *Mary Rose*, had had to make journeys of up to 150 miles to recruit men while Mr. W. Forde, one of the "lodesmen" or navigators, had to spend 40 days in Bristol gathering 28 mariners. Some of the soldiers were recruited in Norfolk, 100 miles from London, and others from as far away as 140 miles. There was no standing army, no network of depots, not even a police force. When they reached the ship they were issued with their uniforms, which were green and white, the Tudor colours. Those for the soldiers were expensive, costing 4s. each, while those for the mariners and gunners cost only 20d., less than half. Probably the sailors needed only working clothing, while the soldiers had to make a show.

Certainly, a German military witness was shortly to be impressed by the men of the English volunteer army, paraded outside a French town they had captured during the campaign: "They are really big strong men having a captain to every hundred, and their pennon on a long spear. Some have English bows, some crossbows, certain of them maces with long handles and certain of them long spears; and almost all are clad in long white coats edged with green cloth and wear breastplates, and steel caps on their heads. For their field music they have a fluteplayer and a bagpiper who play together (and certain of them a trumpet)."

In July the fleet was back, intact and unscarred, to replenish its stores, so Henry rode down to Portsmouth to review his proud ships and offer his captains "a banquet before their setting forward". This time there certainly would be a battle, for the French, with three or four times as numerous a population as the English, were planning a conjunction of their forces. While their Channel fleet was fitting out in the harbours of Normandy and Brittany, the galleys of Prégent de Bidoux, Knight of Rhodes, were coming round from the Mediterranean. The English had no ships to match them, but this trump card of the French had only been played by the sacrifice of some of France's recent conquests in Italy.

We do not know where the Royal banquet was held, possibly in the *Mary Rose* or in the much larger *Regent*. Nor do we know what the *Mary Rose* looked like at this time. There is only one authentic picture and that is after her rebuilding and rearming in 1536. In 1512 she is listed as of 600 tons with a complement of 400 men, now swollen to 431 because she was carrying the staff of the admiral, Sir Edward Howard, and also the staff of Sir Thomas Wyndeham, "treasurer of the army by sea". They included 2 "pylotts", 5 trumpeters and 20 servants.

There is a famous painting which shows the embarkation of Henry VIII at Dover in 1520 for the diplomatic meeting known as the Field of Cloth of Gold. Nautical historians argue that it is fanciful or that it does not represent the actual ships used, which did not exceed 400 tons, but instead portrays the principal warships of the navy at that time, a three-master on the right of the picture being identified as the original *Mary Rose*. Towards the end of my research, having discovered how painfully glib many English nautical historians can be, I set out to check from original documents every statement they made concerning the *Mary Rose*. The inventory, which they had not studied, showed that the *Mary Rose* always was a four-master and that she had carried a formidably heavy armament from the beginning. There was no question of gunports being cut in her sides later, as an afterthought. As none of the ships shown in the picture carries anything like the number of guns which the inventories list for the principal warships, the prosaic truth may be that it represents merely what it is supposed to represent—the smaller vessels of the fleet which actually carried Henry VIII to France. As some are four-masters, it may give a useful idea of the general arrangement and build of Henry's carracks, but no detailed assumptions can be drawn from it as yet.

When Howard sailed after the Royal banquet, his fleet now numbering 25 ships, he found that once again Henry had got off the mark quicker than his opponents, and that he was in time for the French banquet as well. As they closed the French coast off Brest at about eleven o'clock on the morning of 10 August 1512, not only were the galleys of Prégent de Bidoux still far away but 22 French carracks, nefs and barks were anchored near the shore, their crews celebrating the feast of St. Lawrence. And not only that but they were full of visitors from the towns and countryside around. It was Navy Day, almost. The number of guests in the flagship, Vice-Admiral René de Clermont's 790-ton *Grand Luise*, is not known but Captain Hervé de Portzmoguer was entertaining some 300 local dignatories and their wives on board his famous raider, the 700-ton *Marie la Cordelière*. There is a painting of this ship in the Bibliothèque Nationale, Paris, which shows her as a carrack very similar in appearance to those of Henry VIII's. Like them, her castles and fighting tops were pavesaded with shields, but instead of the red cross of the English, the French shields bore the ermine of Brittany or a black cross on a white ground. Instead of Tudor green and white, her crew wore jackets of red with blue or black breeches. Both these ships were fairly modern, having been built about 1498–9, and we know that the *Cordelière* was formidably armed with fifteen "gret brasyn cortawds" and "other gunys of every sorte". She was also packed with fighting men—4 "lords", 800 soldiers and sailors, 400 crossbowmen and between 50 and 100 gunners.

The battle was reported on not merely by Englishmen and Frenchmen but by the agents of some of the Italian states, less likely to show patriotic bias. A Venetian reported that the English first sighted the French at a distance of two leagues and that the attack was led by Howard in the *Mary Rose* and Captain Anthony Ughtred in the *Mary James*, both of them modern ships, the latter being of 400 tons. In accordance with the classical principle of trying to knock out the strongest enemy units first, Howard engaged the French admiral in the *Grand Luise* and Ughtred attacked the *Cordelière* of nearly twice his tonnage in an attempt to cripple her so that the *Sovereign* or the *Regent* should have a chance to finish her off.

The English had the advantage of preparation and surprise. Some of the French ships had to cut their cables and had not hoisted all their fighting sails when they were brought to battle. There were waist cloths and top armings to be rigged —long strips of stiff, painted canvas to hide their crews from view. There were darts and stones to be taken up to the tops and shot of different types to be stacked by the guns: iron shot for smashing or penetrating hulls, stone shot for splintering on impact, crossbar shot for tearing rigging and weakening masts, hollow shot containing "wyldefyre", and bags of rounded lead pellets or square iron dice to spread like hail. In the English ships this would have already been done. The soldiers would have donned their armour, the archers would have selected their shafts, the rough ones for volley fire, the more perfect arrows for individual shooting, with a few incendiary shafts to hand, equipped with special hooks to catch in the enemy's sails or rigging.

The *Mary Rose* fired first, subjecting the larger *Grand Luise* to what the Venetian called "*una grossa bombarda*". The great brass curtalles would have jumped with the shattering recoil of the explosions, running back across the decks, to be swabbed out and reloaded, in the swirling reek of powder smoke. The iron breech-loaders would have cracked fire from their black muzzles, then men would have knocked out the wedges, grabbed the handles of the fouled and empty chambers, swung them clear for cleaning and reloading. Fresh shot would have been placed and wadded, new chambers slammed in, the wedges knocked home. To us, it would seem painfully slow. But it was deadly effective. Within an hour or so, 300 men were down aboard the French flagship, dead or wounded, and her mainmast was knocked to pieces. The *Grand Luise* then fled towards the shore, probably for the protection of the harbour batteries, and some of the French captains were to make official complaint about this desertion by their admiral. But Clermont's retreat may well have saved his ship from capture.

In this mobile battle, in which no rigid formation was used, the English flagship had managed to first "run down" her quarry and then knock her out, apparently without notable loss. It looks as if her designer had achieved a useful balance between speed, nimbleness and gun-power. Almost certainly, this was the first fight between battleships to be decided by fire-power alone.

The only English ship which surviving records show to have been badly hurt by gunfire that day was, not surprisingly, Captain Ughtred's *Mary James*, for he had taken on himself the task of pinning down the *Cordelière* so that she could be finished off by superior numbers of English ships. Apparently, the tactics were to concentrate against the strongest of the French ships and elsewhere Rigault de Barquetot, captain of the nef of Dieppe, was beginning a seven-hour fight against five English ships which were trying to board him. They did not succeed, although they killed 32 of his men and wounded many more. Hervé de Portzmoguer proved elusive also, and, as Cardinal Wolsey wrote, it was only "after innumerabyll shotyng of gonnys and long chasyng one another" that "at the last the Regent most valyently bordyd the gret caryke of Brest". The seamen of Normandy and Brittany were not easy to trap, even when taken at a disadvantage.

However, Captain Ughtred managed to bring the *Cordelière* to a halt by bodily ramming her with his smaller ship and then increased her disorder and confusion by firing his battery guns into her point blank, so that both vessels were wreathed in the reeking powder smoke. Probably the *Mary James* suffered almost as badly as the *Cordelière* in this violent first exchange, but the escape of the Breton ship was checked for long enough to allow Sir Henry Guildford and Sir Charles Brandon to come up in the *Sovereign* and manœuvre for a blocking position ahead of the Frenchman, so that both ships faced each other, fighting castle to fighting castle. And then things went wrong and all Captain Ughtred's daring seemed vain. The *Sovereign*, wrote Holinshed, the sixteenth-century historian, "lay stem to stem with the great carrack of Brest. But by the negligence of the master, or else by smoke of the ordnance, or otherwise, the *Sovereign* was cast at the stern of the carrack, with which advantage the Frenchmen shouted for joy". As the *Sovereign* fell astern, facing the wrong way, the *Cordelière* was free of this formidable opponent.

It was then that the *Regent* entered the battle. Commanded by Sir Thomas Knyvett and Sir John Carew, she had been about to board another great French ship when they saw that Portzmoguer's carrack was about to escape again. Although not rearmed by Henry VIII, so far as we know, the *Regent* was of 1,000 tons and carried more than 700 men, many of them archers wielding the giant Welsh longbow. No one not trained from boyhood could manage them; but for those who could, it was a deadly weapon. The arrows, three feet (a "clothyard") long, were tipped with small iron heads to concentrate the impact; at short range they could penetrate armour or go through an inch-thick plank. Effective range was 250 yards, but their supreme advantage was in their rate of fire. While a continental crossbowman was reloading his cumbersome though effective weapon, the English archer could get away four shafts; a company of longbowmen could produce a positive blizzard of fire. For more than a hundred years, French army after French army had charged to ruin against these bowmen, and in the sea battle of Sluys in 1340 the French and Spanish ships had been overwhelmed by the fire-power of English ships converted to archery platforms, so that they were more easily boarded by the armoured infantry carried in other English vessels. The great *Regent* was several stages beyond that, carrying both archers and armoured men high up in her fighting castle and with many guns to break down the enemy's upperworks and so expose his crew to the arrow storm. As she drove alongside the *Cordelière*, grapnels and hooks were hurled into the Breton carrack and soon the two ships were locked side by side.

Giving up their attempt to escape, the French let go an anchor and the two great towering hulls turned slowly with the run of the tidal stream so that they lay across the wind, the *Regent* in the lee of the *Cordelière*, and only Captain Ughtred in the *Mary James* free to move.

"The fight was very cruel, for the archers of the English part, and the crossbows of the French part, did their uttermost," wrote Holinshed. "But for all that, the Englishmen entered the carrack." Four hundred fighting men poured over the bulwarks of the *Regent* and into the *Cordelière*. Sir Thomas Knyvett was already dead, killed by a gunshot, as the English swarmed on to the Breton carrack, cutting or thrusting with sword or pike as they fought their way across the ruined decks. "Our men so valyently acquyt themselfe that within one ower fygth they had utterly vanquyshyd with shot of gonnys and arrows the said caryke, and slayne moste parte of the men within the same," wrote Cardinal Wolsey to the Bishop of Worcester. And the contemporary Breton chronicler, Alain Bouchart, noted the savagery of the terrible hand-to-hand fight. What was to come now was even more terrible.

Some thought the fire was started by a shot of the *Mary James* into the *Cordelière*, others that "a varlet gunner, being desperate" had deliberately set fire to the French ship. Bouchart wrote that a man in the tops of the *Cordelière* started a fire in the *Regent*, which spread to the powder magazine. A dramatic French painting shows red points of fire racing up the rigging of the *Cordelière*, consuming the sails, while giant flames roar out from the gunports and sailors hurl themselves into the sea.

Victory became tragedy with appalling swiftness. As Wolsey wrote of the French, "And sodenly as they war yelding themsylf, the caryke was one a flamyng fyre, and lyke wyse the Regent within the turning of one hand. . . . So bothe in fyght within three owrys war burnt, and moste parte of the men in them."

As explosions rocked and tore the two flaming hulls, locked together, the battle momentarily ceased. English ships launched their boats, to pick up men who had swum or drifted clear of the inferno, and the battered *Mary James* succeeded in saving some of the Frenchmen she had been trying to kill only minutes before. Her own decks were crowded with dead and wounded, and when she put into port for repairs, 60 of her crew were pensioned off as permanently unfit for sea service. But the tragedy of the *Cordelière* and the *Regent* dwarfed these losses.

All the leaders were dead, both French and English. Knyvett, Carew, Portzmoguer, and many others certainly perished. Their names were published. An early report, based on English interrogation of survivors from the *Cordelière*, stated that a mere 20 Frenchmen remained alive out of the 1,500 in the Breton ship, and that there were only 120 survivors from the *Regent*'s seven or eight hundred. A later report gives the number of French survivors as only six (some may have died of wounds or burns) out of 1,500 men, while stating that 180 English survived from the *Regent*, which lost 600 men. When the two great ships had gone from sight and only the drifting smoke and floating debris marked the scene of disaster, more than 2,000 men had died.

Although the great inferno of the carracks momentarily stunned the French and dismayed the English at their unnecessary loss, the defeat of the French flagship by the *Mary Rose* decided the battle. No accident cancelled out that victory. "The resydue of the French flete, after long chassyng, was by owr folks put to flyght and drevyn of into Brest havyn," wrote Wolsey. "There were 6 as gret shyppes of the sayd flet as the Regent or the Sovereign, howbeyt as cowards they flede." The captain of the nef of Dieppe, saved from defeat only by the arrival of fresh ships from Guernsey, was so furious at being abandoned by the flagship that he challenged René de Clermont to a duel. He cited his own long fight against odds as proof that the French ships, if properly led, could have defeated the English. As it was, Howard cruised off Brest freely for two days afterwards, burning or taking 32 French vessels and capturing 800 men.

The new battle methods first demonstrated off Brest in 1512 were later codified as a fighting instruction, by command of Henry VIII. It was to be firstly a battle of manœuvre for a favourable position with favourable odds against the enemy's most important ships; followed by a stand-off bombardment with heavy siege guns to batter, shock and demolish; and then, when the heavy guns had spoken sufficiently, a deck-sweeping close-quarter fire-fight was to be waged with guns firing stone, hailshot or dice thickened up by hundreds of clothyard shafts from the quick-firing archers; and finally, but only if the defenders had been beaten down and the decks were free of masking gun-smoke, would come the rush of boarders to capture, hold and take away the enemy ship. Later instructions specifically stated that this might not always be possible, in which case the prize was to be sunk after the principal officers had been taken out of her and "the rest committed to the bottome of the sea for els they will turne upon you to your confusion".

These tactics were based on the existing situation—quite small fleets of less than 30 vessels, the ships themselves somewhat cumbersome and leewardly and of greatly varying size and performance. And, taking Clermont's "desertion" with a pinch of salt, an enemy who had very similar ships, generally well and courageously handled by Norman and Breton seamen. Of course, all carracks were clumsy because of their high castles, particularly the great fighting castle at the bow, but the continuing importance of archers to the fire-fight made them necessary at that time. One might as well criticise a modern tank-landing craft for being of unseaworthy design, as object to the carrack in its day. As long as seaborne armies need tanks they will require specialised craft to carry them and as long as the bow was a decisive weapon of war, warships had to be designed to deploy it prominently, even at the expense of building high castles which caught the wind like unfurlable sails. However, they were not required to operate through the harsh conditions of a European winter, because the armies they were supporting fought also on a seasonal basis.

The campaigning season was so busy that although the Mary Rose began her successful battle career in 1512, she did not undergo sea trials until the spring of 1513. And then it was at the direct command of Henry VIII, who had added several important ships to his fleet and wanted a report on comparative performances. The Mary Rose, at 600 tons, was now only the fourth largest of the king's ships, but she was

still the fleet flagship under the command of Sir Edward
Howard. Apart from the rebuilt *Sovereign* now listed at
1,000 tons, Henry had just purchased two large foreign-built
carracks, the 800-ton *Gabryell Royall* from Italy and the 700-
ton *Kathereyn Fortaleza* from Spain. After a royal review off
Greenwich, on 19 March Howard led the English fleet to sea
in the *Mary Rose*. Then, rounding the Foreland into the
Channel, he ordered all ships to make sail simultaneously for
a race through the Straits of Dover.

The *Mary Rose* drove through the water with all sails set,
soon leaving astern the main body of the fleet. Some of the
smaller vessels, which drew less water, cut the corner by going
close inshore and so drew ahead of the flagship, but the race
ended with the *Mary Rose* leading the *Sovereign* by half a
mile. Half a mile behind her was a group of the smaller ships,
followed by the main body of the great ships trailing a full
three miles behind the leader. The *Mary Rose* was "your good
shipp, the flower, I trow, off al ships that ever saylyd", wrote
Howard to the king.

It was not merely speed but manœuvrability and performance at differing angles to wind and sea, which consti-
tuted a full test of a sailing vessel. A difficult situation in the
dangerous Dover Straits immediately tested them all to the
full, the wind changing repeatedly when the ships were in
the narrow channels between the deadly sandbanks, causing
them to tack time after time in shallowing water amid
dangerously high, short seas. Howard thought himself lucky
that all came through safely, and pointed out that "ye commanded me to send Your Gras word how every shipp dyd sail,
and this same was the best tryall that cowd be, for we went
both slakyng and by a bowlyn, and a cool a cors and a bonet,
in such wyse that few shippes lakkyd no water in over the lee
wales. . . . In Christendom owt of one realm was never seen
such a flete as this." Howard listed a few unsatisfactory vessels,
including the 300-ton *Christ*, which "was one off the wurst
that day . . . Sir, she be overladen with ordenauns, beysyd her
hevy toppes, which are byg inough for a shipp of 8 or 900"
(tons). The best, he thought, was his own command, the *Mary
Rose*. "Sir, she is the noblest shipp of sayle and grett shipp at
this hour that I trow be in Christendom. A shipp of 100 tone
wyl not be soner at her . . . abowt then she."

With these qualities, plus proven success in battle, it is not surprising that the design was continued. As replacement for the burnt *Regent*, a scaled-up version of the *Mary Rose* was ordered to be built. Called at first the "Gret carrik" *Imperyall*, she was later named the *Henry Grace de Dieu*, but nowadays is more commonly referred to as the *Henry Grace à Dieu* or *Great Harry*. She is usually listed as of 1,000 tons, occasionally as 1,500 tons. The figures are useful only as a comparison between like ships for the exact meaning of the Tudor "tun" is not known today, although it probably derived from a count of the number of "tuns" (or casks) of ale or wine a cargo ship could actually stow on board. As a warship's cargo consisted of guns, ammunition and armed men, her "tunnage" or "portage" were probably academic. When completed and inventoried in 1514, the *Great Harry* had 184 guns actually on board. No fewer than 24 of the bronze and iron pieces are listed as "grete" and one "grete bumbarde of brass apon iiij trotill wheles" can hardly have been less than a 10-inch or 12-inch gun. But this giant battleship was not ready in time to help Howard during the campaign of 1513.

The orders given to the English admiral were the same as in 1512—dominate the Channel and so prevent the French fleet at Brest from interfering with the transport of the English army overseas for the Picardy campaign. Vice-Admiral René de Clermont was no longer commanding at Brest. He had been given an army command which proved equally unlucky, for in 1513, with many other French noblemen, he was taken prisoner by the English in the cavalry action known as the Battle of the Spurs. Henry VIII was also in Picardy, watching his new bronze guns smashing the walls of fortified French towns. This land campaign depended on the success of Howard's force at Brest, which was carrying out a typical combined operation.

He had his great ships anchored close in, right in the harbour mouth. Beyond, protected by a floating barricade of two dozen hulks chained together and covered by the fire of land batteries on one side, the French northern fleet lay penned like cattle in a semi-open stall. For on the other side of the water was a position held by English soldiers whom Howard had landed from the ships, while English raiding parties were out scouring the countryside. Outside the estuary, along the rocky shallows of the Britanny coast, prowled the formidable fast galleys of the French Mediterranean fleet led by Prégent de Bidoux, which had arrived too late to join the main French force in Brest. Once again, the English sea forces had moved faster than the French and Howard had split the enemy fleet in two. But he had insufficient troops and artillery actually to take Brest and burn its docks and shipping, and the English supply arrangements had been far from admirable. Howard was only hanging on to his position by the strictest rationing of food and drink.

The supply convoy led by Sir Edward Echyngham in the 100-ton *Germyne* did not sight Brest until the morning of 19 April, and even then he turned aside to chase a French ship. He had to break off the pursuit because his Spanish crew had sighted Prégent's galleys in the distance and were muttering, "Now is the day comyng that we shal be fayne to go to the hospital." But the convoy got in safely and Echyngham personally went on board the *Mary Rose* to report to Howard. "I trow there was never knyght more welcome to his sovereign lady than I was to mylord Admyrall and unto all the holl armye, for because I brought the vytlers with me, for of 10 days before . . . all the armye hade but one mele a day and one drynke.'

Three days later Prégent de Bidoux made what may have been an attempt to break through into Brest and join up with the carracks. An early intelligence report had warned the English that each of his four galleys were "fitted with three Venetian basilisks; one shot of these guns can strike through any ship!" The latest news from Italy was that he now had "6 gallioni, 2 nave, 2 barze"; that is, six Mediterranean galleys of the most modern type accompanied by four support craft which the English called "foysts". That report was correct, for, wrote Echyngham, "On the 22th day of Aprill, 6 galyes and 4 foysts came through part of the Kynges navie, and there they sanke the ship that was maister Compton's, and strake through oone of the Kynges new barkes, the which sir Stephyn Bull is capiteyn of, in 7 placys, that they that was within the ship hide much payne to hold her above the watre." Compton's ship appears to have been a smallish merchantman of 160 tons, but Sir Stephen Bull's command was a minor warship, the *Lesse Bark* of 240 tons and 201 men. The Venetian basilisks, high-velocity long guns of bronze, were indeed to be feared. But Prégent did not get into Brest and in the attempt he lost one of his foysts, taken by boats from the English ships. Keeping to the shallows where the English carracks could not approach him, he retired to a rocky bay near Conquet and set up batteries on shore to command the narrow entrance.

Even if the carracks could have been spared from the blockade, the water was too shallow for them even to approach the position. Howard's first plan, a sound one, was to disembark 6,000 men on the shore just out of range of Prégent's batteries, and then take his position from the rear with infantry. But aggressive action by the French land forces in Brest pinned down his troops on the main objective. So he resorted to a risky frontal stroke using six small, shallow-draught oared vessels packed with soldiers, which he would lead in person together with a group of chosen noblemen, to impart the necessary dash and decision which alone might bring victory, for the force lacked fire-power, having only some small guns and few archers, and would have to pass through the narrow entrance singly. It proved a Tudor Gallipoli, for "on both sides of the galyes was made bulwerkes full of ardynaunce, that no boote nor vessel couth comme unto them, but that they must comme betwene the bulwarkes, the which were so thick with gonnes and crosbowis that the quarrelles and the gonstones came together as thick as it hade be haylestones". One vessel which never even reached the galleys nevertheless had every man on board killed or wounded.

But Howard led on with reckless impetuosity and in his small English galley drove through the hail of stone shot and iron bolts to close and board the great galley of Prégent de Bidoux, Knight of Rhodes, Admiral du Levant. An English grappling anchor was thrown into the French vessel, and held. With the fate of the *Regent* much in mind, its cable was attached to the capstan, so that it could be veered out or cut in case of fire in the enemy vessel. Followed by a Spanish officer and sixteen men, Howard jumped the bulwarks into the flag galley. Then the grappling line parted or was cut, and the English vessel drifted away.

Howard was beckoning and shouting, "Comme aborde agayne! Come aborde agayne!" as the gap widened. Then, as the French pinned him up against the rail with the bright points of their pikes, he was seen to take off the golden whistle which was his admiral's insignia and throw it into the sea. "There was oon that lept into my galye with a gilt targett on his arme, the which I cast ouer borde with Morris pikes," recalled Prégent at a parley soon after. "The maryner that I have prysoner told me that that the same man was your Admyrall." One of the boarders had been pulled out of the sea by his comrades. He had eighteen wounds, but was still alive. Sir Edward Howard, however, was certainly dead.

Without orders from the King, the whole fleet abandoned the blockade of Brest and returned to England. A similar mutiny had occurred in the army sent to Spain the previous year. Henry was choleric, but he was also cunning. He sent the fleet a new commander. The man he chose was Sir Thomas Howard, later Earl of Suffolk, a field officer with recent battle command experience in Picardy. He was also the elder brother of the drowned admiral. Riding hard towards Plymouth, where the English ships lay, Sir Thomas Howard reached Dartmouth on the night of 6 May, and next morning took over, not only his dead brother's fleet but his brother's ship to which all the surviving noblemen, captains and shipmasters were summoned.

"At oon of the clock," he reported to Henry VIII, "I assembled in the Mary Rose my lorde Ferres and all oder noblemen and capeteynes and most expert masters of your army, and ther rehersed unto them your commandment yeven unto me, and after that I enquired of them the cause of their comyng from the parties of Breten without your commandement. Unto which they answered with oon hole voyce and all in oon tale they did it upon dyverse and resonable grounds."

Howard found that they had had less than three days' food aboard, with the next convoy remorselessly pinned in West Country ports by unfavourable winds. Those winds would take them back before their rations were completely consumed, so that they had left their station only at the last possible moment.

The second point they made was one which was to plague Henry VIII in the future and was never to be satisfactorily answered in his lifetime. It concerned the modern Mediterranean galley armed with modern bronze guns. Howard went

into this question with care and reported: "All your
capiteynes and masters generally sey, that, and they had con-
tynued there and oon day of calme had cum, if the galyse
being within 3 myle of them wold have doon their worst unto
them, they shuld not a fayled to have sonke such of your ships
as they list to have shot their ordinance unto; which ordinance, if it be such as they report, is a thynge marvelous." Then
Howard made a point which was well answered but which
Henry must have pondered later. He asked, could not the
two small English galleys, the rowbarges, and the boats of the
fleet, have attacked the French galleys? The unanimous reply
was that, in a calm, a single galley could take on the lot of
them. No doubt it was true, but there was the germ of an
idea here, which the ruthless Henry was to seize on and
develop.

Then, in his brother's ship. in his brother's cabin, the
elder Howard put the delicate question. Had these men left
their admiral to be butchered?

A single crayer, it was true, had suffered no casualties at
all; but she had attacked, closed and boarded. It was a fluke.
All the others had taken heavy loss, and in Howard's own
galley only 56 men remained alive out of the 175 who had
gone into the battle. Two-thirds of her crew had been killed
in action in the course of a few hours.

To Cardinal Wolsey, who had to know the truth, Howard
by implication condemned his brother. "I have here fowned
the worst ordered armye and furthest owte of rewle that ever
I saw. . . . Ther is a grete number stolen away. . . . Never
man saw men in greter fere then all the masters and maryners
be off the galies, insomoche that in a maner they had as leve
go into Purgatory as to the Trade."

Howard soon restored confidence and discipline in the
fleet and with it covered first the crossing of the main English
army to Calais for the French campaign and then took his
men and ships north to Scotland, which had entered the war
on the side of France. That was the year of Henry's triumph,
after a bad beginning. The year of fallen French towns, of
fleeing French cavalry, of the bloody defeat of the Scots at
Flodden Field, where Howard led the van. The Tudor king
had helped humble the super power across the Channel and
beaten down unaided his pugnacious northern neighbour.

But in the following year, 1514, Prégent was back in the Channel. They called him Prior John, because he was an officer of that military order, the Knights of Rhodes, soon to be the Knights of Malta.

With his galleys and foists, charged with great basilisks and other artillery, he came on the borders of Sussex in the night season, at a poor village there called Brighthelmstone [Brighton], and burnt it, taking such goods as he found. But when the people began to gather, by firing the beacons, Prior John sounded his trumpet to call his men aboard, and by that time it was day. Then certain archers that kept the watch followed Prior John to the sea, and shot so fast that they beat the galley men from the shore, and wounded many in the foist to which Prior John was constrained to wade, and was shot in the face with an arrow, so that he lost one of his eyes, and was like to have died of the hurt. And therefore he offered his image of wax before Our Lady at Boulogne, with the English arrow in the face for a miracle.

The English avenged the burning of Brighton by sending out a small fleet manned by 800 men under Sir John Wallop to the French coast, where they burnt 21 towns or villages. Prégent returned to the Mediterranean, having given the English an unwelcome taste of the new galley warfare. The next time the galleys came into the Channel, they were to be only part of a great French armada which was to attempt at Portsmouth what the English had failed to do at Brest. And in this battle the *Mary Rose* was sunk.

CHAPTER FOUR

"LEARN THIS FOR A RULE!"

"In no other enterprise, being never so feasible, I will not attempt, *your Majesty being so near*, without first making your Majesty privy thereunto; and not without your Grace's consent thereunto. . . . But have your Grace no doubt of any hasty or unadvised presumptious enterprise that I shall make, having charge of so weighty a matter under your Majesty, without being first well instructed from your Highness; for if I have any knowledge in any kind of thing, I received the same from yourself."
—Lord Lisle, from the *Great Harry*, 21 July, 1545, when putting forward a risky battle plan.

In 1545, just as in 1512, two banquets preceded the battle. Both were infinitely more dramatic, however, and might indeed have been scripted. That given by Francis I in the French flagship was the quiet opening to an event requiring full colour and the widest of wide screens to capture even a fraction of the impact it had in real life, whereas the dinner given by the English king in his flagship was more of a working lunch dramatically interrupted in the most theatrical manner which, at a pinch, could be staged in the living theatre. It is an historical mystery why Drake's undocumented game of bowls has always upstaged these entirely genuine events. For that matter, it is a mystery why the Spanish Armada is remembered and the French Armada forgotten.

The King of Spain sent 30,000 men against England in 136 ships, and not one of the 30,000 got ashore except as a prisoner or survivor from a wreck. Francis sent 30,000 men against England in 235 ships, and many thousands of them got on shore in full fighting order.

It is not as if there was anything unique about any of the favourite Spanish Armada scenes. The beacons flaming the warning of invasion from hilltop to hilltop were old, even in 1514, as we have seen when Prégent raided Brighton. The fire-ships were not a brilliant gimmick dreamt up by Drake, but standard tactics as used by Henry VIII in 1545. Nor was the pre-emptive strike against the gathering invasion force on its own coast a unique stroke of tactical genius, but a commonsense riposte also employed by Henry VIII in 1545. But being Henry, there was no dithering or last-minute cold feet; he hit first, and as hard as he could. Even Drake's gambit of trying to drive the whole Armada ashore on the Selsey peninsula east of Portsmouth was not, as naval historians have thought, an inspired last-minute improvisation by a born sailor. The idea was conceived in the English fleet in 1545 and passed on in writing by the English admiral to Henry VIII for authorisation. In 1588, that letter had been in the records for nearly half a century.

The only really significant difference lay in the weather. The summer of 1588 was like a rather bad winter, with continual gales; good weather for sailing ships, hopeless for galleys. The galleys of the Spanish Mediterranean fleet were all dispersed or wrecked early on. In 1545, however, there were many days of breathless calm, with such oppressive heat that the food in the holds quickly went bad. Perfect weather for galleys, but most awkward conditions for sailing ships which, without a wind, could not move. Moreover, the great carracks of 1545, English and French alike, were more clumsy than the new galleons of the Elizabethan navy so that light winds, although better than a flat calm, were not of much use to them. They needed a really good breeze. The galleys of the French Mediterranean fleet had matters all their own way all too often, hindered only by the new anti-galley ships which Henry was putting into the water as fast as they could be built.

While Francis moved from Paris to Le Havre merely to see his great fleet set sail, Henry came down to Portsmouth to control the battle. He had commanded all the major moves of the campaign so far and liked to keep his senior officers on a tight rein. Some of the noblemen were young and rash, like Howard at Conquet, and most lacked the kind of continuous battle experience which alone produces really professional expertise. Sir Peter Carew, brother of the vice-admiral who was to go down with the *Mary Rose*, had had a taste of his methods the previous year. Henry had begun the war by expanding the Calais bridgehead, virtually all that was left of the conquests of the Hundred Years War, by attacking and taking Boulogne. That gave him two ports on the far side of the Straits of Dover, with which to control the Channel. Francis had reacted violently and during the fighting Sir Charles Brandon, Duke of Suffolk, had given Sir Peter an urgent message which he was to take personally to the king. Handing over his position to his second-in-command Carew had ridden off to deliver the message. Henry immediately demanded to know why he was absent from his post, the castle of Hardelow. Sir Peter replied that it was on the orders of the Duke of Suffolk, commander of the army. The king blazed up. "Learn this for a rule!" he said. "So long as we ourselves are present there is no other general but ourselves. Neither can any man depart from his charge without our special warrant. And therefore you being thus come hither without our commandment, you are not able to answer for the same if we should minister that which by law we may do." Sir Peter had to bow and ask for pardon.

In 1545 Lord Lisle, Lord Admiral of England, had to defer to the king in all major naval matters, as the records show. The timing of a pre-emptive strike, the use of a new stratagem, the selection of new captains for the fleet list, the anchoring positions of the ships for the defensive battle, these were things that Henry decided. He delegated only when he was not present in person. He was squire of the manors of England and Wales and those ships were his personal possession. He acted as if he knew better than anyone else how to use them, and his officers were careful to agree. He was now in his fifties and had studied the matter all his life. He probably did know best. Certainly, all his main decisions were sound. And certainly, no commander had to explain to him the basic principles of war, as the unfortunate Drake had to do with Elizabeth and her Council. Just before the Spanish Armada sailed Drake was vainly urging, "The advantage of time and place in all martial actions is half a victory; which being lost is irrecoverable." No one had to tell her father that. Both in 1512 and in 1513 he had got there first, so that even an inexperienced admiral had had half a victory handed to him on a plate before the battle had even begun.

In 1544 he had not waited to be hit, but had allied himself with the Emperor, Charles V, and struck at two widely separated points in succession, first at one enemy, then at the other. In the spring, his fleet had convoyed 200 troopships to Scotland and the capture of Edinburgh. In July, his army and fleet had besieged and blockaded Boulogne which had surrendered in September. Francis had ordered his western fleet to gather in the Normandy ports, while sending his Mediterranean fleet north to its support, but Henry's fleet controlled the Channel and by Christmas the number of French merchant ships captured by the English privateers totalled 50.

But in 1545 his principal ally, the emperor whose domains included much of present-day Germany, Spain, Hungary and Italy, had not merely pulled out of the war but was being actively encouraged to join France and Scotland against him. England and Wales were left to fight alone against half a continent, with the hostile Scots at their back. It was a situation hardly to be paralleled again until the summer of 1940.

There was one difference. Henry had not neglected to pay his insurance policy. Ever since the breach with Rome in 1534, he had been rearming in step with the continuing rapid development of artillery. The *Mary Rose* had been rebuilt in 1536 and the *Great Harry* shortly afterwards; Leland had seen her stripped frames in Henry VII's great dock at Portsmouth as the shipwrights worked on her. After their rebuild, which brought the *Mary Rose* up to 700 tons from her previous 600 and increased her crew from 400 to 415, both ships were rearmed to a new standard pattern with the latest in bronze muzzle-loaders, together with the most up-to-date range of wrought-iron breech-loading guns. She now carried 91 guns compared to her previous 78, and 50 handguns now supplemented the 250 longbows, 150 Morris pikes and 150 bills ready for issue to her infantry.

The bronze battery pieces are so modern that we know what they are; there is no mystery about a cannon or a demi-cannon. Nor is there about the high-velocity bronze pieces, the culverins, demi-culverins, sakers and falcons. There is no documentation to explain the wrought-iron guns, but a change has obviously taken place. The old names of unknown iron guns have disappeared and their places have been taken by new names referring to guns of equally unknown type. The "great murderers" have been replaced by "port pieces", the "stone guns" by "fowlers", the "serpentines" by "slings"; "bases" and "hailshot pieces" have appeared, and only the "top pieces" remain from the old lists. The inventorist has listed the guns in descending order of weight and stated what type of shot they fired, although not the sizes (see Table 3). Theoretically, a complete excavation of the *Mary Rose* would "crack" the code of the Tudor gun lists. This is happening already and I now know that the heaviest pieces in both the bronze and iron categories were eight-inch guns at least, the former firing cast-iron shot, the latter stone.

Henry had added foreign purchases to his fleet, including great carracks from German, Spanish and Italian shipyards, but they do not carry so heavy an armament as the *Great Harry* and the *Mary Rose*, which are still the principal flagships, and their forecastles lack the elaborate archery tiers of the English-built warships. The king had also added no fewer than three classes of fast, oared vessels to his navy—fifteen "galleasses" of from 140 to 450 tons, ten "pynasses" of from 15 to 80 tons, and thirteen "roobaergys" or rowbarges of 20 tons each. These new vessels were flush-decked or nearly so, lacking the fighting castles necessary for engaging battleships and taking them by boarding; but that was not their purpose. They were to form a "wing" of fast, oared vessels as an anti-galley screen for the battleships. The king's navy now numbered over a hundred ships, more than four times as many as had been at Howard's disposal in 1512.

Its forward bases, particularly Portsmouth, were now protected by a ring of artillery fortifications. The guns of these castles were arranged in superimposed tiers, like a ship, and instead of having four long "curtain" walls, they had not less than a dozen short, angled sides to make them less vulnerable to return fire. This was modern in 1527, when Albrecht Dürer wrote his treatise to explain the new German ideas. They had hardly been formulated before continued progress by the gunfounders made them out of date. Henry's latest castle, brilliantly sited at Southsea and designed in accordance with his detailed instructions, was completed just in time for the battle of 1545. Its narrow, angled bastions were calculated to deflect harmlessly many of the shots which would have damaged the old-fashioned rounded bastion, besides giving inter-

locking fields of fire to its own guns. This basic arrangement
was then to last for three centuries.*

In June 1545 Henry ordered two disruptive strikes to be
made against the gathering French concentration at Le Havre
and other ports on the Normandy coast. Both were abortive.
The first, led by the Lord Admiral, met varying weather.
When it was calm the great French galley force prevented
the raid being pressed home beyond distant gunshot, while a
gale which sent the galleys hurrying to shelter blew onshore
which made matters dangerous in the shallows for the deep-
draught English ships. The second was an attack by thirty
fire-ships with an escort led by Sir John Barkleye in the *Lesse
Galley*. They were to be loosed into the estuary of the Seine
among the massed French shipping. The fire-ships were
recently captured merchantment still with their original
crews on board, and when a gale struck the English fleet on
the night of 21 June they tried to slip away in the darkness.
The *Lesse Galley* led the chase and fired a warning gun, but
at this critical moment the gun burst and Sir John was cut
down by a hurtling fragment of iron. In the confusion, two-
thirds of the fire-ships got away.

By July, the French king's armada was almost complete,
the principal ships being anchored in the wide estuary of the
Seine between the hills of Le Havre and Honfleur. Sieur
Martin du Bellay, an officer of the cavalry force embarked
in the invasion fleet, wrote the most complete account which
survives from the French side.† He stated that there were
235 vessels in all, of which 150 were large "roundships", pre-

---

* In the 1930s, when I used to play schoolboy football in its grounds,
the Henrician core of the fortification had been extended to mount
heavy coastal guns in steel casemates. In May 1940, when from my
window at Southsea I saw with astonishment a Heinkel 111 held in the
searchlights, it was a machine-gun from Southsea Castle which opened
up on it—the first time I ever heard a shot fired in earnest. The thought
that the machine actually contained enemies was almost unbelievable.
The Castle was not demilitarised until after 1945, having seen 400 years'
active service. It is now an artillery museum and contains two rooms
devoted to our recoveries from the *Mary Rose*.

† Published in 1580, I am using a typescript copy of the original sixteenth century MS., kindly supplied by the Curator of Carisbrooke Castle
Museum, Isle of Wight, which I have had freshly translated into suitably
archaic English. There is also an English translation of part of this MS.,
published in 1757 by John Entick in his *A New Naval History*.

sumably carracks, 60 were "flutes", presumably shallow-draught Dutch-built cargo vessels for men, horses and stores, and no fewer than 25 were Mediterranean galleys of the latest and largest type. Commanded by Claude D'Annebault, Baron de Retz, Admiral of France, Marshal of France, Governor of Normandy, this was the greatest fleet ever to be seen in Europe up to that time and for a long time afterwards. Its 30,000 men were to assault and take Portsmouth, the principal English base on the Channel coast and the most heavily defended, at the same time as Marshal du Biez, commanding the French land army, attacked and recaptured Boulogne, which had been refortified by the English.

The French were free to concentrate entirely against England, which perhaps explains why their plan consisted of two unsubtle head-on attacks against defended positions widely separated. One or the other of the two attacks was certainly unnecessary. If the English fleet was defeated and Portsmouth taken, then Boulogne, its communications cut, must fall also. But if everything was turned against Boulogne, and in consequence it fell, then the English fleet would be powerless to help. The obvious move was a combined assault first on Boulogne, then on Calais, to drive the English entirely out of Europe. The French may have calculated that a prior attack on Portsmouth could not fail to affect the carriage of reinforcements and supplies across the Channel into Boulogne. Certainly, as soon as the French king learned, early in July, that Marshal du Biez would be ready to assault Boulogne by mid-August, he ordered the fleet to sail for Portsmouth and rode down to Le Havre with his court to watch it set out.

It would be unfair to say that the principal military feat performed by Francis I was to throw Henry VIII in a wrestling bout, during their younger days; but in French history he is remembered, if at all, for being captured with his whole army at Pavia in 1525. Now, on 6 July 1545 he dined in state together with the ladies of his court on board Admiral D'Annebault's flagship, the 800-ton *Carraquon,* which du Bellay says was the finest ship in Western Europe, carrying 100 bronze guns. Then, while he rode to the heights of Caux Head to get the best view of the fleet putting to sea, the flagship began to heave in her anchor cables. At this moment the cooks, possibly tired and flustered after preparing the royal banquet, had an accident with the oven. The fire spread, as it had in the *Cordelière* and the *Regent,* with terrifying rapidity. There was time enough to save the fleet treasury and for some men to dive overboard and be picked up by the galleys, but when the flames reached the gundecks, the open ports acted like chimneys in creating draughts and then the heated, loaded guns began to explode, hurling their shot in a hail around the ship, forcing the galleys to retire and damaging or sinking a number of neighbouring craft.

D'Annebault transferred his headquarters and the treasury to the next greatest of the carracks, *la Maistresse.* But in going out of Honfleur into the roadstead, she struck the ground. At first, the damage was thought not to be serious and she put to sea at the head of the fleet, setting course for the Isle of Wight.

On Saturday 18 July (which would be 28 July by the modern calendar) King Henry VIII held a business lunch aboard the *Great Harry* at Portsmouth. In the afternoon he had an appointment with the Emperor's ambassador, Francis Vander Delft, who was also being entertained on board the English flagship. The ambassador subsequently reported that "the fleet did not exceed 80 sail but 40 of them were large and beautiful and 60 more were expected from the West." The number of warships was in fact about 60 and 40 more were on their way from West Country ports and from the Thames. The English concentration was not complete. When achieved it would total about 100 ships manned by 12,000 men. Even then, it would be outmatched by the French force of 30,000 men in 235 ships. But if the French came ashore, as they intended to, it would be a different matter. Henry was able to call out 140,000 men of the militia that summer and although he had a Scottish Front as well as a Channel Front to look to, any French success was likely to be local— unless he made a rash move and lost most or all of his fleet. This he was determined not to do, and by laying down precisely the anchoring positions for a defensive battle off Portsmouth and above all, by being present in person as the commanding general, he was making as sure as humanly possible that no over-eager subordinate was likely to lose his fleet for him.

Those present at the lunch included Sir John Dudley, Viscount Lisle, appointed Lord Admiral two years before, Sir George Carew, Lieutenant-General of the Horse (whose appointment as vice-admiral in the *Mary Rose* was made on this day), his uncle, Sir Gawen Carew, who commanded the 600-ton *Matthew Gonson,* and his younger brother, 31-year-old Sir Peter Carew. Sir Peter was still commanding the 700-ton *Great Venetian,* having with "piteous moan" protested against his appointment to one of the new fast galleasses on the grounds that he would see more close action in a great carrack which could board any ship of the enemy. He had begun his military career as an infantry captain before taking over a cavalry command. Not mentioned, but probably present also, was the captain of the *Mary Rose,* Roger Grenville, who was related to the Lisles. His youngest son, Richard Grenville, at this time a child of three, was to take his ship alone into an entire Spanish fleet off the Azores in 1591, possibly not willing to desert some sick men he had left on shore, an action which his contemporary, Sir William Monson, was to describe as "unadvised negligence and wilful obstinacy".

After the meal, the king spoke secretly to the two admirals, Lisle of the *Great Harry* and Carew of the *Mary Rose.* He may have discussed the new fighting instructions, which were not issued as a written order for another four weeks. They were really the old fighting code amended to include the new anti-galley screen. Some of the ships intended for it were still building but enough were present to make new tactics possible. The sheer size of the fleet now demanded that it be sub-divided. There were to be three divisions, each under a separate commander, called the Van, Battle and Wing, each with a different role to play.* The Van contained most of the big ships and was the shock force; it was to engage the enemy's largest vessels, admiral engaging admiral and every captain choosing an opponent of equal size. The Battle was a

---

* Some nautical historians have confused this with the standard march formation for armies, consisting of Van, Battle and Rear, which advanced to contact and then extended in line, Van moving to the right of the Battle, Rear moving to the left of it; i.e. a perfectly ordinary military deployment, to avoid envelopment of flanks. The English sea forces definitely did not intend to fight like this, in line abreast, as a study of the instructions makes clear.

similar but smaller force and would nowadays be regarded as second wave or tactical reserve. The attack of the Van would result in confusion, a smoke-shrouded *mêlée*. The Battle could best affect this fight by keeping together under command and then crashing into it at the decisive moment. Both Van and Battle would have a small, close escort of oared, anti-galley vessels, but the bulk of these would be formed into the distant escort, known as the Wing, which was to keep always to windward of the main action, retaining freedom of movement and not closing, so as to "the better beate off the gallies from the great ships". The vastly increased number of the enemy's galleys, twenty-five as compared to the half-dozen in 1513, made the Wing a very important addition to the organisation and practical tactics of the fleet.

How far the movements of the three divisions could be controlled by signals is not known. The final paragraph of the instructions gave only the secret passwords for use at night. "God save King Henry" was to be the challenge and the reply was to be "Long to raigne over us". After the secret talks the king gave Carew the insignia of his new appointment as vice-admiral, the traditional gold whistle on a chain, with the appropriate congratulations.

Almost certainly, the king had briefed them both on policy matters. Subsequent events and the tenor of the surviving documents makes clear what his intentions were. In plain summary, he must have said: "We are greatly outnumbered and have here only part of our force. We will therefore fight an offensive-defensive. We will do nothing rash. But we must make the enemy pay for what he does. We will give ground only if we are forced to. And if he makes a mistake, we will make him pay for that, too. But mind, when you counter-attack, your stroke will be strictly limited and tightly controlled. We do not have to take risks. We have an excellent defensive position here; the risks are for the French to take. If they choose not to take them, or try and fail, it is all one; to win, we merely have to stay here. To win, they have to succeed in a very great feat of arms, which I do not think they will do."

The king then gave Vander Delft his interview, which was much less cordial. The ambassador could hardly get a word in edgeways for Henry's blistering complaints about the conduct of his master, the emperor, and his speciously liberal pleas for England to make a magnanimous gesture to France by handing over Boulogne were tartly rejected. Vander Delft was alarmed, suspecting double-dealing, his own master being expert at that. But the Tudor king meant what he said. He was not going to back down from a fight, particularly not from a fight he thought he could win.

The ambassador had hardly left the *Great Harry* before Henry ordered a lookout to be sent to the maintop. Sir Peter's biographer wrote:

> The word was no sooner spoke but that Peter Carew was as forward, and forthwith climbeth up to the top of the ship, and there sitting, the King asked him what news, who told him that he had sight of three or four ships, but, as he thought, they were merchants. But it was not long but he had espied a great number, and then he cried out to the King there was, as he thought, a large fleet of men-of-war. The King supposing them to be the French men-of-war, as they were indeed, willed the board to be taken up, and every man to go to his own ship, as also a long boat to come and carry him on land.

Shortly afterwards, and very smartly, the ships began to come out of harbour, passing through the narrow entrance flanked by a round tower and a blockhouse, which could be barred by a great iron chain. They kept close to land on their left-hand side, passing close under the earth-and-timber walls of the town, now lined with guns and armed men. Beyond this was open common land, low-lying and marshy, and beyond this again the gleaming white walls of Southsea Castle with its central tower, almost surrounded by the multi-coloured tents and pavilions of the English army under Sir Charles Brandon, Duke of Suffolk. This was the position chosen by the king for his command post, where he was in control of his army, to which reinforcements were streaming in, and with a direct and unobscured view over the entire battle area to seaward.

The main body of the French force was still distant but D'Annebault had sent forward four galleys under the Baron de la Garde and these were off St. Helens, only three or four miles away. They could see the English just as clearly, and

were impressed. "The enemy's force consisted of sixty picked
ships well arrayed for war, fourteen of which, helped by a
land breeze, came out of Portsmouth with such alacrity and
in such fine order, that one had the impression that they were
going to engage our whole fleet on their own," wrote du
Bellay. "But when our Admiral sent the rest of our galleys
forward, the remainder of their force also came out of harbour
to meet them."

But before the English ships came abreast of the castle,
they put their helms over and steered away towards the south.
These apparently arbitrary actions were dictated by the contours of the seabed. Their keels were following a deep channel
which had been cut through the landscape by a river long ago,
and long since submerged. To left and right were sandbanks
barely covered by the tide at low water, Horse Sand to the
east and Spit Sand to the west, which many thousands of years
ago had been the tops of hills which had lined the now-
drowned river valley. They were steering for a gap where
this invisible river joined an even greater sunken valley, that
of the Solent River leading down from Southampton. Today
it is marked on either side by two nineteenth-century sea
forts, Horse Sand and Noman's Land, where the seabed
changes from a shallow undersea plain to an abrupt slope
into muddy darkness 90 feet below.

Those old rivers still flowed, funnelling the immense
interchange of water caused by the tides twice in every 24
hours through comparatively narrow, deep channels. So the
tidal streams were unusually powerful as well as being complicated. They ran fast enough not merely to be able to halt
a sailing ship trying to stem the current, but could at times
push it bodily backwards. This can be observed today. But,
equally, those who knew the tidal pattern well could use
those forces, to go into harbour or to come out, often in
defiance of the wind. As a battleground for unwieldy sailing
ships it was awkward indeed, and favoured those with the
most precise local knowledge. The king's plan was based on
it and to make matters more difficult for the French, he had
removed the buoys which marked the intricate pattern of
channels and shallows.

The English bore boldly on, opening fire on the vanguard
of the French, but retiring before they could be engaged by

the whole of that immense force. "There was a little skirmish between our ships, being in number 60, but it is true we were too weak and withdrew within the Horse," wrote Sir John Oglander in 1610. A Deputy Governor of Portsmouth, he collected many tales of the battle and probably talked to men who had fought in it. Du Bellay, who was there, wrote:

> After a long fight with gun-shot, the enemy began to slip to the left to the shelter of the land. This was a place where their ships were defended by a few forts that stood on the cliff behind them and on the other side by hidden shoals and rocks, with only a narrow and oblique entrance for a few ships at a time. This withdrawal, and the approaching night, put an end to the first day's fighting, without our having suffered notable loss from their cannon shot.

With his enemy sheltering behind the shallows of the Gosport shore, covered by the fire of three forts behind them and the guns of Portsmouth on one flank, Admiral D'Annebault was presented with a tricky problem. Before he could even attempt to solve it, his flagship sank. *La Maistresse*, probably already strained by bumping on the bar at Honfleur, had developed a leak which could not be checked and she went down in the shallows off St. Helens. The admiral seems to have been away at the time, probably with the galleys, but when he got back he found that her guns, stores and money had been saved by the prompt action of his vice-admiral, de Moüy de la Meilleraye. The ship was salvaged and either beached by Brading harbour or taken back to Le Havre for repair; du Bellay is not clear on this point. In any event, the French commander-in-chief had now lost two flagships and had to choose a third, as well as prepare a battle plan for the morrow.

His decision was to attempt to bring on a general engagement between the two main fleets by using some of his galleys as decoys. These fast, shallow-draught but frail vessels were "to go forward to where the English were anchored, engage them in as fierce a gunfire skirmish as possible, and still fighting, withdraw towards the main fleet", du Bellay recorded.

D'Annebault sub-divided this main force into a centre of 30 picked ships under his own command, which was to be flanked by two wings of 36 ships each. The right wing was

to be led by the Siegneur de Boutiers, second in command
of the army, and the left by Joachim de Chanannes, Baron de
Curton. The 60 English ships were to be sucked forward by
the harassing fire of 25 galleys into more open water, where
102 large warships would converge on them for a decisive
battle. The remaining 107 vessels of the French array were
probably in reserve, ready to intercept any English reinforcements coming from round the Isle of Wight.

It was the sight of the menacing front of the fighting fleet,
facing Portsmouth at a distance of only seven or eight miles,
which greeted Henry VIII's government at dawn on the day
of battle, Sunday, 19 July. His Privy Council, which he carried
to Portsmouth with him, dictated four urgent letters that day,
"signifying that 22 galleys were anchored on this side St.
Ellen's Poynt, and over 100 sail in sight behind them".

CHAPTER FIVE

"TOO MUCH FOLLY"

'But one day of all other, the whole navy of the
Englishmen made out, and purposed to set on the
Frenchmen; but in their setting forward, a goodly
ship of England, called the Mary Rose, was, by too
much folly, drowned in the midst of the haven, for
she was laden with much ordnance, and the ports
left open, which were very low, and the great ordnance unbreached, so that when the ship should
turn, the water entered, and suddenly she sank'.
—Edward Hall's *Chronicle*, 1548.

It was a glorious summer weekend, particularly welcome after
the succession of westerly gales during May and June. Today
it would have brought endless lines of cars heading for the
coast along macadamised or concrete roads, to jam irretriev-
ably in country lanes little changed since the days of the
Normans. In July 1545, instead of the low throb of engines,
there was the high-pitched clatter of hooves, the tramp of
heavily laden men, the roar and rumble of gun-carts and
transport wagons.

The sun glittered on the points of the long pikes which
rose like a forest of steel high above the ranks of the marching
militia and on the flat axe-like blades of the bills. Here and
there were companies of archers with their long yellow bow-
staves held at the slope over their shoulders, short swords
swinging at their waists. At the head of each company strode
its captain, followed by the standard-bearer holding the pole
of the company pennon stiffly in both hands before him. In
battle, the flag would be a rallying and recognition point for
the unit. And these men were marching to battle. The militia
of Sussex and Hampshire, of Wiltshire and the Isle of Wight
were gathering at the coast.

Those marching towards Portsmouth laboured up the
slopes of a long ridge called Portsdown Hill, the last fold of

the South Downs. As they crested the top, they saw a sight to
take away what little breath they had left. The whole of the
coastline from Selsey Bill in Sussex almost to Dorset in the
west was laid out in front of them like a giant, coloured shim-
mering map. Directly below lay the still sheet of water, five
miles long from north to south, which is Portsmouth Harbour,
lapping up to the walls of the old Roman fort at Portchester.
Beyond was the glittering silver-blue of the open sea and
further away the high, rolling downs of the Isle of Wight
blocking the horizon.

What made the sight the more extraordinary were the
ships, not mere cockleshells but high-castled greatships brilliantly painted and gay with flags and topstreamers. There
were hundreds of them, floating like toys on the still water.
No one in living memory had ever seen so many ships. But
they were not toys. They were full of guns and armoured
men. They were death.

The old soldiers knew. The poet George Gascoigne, in his
twenties that day, was to write:

My promise was, and I record it so,
To write in verse (God wot though little worth)
That war seems sweet to such as little know
What comes thereby, what fruits it bringeth forth. . . .
I set aside to tell the restless toil,
The mangled corpse, the lamed limbs at last,
The shortened years by fret of fevers foul.
The smoothest skin with scabs and scars disgraced,
The frolic favour frounst and foul defaced,
The broken sleeps, the dreadful dreams, the woe,
Which one with war and cannot from him go.

It was too far as yet to make out the colours, to tell which
were "ours" and which were "theirs". Which was probably
just as well, for it was by far the smallest group which flew
the red-crossed flag of St. George and long streamers of Tudor
green and white from every mast, under the royal standard.
They lay anchored like a wedge in the triangle of shallow
sea between Portsmouth town and the Gosport shore.

Five or six miles away an immense forest of masts obscured
the eastern tip of the Isle of Wight and occupied the entire
anchorage of St. Helens, where 30,000 men of the French

invasion force waited within close cannon shot of the peaceful fields and smoke from quiet villages rose vertically in the still air. Not a breath of wind stirred the trees. It was from this quarter that the first movement came.

Antoine Escalin, Baron de la Garde, a flamboyant commander popularly known as the "Polin" or "Captain Crossbreed", led the galleys forward from his great flag-galley, the *Reale*, which seated five men to every oar. The other galley squadrons followed his, the soberly decorated vessels of the French unit led by Pierre de Blacas, Chevalier D'Aulps, Knight of Malta, and the Italian galleys of Leone Strozzi, Prior of Capua, Knight of Malta. They were hard and competent men commanding superbly trained and battle-experienced crews. Sails furled to their lateen yards, the long rows of heavy oars rising and falling together like the legs of monstrous centipedes, they advanced, the muzzles of their forward-firing heavy guns pointed at the motionless English ships. The still, blue water, the current almost slack, was perfect for them; and with their shallow draught the shoals where the English lay held no hazard.

A stab of bright flame leapt from the bows of the leading galley and a great cloud of smoke gushed out. Her beakhead drove forward into it, the billowing cloud wreathed her bows and then shrouded the hull for a moment before she emerged from her own battle smoke. Then the other galleys began to open fire. For long seconds, the whole scene appeared to all the distant watchers to be taking place in slow motion and in utter silence.

Then the rumble of the gunfire rolled across the water to them—*duf, duf, duf, duf, duf.** Thud on distant thud as the French fired their heavy ordnance and one by one disappeared in the reeking powder smoke. Soon only the topmasts of the

* The sounds and scenes of a sea battle fought with these weapons were recorded by an anonymous Scottish author a few years later, in 1548, but not published until 1801 as *"The Camplaynt of Scotland"*. He also noted the exact sequence of orders for making sail and engaging an enemy vessel, as well as quoting the work songs. Taken with a surviving "station list" for the *Great Harry*, showing how her work force was organised, this has enabled me to reconstruct the background to the battle. Captain John Smith's *"A Sea Grammar"*, published in 1627, was also useful in outlining and explaining the current battle drill, not very much different then than it had been in Tudor times.

larger English ships could be seen above the billowing clouds
that, in the still morning air, hung over the sea. But experienced men of war could still read the battle through their
ears. Among the slow, thudding detonations of the heavy
artillery came the sharp cracks of the lighter guns firing, *tirduf, tirduf, tirduf,* and now and then the chatter of the swivels
and handguns, *tik-tak, tik-tak, tik-tak,* like a jackdaw knock-
ing on wood. In the ships, the stinking gunpowder smoke
hung like a fog on the decks, so that no man could see his
own length.

Wrote du Bellay:

> Our plans were carried out very boldly, but a change in
> the weather brought such a change in the dangers, that
> one could not judge in such short space of time, to whom
> fortune showed itself more favourable—to them or to us.
> For in the morning with the help of the sea which was calm,
> without wind nor force of current, our galleys could be
> steered and manoeuvred at will to the detriment of the
> enemy. He, unable to move from lack of wind, lay openly
> exposed to the destructive force of our guns, which could
> do more harm to his ships than he could to us; and all the
> more so, as the English ships were higher and bulkier and
> easier to hit while our galleys could, by using their oars,
> manoeuvre so as not to be hit themselves or retreat if neces-
> sary. Fortune supported our force in this way for more
> than one hour: during which time, among other hurt
> suffered by the enemy, the *Great Harry,* which carried their
> admiral, was so damaged, that had she not been supported
> and helped by nearby ships, she would have sunk.

For an hour the English endured it grimly, gunports open,
firing when they could at their elusive targets. Then the wind
came suddenly. The blue water broke up, lost its calm,
ceased to reflect the white clouds of summer. It was blowing
from the north, behind the English. Simultaneously, the time
being after high water, the ebb tide began to run—from the
north; from the English to the French. The sea, bronze-green
now, began to move and ripple past the heavy rope anchor
cables. The great ships began to stir.

Whistles echoed shrill along their decks, and at the
shouted words of command that followed the forecastle and

capstan men began to haul in the dripping anchor cables. The steady chanting of the work parties sounded through the drifting smoke. "Haul one and all! Haul one and all!" More whistles shrilled and the men ran to their stations for loosing sails, hoisting sailyards, and setting sails. They were divided into great gangs of up to 120 men for this heavy labour, and sub-divided into parties for each mast and for each sail on that mast, with "principal" men for the tasks requiring skill and judgement as well as muscle. The roar of the work songs rose and fell. Ending with a great shout, as the foresail billowed out, followed by the fore topsail, followed by the small steering sail on the bonaventure mast at the stern.

Slowly, the *Great Harry* came round before the wind, four men at her helm, but steered more by her fore and aft sails than by her rudder; and after her, the *Mary Rose*, an almost identical ship, but smaller, heeling over now as the wind caught the newly released sails, her four fighting tops with their loads of men, limepots, missiles, swivel-guns and ammunition tilting wildly over. There was confused shouting among the screech of whistles. Men must have found it hard to keep their footing in the four-storey-high fighting castle, itself perched on top of two gundecks. The gunport lids of the lower deck were already open, the sun glinting on the bronze of the great muzzle-loading artillery and on the blue-grey forged ironwork of the big breech-loading quick-firers. It was said afterwards on good authority (Sir Peter Carew's biographer) that half the mariners in the *Mary Rose* were so experienced that they were fit to be shipmasters in their own right; and that, consequently, no man would take orders from another. And it was said also that the heavy guns had not been secured, because of the sense of safety given by the calm sea that hot Sunday morning, and that anyway she was overloaded, bringing the gunports close to the water.

But what the expert witnesses in the nearest ships saw was gross mishandling of the vessel as she hoisted sail and turned towards the enemy. One of the most concerned was Sir Gawen Carew, commanding the 600-ton *Matthew Gonson*, and uncle to Sir George Carew, the vice-admiral. He called his own shipmaster and asked him what the extraordinary manœuvres of the *Mary Rose* meant, to which the man replied briefly that if she carried on heeling like that, "she was like to be cast away". The *Matthew Gonson* passed the wallowing flagship, coming so close that Sir Gawen could call out to Sir George, asking what was the matter. And the last recorded words of Sir George Carew were, "I have the sort of knaves I cannot rule."

Vander Delft, the emperor's ambassador, wrote five days later: "Was told by a Fleming among the survivors that when she heeled over with the wind the water entered by the lowest row of gunports which had been left open after firing. All the 500 men on board were drowned save about 25 or 30 servants, sailors and the like." Du Bellay assumed that she had been sunk by French gunfire and wrote that of her 500–600 men only 35 were saved. Sir Peter Carew, through his biographer, stated that she went down with 700 men, "whereof very few escaped". Certainly, she must have been carrying more than her normal complement of 415, possibly she may have embarked more infantry for a battle so close to base; and the extra weight might have brought her gunports dangerously low. But no one really knows.

From the heights of Southsea Castle, just over a mile away, the tragedy horrified the spectators. Hardly had her gunports dipped under, than the *Mary Rose* rolled right over, so that the watchers were looking down on her decks, packed with men. It is said that one long wailing cry was heard on the shore as the hundreds of hopelessly trapped men went down below the waves in an instant, dying like rats, miserably, without hope of escape or rescue. Stunned, the king and Lady Mary Carew saw now only two crazily heeled masts sticking out of the water, where the vice-flagship had been only a moment before, with some men still clinging to the tops and the yards and a few, a pitifully few, heads of swimmers bobbing in the disturbed water. They were lightly clad servants or sailors. For men in armour, there was no hope. As she realised that she had just seen her husband die in front of her eyes, Lady Carew fainted.

As her brother-in-law's biographer put it, "with that sight she fell into a swooning". And, he added, "The King, being oppressed with sorrow on every side, comforted her, and thanked God for the other,* hoping that of a hard beginning, there would follow a better ending".

* Presumably the king meant Sir Peter, a younger brother who would

Almost immediately, the tide of battle changed. Du Bellay wrote:

> Other more memorable losses they would have suffered if the weather had not changed in their favour. This not only freed them from the danger of our attack, but was favourable for them to attack us, for there rose a land breeze, which together with the current, brought them down under full sail upon our galleys. This change was so sudden, that our men hardly had time to turn the prows round. In the heat of battle during the calm, the galleys had got so close together, that it seemed that the ships coming at them so suddenly and with such force, must inevitably run over them and send them to the bottom, before they could do anything to escape.

The Cowdray engraving shows four galleys arrayed like the spokes of a wheel, two of them bows on to the *Great Harry*, and firing, and with a great cloud of answering gunsmoke thundering out from the bow pieces of the English flagship. This may depict the emergency turn by the galleys, a highly skilled manoeuvre to completely reverse course while stopped, by going ahead with the oars on one side, and going astern with the oars on the other side. This would be difficult to carry out, if the galleys had got themselves bunched together, as du Bellay says, for each long, narrow vessel pivots on herself. Du Belley continues:

> Through the great assurance of the captains, through the skill and experience of the seamen and the galley slaves, power and extreme speed were available to turn round the prows of the galleys. Then our men, by fast rowing and with the help of the sails, moved off within a few hours to where they came within range of the guns of our own fleet. And then they began to space out the strokes, so as to slow down slightly, and tempt the enemy out of his position, as they had been ordered to do.

---

carry on the family line. The biographer was John Hooker, born about 1524. His work was not published until 1857 when, edited by John Maclean, it appeared as *The Life and Times of Sir Peter Carew, Kt. (from the original manuscript).*

Now it was the turn of the galleys to suffer gunfire without reply, for the faster ships of Henry's anti-galley screen were overtaking them.

> Our enemies had special ships, which they call Ramberges. In shape they were long for their breadth and much narrower than the galleys so as to be better steered and controlled in the currents which are common in that sea; and the crews are so skilled that in these ships they can rival the speed of a galley. A few of them followed astern of our galleys at an incredible speed and badly harassed them with their artillery, against which the galleys had no defence, having no artillery astern. Nor could they turn to face their pursuers, for that would allow the enemy fleet to run them down under full sail and capsize them. However, the Prior of Capua, Peter Strozzi, unable to endure this disgrace any longer, and trusting in the agility of his galley, began to wheel round upon the leading English ship which had got ahead of the others and was almost touching with his bows the stern of one of our galleys. But the English ship, being shorter, turned quicker, and steered back towards the English warships. And that ended the chase by all of them. In that whole engagement we suffered the loss of a few convicts and a few private soldiers, but not one man of importance was lost.

However, an English agent later reported from Le Havre the funeral of a galley captain, who "was so hurt, by reason of a shot of the *Great Harry* as they took it, that he died at New Haven and is there buried".

> Admiral D'Annebault had used the wind to get his fleet into their prearranged battle order and was about to give the signal for a general attack on the advancing English fleet when he saw the leading rowbarges turn away. "Now he knew for certain," wrote du Bellay, "that the enemy was hoping that we, trusting in our strength, would rashly go out and pursue them to our disadvantage; that their intention was to chase our galleys only as far they could do so without risk, and that they hoped to lure us forward on to the shoals under the fire of their batteries."

So ended the second day of cautious manœuvring and skirmishing. The results were even, each side having lost a flagship by accident and inflicted some damage on the other by gunfire. But while the French were busy refloating *la Maistresse* behind the cover of their great fleet, the English could not attempt to do the same for their *Mary Rose* until the French were either defeated outright or driven off for good, because to raise such a weight required the lifting power of two other ships of equal size, which could not be spared from the fighting fleet until the crisis was past.

To win, D'Annebault had to do more than skirmish—he had to bring on a battle of main fleet against main fleet and crush the English with his vastly superior numbers. The tempting lure of the galleys having failed, he decided to play another card—his infantry and cavalry—in order to bring on a sea battle in more open water. This game, as he saw it, was psychological warfare. Again, du Bellay writes:

> Our Admiral had had news that the King of England had come to Portsmouth, and he thought that if we made a landing on the Isle of Wight and fired the countryside in the sight of the King, and killed his people only a handsbreadth from him, then the indignation he would feel at such an insult, the pity he would have for the wounding and death of his subjects, and the spectacle of the wasting and burning of his realm, would make him send his ships to the rescue, especially as they were barely two cannon shot away.* But if he did not act, then the displeasure of his subjects, who would see themselves abandoned by their Prince, although he was present, might produce sedition and mutiny. The Admiral ordered the invasion to take place in three different areas simultaneously, so as to divide the enemy's forces.

The three beachheads were to be secured by soldiers landed from the 25 galleys, which were ideal invasion craft because of their shallow draught and ability to go anywhere, regardless of the wind. Two of the beaches to be attacked were fortified. The wide sweep of Sandown Bay, with low-lying ground behind it ideal for disembarking men, horses

---

* The distance was between five and six miles, which suggests that even then the extreme range of artillery was near enough the three miles which was to become for centuries the traditional limit of territorial waters.

and guns, was commanded by one of Henry VIII's new castles
(since swallowed by the sea), while a small fort somewhere
between Bembridge and Seaview commanded the St. Helens
area with its guns. Apparently, the French tried to soften
them up first, for Vander Delft reported, "On Monday firing
on both sides lasted all day and at nightfall one of the French
galleys was damaged." Du Bellay says that the little fort near
St. Helens kept firing into the flanks of the galleys, and
Vander Delft reported later an English assertion to have sunk
one of them.

On Tuesday, 21 July, the French stormed the beaches.
Pietro Strozzi, brother of the Prior of Capua, rushed the little
fort, drove the surviving defenders into the trees beyond and
fired ten or a dozen houses of the nearest village. The smoke
of burning homes went billowing up into the English sky.
At Sandown, the galley captains Marsay and Pierrebon led
their troops against the castle. Both leaders fell, wounded.
The assault failed.

But the main attack, directed against the southern heights
of the island at Bonchurch, the really serious assault of the
day, went in against no opposition. The importance of this
stroke is evident by the rank and quality of the two men who
led it—the Seigneur de Tais, Colonel-General of the infantry,
commander of the French army embarked in D'Annebault's
ships, and the Baron de la Garde, the flamboyant "Captain
Polin", commander of the entire galley force. Their men got
ashore without loss, at the foot of high, crumbling cliffs. Led
by the Seigneur de Moneins, their advance guard scrambled
up the broken, partly wooded incline towards their first objective, the road to Newport, the central town of the island.
There was no sign of the English at all, until the whip and
howl of an arrow storm from unseen archers engulfed them.
De Moneins had his right hand transfixed and the advance
came to a halt. "Confident in their position, they showed a
bold front to our men," wrote du Bellay, who seems to have
been an eye-witness of the Bonchurch fighting.

Now that the position of the defenders had been revealed,
the main French force formed up and attacked. "We made
them abandon their position and retire in confusion," du
Bellay went on; "but could only follow them by breaking
ranks and advancing in single file". Writing from the

memories of old men who had fought there, Sir John Oglander reported that "There was a hot skirmish between them and us and many were slain." All the fighting was uphill, favouring the younger, fitter men. A stout officer of the Wiltshire militia, Captain Fischer, seeing himself being overtaken by the leading French, was heard to shout desperately, "A hundred pounds for a horse!" He was never seen again, but his cry for help was remembered and Oglander recorded it, with his own comment, "but in that confusion, no horse could be had, not for a Kingdom".* The French burst into Bonchurch, and soon the flames were crackling and hissing among the houses and the farms, and more clouds of smoke were rising above the hills of the Isle of Wight to signal the French success.

D'Annebault would have been astounded to learn of Henry VIII's reaction, as recorded by Oglander. "Our King also sent word to us that we should retreat in order, seeking to draw all their strength ashore far from their ships, hoping for a favourable opportunity to surprise their fleet." The Privy Council minutes this day, 21 July, confirm that Henry saw how the invasion must weaken the French and sought to take advantage of it, offensively. The Lord Admiral was told that "if the Frenchmen continue landing men in the Isle and so disfurnish their galleys, he might essay some attempt against them".

By risking his galleys, without which his great force was a blunt instrument indeed, the French admiral had sadly misjudged both the temper of the English and the real character of Henry VIII. The island's garrison was small, but the king promptly reinforced it. Sir Richard Worsley, Captain of the Isle of Wight, had called out 1,500 men of the local militia to support the 50-strong garrison of the forts and the 234 workmen labouring on the defences. Henry now sent over to Wight from the mainland 2,700 of the Hampshire militia and 900 from Wiltshire, together with an army headquarters to control them under Edward Bellingham. The two orthodox gambits, defend all the beaches or concentrate after the landings, were impossible—the numbers were too few for the first, the roads too bad for the second. Bellingham's 5,400 men were ordered

* Presumably, the story was told long after and came to the notice of William Shakespeare.

to hold in groups only the high ground, talking to each other across the undefended countryside between by means of hill-top beacons for which the king had devised a code signalling system.

The main French army was still afloat, not yet committed. The 500 light horsemen and their mounts were also still aboard the transports. If they could get ashore, the French army would have a marked advantage in mobility over the infantry of the part-time English militia. All were being held back for the right place and the right moment—the calculated stroke. Unlike most of their opponents, they were fully trained soldiers and in high spirits, too, full of confidence and eager to fight. Much more eager than their commanders. First, they had been mere spectators of the sea skirmishing at Spithead, with no general attack permitted although they outnumbered their enemies by four to one. Now, they were still being kept penned in their ships. What was their admiral afraid of? One could walk ashore and go for a stroll, for all the enemy could do. The sight of the empty beaches and the smoke rising above the trees from both Bembridge on their right and Bonchurch on their left, where their comrades were burning and pillaging at will, was finally too much.

Many of them, possibly as many as 2,000 men, swarmed into the boats and made for the shore, probably in Whitecliff Bay.* Probably, the unofficial landing was led by officers, for above the sheer white face of Culver Cliff on their left rose the long whaleback of Bembridge Down, with no one moving on it, not an Englishman in sight. One of the highest points in Wight, it commanded all the invasion area, including the great prize of Sandown Bay and the low ground behind. Under no particular commander, so far as du Bellay knew, and certainly in no particular order, they struggled up the cliff paths and then across the fields for the base of Bembridge Down.

The English militia were inexperienced soldiers, but not such novices as to poise their lookouts dramatically on the crest. They saw, but they were not seen. Masked by the whale-

---

* Although as a boy I lived at Bembridge and often swam in White-cliff Bay, my identifications are those given by C. T. Witherby in his two invaluable works, *The Battle of Bonchurch* (privately published, 1962) and *Invasion of England: 1545* (unpublished MS., 1964).

back of the down, they even had time to unharness some of the carthorses belonging to the transport wagons and with these form an improvised cavalry troop, which they also kept hidden. Their orders were to hold the heights and if attacked retire steadily and draw the French away from the beaches and their ships. But the disorganised, breathless mob in front of them was too tempting. They also disobeyed orders. Instead of retiring, they attacked. As the leading French soldiers reached the summit, the militia came out of the screening hedges with a yell, the lumbering carthorse cavalry among them.

"We killed many, took many prisoners, and drove the rest down as far as the ships, killing all the way,' recorded Oglander. Du Bellay wrote of "a fierce attack by horse and foot soldiers" which slaughtered or captured many of the impetuous French and "drove the rest in disorder down to the foot of the mountain near the ships". Here, worse was to come, for their comrades were enraged by this reverse and yet more men poured ashore from the ships and soon a general, disorganised French attack was once again swarming up Bembridge Down. The militia retired at once right over the summit, crossed a river on the far side and broke the bridge behind them. This is what Henry wanted, but it was far more than he had dreamed of. A chaotic and totally uncontrolled rush inland of a large part of the French army. D'Annebault took drastic action. He pulled his Colonel-General, de Tais, out of the middle of the failing battle of Bonchurch, with his force stuck well short of the strategic summit of St. Boniface Down, and sent him round to Whitecliff Bay to get the disorderly soldiers off Bembridge Down and back to their ships.

The winds had become strong westerly on 20 July. On the evening of the 21st, with the French now ashore at Bonchurch, Whitecliff and Bembridge, Lord Lisle proposed to Henry that advantage be taken of it. His shipmasters had suggested a headlong attack by the English fleet on the French. They were certain that this would cause the French to up-anchor and be blown in confusion far away from their embattled troops now well ashore in Wight. They stated flatly, "If we come under sail towards them they must loose anchor and abide us under their small sails; and, once loosed, they could not with that strainable wind fetch the Wight again

and would have much ado to escape a danger called the
Awers." The Owers bank, projecting far out underwater from
the tip of the Selsey peninsula, would be directly in the path
of any fleet forced out of the protected St. Helens anchorage
into the full force of a strong westerly wind. They could never
make heading against it, but must be blown up-Channel towards Dover and Calais, even if they escaped the ship trap of
the Owers. Lisle date-timed this proposal 21 July, 8 p.m., in
the *Great Harry*, but before the king could give permission
for the attack, the favourable westerly died away and another
calm set in.

In the French flagship, conference after conference was
held, with bitter but unspoken accusations of cowardice dis-
torting the debate. The soldiers saw only the advantage of
numbers, overwhelmingly on their side. There must be some
way of getting at the English fleet. The sailors and pilots, on
the defensive, claimed that there was only one way into Portsmouth and that only four ships abreast could use it, and that
this would bring them into the converging, concentrated fire
of both the land forts and the English ships. Losses would be
heavy, the chances of success slight. If wind or tide were
against them, they could not get in at all; but if wind or tide
were with them, the current was so fast there that it would
take charge. Any mishap could result in complete disaster.
An angry voice suggested anchoring. No, said the sailors. If
the anchors held, then the ships would swing round and present their vulnerable sterns to the enemy. But they would not
hold long, they would drag or break and a hundred ships
would pile up on each other or go aground right under the
muzzles of the enemy's guns.

"These fellows don't like the thought of gunfire" was the
judgement of the military leaders. They demanded a night
reconnaissance of the channels and insisted that an army
officer of not less than captain's rank should be in each of the
three boats sent out, so that each pilot would have a senior
soldier at his elbow. When the boats returned next morning,
there were no more disagreements. The pilots' original esti-
mate, made under pressure, that as many as four ships could
enter abreast, was clearly the wildest optimism. The reports
were unanimous: Only one ship could enter at a time, and
then only if she had a local pilot and was coming in peace-

fully, for the channel was not merely narrow but winding, and it led in right under the guns of Southsea Castle. The position Henry VIII had chosen for anchoring his fleet was impregnable.

Only one offensive move was now open to the French: to turn their bridgeheads in Wight into a real attempt to capture and occupy the whole of the island. The optimists argued that then Portsmouth would fall and French control of the Channel would be gained. At the very least, the English would be forced into ruinous attempts to recapture or seal off this French fortress set on English soil. The weather was still very calm, and the English fleet could not interevene now, even if it wanted to.

Henry realised that the crisis of the campaign was at hand and that it would be waged on land. He had already built up his force in Wight to 8,000 men. Now he committed his strategic reserve, held back in the capital. On 23 July the Lord Mayor of London was ordered to send 2,000 "able men" to Portsmouth and an officer of the Board of Ordnance at the Tower of London, Anthony Anthony,* was commanded to send down every last cannon, demi-cannon, culverin and demi-culverin he had, together with shot, powder and munitions. The Captain of the Wight was warned that the French would attempt to take Sandown Castle by surprise assault, and so open a road into the island for the French artillery and cavalry. Rightly, Henry was preparing for the worst.

This time, however, the pessimists in the French fleet included the senior generals, who put forward some depressing arithmetic. Both de Tais, general of infantry, and Saint-Remy, general of artillery, specified three forts to defend the essential anchorage at St. Helens, three months to build them, 6,000 pioneers to do the work, 6,000 front-line soldiers to protect them meanwhile, and adequate tenting and bedding for all these 12,000 men. With the English fleet still strong, so many men could not be spared out of the French ships, while neither tenting nor bedding existed on this scale. The sailors mentioned the autumn gales. One good blow from the south-

---

* This officer was responsible for producing in 1546 a picture list and part-inventory of the "Kyng's Majestie's own shyppes" which contains the only known authentic picture of the *Mary Rose*, not yet given up for lost.

east would create havoc in the St. Helens anchorage, while a strong northerly would be almost as bad. D'Annebault sent a letter to King Francis, asking if he should capture the Isle of Wight with his great armament, or sail up Channel to Boulogne to harass the English there. But everyone knew that this was mere formality. It only remained to bring off the troops still ashore in Wight and at the same time refill the watercasks of the galleys.

This took place during the withdrawal from the Bonchurch bridgehead. It was covered to seaward by the guns of the ships and to landward by a screening force of foot soldiers under Pierre de Blacas, Chevalier D'Aulps, Knight of Malta, whom the English called Chevalier D'Aux. He was the commander of the six new galleys from Normandy and a sober, conscientious soldier concerned to place his outposts a sufficient distance from the working parties they were to protect. He led on up the hill, like de Moneins before him, until once again a storm of arrows from unseen English longbowmen whipped and howled into another French advance guard. "He climbed to the top of the hill and there he found English soldiers in ambush," wrote du Bellay. "They attacked so fiercely that his men took flight and abandoned him. At that moment, he was hit in the knee by an arrow, which made him stumble. Then, as he was picking himself up, he was struck such a blow on the head with a bill, that his morion flew off, and he stumbled a second time. There he was dealt another blow with a bill, which spilled his brains on the ground." Sir John Oglander grumblingly relates that the Chevalier called for ransom, "whereupon some country fellow (I can imagine him no better) clove his head with a brown bill". Mr. Sands of the Hampshire militia collected the dead man's armour and sent it over to Portsmouth for Henry VIII to see.

D'Annebault, in one of the ships lying just off-shore, witnessed this last rout of his troops by local militia and, once again, sent the Seigneur de Tais, Colonel-General of infantry, to organise an orderly withdrawal. Leone Strozzi, Prior of Capua, required no such help in his disembarkation from the Bembridge area. The expected attack by the English was met by prompt counter-attack. "After putting more than thirty to the sword, he routed the remainder," wrote du Bellay. The men of Wight had not mutinied, as D'Annebault had expected, but had fought hard against a fully professional invading army. Their losses were high. "There was not any family of any account on the Island but lost a father, brother or uncle," wrote Sir John Oglander. "Ower family lost two younger gentlemen, Hugh George and Richard Oglander."

What may be the last stage of a Bembridge area withdrawal is depicted in a finely detailed near-contemporary drawing, which shows English militia in block formation and armed with bills, pikes and a few handguns, advancing down a slope to a beach, which is clear of French. Just off-shore lie three galleys, bows on to the beach, firing their heavy forward armament, while beside them is a large carrack stern on to the shore and firing the heavy bronze stern guns as well as the swivels higher up. Her ports are open to show a broadside armament of four guns, bronze and iron arranged alternately, with two long rows of swivel-guns mounted on the decks above. The leading English have reached the water's edge and the French are moving away, the carrack with all sails set and drawing, the galleys backing their oars so as to keep their bow guns in action until the last moment. This was probably the scene on 24 July, when Vander Delft, who noted that "the wind had always been in favour of the French", reported also that "the fleets face each other still; but on the flagships coming nearer together the French flagship and fleet drew away". According to du Bellay, the French began this disengagement just before nightfall and, aided by a most favourable wind, ran before it so fast the following morning that they had got fourteen leagues away from Portsmouth before even their own galleys could catch up with them.

At Henry VIII's headquarters on Southsea common the Privy Council were busy cancelling the orders for reinforcements to be directed towards Portsmouth while at the same time trying to organise a major salvage operation at Spithead. The raising of the *Mary Rose*.

CHAPTER SIX

"HAST, HAST, POST HAST!"

> "Occasionally it happens that large ships are lost
> as a result of bad weather, or are wrecked, even
> whilst in the safety of a harbour and in good
> weather, as a result of carelessness. When this
> happens, it is customary to place two or four
> special ships above the wreck, fill them with water
> and let skilled divers pass strong ropes under the
> wreck and fasten them to the ships. The ships are
> then baled out with the result that they start
> rising, thus bringing the wreck to the surface. The
> possibilities for raising sunken warships, however,
> are small seeing that they are loaded with cannon
> of copper and iron and stone balls."
>
> —Olaus Magnus, *Historia de gentibus*
> *sepentrionalibus,* 1555.

At sunrise on 25 July the watchers over Seaford Bay in Sussex,
east of Brighton and nearly 40 miles from Portsmouth, saw an
intimidating awesome spectacle. The whole of the French seaborne armament, the greatest fleet ever seen, was riding into
the bay and by 10 o'clock they were landing soldiers, some
1,500 men in the first wave. The lookouts stayed to number
them accurately in round figures as "twelve score French sails
. . . and above 20,000 men, if each ship carry his full freight".
When a Sussex courtier, then at Portsmouth, heard of it next
day he lamented "I think not the contrary but that my house
is burnt already." The man on the spot, Edward Gawge,
penning a note asking for the aid of the Kent militia (the
men of Sussex being mostly now at Portsmouth), added an
injunction: "Hast, hast, post hast, for thy lyff, hast."

His letter reached the justices of the peace in Kent at 10
o'clock that night, twelve hours on the road. They had already
received a verbal message of "great alarm", but had ignored
it. They wanted a request in writing. Now they had it, they

"rang the alarm and fired all the beacons". The clashing of the church bells echoed over the rooftops in the summer dusk and was taken up in village after village. The beacons flared and from each hilltop a spreading crimson glow began to stain the darkening sky. Men buckled on such armour as they had, shouldered bills or bows, and tramped through the streets to the places of assembly. Soon, they were marching through the night towards Sussex.

Near Seaford, the first fires had flared soon after ten that morning, the yellow flames pale in the sunlight, but crackling and hissing and sending up gouts of black smoke, as the French burst into the first village inland and, meeting no resistance, broke up in search of plunder. It was Whitecliff Bay all over again. The beaches, here temptingly flat, open and empty of defence, had infuriated the fighting men. The evidence of French power, the hundreds of mighty ships, with their thousands of guns and tens of thousands of armed and armoured soldiers, had been around them for weeks, but few of those guns had fired and most of the men had not fought. Always, their admiral had held them back. Now, some 1,500 of them plunged ashore on their own, to make war on their own, to leave some scar on England to mark their passing and to get something, be it never so worthless, to bring back to France as proof of individual valour.

They came into that village like a wave, stopped, fired it, and then poured onwards again, over a light wooden bridge spanning a deep, fast-flowing tidal river. As the leaders spread out on the far bank, some of them tumbled and fell, jerking and clutching at the clothyard shafts suddenly embedded in their bodies. The howl and whip of the arrow volley ceased and there came a rush of English militia from the cover of a small fort hidden until now by the bridge itself. Some used their sharp, glittering, axe-like bills on the French, others broke the planks of the bridge behind the backs of their enemies, leaving it unusable. Then they all closed in on the invaders and drove them into the river. In minutes, the bank was covered by the bodies of the fallen and the water was choked with men in armour struggling to stand in the pouring current. A hundred of them were shot down, cut down or drowned. Only hours later was D'Annebault able to extricate the survivors, and to do it he had to land artillery and batter the English fort. He then set sail direct for Boulogne, without attempting a landing in Kent. By an oversight, however, that Mr. Gawge who had so frantically written for help in the morning failed to cancel his message once the danger was past, and the Kent militia kept on marching to his aid. It was two days before they learned that their services were no longer required, whereupon they in turn composed a letter, informing the army commander personally that "being so many gentlemen", they had not been "gently handled".

At the end of July D'Annebault landed 7,000 men, but not in England. The 4,000 soldiers and 3,000 pioneers were landed in France, behind the French lines, to assist in the coming assault on English-held Boulogne. Du Bellay and other leaders in the fleet began to remark bitterly that these numbers, if put ashore in Wight, would have sufficed to hold that island for France. This was a doubtful proposition, considering the rough handling the invaders had received from comparatively small bodies of militia, and that Henry had 8,000 men in Wight already and 2,000 more were on the way when the French gave up. Whereas by remaining off Boulogne with his fleet and relieving the overcrowding and consequent sickness in his ships by sending a substantial reinforcement to the French beseigers of the town, D'Annebault was doing real service. The French siege works were so far advanced that they were menacing the English garrison's communications with England, and the English commander had asked for 5,000 infantry to be sent across the Channel so that he could storm those positions. These soldiers, recruited from Norfolk, Suffolk and London, were ready but could not be sent overseas as long as D'Annebault's great fleet lay anchored off Boulogne, commanding the Straits of Dover. Communications between England and her beleaguered forces on the continent were cut, as were those by sea between London and Portsmouth. The victuals for Lord Lisle's fleet could get through, neither could the ships being readied for him in the Thames. In order to safeguard his continental operations, Henry VIII was committed to a sea action against a fleet still numbering over 230 ships and carrying a still formidable force of 23,000 men.

By 10 August he had increased the strength of the English fleet to 104 ships manned by 13,748 men. The vessels he had obtained by requisitioning the largest and strongest of the merchant ships, regardless of nationality, then in English ports. Many were German, many others did not pass an inspection by his officers. Among their reports are revealing notes condemning clinker-building: "clynchers, very weak"; "clenchers, feeble and old fashioned"; "clenchers, which cannot abide the boarding with another ship without danger of perishing". The pace of technical development had been so fast that no longer could any large merchant vessel be converted to a warship. Even those basically suitable required a lot of work done on them before they were fit to fight. But by one means or another he increased his numbers so that for every ship he had, the French had only two. To get the men to man them, the coastal villages were depopulated and for a time all fishing ceased. There were no able-bodied men left. Then the boats began to go out again and Lord John Russell reported on 22 August that he had seen with his own eyes that the fishing craft were now crewed almost entirely by women, helped here and there by a few old men or young boys. Nor did they stay inshore, but ventured out as far as 20 miles. Some had already been chased by French privateers, but by smart handling of their heavy boats had got away.

There was the additional danger of the galleys, in effect the "battlecruisers" of the French fleet, which carried out armed reconnaissance all along the coasts of Kent, Sussex and Hampshire as well as keeping detachments prowling close inshore off English-held Calais and Boulogne. These became so confident that they drove two small English vessels aground by Boulogne and sent in soldiers to burn the stranded hulls. They were met by soldiers of the English expeditionary force under Lord Poynings, who was able to report that "we gave them so sharp an onset that, notwithstanding all the shot of the great ordnance, which was as much as they could make, we forced divers of the galley men to seek their swimming under the water and killed of them when our men stood almost to the chin in the sea".

On 6 August three of the galleys looked into Portsmouth to count the growing number of Lord Lisle's fleet. It was yet another breathless summer day of the sort that was spoiling the victuals in the holds and causing sickness and dysentery. The galleys boldly drove up to St. Helens Point and amused themselves by chasing a small English vessel right into the

anchorage, very nearly catching it. Over by the Southsea shore
a cluster of large vessels, motionless on the still water, showed
where an attempt was being made to raise the *Mary Rose*.
They were a tempting target but the galleys, having no great
fleet to fall back on now, were unable to range at will. Four
fast vessels of Henry's newly organised "wing" of oar-
propelled craft came out against them. The *Grand Mistress*
and the *Anne Gallant* were galleasses of 450 tons and 250 men,
the *Greyhound* was a galleasse of 200 tons and 140 men, and the
Falcon was a rowbarge of 20 tons and 45 men. The two largest
carried 30 gunners (as many as the 700-ton *Mary Rose* had
done), while the two smaller vessels carried 16 and 4 respectively. The spell of calm must have been broken by a breeze,
for Lisle reported that the three galleys were "canvassed away
again" by the four English ships. Like the galleys they were
designed to deal with, the galleasses achieved their speed
partly through their light construction, low build and great
length. They could hit fairly hard with their broadside guns,
mounted above the rowing deck, but would be easily smashed
or taken if they tried to close a great ship. In effect, they too
were battlecruisers, not battleships, but out of them may have
come the galleon, a warship fast and manœuvrable under sail
alone.

In the second week of August came a wind fair for France
and with it the English fleet sailed out of Portsmouth, 100
strong without including the great hulks and hoys clustered
round the wreck of the *Mary Rose*. "Such a puissant navy as
has not been assembled within the remembrance of man,"
according to the Privy Council in their request to Archbishop
Cranmer for a national day of prayer for the navy "to be sung
or said . . . in the English tongue". When D'Annebault had
news of this, thought Lisle, "he will not tarry in the Narrow
Seas". The lurking galleys were still outside the anchorage,
but they were not satisfied merely to count the numbers of
the English ships. As soon as night came on and they noticed
a requisitioned Dutch vessel trying to steal away from Lisle's
fleet, they raced down on it, boarded, bundled the master
out of it and into a galley, and were away before the pursuing
English ran alongside to recapture the ship and its crew.
The Flemish shipmaster knew nothing of the English navy,
but he did know its intention, the most vital information of

all. With the strong westerly wind then blowing and the very rough sea that was running, Lisle hoped for a decisive encounter with the French great ships, unhampered by the galleys which would soon have to seek shelter.

This news reached D'Annebault within hours. He was not off faraway Boulogne, as Lisle believed, but close at hand off the Sussex coast. He just had time enough to make a plan, before the English would be down on him, the wind behind them. He ordered his galleys to go upwind and shelter from the rough seas in the lee of the Selsey peninsula. Then the main fleet anchored where it was, an insecure position because if attacked they might be driven ashore or on to Beachy Head behind them. But first, the English would have to sail downwind of the galleys and be caught between the two French forces. He excluded the option of a running battle with both fleets going downwind on parallel courses, for they could all be blown through the Straits past Boulogne and be unable to get back. Anyway, the wind might drop or change and allow the French to use the tidal streams to drift them to windward of the English. And that is what it did do, swung round from westerly to E.S.E., dying away as it did so. Lisle complained bitterly that until God gave him a wind that would last at least a day and night, he could achieve nothing against the French, while du Bellay wrote "by degrees, it became so calm that before noon we wished nothing more than to meet those who just before had threatened us". That was on 14 August, with the rival fleets still out of sight of each other. It was as if, in a modern naval engagement, all the major units on both sides had suffered almost complete engine failure, simultaneously. The only thing they could do was to use the currents, anchoring when they were adverse, to move the great ships onwards parallel to the coast.

At dawn on 15 August the French galleys sighted the English ships, which began to tack slowly south across a light breeze for what little windward position there was. "The English stood out, with their heads towards the sea, and made a show of being desirous to engage," noted du Bellay. Lisle, however, was impressed by the strength of the French: "They seem to be many more ships than we, but victory rests with God, and we will do our duty if it please Him to send a commodious wind. But they do not seem disposed to fight, and we may dally with them a day or two before we need fight except we see a better advantage."

The only vessels which could really move in these conditions were the galleys of the Baron de la Garde and the oared vessels of the English "wing" under William Tyrell, described as "a man that hath seen the feat of the galleys and is a sure man and diligent in anything that he is committed unto". These rival screening forces rowed seaward for the windward position, and late that morning the grumble and thump of distant gunfire out at sea showed that they were engaging. The Baron de la Garde had made a thrust with his whole galley force at some detached ships, intending to pin down the English so that D'Annebault's fleet might drift towards them with the eastward-setting tidal stream aided by what little wind there was. But Tyrell blocked his move and broke it up well clear of the battle fleet.

"Thinking that you heard part of the shot between us and the Frenchmen yesterday, and might think that some great feat was done," wrote Lisle to General Bellingham; "I assure you that it was but a bravery of their galleys, which, following us all yesterday, and having the wind of us and their fleet the wind of them, about noon set upon us and continued shooting until night. Not a ship was struck, and all they did was to break three oars in the Mistress; and yet they bestowed among us 200 cannon shot" (du Bellay says 300). He added that the galleasses *Mistress, Anne Gallant* and *Greyhound,* and all the "shalupes" and rowing pieces had done "right well". Sir William Paget reported 1,000 shots fired in all, "our ordinaunce harde rasheng in their shippes and galees . . . for they approached so nigh as to be reached with our iron slings". Du Bellay reported "a very fierce skirmish" at close quarters for two hours with "the fury of the English artillery" passing mostly over the low-built galleys, and next morning a sea covered with broken timber mixed with a few drifting bodies.

By midnight on the 15th it had begun to blow harder, with the two fleets anchored a mile or so distant, and Lisle had ordered a dawn attack. But at daybreak the French ships were so far away that even that great cloud of tall sails could be seen only from the maintop of the *Great Harry.* "They approached like a wood, but in their removing kept no order," wrote Lisle. The French could have attacked the previous evening, because the current was bringing them down towards Lisle, but had anchored instead. He was convinced now that D'Annebault would never fight. "A more commodious day for their advantage they shall never see again: their demeanour that day was shameful."

Five weeks after it had sailed from Le Havre under the eyes of the king and his court, the French fleet returned. On 17 August an English ship counted 200 sails in the estuary of the Seine and captured a Flemish merchant ship coming out. The master stated that the French fleet was landing great numbers of sick and starting to disperse; that the crews "had rather be hanged than go forth again"; and that "the common people grudge that their King has been at great charge and nothing done". That was true and partly the fault of Francis himself, for countenancing an over-ambitious plan. But only partly, for had Henry VIII not kept firm control over his own forces and deftly blocked every move that D'Annebault made, the French might well have scored an overwhelming victory at Portsmouth.

It was the last duel in which the two monarchs were to indulge and it was Henry who rounded it off. With the French dispirited and dispersed, he launched his own invasion. In September he landed 6,000 soldiers near Tréport in Normandy, defeated the local French forces, burnt the town and 30 ships, and lost only 14 men killed in action. But the "overfair summer season" had resulted in many sick of the "plague" and the "bloody flux", in the English ships as in the French, and the campaign was over for the year. Now, wrote the English ambassador in Venice, he was glad to learn that enemy claims to have won a sea battle and captured the Isle of Wight were untrue and "to see th' intollerable crakes of Frenchmen reducid to vaine ostentacion and coardnes". He had one regret: "the' infortunable case of Sir George Carow is by negligence so miserablye success'd". Only the loss of the *Mary Rose* had marred a skilfuly executed campaign by land and sea against much superior French forces.

The *Mary Rose* had sunk on Sunday, 19 July and the long spells of hot, breathlessly calm weather which had so frustrated the fleet were extremely favourable for a salvage attempt. The hull was undamaged, so far as we know, and lay in shallow water where the tops of the fore and main masts were visible above the waves. As early as 23 July Lord John Russell, the Privy Seal, had had letters from Sir William Paget, the Secretary of State, condemning the "rashness and great negligence" which had caused the disaster but giving "good hope" that the ship would be recovered. Lord Russell had replied at once, his letter being the first of ten addressed by various persons to the Secretary of State between 23 July and 9 August, which survive to tell the story.

The two main organisers were the naval and military commanders, Viscount Lisle the Lord Admiral, and Sir Charles Brandon, Duke of Suffolk. The actual directors of the salvage operation were two Venetians, Petre de Andreas and Symonde de Maryne, the latter being owner and master of a foyst which seems to have carried 31 men. Their ship may have been detained at Southampton, a port which had had regular commerce with Venice and Genoa for centuries; but what salvage experience they had is unknown. All that has survived is a lengthy list of stores which they required from the English authorities. On 31 July Suffolk told Paget that he would with speed set men to the weighing of the *Mary Rose* and next day was able to report that plans had been agreed with the Venetians and to enclose a list of the ships, equipment and men thought necessary for the task. There is no mention of diving equipment and although diving bells had long been used in the Mediterranean and could be fairly quickly improvised, they would be difficult to position over the *Mary Rose* as she then lay and it would be even harder to maintain that position for any length of time, owing to the push of the complex tidal streams at that point.

But the very fact of the area being tidal gave the salvors a great advantage, which they would not have had in the Mediterranean or in the Baltic. So they planned an orthodox tidal lift, employing the same principles as would be used today. By Tudor reckoning the *Mary Rose* was of 700 tons, so they planned to place on either side of her two empty ships also of 700 tons, secure them to the sunken vessel by strong cables, and at low water haul those cables taut with capstans. When the tide rose, the two empty ships would lift with it, bringing the *Mary Rose* off the bottom, still submerged, but hanging free of the mud. Then the two lifting ships, the *Mary*

Rose hanging betwen them in her cradle of cables, would be moved to shallower water until the sunken hull grounded again. That operation would be repeated ten or even twenty times until the *Mary Rose* was stranded in such shallow water that she might even dry out partially at low water springs and could now be lightened by the removal of her guns. Then the gunports would be closed, as much of the water as possible pumped out, and the wreck would come afloat, sluggishly.

The two great vessels moored over the *Mary Rose* to lift her were 700-ton carracks with crews of 300 men, recently bought for the navy but not yet converted by the dockyard into battleships. They were the *Sampson,* master Thomas Bell, and the *Jesus of Lubeck,* master John Seintclier, a Hanseatic trader which was to see much service under four Tudor monarchs. She was trapped and captured by the Spaniards from John Hawkins in 1568 at San Juan de Ulua, the disaster which set the young Francis Drake on his career of revenge. In her first venture under the Tudor colours she was turned into a mere pontoon by the removal of her ballast, guns and stores to give maximum buoyancy and lifting power. On 1 August, after the *Mary Rose* had been on the bottom for just two weeks, both pontoons were in position by the wreck, together with some smaller hulks from the dockyard and four large hoys, probably fitted with sweeps to act as tugs and hufflers. In addition to the crews of these vessels, the salvage team proper numbered 31 Venetian and 60 English mariners. They had to lay out and handle the moorings and lifting gear which consisted of 5 great cables, 10 great hawsers, 10 new capstans, 70 pulleys and a great quantity of cordage, as well as tallow and ballast baskets. Late that Saturday evening, Suffolk wrote to Paget, "I trust by Monday or Twisday at the furthest, the Mary Rose shalbe wayed upp, and saved".

The Lord Admiral was worried by this diversion of resources at a time when a vastly superior French fleet was in the Channel. "The worste ys, we must forebere thre of the greatest hulkes of the flete, tyll the things be don, which wilbe a great weakening to the navye, yf any thing in the meane tyme shall happen". The third hulk was Sir Peter Carew's *Great Venetian,* but Lisle consoled himself with the thought that the *Sampson* and the *Jesus* at least were useless as warships, for they "must have sparre decks and wast nettyng with pourtes cut", a partial rebuild which could not be carried out quickly, even if resources were available. By 5 August he was lamenting that salvage demands had "so charged all the Kynges Majesties shipwryghtes with makyng engyns for the same, that they have had no leisure to attend any other thyng". And still the *Mary Rose* had not come up. She had not even been righted yet.

However, later that same day, Wednesday, 5 August, he was able to report to the Secretary of State: "And as touching the Mary Rose, her sailes and saile yards be layd on land, and to her mastes there is tyd three cables, with other ingens to wey her upp, and on every syde of her a hulk to sett her uppright, which is thought by the doers thereof, God willing, to be doon tomorrow, one tyme in the day; and that doon, they purpose to discharg her of water, ordenaunce, and other thinges, with as moch diligence as is possible, and, by litell and litle, to bring her nerer to the shore. . . ."

Although the removal of the great sailyards enabled the salvage craft to move in closer to the wreck, they failed to right her on 6 August, but prospects still looked promising. On Friday, at lunch, Lisle told Suffolk that she might be up that afternoon, or at the latest the following day. But on Sunday, 9 August, a depressed group of Italians went ashore. Lisle reported that they had come "to signify vnto vs that after this sourt which they haue followed hetherto they can by no meanes recouer her, for they haue alredye broken her fore-mast . . . and now they desyr to prove an another waye, which ys to dragg her as she lyeth vntill she came into shallow ground, and so to set her upright, and to this they axe vj days prouf". Lisle did not record what the new method was, but agreed to the six further days they requested. Probably the Venetians intended to lay out heavy anchors shoreward and try to drag the wreck across the bottom by hauling in on the cables. The Cowdray engraving shows the ship lying on the bottom heeled over at an angle of some 40 degrees towards Southsea, and although the Venetians may have corrected part of this heel, there is no record that they did so. The only surviving document after 9 August is a warrant of 8 December, 1545, to "pay Petre de Andreas and Symonde de Maryne, Venetians, 40 marks in reward for their pains about the weighing of the Mary Rose".

Small-scale salvage of guns went on for four years, but the evidence is sparse, merely entries of payments on the "Rolls", long sheets of parchment allowed to curl up like large charts. One entry merely records the payment of £57 11s. 5d. to Peter Paul, an Italian, in 1547 for recovering guns from the wreck; another in 1549 of £50 to the same person. There is no record of what method he used or of exactly what sort of guns he recovered. At the time the *Mary Rose* was built a great bronze gun cost about £35, a great iron gun (if not a sling) about £13; but there had been some inflation since then which had caused Henry VIII to increase his pay scales for the armed forces, which were now permanent bodies.

The last reference to the wreck as it appeared in Tudor times was not published until 1623, when Admiral Sir William Monson printed his Naval tracts (reprinted in 1902 by the Navy Records Society, edited by M. Oppenheim). Monson wrote: "The Mary Rose, next to the Regent in bigness and goodness, after this was cast away betwixt Portsmouth and the Isle of Wight, the very same day King Henry boarded her, and dined in her. Part of the ribs of this ship I have seen with my own eyes; there perished in her four hundred persons." Monson was born in 1569, after the *Mary Rose* had been on the bottom for 25 years. Another 15 or 25 years may have passed before the young Monson saw some part of her hull, perhaps the shallowly submerged ruins of her upperworks on a day when the water was particularly clear. I have myself seen the weed, sand and shingle down through the water when passing over the shallows of Spit Bank on my way to the *Mary Rose*. Certainly, the hull must have remained intact for a very long time, the currents swirling and boiling around it, scouring out deep pits and helping to dig the great oak structure deeper still into the mud.

So long as the *Mary Rose* remained a substantial obstruction above the seabed, oysters would grow on her timbers, lobsters and congers would live in the caverns of her hull, fish would surround the weed-covered wreck in glittering shoals. And local fishermen would know the location of the site by "marks" on land. But when the protruding parts of the hull collapsed or were eaten away and all that remained was swallowed by the mud, the fish would leave and so would the fishermen. Indeed, they would now avoid the site because the few timbers which still showed would be only a damaging obstruction to their nets and lines. And after a time the very name of the ship which lay buried there would be forgotten, like the identity of the men who had died in her.

Part II

JOHN DEANE'S DISCOVERY

CHAPTER SEVEN

"SOME WRECK, COMPLETELY BURIED IN THE SAND"

"The merit of having first introduced the diving helmet into general use, and applied it to practical purposes of a most important nature, is due to Messrs. Charles and John Deane, and their apparatus is the simplest that has yet been suggested, and is very servicable for general purposes as it never fails, excepting when the diver's head by any accident comes lower than his body, in which case the water must necessarily enter, and drive out the air, upon which his safety depends".
—*The Hampshire Telegraph,* 21 September, 1840.

The Italian salvagers of the sixteenth century may have had no more in the way of underwater equipment than a glass-bottomed bucket and an assortment of grappling instruments. Mediterranean diving techniques, even if they had possessed them, would not have been effective at Spithead, with its rapid and complicated tidal streams combined with capricious weather and cold, murky water. No really efficient and economic apparatus suitable for "open water" diving around the British Isles was available until 1828. And this had been developed at Whitstable in Kent as a result of a fire in one of the outbuildings of a local farmhouse some ten years earlier.

In an attempt to save the horses tethered in a burning barn, the farmer brought into action an old pump and hose pipe; but the weak jet it threw did not dowse the flames, while the dense smoke prevented anyone from getting into the barn without suffocating. It was then that an idea occurred to a friend of the farmer, a young man called John Deane who remembered noticing an old suit of armour in the farmhouse. He took the helmet off it and suggested to the farmer that the pump and hose should be used to pump, not water, but air; then, if he wore the helmet and stuck the end of the hosepipe underneath, he would be able to breathe fresh air even when enveloped in the suffocating smoke inside the barn. Thus equipped, he went safely inside and one by one brought out all the horses.

John, who was then only eighteen, discussed the matter with his elder brother, Charles Anthony, and they decided that his impromptu idea could be of universal application in fire-fighting. In 1823 they secured the patent rights for an "Apparatus to be Worn by Persons Entering Rooms filled with Smoke, &c." The patented drawings of a man wearing purpose-built helmet-and-breastplate with hose attached, plus a heavy-duty jacket and trousers, look almost exactly like a picture of a helmet diver. This is no coincidence, because the one led directly to the other, and in modern times ordinary self-contained diving gear is used by Fire Brigades when smoke-filled premises have to be entered.

The father of the two young men was a Deptford shipbuilder, a descendant of Sir Anthony Deane, the friend of Samuel Pepys, and responsible for vastly improving the design of British 60- and 70-gun ships. Therefore, they saw immediately the underwater potential of their smoke helmet. But it took five years of wary and dangerous practical experiment before they achieved a safe and simple diving system. John first tried out the smoke helmet by just walking into the sea from the beach at high water, but turned upside down as soon as he got out of his depth. The helmet was attached to a jacket, which also filled with air, and the diver, struggling with his own buoyancy in the waves, became an unmanageable balloon. Weighted shoes were the answer. In its final form, the jacket was discarded entirely and the diving apparatus, as such, consisted of an open helmet with breast and back plates, plus airhose and signal line. This had the advantage of utter simplicity. It could be put on and taken off in an instant, and the main weights, secured to the breast and back plates by a rope with a quick-release knot, enabled these to be "ditched" instantly in an emergency. Quite separate from the diving helmet was the protective clothing which is required for any serious underwater work around the British Isles, even in summer. This consisted of two layers of warm underclothing worn under a watertight, india-rubber dress which, being liable to tear easily, was in turn worn under heavy canvas trousers and jacket. These were held up around the neck by a tied handkerchief, so that they would be inside the air-filled helmet when the diver stood upright, or nearly so. If he stooped down too much, the helmet would admit water to the diver's face and also flood his suit, which would be uncomfortable, and therefore a series of safety precautions had to be worked out and followed, including a nearly vertical descent and ascent on a rope ladder weighted at the bottom and suspended a few feet above the seabed or the wreck being worked.

During their time of experiment the brothers went out with the "sweepers" off the Kent coast; these were boatmen who made a living by dragging for lost anchors and so on. Then, gaining confidence, they tried a wreck and were successful again. When, by degrees, they had learnt all the hazards and worked out ways of dealing with them, they joined with William Edwards, owner of the Ramsgate smack *Mary,* and his crew, and set up in business as "submarine engineers". Among the larger wrecks to be worked by this team were the four wooden battleships *Royal George* (Spithead, 1782), *Boyne* (Southsea Castle, 1795), *Colossus* (Scilly Isles, 1798), and *Venerable* (Torbay, 1804); the four East Indiamen *Hindostan* (Margate, 1803), *Earl of Abergavenny* (Portland, 1805), *Carnbrea Castle* (Chilton Chine, Isle of Wight, 1829); and *Enterprize*; and the ordnance transport *Guernsey Lily* (Yarmouth, Isle of Wight, 1799). In his mid-fifties John Deane was still diving, raising bronze guns from Russian ships sunk under the ice of a Crimean winter and being shot at by Cossacks on occasion. He died in bed, aged 84.

In addition to bronze guns, the Crimean wrecks of 1855–6 had steam engines with brass and copper pipes and fittings to attract salvagers, while the sail-driven vessels of an earlier era had copper sheathing and sometimes bronze guns or rich cargoes in addition. It was the concentration of such wrecks in the Portsmouth–Isle of Wight area which persuaded the team to move their base of operations there in 1832. They began with the *Boyne,* the *Royal George* and the *Guernsey Lily.* In their day, these were all fairly recent wrecks, standing high off the bottom and marked by wreck buoys. They were all of well-known construction, with builders' plans and models available, if necessary; indeed, they differed hardly at all from the most recently launched vessels, for the navy still consisted of "wooden walls" powered by the wind. Although steam machinery had been introduced into Portsmouth Dockyard in about 1800, it was still a poor form of motive power for ships, and only special craft, such as tugs and fast packets, employed steam to turn large paddlewheels. The Deanes' own diving boat was wind-driven, making a strange contrast with their diving gear, parts of which owed their efficiency if not their very existence to the Industrial Revolution. The pump, the airhose and the watertight suit were all of a quality impossible for eighteenth century technology to achieve, and this was very necessary with such deep wrecks as the *Royal George,* covered by up to 90 feet of water at high tide; to pump an adequate supply of compressed air into the helmet of a diver working at that depth required a very efficient and reliable supply system. The air had to be delivered with sufficient force to overcome the pressure of a column of water 90 feet high; the air to roar into the helmet, filling it almost completely and escaping from underneath in a continuous surge of artificial power.

It was very cold and very dark down on the *Royal George,* and very dangerous, with the pull of the current on the great length of airhose, and on the anchor cables of the boat on which the diver's life depended. And when he worked on the upper parts of the grisly ruin, the tomb for half a century of nearly 900 men, women and children, there was the ever-present hazard in that dim light and low visibility of the diver stepping into space, into a hatchway, or over the side, and in his fall flooding the helmet. Or, a part of the wreck might simply collapse beneath him, or on to him, sliding slowly down without a warning and without a sound. To John Deane the ship appeared "one huge, indescribable mass of old, decayed timbers and materials confusedly mixed and intermingled with mud, clay, sand, etc."

Divers who had gone down within a year of the sinking in 1782, when the *Royal George* was intact, with her taffrail only 12 feet below the surface at low water, had been able to recover only a few of the lighter, easier guns from the upper deck—fifteen 12-pounders in all. However, John and Charles Deane worked the forbidding, weed-wreathed carcase of the great battleship from 1832 to 1836 and raised 30 guns—3 bronze 18-pounders, 19 bronze 24-pounders and 8 iron 32-

pounders. As they were receiving from the Government only half the value of the bronze pieces, and without any allowance for their costs, they were feeling aggrieved when, on 16 June 1836, there came an interruption.

In the Spithead anchorage that day lay the 74-gun two-decker H.M.S. *Pembroke*. About half a cable's length ahead of her bows a fishing boat, probably trawling for "flatties", had come to a dead stop in the water. It was manned by five Gosport men, John and Jasper Richard, Job Redman, and the two Burnetts, William senior and William junior. Buoying their snagged gear, they came across to where John Deane's diving boat was moored over the *Royal George*. And they put a business proposition to him. They had snagged again on a well-known "fastener" which was probably a wreck, because it was on a flat bottom well clear of the area of generally "fasty ground" off Spit Tail. But because nothing had ever come up from it, they could not prove that the obstruction was a wreck. But if it was, it had never been worked by anyone, and they proposed that Deane should go down and examine the mysterious object and if it was indeed a wreck, then the proceeds should be split fifty-fifty between themselves, the finders, and Deane's party, the salvagers. The prospect of the unknown is always tempting, and Deane agreed, although it was his life which would be at great risk, not theirs.

Clearing a snagged net is always an interesting proposition, even today, and in Deane's time would have been even more critical. Probably, the fishermen's boat hauled up on the net until it came vertical in the water, while Deane's boat anchored alongside and put down the weighted rope diving ladder, bouncing it off the bottom until it hung just clear of the seabed, because if it trailed along the bottom the diver was likely to get his feet tangled, particularly if visibility was so bad that he could not see the bottom anyway. However, June is often a good month both for visibility and brightness of the light underwater at Spithead. Deane stepped carefully off the end of the ladder, his feet raising a cloud of fine sediment which wreathed his legs, and put one hand on the signal line which was secured under his armpits and then led up vertically past the front glass of his helmet. He gave one sharp pull, instantly answered by a similar pull from the signal man in the smack *Mary* many fathoms above him. This told the signal man that he was safely on the bottom and about to begin his underwater walk. As Deane went forward, the signal man gradually paid out more line, but keeping the line taut all the time as a precaution if the diver stumbled and fell. A continuous series of jerks on the line were Deane's signal that he was in danger and must be hauled up at once.

But the seabed was a barren plain of clay and mud with a little fine sand. No wreck loomed as a menacing shadow ahead. All that had caught the fishermen's gear was a single, softened, blackened timber barely protruding from the grey mud. He freed the lines from it and then, casting around to see if the timber was only an isolated piece of driftwood, he found several more like it, so nearly flush with the bottom that they were hardly visible. There *was* a wreck here, but it was completely buried. A trawl could go right over it and nine times out of ten, snag nothing. Deane had never seen anything like this before, but it seemed that the wreck must be very old. Prospecting further, he noticed another dark shadow, prominent in that dull, grey desert because it came up out of the ground about a foot. He knelt carefully, bending his head only slightly, and touched it. The thing was firm and unyielding. He does not tell us so, but he probably took the knife out of the front pocket of his canvas jacket and scraped at the vaguely cylindrical mass. It was metal, and it was green. Copper or bronze.

The rest was routine for a team which had raised so many guns from the *Royal George*, and had the necessary heavy lifting gear on board. When the 54 cwt. gun broke surface that day and was laid on deck, it proved to be over 12 feet long, including the cascable, with a bore of slightly more than six inches. The shot, wad and powder were still in place. Moulded prominently behind the two lion's head trunnions was the Tudor Rose. Even the inscription could be read:

HENRICVS VIII
ANGLIE. FRAN
CIE. ET. HIBERN
IE. REX. FIDEI. DE
FENSOR. INVICT
ISSIMVS. F.F.

ARCANVS DE ARCANIS
CESENEN FECIT

MDXXXXII
HR. VIII

Without any doubt whatever the gun was a bronze demi-cannon cast by an Italian founder in 1542 for Henry VIII, King of England, France and Ireland, Invincible Defender of the Faith. And it had been under the sea for a very long time, because there were several small holes in the metal, apparently from corrosion, or so the experts at Portsmouth Gunwharf thought when it was handed over to them on 18 June 1836. This was the local office of that Board of Ordnance, its headquarters still in the Tower, which Henry VIII had set up nearly 300 years before and which was to last in the form he gave it until 1855, the year John Deane was diving under the Crimean ice.

In England, the nineteenth century was the time of the antiquarians, people of some wealth and leisure with a general, but not methodical, interest in the past. When Deane's report of his find reached the Tower, its historical importance was realised instantly and a copy of his letter made and sent to the king. At the same time, because Deane was claiming full salvage on the grounds that the gun came from an unknown wreck which might be a private, and not a Royal, ship, a committee was set up under a major-general to study the gun and establish identity of the wreck. In August, while John Deane was away in Ireland but his team of divers were working both the *Royal George* and the newly discovered wreck, more evidence was found. On 15 August a whole batch of historic ordnance was landed at the Gunwharf. One was a cast-iron 32-pounder of the reign of George III, raised from the *Royal George*. The others were all from the new site, which had still not been identified, the *Hampshire Telegraph* being able to report only that they had been discovered "resting on some wreck, which was so completely buried in the sand that the diver could find nothing to which he could affix a rope". Of these four guns two were bronze with the Tudor Rose plain for all to see and two were of wrought-iron and of such antique construction that the general reaction to them was amazement.

One of the bronze guns, a cannon royal, was of heavier calibre than anything carried by the great eighteenth-century three-decker flagship *Royal George*. It had a bore of just over 8 inches for a total length, including cascable, of 10 feet, and weighed rather more than 42 cwt. It was an exceedingly powerful short-range battering piece made for Henry VIII by Robert and John Owen in 1535, the year before the *Mary Rose* was rebuilt and rearmed. The second of the bronze pieces, instead of being round, was a long cylinder with twelve flat faces. Although almost the same length as the 68-pounder cannon royal, it had the comparatively small bore of $4\frac{1}{2}$ inches for a weight of just over 23 cwt. and was obviously a long-range, high-velocity piece. Apart from the inscription "H R" flanking the Tudor Rose, the only legible moulding was the uninformative line "THYS COLVERYN BASTARD WEYS ZZ99". There was no date or maker's name.

But it was the iron guns which caused the furore. One was intact, the other consisted only of a length of broken barrel. Like the bronze guns, both were loaded, but with stone shot instead of cast-iron balls; their barrels had not been "cast" in one piece, but had been "built-up" of many staves and hoops of wrought-iron; and they were breech-loaders. The intact gun had an 8-inch bore and was $9\frac{1}{2}$ feet long; it was still mounted on a wooden bed, without wheels, giving a total length of 13 feet. The *Hampshire Telegraph* described them as "objects of great curiosity", for the fact that such guns had ever existed had been long forgotten, and when old histories were looked up, the references were depressingly sparse, bare and vague. And still are. Consequently, theorists were not lacking, and at that time a Mr. C. D. Archibald was engaged in writing a thesis to prove that, although the first guns to be cast in England were made by John Owen in 1521, on the continent ordnance of cast bronze and cast iron had been known before the end of the fourteenth century and by the beginning of the fifteenth century, the great majority of guns in use were cast pieces.

The new evidence from Spithead did not alter Mr. Archibald's opinion, but it did cause him to add a lengthy footnote to his article published in *Archaeologia*, Volume XXVIII, which concluded:

The one of them is of great length, formed of bars and hoops of iron, and is firmly imbedded in a large and heavy piece of timber. It must at all times have been an unwieldy and inefficient engine, and I cannot imagine that it could have co-existed, for purposes of active service on shipboard, with those highly finished pieces (of bronze) just mentioned. The gunpowder which would be suitable for the one would blow the other to pieces, and the gunners accustomed to the former would hardly be persuaded to run the risk of discharging the latter. It seems to me, therefore, that these rude pieces of the olden time, if indeed they were ever on board the *Mary Rose*, must have been used for ballast or some other illegitimate purpose.

The urgent convolutions of scholars in danger of being proved wrong are always interesting to watch, and to be fair to Mr. Archibald, his quite desperate theory about the guns being "illegitimate ballast" was restated as late as 1971, by an academic anxious to show that I was wasting my time on a wreck long since blown to pieces by John Deane and others.

In the category of serious research was the work of the Board of Ordnance committee, composed of Major-General W. Millar, Colonel Sir Alexander Dickson, K.C.B., and Major W. Dundas, which delivered a 13-page report on 30 September 1836. They had consulted the works of early historians such as Holinshed, Monson and Derrick, and combed through the recently published State Papers of Henry VIII, which transcribed the correspondence in full (unlike the currently available volumes in which proceedings are merely "calendared" in briefly summarised form). They were not misled by Holinshed's vague position indication, "drowned in the middest of the Haven", which led many then and since to assume that he meant Portsmouth Harbour, and they regarded Monson's testimony as decisive. They concluded: "It appears quite certain that the *Mary Rose* was lost at Spithead, that the Ship never was weighed up, and from the description of the Guns lately discovered there is every reason to believe that they formed part of her Armament."

They further concluded that not only more guns but artefacts of at least equal historic value, might still be recovered from the *Mary Rose*, and indeed from other very old wrecks such as the *Edgar*, also lost at Spithead, "to which it would be advisable that the attention of Mr. Deane be called and that every encouragement be given to him". This was an enlightened view for the time, markedly in advance of the modern laws of England regarding salvage. But systematic excavation on land was then hardly known and excavation underwater unheard of. Indeed, John Deane was a pioneer, not only of underwater invention and salvage but of recording. The guns he raised from the *Mary Rose*, as well as objects he recovered from ships of small historic value, were most carefully drawn and coloured, exactly as they had come from the sea, with the intention of publication in a book to be titled *John Deane's Cabinet of Submarine recoveries, relics and antiquities*. But the recovery and recording of objects, if that is all that is done, misses the more complete knowledge to be obtained from a methodical excavation in which the original position of each item is noted before it is removed. Guns from the *Mary Rose* are extremely interesting in themselves, as examples of the development of ordnance, but their original siting in the ship, if known, would tell us very much more. Of course, such an excavation was totally beyond any resources Deane could command; even digging for further artefacts in a totally buried wreck was an uneconomical chore. He did not recover anything more from the *Mary Rose* until 1840, when he referred to "repeated attempts and failures of discovery" which preceded a successful conclusion to this last season on the wreck.

The most spectacular find was another great bronze gun, a whole culverin weighing over 43 cwt., which was nearly 12 feet long, with the comparatively small bore of $5\frac{1}{4}$ inches. It was a long-range, high-velocity weapon of the same date and make as the demi-cannon which Deane had found on his first visit to the wreck in 1836. That is, it had been made by Arcanus de Arcanis of Cesenen in Italy in 1542, proving that rearmament was a continuous process in Henry VIII's navy. As soon as improved guns became available, they were put into the ships. This escapes some of the scholars, who still regard the rearming of the *Mary Rose* as having been confined to 1536. The discovery of the bronze culverin was reported to the Board of Ordnance on 5 September, together with four more of the wrought-iron "built-up" guns some 6 to 8 feet long. There were also what Deane referred to as "several smaller guns, swivels and parts of the same make". These were duly listed, measured and described by the Board's officials. Also landed, but naturally not handed over to the Board, was a small quantity of timber from the wreck, a "perfect human skull", and two longbows. These were the first, fully authenticated examples of the English longbow ever to be unearthed. Unlike swords, pikes and indeed armour, a worn or broken bow was not thought worth preserving and went on the fire, and although bows have been found on battlefields it has proved impossible to relate them with certainty to the battle.

On 13 October, with the diving season coming to an end and having still barely scratched the hull of the buried *Mary Rose*, Deane decided to try small charges of gunpowder. He asked the Board to supply him with "a few old condemned bomb shell (13 in.)" and was duly authorised to draw six of them from Gunwharf. These were hollow cannon balls ("shells") of 13-inch diameter, with 2-inch-thick walls, having a small hole for the insertion of a fuse which was ignited when the gun fired. To ignite them underwater, a long tube had to be fitted into the fuse hole beforehand, the open end remaining in the boat, which was directly above the explosion which resulted when a match was put down the tube. As the explosions were necessarily of low power, the procedure was safe except in very shallow water, and for maximum effect Deane first dug them into the seabed with a spade. He probably exploded most of them in the same place, although not at the same time, for he produced "a crater of large dimensions".

On 30 October he reported that after "three months labour and expediture" he was discontinuing operations for the year, and had recovered "two more large iron guns, and several parts of others". But he had also obtained a haul of artefacts from the crater, which he could sell at public auction. This was held at Portsmouth Point (the "old Portsmouth" of Henry VIII's time, not the new Portsmouth which had grown up outside it) on 12 November. There were now 8 "warrior's bows", which sold for between 10s. and 15s., as did the "common glass bottles"; "iron and granite shot" reached 20s. to 30s.; while "15 ft. of the mainmast" brought in £30. There was also an "anchor" (a watercolour shows that it was really a grapnel) and "part of a pump". "A few lots of Oak Timber" were also for sale, it being noted that: "The wood is in a high state of preservation and calculated for converting into ladies' work tables and boxes, picture frames, and any fancy articles and models." Most of the timber seems to have been recovered in August, and it was this sale which caused a contemporary nautical historian to write that "the hull has been recently broken up". His conclusion, but not the basis for it, remained in print to mislead later scholars.

Some of the items were bought by museums, but many went into private hands and effectively disappeared from sight. The museum purchases fared little better, being subject to accidental fires and the bombings of the Second World War, but above all from lack of any knowledge of how to conserve materials raised from the seabed. Indeed, no one realised that there was a problem at all, until some of the objects started to fall to pieces. At first, it was noticed only as a curiosity that the cast-iron shot weighed much less than their size suggested they should. For instance, the shot of the demi-cannon, about a 32-pounder in size, actually weighed only 19 lbs, the shot of the 68-pounder cannon royal only 45 lb. Obviously, a chemical change had taken place, but what this was, or how to arrest it, let alone reverse the process so as to make the object chemically "stable" once more, was quite beyond nineteenth-century science.

But what did strike knowledgeable men of the time, and as far as smooth-bore ordnance was concerned they knew a great deal more than we can ever do now, was the power of the *Mary Rose's* armament. A contributor to Colburn's *United Service Magazine* wrote in 1844:

> On a recent occasion we visited Woolwich, to see one of our large steamers on her return from abroad. She was lying in the magnificent new floating-dock, and presented a formidable appearance. On examining her ordnance, and seeing the 68-pounder shot, we could not but draw comparisons with the old war-officer who kindly "showed us round", on the difference of handling those massy balls and the 18-pounder ones which were ranged round the coomings of our line-of-battle ships' main-decks, and those of the smartest frigates in the Service, during the late wars. In

the course of the discussion the arguments ran, as arguments usually do, *pro et con*; and the assertion of giving a smashing blow being more advantageous than riddling, was met by the opinion that celerity and number would more than compensate for the smash, and could be effected with less fatigue, greater certainty, and few hands. After a discussion in which neither party convinced the other, we returned to the shore, and wended our way to that very interesting museum, the Repository of the Royal Artillery, on Woolwich Common. But the thoughts of the heavy armament of ships engrossed our mind, and those 68-pounders in a steamer were uppermost.

On arriving at the entrance of the Repository, being pretty well known there, we asked,—

"Is there anything new lately?"

"No, Sir," said the Serjeant, "nothing *very* new: unless," added he, "those guns from the *Mary Rose* have been brought since you were here," pointing at the same time to two large pieces of ordnance near the door.

Being aware of Mr. Deane's diving exploits in 1835, [*sic*] the dexterity he had manifested, and the vexatious interruptions he had met with, we were, of course, curious to examine such trophies of his address, and therefore immediately went to them. But what was our surprise on seeing guns of the heaviest calibre, with bores of upwards of eight inches.

"Why these must have sent pretty large shot," we remarked.

"68-pounders, Sir," answered the Serjeant, "the guns were loaded, and the drawn charge is now there," pointing to a table near the door.

We therefore strictly examined the shot, and also the powder, after their 290 years' submergement, and we are quite satisfied that Solomon was right in asserting that "there is nothing new under the sun."

The Anthony Roll list shows that both these apparently rival theories of gunnery were employed in arming the *Mary Rose*—the cannon-class guns for "smashing", the culverin-class guns for "riddling"; while the stone-firing iron guns recovered by Deane show as a third class—anti-personnel

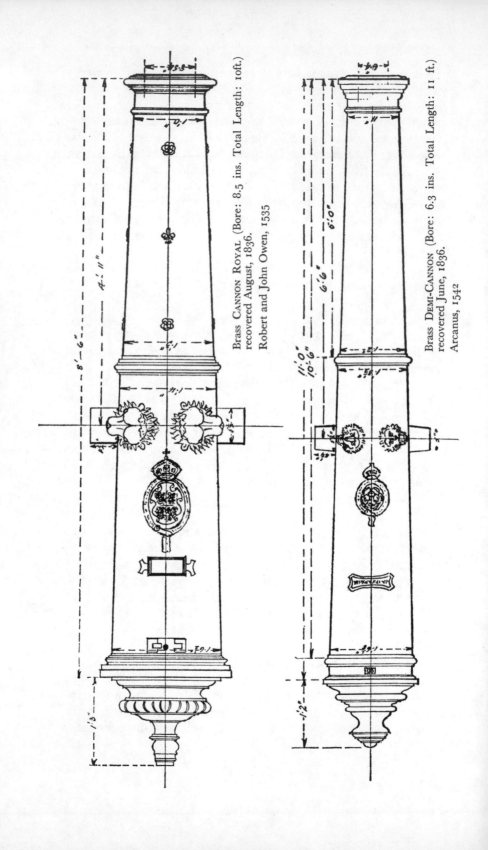

Brass CANNON ROYAL. (Bore: 8.5 ins. Total Length: 10ft.)
recovered August, 1836.
Robert and John Owen, 1535

Brass DEMI-CANNON (Bore: 6.3 ins. Total Length: 11 ft.)
recovered June, 1836.
Arcanus, 1542

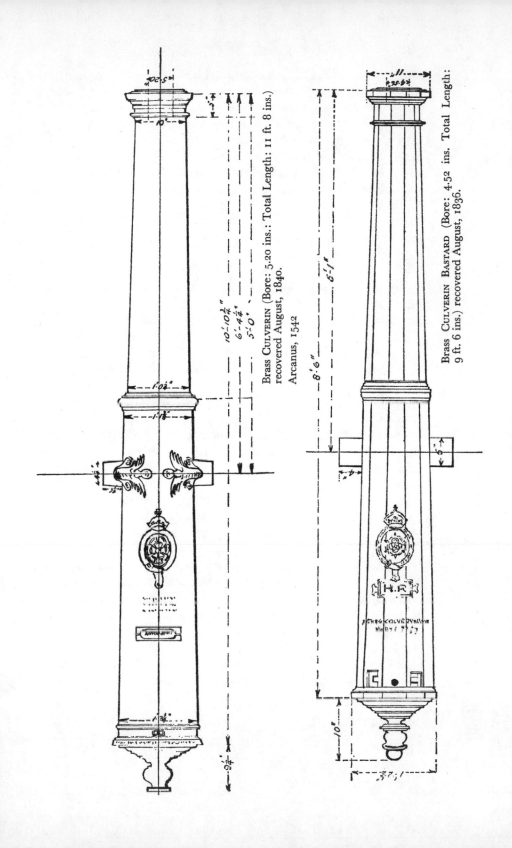

Brass CULVERIN (Bore: 5.20 ins.: Total Length: 11 ft. 8 ins.)
recovered August, 1840.
Arcanus, 1542

Brass CULVERIN BASTARD (Bore: 4.52 ins. Total Length:
9 ft. 6 ins.) recovered August, 1836.

rather than anti-ship. A comparison between the Anthony Roll (Table 3) and the guns recovered by Deane (Table 4) show that he had raised 4 out of the 15 bronze guns and at least 11 of the 76 iron guns, plus 9 "parts", most of which were probably spare chambers (each gun having two chambers). In all, his recoveries probably amounted to some 16 guns out of the 91 guns shown on the Roll. Of the warlike and other stores he had got nothing, except possibly some of the bows and the shot. The implications were not realised at the time and no comparison was ever made; indeed, most of the crop of late nineteenth and early twentieth century nautical historians who wrote about Tudor ship guns did not bother even to look at the actual examples Deane had given them, let alone start searching for lost files in Ordnance Board records.

Deane himself was soon forgotten. His book was never published, the manuscript lost, the watercolour sketches scattered among his relatives. Even the fact of the invention of the diving helmet by the two brothers went into historical limbo, for Charles Anthony Deane sold the rights to the engineer Augustus Siebe and collaborated with him on a "closed" version of it, in which the helmet was screwed to a breastplate fixed to the suit and the air escaped, not under the helmet but from a non-return valve in it. This soon became the "standard" dress for divers and achieved worldwide fame as a result of the exciting explosive demolition by Colonel C. W. Pasley's divers during the early 1840s of the two Spithead wrecks, *Royal George* and *Edgar*. Even the fact that they had initially, in 1839, used Deane's helmet and dress was soon obliterated, as was Deane's discovery of the *Mary Rose,* which was soon attributed to Colonel Pasley's Royal Enginers, and from there it was but a short step to a general acceptance that the *Mary Rose* had been blown up with one-ton charges laid under Pasley's direction. And as nothing now protruded from the seabed to show the place where Henry VIII's great battleship had foundered, no wreck buoy was thought necessary and all knowledge of the site was forgotten, for the second time since 1545.

Part III

THE SEARCH
FOR THE MARY ROSE

CHAPTER EIGHT

PROJECT "SOLENT SHIPS"

"Southsea Branch of the British Sub-Aqua Club
are undertaking this year a survey of historic
wrecks in the Solent, starting with the *Boyne* and
Royal George, the exact locations of which we
already have. These, however, are merely dummy
runs for the one really important wreck, that of
the *Mary Rose,* sunk 19 July 1545, which would
merit a proper archaeological investigation. Apart
from the fact that she is believed to lie not far
from the *Royal George,* we have no idea of the
location."

—Letter to Hydrographer of the Navy,
8 February 1965.

"Made it clear the *Mary Rose* was only 3 of 1-2-3
and an outsider at that."

—Note of telephone conversation,
mid-February, 1965.

When Project "Solent Ships" began in 1965, the *Mary Rose*
was 455 years old, had been on the bottom for 420 years, and
125 years had elapsed since John Deane had seen her. And
much of this book could not have been written. John and
Charles Anthony Deane had been eliminated from the record.
The nautical background was sub-standard. Because the ships
and the battles of the period were vague, no full-scale study
had been attempted, and most accounts were brief and super-
ficial, sometimes misleading. On the subject of early Tudor
ship guns, I found only one historian worth reading, L. G.
Carr Laughton. A great deal of the secondary written evidence
was false, distorted, inadequate, or the product of ignorance.
And all position indications for the wreck were not merely
wrong but wildly inaccurate.

I suspected that much of the information was unreliable
and that the *Mary Rose* enquiry would have to consist of
original historical research. This I listed under six headings:

(a) the ship; (b) the battle; (c) the early divers, and the damage they did; (d) the guns and artefacts they raised, and their present whereabouts; (e) the fluctuating and complex marine biology of the Solent Area; (f) the wreck position, either (i) by deduction from a study of the battle or (ii) from the clues given by the early divers.

I had the advantage of being a professional military historian—not an academic. I had taken a brief course in helmet diving with the Royal Enginers in Hamburg during 1951 and 1952, so I understood the problems of that type of diving. I had taken to mask and flippers in 1958 and had joined the local branch of the British Sub-Aqua Club in 1959, in order to learn the aqualung, when I was 40 years old. I had become involved almost at once in an archaeological project—the study of buildings submerged in Hayling Bay during the inundations of the Middle Ages. Later I had acquired a little knowledge of marine life and of submarine geology. I had also learnt the simple methods of the inshore fishermen for accurate position finding at sea. And I had, meanwhile, gained an adequate although strictly amateur experience of aqualung diving, as well as some ability with an underwater camera in conditions not always wholly suitable.

Basic to the situation was the existence of a 200-strong branch of the B.S.-A.C. in Southsea, founded some ten years previously. Although many members were tied to the training programme, either as instructors or trainees, a number were not content with simple sport diving but preferred the wider objects of the club which were to encourage underwater exploration. Among them were the group which had been concerned since 1960 with the Hayling "Church Rocks" project, eventually under my direction. We had been faced with the difficult problem of recognising the remains of "robbed out" buildings erected originally on natural rock strata, and although the object of this enquiry had been to establish the cause of the inundations, it had been a useful introduction to work of a generally archaeological nature. So there was a nucleus of amateur divers with some five years' experience of practical archaeology in British waters. Apart from this, the branch provided the vital compressor for filling the aqualung cylinders, there was a branch boat, and some of the members had their own private boats.

By herself, the *Mary Rose* was too much of a long shot to be worth an enquiry by such a team, but if by any chance we did find her, we might not know enough ship archaeology to make a proper appraisal. Therefore I put to Southsea Branch a more general project, which they agreed was viable. I jotted down some notes to record our intentions:

Basically, to "write the book" (believing that it had not yet been written). In detail, to locate, survey and assess the remains of some of the 13 known historic wrecks in the Solent area, taking the easy ones first, in order to establish (*a*) what such a wreck actually looked like; (*b*) which, if any, might merit excavation or salvage; (*c*) what methods of excavation or salvage might be appropriate, bearing in mind that no one has ever assessed an historic shipwreck in British waters. It would not be too much to claim that no one has even *seen* such a wreck, because the divers saw only the obvious—the armament—and appropriated it if they could. Bearing in mind also that Mediterranean experience might not be a valid guide to very different types of ship sunk in very different conditions. The British wrecks are mostly warships, large or very large; whereas the Mediterranean wrecks are all merchant ships, small or very small. Further, most of the Solent Ships, being in an anchorage, have been blown in varying degrees, as a result of underwater demolition lasting anything from 5 weeks to 5 years. Finally, with but few exceptions, the Mediterranean work has been but indifferently done.

The method to be used was as follows:

To begin with, very accurate historical information on the degree of demolition carried out, plus very accurate location, because of the obvious danger that so little might now remain that we should fail to recognise a wreck site when we saw one. Once the first two or three had been probed, however, we should have amassed enough experience to read the signs. Proceed as for the tracking of animals or a detective enquiry. A fast, seaworthy, very mobile diving boat with echo-sounder. Slack water for small-area searches, but use fast tides and mobility of aqualung gear supported by small mobile diving boat to cover the large

areas, especially in delimitation. Divers and boat handlers
to be practised in working together; all divers to have practical underwater archaeological experience and to be well
briefed for each separate wreck; land archaeologists with
some understanding of the special problems to be carried
in the boat whenever possible, and ultimately expected to
dive. Basic assumption that the most important part of a
wreck search *is to go where there is no wreck,* so that the
characteristics of the natural seabed surrounding the wreck
area are early established.

The required historical information regarding many of
these wrecks was already on file in my office, as were their
positions. The earliest large-scale Admiralty chart I had for
the *Royal George,* for instance, was dated 1784, two years after
the sinking. I had written several studies of this affair, including a TV script, long before I had begun to dive, let alone
consider actually visiting the wreck. Her hull really had been
broken up, between 1839 and 1843, leaving only a low mound
which had ben raked again and again by half-anchor creepers
and an ingenious underwater rake, so as to spread the remains.
The *Boyne* had first caught fire at Spithead, then drifted on
to the Horse Sand off Southsea Castle, where the after hanging
magazine had blown up, and she had subsequently burnt
almost to the waterline. The underwater demolition on her
had not been so thorough, however, because the spot was a
nasty place for divers. The nearest navigational channel buoy
was still marked *Boyne,* although I knew that it was not
actually on the wreck. The interest of these two eighteenth
century three-deckers lay in what had happened to them after
demolition, in the way of sedimentation and deterioration
of dated materials. The ships themselves were of no
importance.

The *Mary Rose* was different in every respect. I had been
interested in her for a very long time and the earliest news-
paper article in my files was a wartime cutting from the
Portsmouth *Evening News* of 12 February 1941. Written by
James Bayes from the memoirs of du Bellay and Oglander,
it had the then-topical title: "THE LAST TIME INVASION
WAS ATTEMPTED: Battle off Portsmouth in 1545". As
Bayes observed: "Few history books record the events of July

1545 . . . the odds, were, in fact, much the same as those our Air Force is said to have faced during the evacuation of Dunkirk". That is, ten months before. At that time, the Channel was not English, it was no-man's-land; to the south there was only the enemy, and beaches were covered with oil and wreckage from countless recently sunken ships. By 1965, this had been long forgotten, and in order to visit the continent it was no longer necessary to be accompanied by a million armed men. However, the possibility of unwittingly blundering into unexploded bombs, mines and shells in probably semi-darkness at Spithead was a factor which had to be considered, as well as the results of the pre-invasion build-up for D-Day, also the various Coronation and Fleet Reviews, for on all these occasions many hundreds of ships were anchored at Spithead. There was no knowing what damage their heavy steel hooks might have done and there was the certainty that the whole area was bound to be littered with the ships' garbage of many centuries, which could confuse the identification of any wreck we might find.

But I still had no idea where the *Mary Rose* was. Enquiries made with Siebe, Gorman in 1962 and locally in 1963 had produced no result. No one seemed to know, and I was left with the alternatives presented by the orthodox authorities:

". . . the Mary Rose sank *in the mouth of Portsmouth Harbour* in 1545."
>(G. S. Laird Clowes in "Sailing Ships", Science Museum, 1932-62.)

". . . the Mary Rose which capsized *off Brading* on 20th July, 1545, when getting under way."
>(M. Oppenheim in "Administration of the Royal Navy", N.R.S., 1896.)

". . . the Mary Rose, 60 guns, Captain Sir George Carew, sunk in action with the French Fleet *off St. Helens, Isle of Wight*, 20th July, 1545, with the loss of all hands."
(Catalogue of Dockyard Museum, Portsmouth, 1919.)

"The wreck was abandoned and forgotten until, during the *Royal George* operations, divers came *accidentally* upon the remains of the ship sunk 237 years earlier, *lying but a short distance away.*"

(Sir Robert Davis in "Deep Diving and Submarine Operations", 1962.)

This selection (the italics are mine) did not inspire confidence, even disregarding the small slips regarding the date,
the guns, the captain, and the casualties. The distance between the mouth of Portsmouth Harbour (favoured by one
reputable naval historian) and the St. Helens/Brading coast
of the Isle of Wight (favoured by another of equal repute) is
some six sea miles. Both could not be right; in fact, neither
was. The Cowdray picture ruled them out absolutely. This
was contemporary and showed the *Mary Rose* quite plainly
as sunk along a line running roughly from Southsea Castle to
Ryde in the Isle of Wight, but much nearer to the Southsea
shore than to Wight. But the sixteenth century painting had
been drawn according to sixteenth century conventions, virtually without perspective, and I could not quite make up my
mind about it. It appeared, almost, to be a chart. Dare I take
it literally? It certainly agreed with Monson's statement: "Part
of the ribs of this ship I have seen with my own eyes," for it
indicated a comparatively shallow area of Spithead.

But to someone in as much doubt as I then was, it did
not rule out Sir Robert Davis entirely, for the line Southsea
Castle–Ryde runs also almost through the position of the
Royal George, which lies, however, much nearer to the halfway mark and in much deeper water, about 75 feet at average
low tide, nearer to 90 feet at high. Assuming that the Cowdray
picture was somewhat inaccurate or, more likely, that I did
not fully understand the conventions the artist had employed,
it was just possible that Pasley's divers, while working on the
Royal George, had blundered on to the *Mary Rose.* And in
that case, the two wrecks must be close. Apparent confirma-
tion of Davis's story was given by a local historian, W. H.
Saunders, who published his *Annals of Portsmouth* in 1880
and would have remembered Pasley's work. He wrote,
". . . but the occasion was rendered memorable by a mis-
fortune, the total loss of the *Mary Rose,* which was the more
remarkable as having occurred on nearly the same spot, when
at a later date the *Royal George,* from a similar cause, went

Fig. 1. An English four-masted carrack, similar in design to the *Mary
Rose*, at Dover in 1520.

Fig. 2. The *Cordelière* and the *Regent* locked together and burning during the Battle of Brest in 1512.

Fig. 3. Sir Peter Carew, younger brother of Vice-Admiral Sir George Carew, was present at the battle in 1545 and later described the sinking of the *Mary Rose* to his biographer.

Fig. 4. A French carrack and three galleys retiring from the beaches of the Isle of Wight under fire from the advancing English militia. Newport and Carisbrook are shown symbolically as on the coast, although both are inland.

Fig. 5. Watercolour from John Deane's portfolio of the three brass guns he raised from the *Mary Rose* in 1836. They are of three distinct types. *Top*: 68-pdr Cannon Royal (heavy shot, short range); *bottom*: 32-pdr Demi-Cannon (medium shot, medium range); *centre*: 9-pdr Culverin Bastard (light shot, long range).

Photo: Alexander McKee

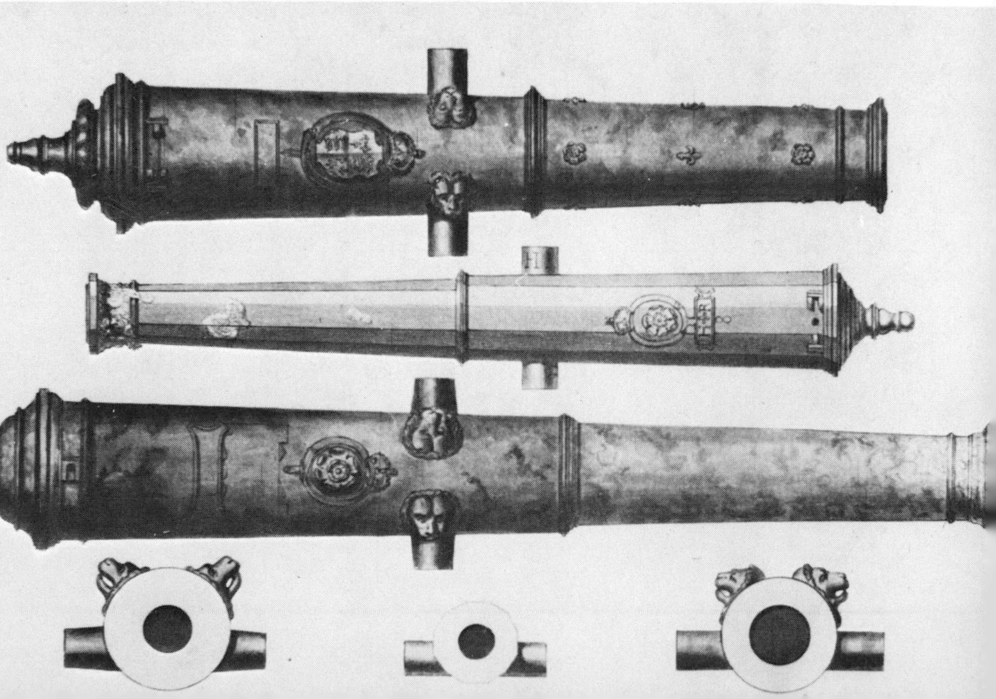

down". Now, while the Cowdray picture indicated only a large, vague area, Sir Robert Davis's story could be checked by relocating the *Royal George* and using her as a start point for a bottom search.

Meanwhile, between the meeting with Southsea branch representatives on 2 January to initiate the project and the first diving operation with them on 24 April, local research had produced an unexpected and astonishing "twist" to the story. I had for the moment turned my attentions to the exploits of the early divers at Spithead, which had been famous in their time, and ought to be well-documented locally. They were. But the story they told was not that expounded originally by Sir Robert Davis and then "lifted" by almost every author of underwater books who came after him. These had a section devoted to the development of diving apparatus, in which the invention of, first, the "open" diving helmet and, second, the "closed" type which succeeded it, were credited to Augustus Siebe and their first practical use credited to Colonel Pasley and his Royal Enginers during their demolition of the *Royal George*. But regardless of whether the authors of these books were English, American, French, Dutch, Italian, or whatever, their main source was Sir Robert Davis. And Davis was wrong. This was appalling, for not only had I believed Davis but had actually quoted him recently in a public request for information. As I turned up reference after contemporary reference, it became clear that the author of *Deep Diving and Submarine Operations* was not even the earliest historian of diving, for that honour also belonged to one of the Deane brothers!

Now, from the *Hampshire Telegraph* of 22 March 1841, I learnt that:

Mr. Deane, of Gosport, delivered a lecture before the Philosophical Society yesterday evening, "on Submarine Operations and Researches" illustrated with excellent diagrams and working models. Commencing with an historical review of the different kinds of diving bells and other apparatus, which had been invented for the purpose, he particularly treated of Halley's, Spalding's, Walker's, Borelli's and several others; showing their relative advantages and disadvantage. He then related the manner in

which he and his brother had proceeded in the invention of
their own. . . . In narrating some of the submarine enter-
prises which they had successfully carried on, his recital,
simple and matter of fact, assumed an air of romantic
adventures; and kept a crowded audience fixed in interest
till an unusually late hour. . . .

This was tantalising, for I did not know then exactly how
Deane's apparatus worked, which was anyway a sideline, for
what I was really after was a fully detailed description of
what the *Mary Rose* wreck site had looked like in 1840, where
it was, what Deane had done to the wreck and the present
whereabouts of the artefacts he had recovered.

I was still two years away from possessing full technical
details, not only of Deane's apparatus but of other contemporary diving gear not mentioned by Davis. I did not know
even that there were two Deanes or that they came originally
from Kent. But I did know that the Davis story itself was
muddled and contradictory, two sections of a massive and
valuable textbook being devoted to the history of salvage
and the development of diving gear. These historical sections
(but not the textbook itself) showed all the signs of scrappy
compilation by a busy man over a long period, without final
co-ordination or tight scrutiny. Even the picture of the *Mary
Rose,* which headed the historical salvage section, was in fact
a poor likeness of the *Great Harry* borrowed from Derrick.
Deane was not mentioned as an inventor of diving gear in one
section, but merely as the user of an apparatus invented by
Siebe, and in the other section he was not mentioned at all.
But at the very back of the book, among the appendices, was
a *Brief History of the Firm of Siebe, Gorman & Co. Ltd.,*
which gave a different version and said of Siebe:

> It is, however, through the invention of his diving appar-
> atus that his name will live. He made the acquaintance of
> a working diver named Deane, who was using a very crude
> dress of the "open" type. Siebe produced an improved
> version of this type consisting of a metal helmet attached
> by rivets to a jacket extending to below the waist. Air was
> supplied through a hose by a force pump, the surplus air
> escaping at the bottom of the jacket; it acted, in fact, on
> the principle of the diving bell.

Even this condescending reference to Deane was incorrect, judged by the secondary accounts which were all I had then. But I did not discover what an awful, meaningless muddle it really was until later, when a series of fortunate discoveries put all the basic original documents into my hands. These were to include Deane's own Diving Manual of 1836, which he sold with the apparatus; Colonel Pasley's own lengthy technical report on the merits and demerits of the main types of diving gear available to him in 1840; and an official list of patents for diving gear going back as far as 1632. Briefly, the Deanes were the inventors of the first practical diving helmet, which was not as described and illustrated by Sir Robert Davis, for it was *not* attached to a jacket. It was just a weighted helmet, exactly as used today for some forms of shallow water diving, particularly in America. However, there did exist not one, but two, quite distinct types of apparatus of the sort described by Davis as the single invention of Augustus Siebe. The earliest was a smoke helmet and jacket for fire-fighting, for which Patent No. 4869 had been issued on 20 November 1823 to Charles Anthony Deane, of Deptford, in the County of Kent, Ship Caulker. The latest was a similar specification, but intended for diving, for which Patent No. 63 had been issued on 9 July 1853 to John Deane, of Whitstable, in the County of Kent, Submarine Surveyor. Her Majesty's Patent Office contained no record of a patent granted in respect of the invention of any diving apparatus whatever to anyone at all bearing the name of Augustus Siebe. We had all been well and truly hoaxed.

In the 1830s and 1840s, the Deanes' helmet and separate waterproof suit was known as the Common Diving Dress and was sold by them as such. But there also appeared during this time what was then called the Tight Diving Dress. Sir Robert Davis, misunderstanding Deane's design, distinguished between them by calling the first the "open" dress and the second the "closed" dress. The "closed" dress, which is that still used for deep diving and some shallow water work as well, is really only the Deanes' helmet fastened to the Deanes' dress by screws—instead of merely resting on the diver's shoulders. Nothing more, for the Deanes' helmet had an outlet valve already for getting rid of stale or excess air upwards as well as under the helmet. This "closed" design allowed the diver to lean forward or even lie down without flooding the helmet and dress, but took much longer to put on and take off. In all the world's underwater books, the invention of a diving dress on the "closed" principle is dated to 1837 and the inventor is stated to be Siebe. But the authority for this sweeping statement is, again, Sir Robert Davis. And again, Davis is in error.

There is no record of a patent for a "closed" dress in 1837, or any other year, in the name of Augustus Siebe. There are, however, no fewer than two patents for apparatus of the "closed" type dated 1835, two years earlier, in the names of John Bethell and John William Fraser. These share one main characteristic, that the "dress"—or waterproof suit—is made in two parts, a pair of trousers and a jacket to which the helmet is permanently attached. This involved making a watertight seal over a metal band round the waist. Pasley's divers used a Bethell suit in 1839, and hated it because when merely waiting to dive they liked to have their helmets off. With Bethell's apparatus this took 20 minutes, and as they were making repeated dives of short duration, it was impossible to take the helmet off and allow them to breathe unsullied air for a change. Pasley promptly cut the helmet off the jacket and converted Bethell's apparatus into Deane's.

Pasley is very hesitant about Siebe, who, he says, was recommended to him on the grounds of his good "workmanship" in the manufacture of diving gear, and he goes on to warn that, "It is proper to remark that the whole of the details of this construction are not entirely Mr. Siebe's own invention, as he was assisted by Mr. Edwards, and part of it may have been copied from other Diving dresses, for a great number of ingenious men have proposed improvements, and several patents have been taken out, with all of which I do not profess to be acquainted." No patent ever was taken out by Siebe, but there was a row between the two Deane brothers at about this time, because of some "rights" sold by Charles Anthony Deane to Siebe, a transaction which John Deane thought was unwise. I was unable to obtain details, but it was probably the simple idea of starting with the Deane suit and the Deane helmet and then screwing them together. The Deane suit was in one piece, so that the diver had to get into it via the neck, as he does today. The only modification required to turn it into a "closed" type was to arrange for the helmet, when put over the diver's head, to be clamped tightly by screws to a collar fitted to the neck of the suit. This watertight join at the neck, achieved by a collar, a corselet and a few screws, is the only difference between the "Common Diving Apparatus" invented by the Deanes' and the modern helmet diving dress familiar to everyone.

This long-term study of early underwater gear, made intelligible because I had myself had some experience of the "closed" dress, and undertaken while I was diving in the same area with an aqualung, had two direct bearings on the search. The first, and most immediate, was that in advance of finding any wreck site, I had some information, varying from meagre to excellent, of what that wreck had looked like when last seen by a helmet diver more than a hundred years before. This did not mean that the site was going to look like that now, but that a comparison was possible which would provide information on sedimentation, marine life and growth and the local underwater environment generally. These were all prime points in the reconnaissance plan. Secondly, where a wreck had not yet been found, and the damage done to it with explosive or otherwise by the early divers was in dispute, I was soon to have a fairly accurate idea of what could, or could not, be done with the apparatus and resources they had had available.

The old-time divers would have died of laughter at the sight of our first operation to locate the *Royal George*. There were five of us in an open bass boat which might have been as long as 16 feet and might have had as much freeboard as 2 feet, proceeding at a snail's pace out of Langstone Harbour to reach Spithead 2 hours later, because any greater speed would have swamped the craft. But this was an emergency. We had planned to start in May with a larger craft fitted with "command post" facilities for navigation and note-taking, but in the last week of April an exceptionally weak neap tide had coincided with a light northerly wind following a long period of low rainfall. This should mean that maximum underwater visibility would be combined with minimum current flow, the optimum conditions for operating in the Solent area. So we went while the going was good, in what we could get.

But in its way this effort was an excellent demonstration

of the practical difference between helmet diving gear and the aqualung. Our boat was too small to carry the pump to supply even one helmet diver, but we had five divers of whom, with seven years' experience, I was the "novice". We could rely on an anchor which, if it dragged, would cause no real inconvenience, but if a helmet diver's boat dragged the helmet diver was as good as dead. Whereas we could search a wide area, leaving behind us the sediment stirred up by our fins, a helmet diver could move only with difficulty and in the middle of a cloud of muddied water of his own creation. And, also, he could lower his face-glass to the seabed for a close inspection only with difficulty and at some risk of inadvertently blowing himself to the surface with an inflated suit. We could stand on our heads if we wanted, or swim five feet up or five inches up, as the nature of the search dictated. We could not stay down as long as he could, but in any sudden emergency we did not have to rely upon others, but could go for the surface at once under our own power, unhindered by lines and hoses.

Where we were really out on a limb, though, was in searching out from the boat in the shipping lanes, for although this was part of the Spithead anchorage it was also the deepest part, much used by traffic of the larger sort, liners and super-tankers going up to Southampton, as well as the Isle of Wight ferry service and miscellaneous warships of all nations. For this reason, among others, each diving team would tow a large marker buoy so that we could track them and check their search pattern. As we came up to Spithead, John Towse and I compared notes on the position for the *Royal George*. We were operating a double-check system, where both of us had worked out "marks" independently, Towse from an old chart, I from two other old charts, both of us having first transferred the position to our own copies of the largest scale modern charts available. Only when we got out on site and could actually see the marks we had chosen as they really were did we discuss the matter. There was little to discuss, most of the more obviously useful marks having been spotted by both of us, and we simply tried them out, brought one set of transits in line and then ran until the second set were also in line; when we had done this a few times, travelling very slowly, we cut the motor and dropped the anchor.

John Baldry and Roger Hale did a square search north of the boat, which was the most likely area. After a few minutes they came across the right sort of remains, and brought some back as samples. These included a 32-pounder iron cannon-ball, a length of tarred standing rigging, and a carving on what looked like whalebone, found in an area of small mounds, with many animal bones lying about. They reported a large stone shot near the anchor.

None of us had dived Spithead before, and for all we knew the entire anchorage might be littered with such items. For my search with Alan Lee I therefore turned my back on what Baldry mockingly called the "mother lode", the undulating area where he had found the ship artefacts, and toured in the opposite direction. The rather cold water was as clear as a bell just below the surface, but at 20 feet we ran into a layer of green peasoup, which shortly gave way to an almost complete blackout, which only lightened when we arrived on the bottom at about 80 feet. Effective horizontal visibility was about 6 feet, although one could dimly see a diver 10 feet away as a blurred shadow. This was ample for our purpose and quite safe in the event of encountering unknown obstructions. The light level was too low for photography and there was no contrast in it, so that everything appeared flat. As we were anyway touring a flat plain with none of the undulations and mounds that marked Baldry's "mother lode", the impression was of a grey clay desert littered with cast-off debris. There were no fish, there was no weed; hardly any life at all apart from a few nervous hermit crabs and pale anemones, and what was probably a seamouse. There was a light scatter of small transit shingle and dead shells of the American slipper limpet, which had not been present in Deane's time. But the principal items of litter, excluding a motor car tyre, were all ships' garbage—an empty toothpaste tube, a spoon, a fork, bits of plates, cups and bottles—the sort of object we classified as "anchorage gash". There were no parts of ships, or ships' fittings, let alone anything indicative of a wooden warship wreck. I therefore concluded that this was unsullied Spithead in its natural state, and that the mounds to the north, containing the right sort of artefact, probably did represent outlying wreckage from the *Royal George*.

Because of the ever-present ship danger, we returned to our boat by navigating along the bottom. This was just as well, for the surface party saw a NATO squadron of destroyers and frigates steam over us—the British *Leander*, the American *Hammerberg*, the Dutch *Overijssel* and the *Canadian Columbia*.

The next operation was directed primarily at the *Boyne* and carefully timed because the hazards from the ships and the fast tidal stream had to be taken even more seriously. In addition, there was a nasty sea and poor visibility, due to a south-east wind occurring on the ebb. I had to be satisfied with a solo dive, starting off the wreck and then moving on to it. The natural bottom was light shingle mixed with dead oyster shells, no weed at all, very little modern "gash", but some small pieces of splintered wood. Then, as I turned in towards where I knew the wreck must be, the seabed started to rise up in a great mount, patches of weed appeared, and the light got brighter. I checked each weed-patch and in each case the holdfasts were grown on to heavy, solid objects, which were of iron covered in natural concretion. The concretion rendered them shapeless, although one seemed to be a hollow tube, just possibly a cannon. A quick scrape with my knife produced no effect beyond the panic evacuation of the interior by several crabs. The mound can hardly have been less than 10 feet high, and I concluded that the demolition had been perfunctory and the remains had become encased in a large shoal of shingle, now a permanent feature of the seabed at the side of the navigational channel.

It was rapidly becoming unsafe to continue on the *Boyne*, so we went straight on to the *Royal George*. Inevitably, the fast tide run had begun there, too, although sea conditions were better. Maurice Harknett, whose boat we were using, decided that an anchor drift was the only way to cope with the various hazards which were coming together in dangerous combination, so he dived with Jim Dipnell, both under-weighted, and when they arrived at the anchor they lifted it for a free ride. I relaxed, with my back to the bow cabin (because we were drifting stern-first) and began to chat to Margaret Rule, a land archaeologist, whose first trip to Spithead this was. Then we both heard a booming noise close on the port side and, turning my head, I was astonished to see

the great whaleback and high "sail" of an enormous underwater monster sliding past on the surface, apparently about
100 feet away. It was the biggest submarine I had seen since
the old X.1 at Malta in the 1920s, but I had never heard one
make a noise like that before, not surprisingly, for this vessel
was nuclear-powered. The "boat" was H.M.S. *Dreadnought*,
of 3,000 tons displacement, representing yet another phase of
the technological revolution which in John Deane's day was
represented by the steam paddle-ships.

The divers, who were being dragged at speed over the
bottom, were in no danger as long as they held on to the
anchor and ascended by the anchor line. They reported
having crossed an undulating seabed where scattered mounds
were littered with debris, but had no opportunity to inspect
it. I began my dive from their original start point, but was
unable to lift the anchor single-handed and was therefore
forced to attempt a swim up-tide, unconnected to the boat.
On the bottom, visibility was poor and the light so bad that
it was hard to read the compass. However, I progressed slowly
forward, swimming very hard but not moving much, ignoring
the clay plains and searching the mounds. A newspaper came
bowling along the bottom, followed by drifting weed which
wrapped itself round my mask and blacked me out momentarily. This current, which was running at nowhere near
maximum, is probably the principal agent in the slow movement of shells, shingle and light artefacts along the bottom,
which is a feature of the English Channel and similar areas,
and has to be considered in relation to archaeological sites.
The mounds, unlike the plains, were oases of minor plant
life and the whole area was thickly littered with anchorage
artefacts, mainly damaged pottery or sherds, in the ratio of
one item to every square yard. These were, as usual, simply
lying on the surface like leaves in a park in autumn, entirely
without burial, and I ignored them. But after covering 50
feet, and nearly exhausting my air, I noticed something
different, the rim of a little pot which was in rather than on
a mound, being largely buried. The fact of mound burial
struck me as being significant, and for this reason alone I
collected it. The pot proved to be intact—that is, probably
not discarded—and of late eighteenth century date, the period
of the sinking of the *Royal George*.

For the third and final operation on the *Royal George* we had to wait for the good underwater visibility which comes on the neap tides of June, because the search which I then planned demanded it. This required six divers to take turns to carry out three parallel tide-rides from south-west on the *Royal George* site to north-east of it in the direction I believed the *Mary Rose* must lie. These lines were to be 100 feet apart, so as to cover as large an area as possible. From the Cowdray engraving, the alignment of the *Mary Rose* wreck was some-where between south and south-east, and therefore we would be approaching her on the broadside. As she could hardly be less than 150 feet long and the site itself would be larger than this, we could hardly miss seeing her—if she was there. But, to be effective, the first parallel had to start on the *Royal George*, quite definitely, and therefore this was planned for slack water to allow for careful inspection of the mounds and the selection of further sample artefacts. I led the first pair because I wanted to be sure in my own mind that the whole search pattern was indeed firmly anchored on at least an out-lying part of the *Royal George* site. To assist with the de-briefings and identification of artefacts, Margaret Rule again accompanied us.

Jim Dipnell and I dived with a 120 ft. buoy-line and waited two minutes at the anchor in order to allow our eyes to become accustomed to the gloom. This time, the light was exceptionally good (late morning, summer, sun high, calm sea, plus visibility of 15–20 ft.). We then lined up on a com-pass bearing of north-east, Jim holding the weighted end of the buoy-line, I grasping the line about 6 feet away from him and keeping the line parallel to the seabed. Thus spaced out, the two of us would be able to scan a combined path about 35 to 40 feet wide along our course, while the buoy above would enable Harknett to follow us with the boat. We were already on the small mounds to start with, and when I picked up an obviously modern fork the light was so good that I could read the date on it—1957. As before, such artefacts were simply lying about, unburied.

Finning slowly, spread out, we passed over more of the small mounds, which I thought likely to be the residue of the raking and dragging Colonel Pasley had carried out after each of his big explosions. These had become increasingly unprofitable, as the *Royal George* collapsed into the surrounding mudbank, eventually leaving a well-spread-out mound only some three feet high, with all obstructions removed. That is, according to Colonel Pasley. Contemporary trawlermen had disagreed.

Within a minute or so of leaving the anchor, the small mounds gave way to a massive bank some five or six feet high aligned at a slight angle to the current. For a moment, I had a wild vision of finding the *Mary Rose,* but the alignment of this huge mound, more or less east–west, did not allow it. I was looking at the real *Royal George*, the main wreck mound and not the "spread" which was all we had seen so far. It was much as the last Royal Engineer divers had described it in 1843, only twice the height. Nor was it devoid of wreckage, for simultaneously Dipnell on the left and I on the right saw large clumps of weed. Instantly, but keeping in touch via the buoy-line, we separated to inspect them. Both clumps were attached to large masses of heavily concreted ironwork which were deeply and immovably buried in the mud and clay of the mound. My attempt at a snap inspection raised such a grey cloud of sediment that I moved away, head down, looking at the composition of the mound. Ignoring the light scatter of anchorage artefacts on its surface, I found traces of buried objects and a high concentration of shingle. One sample I took was of iron attached to wood, the top barely visible, the lower part well buried. The mound was less a ship than a compost heap. The shingle could have come from the ballast but, like some odd pieces of wood lying around the base of the mound, might possibly be attributed to the effect of the currents, which can move such items along the bottom. A mound or bank would tend to trap these. The height of the mound, twice that reported in 1843, could represent natural build-up since then, although all along I had suspected that Colonel Pasley had been under unfair pressure to exaggerate the extent to which the *Royal George* had been removed. To collapse a free-standing wreck is easy; to recover all the wreckage left in the resulting heap is impossible. Or so I believed.

Dipnell's finds had included animal bones with the marks of butchery on them, but it was impossible to say whether these were "gash" or from the meat casks once stored in the hold of the ship. There may have been a temptation to explore

the wreck further, and it says a great deal for the team that
no one suggested this. Instead we carried on with the search
pattern, using the exceptionally favourable visibility to establish once and for all whether or not there was any truth in
Davis's story, that the *Mary Rose* lay close to the *Royal
George*. With the main wreck mound as anchor point for the
pattern, we should be able to get a decisive result.

We moved south 100 feet and Maurice Harknett set off
with Tony Bye on their anchor-ride towards Southsea. They
reported a flat, featureless bottom, with no mounds of any
sort, large or small, and no ship wreckage or artefacts either.
A complete and definite negative. The third run was a tide-
ride by Jim and myself again, using the buoyline method as
before. Once more we waited two minutes at the anchor
before setting off, to accustom ourselves to the light on the
bottom. It was still bright, with visibility better than 15 feet.
We were on a nearly barren plain of mud, clay and ooze
littered mainly with the shells of molluscs, mostly empty.
There was no weed, because there was nothing for the holdfasts to cling to. Nor was there any shingle. We set off, finning
lazily and being carried fast by the current, peering ahead
into the green "fog" for a distinctive wreck mound or the
shadow of weed marking something substantial. There was
nothing, except the scatter of modern anchorage artefacts
lying fully exposed on the surface. There were no outliers
from the *Royal George*, and there was no sign of the *Mary
Rose*. A definite negative for both wrecks, with good conditions making a mistake impossible.

The day's work convinced me that Davis also was wrong,
as well as the academic historians. In a state of slightly
suppressed fury, I decided that the only guide worth having
now was contemporary evidence—Monson, the Cowdray
engraving, the course of the battle itself. If I was to be misled
in future, then it must be from a genuine sixteenth century
error.

CHAPTER NINE

"X" MARKS THE SPOT

Superficially, our findings on wreck formations appeared to confirm the existence of the classic "wreck mound" in British waters as well as in the Mediterranean. But this was not really so. Both the *Royal George* and the *Boyne* had indeed collapsed and been so thoroughly assimilated that their remains could have been mistaken for natural features of the seabed by anyone who had swum over them casually, without really looking. However, the process by which they had arrived at this state was utterly different to that which had resulted in the Mediterranean wreck mounds. Nor were Mediterranean laws of more than merely local application, for wreck remains in coral seas like the Caribbean or almost land-locked freshwater areas like the Baltic were different again, and different also from each other. In any event, Mediterranean experience was very limited and what the aqualung pioneers described as "utterly atypical" wreck sites, were really no such thing.

When Cousteau wrote his classic book, *The Silent World*, the number of wrecks his team had seen totalled only 25, ancient and modern, but mostly modern. And the ancient were all very old—Roman or Greek—while the modern were very new, mostly from the Second World War. There was virtually nothing in between. From this unrepresentative and relatively tiny number of sites, located in a tideless and utterly atypical sea, they put forward various propositions regarding the lengths of time various main materials were likely to last underwater and consequently how much, or rather, how little of really important ships was likely to remain. And often where, rightly and cautiously, the pioneers themselves had prefaced their discovered principles with the warning note, "In the Mediterranean . . .", their foreign admirers from colder climes had been more hasty and were found grandly proclaiming that, "In the Sea . . ." so-and-so must happen after X, Y, Z number of years, citing as incontrovertible evidence the immense experience of pioneers who had seen, comparatively speaking, hardly any wrecks at all at the time they wrote.

A more considered view was expressed by Frederic Dumas, the most archaeologically minded member of the Cousteau team, in his handbook, *Deep-Water Archaeology*, written much later and published in England in 1962. As "a good example" of the rapid disintegration of wooden ships, he documented the *Panama*, a wooden-hulled paddle frigate launched in 1843 and sunk off Toulon in 55 metres of water in 1896. She was a sizable vessel of 3,873 tons, but when Dumas saw her she could hardly be seen. "Only a table of mud, about 1 metre high out of which sundry almost un-recognisable objects protrude, distinguishes her from the sur-rounding, uninterrupted expanse of bottom." The exposed woodwork, he thought, must have been consumed by marine life "after a few years", but even the exposed ironwork had gone after some 60 years. Although imprecise, this is a generally true picture of the effect of "average" Mediter-ranean seawater on a wreck which ends up at that depth on a fairly firm seabed. Dumas then went on to mention a visit to the site of the battle of Navarino, fought in 1827, where he saw "enormous pieces of rotten wood" lying on rocks down to 40 metres. But the startling discrepancy between the two sites, at opposite ends of the Mediterranean, did not seem to worry him; at any rate, he did not comment on it (and, as far as I know, it still has to be explained).

The original thinker on this subject had been Anders Franzén, the deliberate discoverer in 1956 of the *Vasa*, a Swedish galleon which capsized in Stockholm Harbour on her maiden voyage in 1628. He had proceeded in a logical manner, starting with the premise that wooden ships do not just fade away, but are actually consumed by various marine organisms of which the best-known and one of the most damaging is *Teredo navalis*, a species of boring mollusc usually called a "shipworm". But, like most shellfish, this mollusc is very particular about its environment and could not live in the Baltic. The low salt content of the water is one factor, but there may be others. Franzén reasoned: if there is no Teredo to eat wooden ships, the wooden ships will still exist. The matter is more complicated than that, but broadly speaking he was right. He then made a list of the dozen or so most important historic wrecks in Swedish history, crossed out some which were likely to have suffered damage from other causes, such as winter ice or heavy, breaking seas in shallow areas, and finally narrowed his list to one prime object of search, the *Vasa*, which was in deep, protected water near his home. After a three-year survey, during which he was widely regarded as gone in the head, and undeterred by numerous false clues, he at length found the *Vasa*. And she was towering up out of the mud to the height of her upper deck. One of her masts, even, was still standing. Then, with the help of a willing salvage company and other individuals as far-sighted as himself, the *Vasa* was raised, brought into dock, and the immensely difficult process of conserving the huge hull and all its many different materials was begun.

The contrast with the exploits of the Mediterranean divers was striking. Their finds were accidental and when they blundered into them they did not know what to do. They did not know, even, that materials which have been underwater a long time have reached equilibrium, and that if they are returned to the surface that balance is broken and in many cases irreversible decay sets in. Wild with enthusiasm for antiquity, the pioneers had found part of the woodwork from the hulls of Roman ships still preserved, where these had been buried deep under the sand below a heap of cargo, and they obeyed their first instinct, to raise them regardless. And as the Mediterranean museums had no means of conserving them, the woodwork soon shrank and cracked. The so-called "excavations" from which they came were normally little better than mobile craters dug at random through a mound of amphorae; after a little while, the pioneers gave up, and the site was abandoned to the looters who raided it for souvenirs. This was the pathetic record of "underwater archaeology" in the Mediterranean for many, many years. Most of the work was carried out by amateur sports divers, but in some cases larger projects had been directed (exclusively from the surface, sometimes with underwater television) by professional French and Italian archaeologists. The results were exactly the same, except that the size of the craters and the damage they caused matched the resources—that is, the craters were larger and the damage greater. With very few exceptions, until the Americans came to the Mediterranean in the late 1950s, "sea digging" was a primitive exercise on the theme of how not to do it. No formally trained Mediterranean archaeologist could be persuaded to go underwater, although the conditions were simply wonderful, and to the best of my knowledge the first to do so was the American specialist, Dr. George Bass, who had no previous diving experience at all when he began work in 1960 on a Bronze Age wreck previously- reconnoitred by another American, Peter Throckmorton.

In American waters, however, the American record was marred by the lure of treasure from the wrecks of vessels from the Spanish Plate Fleets, mostly in the Caribbean and off Florida, although some were in the Pacific. The Spanish colonisation had taken place at the same time as Henry VIII was building up what was purely a Home Fleet, intended for use solely in European waters, and some of the early Spanish wrecks on the coasts of the New World were historically important. But the effect of treasure hunting was to destroy any old wreck in a frenzy, even before it had been identified, let alone recorded. There were some very sharp operators at work and the net result was similar to the effect created by the Mediterranean "sea diggers", but because the Americans were much more efficient, the damage was worse. All that could be gleaned of wreck formations was that anything not instantly buried was likely to be eaten by shipworms or grown on by coral, and that a typical Plate Fleet wreck was just a pile of large ballest stones with cannon lying about, often partially or wholly camouflaged by coral. These were mostly shallow water wrecks anyway which had suffered initially by being smashed to bits on reefs by hurricane force winds, the wreckage thereafter being subject to frequent hurricane disturbance.

In some cases there was more, much more, still remaining than anyone had any right to expect, both in the Caribbean and the Mediterranean, but the individuals who were to probe such sites thoroughly were only just beginning. At that time, the only serious information came from the Pacific and from a government agency unconnected with the study of wrecks. This was the Department of Fish and Game of the Resources Agency of California which, with minute resources in finance, materials and underwater scientists—three divers and a dinghy—was studying the effect of artificial reefs in attracting and building up fish populations. Their first report, dated 1964, showed that different types of reef material had been chosen for test—specially designed concrete blocks, old motor cars, and old wooden tramcars. They also fixed test strips of wood to the trams in order to find out exactly what happened and how long it took. The effect of that particular Pacific environment on wood and light metal was appalling. The car bodies completely collapsed from corrosion within a period of 3 to 5 years, and the wooden trams were eaten to destruction in a similar short period of time. A species of the famous Teredo, however, came only a bad second in the eating stakes, limping home long after the champion, a borer called *Bankia setacea*, whose wormlike body quickly grew to lengths of 12 to 13 inches on a nourishing diet of old tram and fresh pinewood blocks.

The point which emerged from a survey of available evidence world wide was that there was no such thing as "The Sea". Instead, there was a multitude of widely differing environments, many of theme extremely local. And the question to ask, which we did ask with Project "Solent Ships", was: "What sort of environment have we got?" The answer to that would tell us whether or not it was really worth while to go on looking for the *Mary Rose,* possibly for years. Therefore a great number of local wrecks were studied, not only those already known to us but others which had to be the object of deliberate search. We could not afford to put down artificial reefs and then study their deterioration year by year, but it was perfectly possible, given good wreck-finding techniques, to treat the local sea as a laboratory filled with man-made materials whose date of final immersion, if not already known, could in most cases be discovered after a little research. Further, various types of materials could be studied in relation to the marine organisms which were actually attacking them.

Another line of approach was through descriptions of the state of wrecks given by the early divers, which I was now uncovering in quantity. Although the *Royal George* and *Boyne* were now wreck mounds, and presumably the *Edgar* also, they had not reached that sad state through any Mediterranean, Pacific or Caribbean process, they had been demolished by repeated gunpowder explosions, precisely because the natural process of decay had *not* collapsed them. Before demolition, the burnt-out 3-decker *Boyne* had been a hull rearing up 8 or 10 feet at least above the seabed after 45 years underwater; the 3-decker *Royal George* had towered to between 33 and 36 feet, although the upper decks had mostly fallen in and the port side was distorted; and even the 2-decker *Edgar* had stood $13\frac{1}{2}$ feet, or nearly two gundecks high, above the seafloor after 133 years. The timber of the *Edgar* was in a very fragile state, not surprisingly, but it seemed hardly possible that she could have been attacked by Teredo. It was more likely that only the gribble, a tiny, debased crustacean borer, had been around to take advantage of the softening of the wood, first by bacilli and then by fungi, which initially opens it to attack, in British waters, after about five years.

We knew we had a very remarkable and interesting sea area to deal with, and the ship project, from the start, was tied in with a study of local marine life, in which we were guided by Mr. R. V. Wells, who was then helping to organise part of a nation-wide shellfish survey. This was a more important study than might appear, because the molluscs, being extremely choosy about their environment, are "indicator animals" to what sort of sea you have. If, on returning from the moon, your space capsule got off course and bumped down in an unknown area of the globe, but was then approached by a large polar bear, this would tell you roughly where you were, and a lot about the climate and the other types of animals you might expect to see around. Similarly, if the animal was not a bear but a camel, the beast would be a kind of shorthand as to what lay outside. Just so with the shellfish.

The marine naturalists were aware already that the Solent area was very special, considered as an undersea environment, and also that its patterns were liable to violent fluctuation, but not very much was known about it because there was no local fishing industry of any importance. Therefore there were no funds for a marine biological station. This situation changed during the years we worked at Spithead and there is now such a station on Hayling Island, staffed by specialist scientists, some of whom are divers. But when we began it was a case of do-it-yourself marine biology by rank amateurs; or nothing at all. We were told that there was a mysterious difference between the water content west of the Isle of Wight and that to the east of it, the dividing line being famous as the Isle of Wight "cut-off". The difference was so subtle that it could not be detected by instruments, but the shellfish were in no doubt about it. Nor were we, for we had actually seen it—or, rather, its more spectacular results—and could place the dividing line with fair accuracy along Bembridge Ledge. Now, thinking it over, we could see that west of the ledge was basically West Country scenery, broadly similar to Dorset underwater, with good visibility and a wide range of exotic seaweeds and other plants which completely vanished east of the ledge. This, we now found, was true also of the shellfish. There was some sort of underwater barrier, an invisible "Iron Curtain", which excluded some animals and plants, but not others. For archaeology, this meant that some of the species which rapidly consumed old ships might not be present east of Bembridge Ledge. As we went into the matter, it became apparent to me that the area between Bembridge and Selsey Bill could be further sub-divided into four separate areas, so that the preservation of ship material might well vary considerably within the space of even a few miles.

I could do no more than suspect that the cause of the broad division between east and west was a matter of underwater geography. Geologically, what we were dealing with was a major drowned river valley—that of the former Solent River—into which led other drowned river valleys now known as Southampton Water, Portsmouth, Langstone and Chichester Harbours. The Solent River had been breached long ago west of the Isle of Wight by one of the many alterations in sea and land levels, so that it was now salt water instead of fresh which flowed north around the Isle of Wight. At one time, sea level had been very much higher—there are traces of a beach halfway up Portsdown Hill. At another time, it had been very much lower—and Spithead itself had been a hillside. As we were soon to find out, there had even been a freshwater lake near the hilltop—which was now Spit Sand.

The point that struck me was that most of the rivers which had once fed the great Solent River still flowed into it, mixing fresh water with salt; and also, because of the tremendous, scouring currents caused by the narrow channels of the drowned river mouths, they fed it now with vast amounts of mud also; quite apart from such by-products of man as masses of untreated sewage and chemical waste. All this might well change the "vitamin content" of basically clean Atlantic water coming up-Channel from the west. And this might well discourage some species of animals totally (it discouraged us quite a lot). And that might well be good news for the survival value of ancient wrecks.

This three-dimensional mental picture of the Solent area in terms not only of a static geographical relief map but also as a working model of a rapid water-interchange system, was basic to the next stage in the search for the *Mary Rose,* which was a study of the battle and of the various moves which had been made by both sides on 19 July, 1545, Given that the *Mary Rose* had to go from A to B just after high water, which path would she take—via X or via Y? She certainly could not go direct, without running aground. And had she turned— apparently to port—shortly before the capsize? Where, in those conditions, would she have made her turn? And how far would she have gone, on her new course, before her heel brought her over to an impossible angle and her lower gunports went under? I decided that she had gone down the Swashway towards Ryde, following the *Great Harry,* rather than round Spit Sand by the main channel, and had turned towards the French galleys at No-man's-land earlier than the much larger and deeper-draught ship, probably down an unmarked channel which has no name, but which I will call the sub-Swashway. How far along this track did she go before she rolled over? That was more difficult, but clearly her capsize was not immediate. There was time for Sir Gawen Carew to become worried and even to overtake and shout out to Sir George. That still left an uncomfortably large area to search, so I looked at the largest scale chart to see if any moundlike anomalies or odd obstructions were marked. I found four and decided to test them, provided I could find anyone willing to help me with a survey which must produce three negatives, and might produce four. However, they would be negatives only in the most dramatic sense, that of not finding the *Mary Rose*; in terms of exploring the nature of the seabed and of the marine life there, the time would not be wasted.

Such a close and intense study of the battle, with a real penalty for error or even a failure of understanding on my part, led me to firm conclusions which differed markedly from those of most British nautical historians. I could find no fault with the restraint shown by Henry VIII as an admiral, nor could I criticise D'Annebault's decision not to attack head on; indeed I sympathised with him in his dilemma. Not so the academic historians, who were irritated by the "feeble" result of the meeting of these two great fleets (and conveniently forgetting how very much greater than the English the French fleet had been). All had wanted a decisive battle at Spithead and some even thought it should have been conducted in fleet-line-ahead, the classic tactics developed much later which led almost inevitably to indecisive battles of manœuvre. Angrily, the scholars denounced Henry VIII for apparently failing to understand that line ahead was the only possible formation in which a fleet of broadside-gunned ships could come into action properly. Sometimes, I rather wished that he had, for the deep water channels in the area are so restricted that a fleet action conducted on those scholarly lines could have resulted in the running aground of hardly less than 150 ships, and all those wrecks would have made a most interesting study for marine archaeologists in this century.

The search in shallow water inside the Tail of the Spit was carried out as economically as the rest of the enquiry up to now; only two half-days were spent on it. The clues were very vague and it was worth no more. I reworked the Cowdray engraving several ways and could decide only that the *Mary Rose* was shown as lying between one-fifth and one-third of the distance out from Southsea Castle along the approximate line Southsea–Ryde. I looked for hints either directly from John Deane or from those in contact with him, and what turned up was as vague and inaccurate as one would expect. Deane would have had no desire to give away, publicly, the exact position of his valuable new find. There were two such "clues". First, "between the *Royal George* and the buoy of the *Edgar*". Rather too far off the admittedly rough line Southsea–Ryde, and rather too deep. Second, "a mile from the *Royal George*". Too far; that would put the position as on the Southsea side of Spit Sand, which was impossible. But I decided to start as far away from the *Royal George* as the depths would allow, in the north-east arc from her, and then work back into deeper water. That was about three-quarters of a mile away, where two mounds and one "obstruction" were marked on the largest scale Admiralty chart.

None was necessarily the *Mary Rose*, although the "obstruction" must be something. I looked at the area of the first mound with Tony Bye, and it was really no such thing, although one could see why a height variation could have been obtained. In 25 to 30 feet of water and good visibility of 12 feet or so, we noted that this seabed was quite different from Spithead; it was loose, light clay containing some harder conglomerations, and arranged in a series of linear mounds running very roughly north–south. Some of these mounds were of bare clay a foot high, while others were piled higher with thick beds of slipper limpet, clear evidence of wave effect. Here and there were single fronds of laminaria weed, but in every case they were attached to groups of live limpets and not to rock or wreckage. There was no shingle whatever on the surface and only one artefact. This was a modern milk bottle with a fish inside. In his transparent "home" he had perfect all-round vision and yet was safe from large predators. Both Tony and I carried out trial digs, with hand and knife, showing that the bottom was extremely loose and soft. I then did an anchor-ride over the next search area, and leapt from the anchor when a steep slope downwards coincided with a suspicious clump of laminaria, but these proved to be attached once more only to groups of slipper limpet, the American *Crepidula fornicata*, which cling together in chains and have so peculiar a sex-life that not even British television had yet dared to screen it. I surfaced to report a non-significant drop off, probably the slope of Spit Sand itself, but in the boat they reported that the echo-sounder had shown a mound 13 feet high.

That had to be checked on the next occasion, which we combined also with an effort to locate the "obstruction" marked as being nearby. This was found some 40 yards from where we had anchored and was a real pin-point in the sea. We christened it the "Dalek" because it was a metal, dustbin-shaped object about six feet high set on three widespread metal legs. I spent about three-quarters of an hour cruising, observing, and carrying out trial digs with an entrenching tool. The seabed was basically a series of terraces, like sunken beaches, probably created by wave action. Surface artefacts were few, mostly light clinker from boiler cleaning. Digging in this soil was incredibly easy. With one stroke, a foot-deep trench could be made in the grey clay which covered a layer of black, sticky mud. In a few minutes, one was down to two feet. That the "mound" recorded by the echo-sounder had obviously been the steep slope of Spit Sand bothered me not at all, but the immediate implications of the trial digs led to an immense feeling of depression. Any heavy ship sinking on to a seabed like this would go in deep and be well preserved, which was good news for the long term, but in the short term it would be difficult, if not impossible, to find by purely visual search. Bitterly, I wrote in my log: "But with this composition, may be no mound. *Most* unsatisfactory." I decided to call off all direct search for the *Mary Rose* unless, or until, I could get the loan of scientific search instruments which were just then being perfected but had not been used for archaeology. In the meantime the general survey of wrecks and marine life would continue. This was on 7 August 1965, three and a half months after we had started.

My decision was reinforced by the results of a branch dive next day on a wreck off the Isle of Wight. This was a steel freighter, probably of about 700 tons, sunk on soft clay and in the fast tidal stream area of the Princessa Shoal. It had been found in 1964 but only casually looked over. But the mood was now for a proper inspection, so as to squeeze every available piece of information out of the site, and John Towse was able to give a detailed report of observations made in truly wonderful visibility of 35 feet (the ship was in "West Country" water on the far side of the "cut-off"). The ship lay in a "dish" dug out of the surrounding clay by tidal scour. Average seabed level was 35 feet at the time, the depth of water over the wreck was 32 feet, but the depth of water around the exposed base of the wreck was 40 feet. The ship looked rather like a castle, sticking up 3 feet above the level of the seabed, but surrounded by a 5-foot-deep "moat" scoured out by the currents. This scour was probably helping to dig the ship into the seabed and in course of time, probably only a few years hence, it would have disappeared completely—a steel cargo ship entombed without trace, not just under the sea but under the seabed. A piece of chewing gum found on a porthole suggested that the ship was modern, but in order

to date the process of burial it was necessary to identify the
vessel, so Jack Millgate had taken a manufacturer's plate
from the engine room. This in due course gave the name of
the ship, the *France Aimee* (ex-*Laura*), and the date of sinking as April 1918, from collision. That is, 47 years before.

These two results, from Spit Sand on 7 August and the
Princessa Shoal on 8 August, were decisive. It told us where
many old wrecks had gone, not corroded or eaten away but
buried. This could happen only where the seabed was composed of soft, light materials to a considerable depth, but
where these conditions obtained the amount of the hull remaining would be decided by two factors, the first being the
rate at which the hull disappeared, the second being the rate
at which the exposed portions of it were corroded or eaten
away, and this latter depended on the chemical constituents
of the water and the marine organisms present in it.

There would be a race between the disappearance of the
ship under soft clay in which no oxygen-breathing animal
could exist, and the attack of such organisms on the exposed
portions of the wreck. And a race also between the ravages of
the chemical changes taking place in metals surrounded by
seawater and the comparative sterilisation which might result
when by burial the water was excluded. The lower part of
the hull, which would disappear at once, should be almost in
mint condition; the parts immediately above might have
suffered slightly; but at some point in time, determined by
the particular sea environment in which the wreck lay, all
exposed materials would be completely destroyed, the exposed
portion eventually vanishing as if cut off by a knife. If the
environment was similiar to that of the Pacific, Caribbean or
Mediterranean, much less time would be available for the
long-drawn-out burial process and the general auguries would
be unfavourable. But if, as seemed to be the case in the Solent
area, the corrosion of metals and the consumption of timber
was a slow process, there might very well be a worthwhile
amount of hull structure left, together with much of its contents, and because the *Mary Rose* was a solidly built battleship the hull might still retain its original form. But even
if a hard layer of sub-strata, rock or sand perhaps, lay close
to the surface of the seabed, there was still the point that the
Cowdray engraving showed the wreck as heeled over 40

degrees and it was known that Venetian salvagers had failed to bring her upright. Even if one side of the ship was gone, the other side should certainly remain; and from this the missing portions could be reconstructed. This assessment, which some considered to be rashly optimistic, was the basis of my determination to continue, when instruments became available.

The use of instruments had been in my mind from the beginning, but they were rare and expensive; it was one thing to want them, quite another to get them. At least, when you had no money to pay for them. Up to now, I had been financing the project out of my own pocket and trying to recoup with the occasional magazine article, but the sums involved were minute. The most valuable instruments were those used for geological surveys such as were required by the undersea oil industry, and their cost was in proportion. Comparatively astronomical. Astonishingly, there was then a prejudice against their use in underwater archaeology, which stemmed from the Mediterranean pioneers and was reflected by some of their disciples in London. Dumas had written in *Deep-Water Archaeology*, "Let the reader have no illusions about electronic detectors, supersonic sounders, Asdic and so on," and his translator, Miss Honor Frost, was to echo him for many years. What they had in mind were cheap versions of prehistoric devices dating back to the 1920s. There had been very considerable advances since then and if the unsentimental gentlemen of the North American oil industry were prepared to shell out good dollars for these devices, it was not only possible that they worked but that they might work for us too. At least, if I could get hold of some (there was a range of devices, not just one) I thought I would be able to put them to the best possible use, in the right area.

But there was now a good deal of controversy as to which was the right area, which stemmed from the fact that there was a rival team in the field and that they had a tenuous connection with a loose body of miscellaneous, well-meaning people who had come together in London to co-ordinate the growing interest among amateur divers in archaeology and to introduce them to archaeologists and naval historians of the London "Establishment". Where shipwrecks were concerned there had to be a three-way traffic because most divers knew about wrecks, but not about historic ships or archaeological thinking and method; most archaeologists knew nothing whatever either about the sea or any sort of ship at all; the nautical experts knew about some types of historic ship, but nothing about wrecked ships and very little about the sea or archaeology. There were very few people who could combine a working background knowledge of all three separate spheres, without which no one can really claim to be an "underwater archaeologist". Even now, strictly speaking, there is really no such thing, academically, because no university is yet able to run a course in the subject and award a degree. It is still a question of learning by doing—and learning also by contacting and corresponding with leaders of other groups all over the world who are engaged in similar tasks and whose work one respects. Up to now, the principal forum for this in Britain was the annual conference of the British Sub-Aqua Club organised by our neighbours at Brighton. This was devoted, not just to archaeology but to the entire underwater scene on a world-wide basis, with an international panel of lecturers.

At the latest conference, held in March 1965, the formation had been announced of a Committee for Nautical Archaeology with its headquarters at the Institute of Archaeology in the University of London. Its guiding light in those early years was the excellent Joan du Plat Taylor, who had carried out the conservation work during the classic excavation of the Bronze Age wreck off Cape Gelidonya by George Bass and Peter Throckmorton, in which Frederic Dumas and Honor Frost had also taken part. Miss Taylor was to do the really valuable and essential work of making the C.N.A. a forum for the dissemination of knowledge, guidance and useful introductions. The Committee also included representatives from the Services, the B.S.-A.C., and a number of the London museums. Most of the academics were then unknown to me, but the one exception, met professionally many years before, had produced a highly unfavourable impression, in that he regarded himself an expert on everything, even in fields well outside his experience, but not of mine. Now, as far as I could gather, there had been a division of opinion within C.N.A. soon after its formation in 1964, between those who thought the body should provide a forum and encourage the practical workers already in the field and .those who thought C.N.A. should initiate its own project, with hastily recruited personnel; and preferably a project of such vital importance that it would attract great publicity and establish C.N.A. as a forceful body of international repute. And the project which was suggested was the search for, and discovery of, the *Mary Rose*!

These discussions took place without my knowledge, and unknown to Southsea branch, at the same time as we were planning to do the same thing, but from local resources and with a well-tried team which had five years' experience of practical underwater archaeology behind them, and would be accompanied by a trained archaeological conservationist, Margaret Rule. The C.N.A. planned to use a Royal Navy boat with navy divers untrained in archaeology, but using Service methods of search and diving, together with amateur divers of the B.S.-A.C. from inland branches, who had been trained in different methods and had little sea diving experience, none whatever of archaeology. And, as I made it my business to find out, none of their personnel had any knowledge at all of historic ships and their armament even of the Napoleonic war period, let alone the immensely baffling subject of the Tudor navy. As soon as I heard about their project, I had an early meeting to check on this, to me, all-important point. If they were really knowledgeable enthusiasts, I was all for co-operation, if possible, but a few leading questions of an elementary cat-sat-on-the-mat nature produced blank stares. They were totally ignorant of the ships they were searching for and the subject they were supposed to be studying. And in view of that, and the cumbersome nature of their search methods, I decided that we had better operate independently; although I would keep Miss Taylor closely in touch with what we were doing and what our results were.

The situation was not improved by their attempts to intrigue at the London level of the B.S.-A.C. and also in the local branch; no doubt they had learned this from the academics, who are usually past-masters in the art. The attempts were counter-productive, because they sent a C.N.A. member, Lieutenant-Commander Alan Bax, R.N., to lecture Southsea branch on search techniques. He told them that fishermen's "marks" were no good, and that they must use

sextants and so on to obtain real accuracy. This was the big
ship Navy method; the rich man's method too. A big ship is
a stable platform, quite apart from having plenty of space,
but our work had to be done from small, cramped boats often
rolling and pitching in a heavy sea. Even if you could afford
a sextant, and managed to keep it unbroken and dry in these
conditions, it would be of little use. The only completely
reliable and extremely accurate method was that traditionally
used by the inshore fishermen, which had the additional
advantage that it cost nothing: the only instrument employed
was the human eye. But, like the longbow, it did require considerable experience and practice to obtain results. However,
as we had been finding particular rocks with it, miles out to
sea, for many years, we were confident that we might be able to
find our way about Spithead. Like us, they started off by
looking for the *Royal George* and a Southsea branch observer
on board reported that they had dived two locations, one of
which gave 40 feet and the other 110 feet. The chart depth
of the *Royal George* is 72 feet at low water and the actual
depth range is about 75 to just under 90 feet. They appeared
to be having navigational problems.

Their own reports later showed them consistently too deep
—90 to 105 feet—with extremely odd figures of 40, 45, and
53 feet popping up occasionally in what was supposed to be a
methodical mapping of the area between the *Royal George*
and the *Edgar,* where they thought the *Mary Rose* was. Their
echo-sounder had picked up several mounds, which they had
tried to core, but when I saw their results in plan it was clear
that what they were mapping were not ship mounds but the
contours of the sunken Spithead hill range. Whenever they
found wood on the bottom, they assumed it was evidence of a
ship, whereas we had always disregarded this because scattered
fragments lying on the surface were most likely to be driftwood in transit. They had a chart position for the *Royal
George* which, being dived, gave a depth of 100 feet and produced several small "old looking pieces of wood". This, they
assumed, reresented some remains of Admiral Kempenfelt's
flagship. There was no mound at that place, or any other
physical evidence, and the depth was too great, according
to my charts, so their *Royal George* was a highly hypothetical
site. They were obstinate in their faith in Davis and were

prepared to assume that if nothing was found near their theo-retical *Royal George*, then "the *Mary Rose* must be no more". Talking to them made me tired, and I think now they were blindly following the advice of their London nautical experts, who seem to have been united in a general belief that the *Mary Rose* was next door to the *Royal George* and had pre-sumably been blown up and largely destroyed at the same time by Colonel Pasley's divers. I suppose the academics thought that there could be little harm in untrained divers raking around in the wreckage, as nothing of significance would be left, apart from the publicity.

The year 1966 was likely to be an interesting one, with Miss Taylor trying to obtain instruments for us and inaugur-ating also a scheme for the dive training of student archae-ologist, but first she called a meeting at Guildford on 5 Feb-ruary, at which, she hoped, the differences of the 1965 season might be resolved. It was a vain hope. I found myself in a minority of one, arguing that Davis was wrong and that the *Mary Rose* lay in the north-east arc from her in shallower water. The others would have none of it. They snorted angrily at the very suggestion, as though the authenticity of holy writ was in question. They thought my *Royal George* was some other wreck, and that their position must be right, in spite of their lack of any evidence for a wreck at all at that point. And if I was wrong in my *Royal George* identification, then our delimitation for the *Mary Rose*, based on that point, was invalid. As for Monson and the Cowdray engraving, they brushed them aside. They were of no consequence. The *Mary Rose* was deep, near the *Royal George*. As I would not budge either, it was obvious that our teams would have to continue to work separately, and therefore we divided Spithead be-tween us, according to our rival theories, they to take the 10-fathom line and everything deeper, we to stay inside the 10-fathom line nearer to Southsea. Because I do not always express myself forcefully in conversations, and because I did not want any mistake, or any subsequent recriminations, I gave them shortly afterwards my reasons in writing why I thought that the *Mary Rose* was most certainly in the area they were prepared to cede to me. That had no effect, either; but after that, they could have no complaint if they were wrong, which I was certain they were.

The only matter of technical interest which might be rapidly resolved was the discrepancy apparent between their position for the *Royal George* and my position for it. My position, based on two charts, had a ship mound and the right depth range; theirs had neither—it was 600 feet south-west in 14 fathoms instead of 12 fathoms. We decided to compare charts, to establish where the discrepancy lay, and John Towse and I arranged to meet Alan Bax at the Navy's Hydographic Department in London to inspect the original of the chart he had used for the search supported by the Committee for Nautical Archaeology. But on the day in question, 10 May, he was too busy to get away and Towse and I went up by ourselves to the Hydrographer's, where everything had been laid on for us, including a cup of tea, and a pile of Spithead charts. These included the original of my own main chart, Mackenzie's survey of 1784, of which I had only a photostat copy left over from the Hayling Bay Church Rocks enquiry. Then we looked at the main chart C.N.A. had used. This was Commander Sheringham's survey of "Spithead with the Entrances to Portsmouth and Langstone Harbours", 1841. I had bought photostats of the Langstone Harbour sections of this years before, again in connection with the Church Rocks enquiry, but the bother and expense of obtaining copies had deterred me from getting the Spithead section. The originals were extremely large and had to be held down at the corners by heavy weights; in order to see the centre of a chart, one had to lean right forward over the table.

Sheringham's took about ten seconds to unroll and then Towse and I leaned forward, taking in the red cross and name *Royal George* (in 12 fathoms, not 14, the same as Mackenzie), then sliding down to the right to where we saw the red cross and the name *Edgar* in 12–13 fathoms; and finally, almost automatically, going back to the *Royal George* and then looking up in the north-east arc towards the shallows of Spit Sand into our own search area. And there it was. A red cross and the name *Mary Rose*. In 6 fathoms. Towse gave an audible gasp. I thought I had been tricked, that Bax and the rest of C.N.A. had been working some complicated ploy in pretending that the *Mary Rose* was near the *Royal George,* when their own chart showed her as more than half a mile away in 36 feet of water at extreme low tide. The distance between the red crosses denoting the two wrecks on the actual chart was only $3\frac{3}{4}$ inches. No one, I thought, studying that chart for a search aimed at the *Mary Rose* could fail to see that the words "Mary Rose", in red, were written on it. But they had.

Fifteen seconds had now elapsed, from start to finish, from beginning to unroll the stiff canvas of the chart to making the astounding discovery. Then we began feverishly to transfer the *Mary Rose* position to our own charts, by our own separate methods, so that search could begin at once. There was some discrepancy between Sheringham and the modern chart, although the large scale was similar. It might have been due to shrinkage of the fabric or use of a different projection. I ordered a photostat copy and we asked the Hydrographic Department to transfer the *Mary Rose* position to a modern chart position, as a check on our own necessarily hurried working.

But what were we to do about Bax and C.N.A.? Less than three months before, they had vehemently restricted themselves to the deeper water beyond the 10-fathom line where the *Royal George* and *Edgar* lay. They had been impervious even to a written statement of my case. They had of their own free will, and in full possession of their senses, entirely excluded themselves from any chance of discovery. The *Mary Rose,* in 6 fathoms, was in the centre of our search area, some 300 yards from a charted mound which I had been about to examine when it had become obvious that visual search was useless and that we must go over the area with instruments. But without the facilities Bax had obtained for us at the Hydrographer's we would not have found the exact position so easily. We would have to tell him, but we did not want masses of bull-at-a-gate divers tearing away at the wreck, with delighted London academics learnedly discussing it, in bland ignorance up top.

And now there arose, too, the spectre of the lack of legal protection. The position had to be kept secret and that meant confining our efforts to a small team of reliable people. From now on, the *Mary Rose* was to become for me less of an interesting exercise in undersea detection and more of a worry, a responsibility. The pattern of destruction in the Mediterranean, some of which I had witnessed for myself, was still all too recent. Outright unscrupulous "amphorae pirates", enthusiastic sports divers and worthy, well-meaning scholars had all contributed. Nothing like this had yet occurred in British waters, and I hoped it never would. But pious hopes were superfluous—there were plenty of them about. Something had to be done.

Fig. 6. Professor Harold Edgerton operating one of his special "pingers" at Spithead in July, 1968.

Fig. 7. "Pinger" graph of the *Mary Rose* site at Spithead showing the "W"-shaped anomaly underlying the mounds-and-depression left on the seabed above. The ship is below the "W" and does not show at all except for faint indications of the port and starboard sides, but clearly the seabed itself and the sub-mud strata have been greatly disturbed by an unnatural object.

Fig. 8. Sidescan graph of a half a mile of seabed at Spithead, showing in the top left corner a distinctive anomaly among the natural ripple patterns of the mud and clay. It proved to be two long mounds with a depression in between—the scour mark left by the wreck of the *Mary Rose* before she disappeared completely.

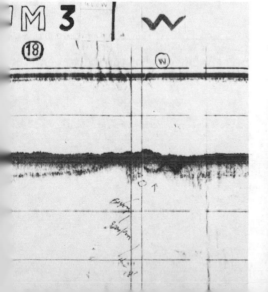

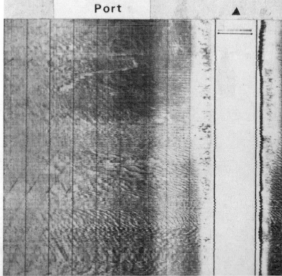

Fig. 9. Fire Brigade hose, rigid with the water being pumped through it at high pressure, photographed just under the surface of Spithead.

Fig. 10. George Clark, with the hose over his left shoulder, digging a 6 ft. deep trench 50 feet underwater.

CHAPTER TEN

THE DEPRESSION

Overnight, the long calm had broken. Now, down by the
Ferryboat Inn on Langstone Harbour, the wind was rising
to gale force and veering round to east, so that the harbour
entrance was a mass of breakers. The April wind was deathly
chill, the first snow of the coming blizzard only minutes away.
As we moved out across the harbour in Harknett's boat the
entrance vanished in driving snow and soon afterwards what
little land we could see had turned white. The tide was pouring past the broken-backed 6,000-ton concrete caisson which
had never made Normandy in 1944, but Harknett nosed his
boat gently through the eddies and into the lee of the stranded
"Mulberry". Now Margot Varese and I had to undress in a
blizzard of snowflakes before suiting up and getting into the
water. Incautiously, Harknett was telling Bob Hurst about
the congers down there, hiding in the dark crevices of the
broken concrete. Miss Joan du Plat Taylor's bright idea for
the training of young underwater archaeologists had come to
fruition.

It was really a victory for those in C.N.A. who thought
that its proper role was co-ordination, guidance and training.
There had long been a complaint that "most divers are not
archaeologists and most archaeologists are not divers", but it
was too much to expect busy people, many of them elderly,
to go through the rigorous training and tests devised by the
B.S.-A.C. for open water sport diving. Miss Taylor's idea was
to recruit young archaeologists, still studying at university,
have them put through an abbreviated B.S.-A.C. course in a
London swimming pool, introduce them to open water under
a competent instructor, and then pass them on to a B.S.-A.C.
branch which was already running an archaeological project.
By April 1966 she had four students from the University of
London, and one member of the staff, Margot, who had an
extra-mural diploma in archaeology, with prehistoric Britain
as her final subject. Bob was one of the students, already with

a B.A. in anthropology, who was working for his postgraduate diploma in the archaeology of Mesopotamia. But as he had no neoprene suit, there was no question of his diving in this weather, which made a strong contrast to the seas of his native Florida.

That dismal morning was also a climax to my own efforts over some years to encourage the right sort of person to dive with us, for although I had long been interested in archaeology, I was only an amateur. What I felt I required was a professional who could go underwater with me and then with whom I could discuss all the problems special to an undersea environment. Margaret Rule did not yet fulfil that function, for although I learned much from her she had to rely solely on my descriptions and those of the other divers. Her basic role was conservation, an important one, because some materials when raised from the sea require immediate treatment; in some cases, a wait of five minutes might produce an irreversible deterioration. She had been with us since 1964, when we had been carrying out a geological survey in Bracklesham Bay, where she had had a useful introduction to underwater work with the simple basic equipment of fins, mask and snorkel, which usually leads to the confident use of the aqualung, but had not then progressed beyond snorkel diving.

Women have an advantage over men when using the aqualung because their smaller lungs use correspondingly less air, thus increasing their endurance; but few women dive. I believe it may be because of the emotional menace suggested by low visibility and dim light. This is particularly apparent with free-standing wrecks which loom initially as an intimidating black mass, before the diver moves in closer and everything comes into focus. More women divers than men tend to get hung up the moment they see the first huge shadow, with its suggestion of unknown peril, and retreat; so they never realise, as they would if the visibility was good and they had pressed on for a few seconds more, that it was only an overgrown heap of old junk, after all, sometimes looking quite beautiful with its garlands of weed and surrounding shoals of fish. Nevertheless, wrecks are dangerous and need to be approached with caution even in the best possible conditions.

But on this day conditions were to be the worst possible— and the dive was to be on a wreck. And that had not been planned. I had chosen this Saturday because it was the best neap tide which would occur in the whole of 1966, and neap tides usually give the best visibility. Harknett and I had intended to take the students to two comparatively easy and safe areas, Church Rocks in Hayling Bay and the geological "amphitheatre" in Bracklesham Bay, where the scenery is interesting and if the visibility is good, can be marvellous. We did not intend to visit a wreck. It was to be an easy, interesting introduction. Now, we could not even get out of harbour and the only possible diving site was in the lee of the Phoenix caisson, where the current was not so strong. Even this was outside Margot's experience, which had consisted of a dozen summer dives in shallow, protected water. We were both shivering when we had got into our suits, and the snow was still whirling past with the easterly gale. We swam to a wire leading from the side of the "Mulberry" down to the bottom about 18 feet below, and descended it. Being in shadow here, visibility seemed only a few feet, but when our eyes got used to the gloom we could see further. The black, tide-scoured gap under the concrete hull, where the congers and lobsters hide out, was too dark for us to make out whether there were any there or not. After an extremely dismal dive, we packed up for the day. I was pleased, and had every right to be. With a little more experience, Margot could take the ship hazards of Spithead in her stride. And then we should have a genuine underwater archaeologist in the team, as well as a professional archaeological conservationist.

We were therefore on the way to being well set up on the archaeological side before the discovery of the exact chart position on 10 May. And on the very day following that, there was a meeting of yet another newly formed body designed to bring together various organisations interested in the subject. This was the Co-ordinating Committee on Maritime Archaeology, which had been born at the University of Southampton and was to limit itself to the Solent area, roughly from Selsey Bill in the east to Swanage in the west. Some vital help was to come from this source in the future, but the first meeting was rather light on land archaeologists and museum people generally, although it did bring the diving groups together. For the first time I met Maurice Young of Southampton B.S.-

A.C., and was impressed to learn that he led the team who had surveyed the River Itchen for evidence of Roman construction and were at present engaged on a search for an early eighteenth-century frigate off the Needles. This meant not only that they had some years of practical experience but that they were in earnest. Groping in darkness on the bed of a foul-smelling, muddy river tends to exclude romantics, exhibitionists and the over-ambitious; and to retain only the people who have reached the stage of becoming bored with diving as a mere sport and are looking for serious work to do. And the fact that they explored the Needles, which they called "Sea Area Clammy Death" because of the underwater fog created there by the mixing of the fresh with the salt water, meant that their standards of diving and of controlled courage must be high. Apart from this, Morrie Young himself was a shipwright by profession. Archaeologists can be valuable under water—just how valuable Margot was shortly to show us—but they have no knowledge of ships. Buildings are their business. I had a reasonable background knowledge, but because I was a military historian I tended to know more about how they were used rather than how they were built. I noted in my records: "Only about half a dozen of them really interested as yet. Worth cultivating , I would say," which was the understatement of the year; they were to prove the essential backbone of the project for many years and see it through to triumph.

I had a tiresome habit of putting my thoughts on paper at decisive junctions, partly to clarify my ideas but also to codify them for reference, so that the objective would be set, clear in my own mind to start with. I could then try to convince others, noting as I went along their reactions and suggestions, so that there would be no doubt in later years as to exactly what was known, and intended, at any particular time and how the credit should be distributed. Credit was the most any of us was ever likely to get, apart from overdrafts, for we had to finance the project ourselves; and this at a time when most of the competent diving teams around, equally with us, were looking for serious work. By that, most of them meant hard cash, either modern treasure hunting for wrecks containing copper and brass fittings, or the old-fashioned kind for "sunken gold". That could turn them into competent opponents, for although the *Mary Rose,* fortunately, was no "treasure ship", they all knew about the bronze guns and some were more than capable of destroying the ship in order to find them. And, as the law then stood, they could even do this legally with the full encouragement of existing government bodies bound by old-fashioned regulations set down when no one dreamed of the possibilities of underwater archaeology.

I circulated copies of my notes to Joan du Plat Taylor and Margaret Rule, among others, and at this time we were still hoping that C.N.A., in London, could deal with the London authorities at their own level in order to reduce the danger of outright pillage, as well as the hazards of a too-hastily mounted excavation. I urged:

> Can we now declare *Mary Rose* a protected site? Can we forbid all excavation until Miss Taylor has been able to assess the actual site (after discovery) and work out whether or not a decent job can be done? Too much haste, now, could make our archaeological names, true, but in quite the wrong way. No bosh shots. Importance of adequate finance. Factor of weather. If a gale caught you in the middle of a delicate bit of work, what then? Any programme which ignores these fundamental factors is doomed to ruin the site for good. To my mind, this thing is on the scale of the *Vasa,* and would require the same resources at least, as the site is unprotected from weather. If resources not available, no picking around. Can we have security on site location? To avoid pillaging of brass guns. My feeling is, this is a case for minimum, not maximum effort. Keep the numbers as low as possible, for security, and as experienced as possible, for efficiency and reliability. THIS is the point where, if we are ever to go seriously wrong, we do so!

"Minimum effort" was easy to achieve. Few people cared for the humdrum probing of a barren and dismally uninteresting seabed, when so much of the Solent area was still unexplored. The first search of the chart position consisted of one dive on 14 May by John Towse and myself from Harknett's boat in an effective visibility of about 18 inches, although one could see dimly for about 5 feet, but with virtually no light at

all whenever the sun went behind a cloud. It was that peculiarly unfocused visibility which seems to suggest that the seabed itself has temporarily gone into suspension. The odd thing
was that all our observations, and the conclusions drawn from
them, proved years later to be absolutely correct.

To start with, came the routine navigational exercise on
the double-check system, Towse and I having worked out the
problems separately and comparing notes only when we
arrived on site. The drill is to be able to draw two intersecting
lines on the chart, each line being based on two features on
the land, some distance apart, which are in line and give a
crisp indication of it. The wreck should be at the intersection.
This is extremely easy when working backwards from a discovered wreck to the "marks" which can be observed to bear
from it; more difficult, when working the other way round,
from the chart to the wreck. Firstly, no map or chart is accurate entirely, because the earth is a globe and cannot be
represented exactly on a flat surface; the type of projection
used by the particular chart has to be borne in mind.
Secondly, the land features shown on the Admiralty charts
of that time were years out of date; much destruction, rebuilding and new building had taken place. Thirdly,
"transits" which look good on a chart can be impossible at
sea, perhaps because they are obscured by trees or do not give
a fine indication of when they are "on". So you select a large
number of possible "transits" and then try them out. In principle, I cared much less than Towse about obtaining "transits" which gave lines apparently running right through the
wreck. I was quite happy to accept crisp "marks" which ran
to one side or the other, provided I knew which side it was,
for then you had what is called "an error in a known direction". In practice, the only difference is that in the former
the bottom search will be in a square or circular pattern from
a fixed point, and in the latter it will be line abreast in a
particular direction. But on this morning we had a surprise
for each other, based on the fact that we did not really believe
in our own positions for the wreck and were still waiting for
the Hydrographer to make the transfer to the modern chart.

Towse, who is an Admiralty scientist by profession, explained at some length that all wrecks in the Solent area were
surrounded by scour-pits, of which the "Norman Castle"

wreck he had recently discovered on the Princessa Shoal was
an excellent example. I nodded, because I knew how the
mechanism worked and had even photographed it some years
before, using the datable boom defences off Southsea beach as
my models. Each iron pile (Second World War) had a scour-
pit at its base and when the current ran the eddy could
actually be seen at work digging the pit, marked by a revolving
cloud of sand; higher up, particularly just under the surface,
there was no sediment but the disturbed pattern of whirling
water was so clear that it could be photographed distinctly.
Each concrete block (First World War) also had a scour-pit,
and was actually eroded at seabed level, having been undercut
some six inches, and what had been cut back was the concrete
as well as the mobile seabed. Briefly, a wreck, a rock or any
other similar object is an obstruction to the tidal stream, and,
as water is almost incompressible, it is forced to speed up at
that point, the energy so created triggering off these whirling
eddies, which are natural eroding and excavation machines.
Harknett, who is a lecturer in electronics, listened in bored
fashion to our crude discussion of the obvious (but I include
it, because I find that to many people it is not as obvious as
all that).

Now, said Towse, on a cohesive clay seabed, these scour-
pits may remain long after the wreck has dug itself by this
means downwards and out of sight, as may soon happen with
the *France Aimee*. Therefore, said he, what we are really looking for is a scour-trace such as a big ship might leave behind;
and, he went on, there are *two* such marks near the *Mary Rose*
position. To this rabbit from his hat I silently produced my
counter-rabbit—my chart, with just those two features already
boldly outlined in yellow crayon. I put my finger on the most
northerly of the two and explained why, because of its shape,
alignment and position, I would bet my money there. Towse,
it appeared, already had his money on it, and therefore there
was nothing to do but go down and look. The position was
fixed by my best "mark" on the Southsea side and John's best
"mark" on the Gosport side. He also pointed out another
Southsea "mark" which might be on or near part of the site
and was particularly crisp and accurate. All these "marks"
later became standard navigational practice.

The seabed proved to be of a complicated nature, consisting of very soft harbour mud, eroded and upstanding lumps of clay, beds of slipper limpet in layer lines, and, occasionally, "quite wide pools of sand". It was the latter which set all bells ringing. Neither in the deep water of Spithead nor in the shallow water of Spit Sand had there been sand; but Deane had mentioned sand at the *Mary Rose* site. The mud was the softest we had ever seen. I noted:

> You didn't need a probe. To show it, Towse just thrust his hand down into it anywhere he liked, and his arm promptly disappeared as far up as the shoulder. Very few anchorage artefacts seen—and all light stuff—a large tin can, a scrubbing brush, a light carrier bag in blue, a piece of coal and a portion of clinker. There was nothing else, whereas Spithead is littered with the stuff. Does it sink in here? or don't many ships anchor here? Both, I should think! After one look at that lot, neither us thought we were going to find the *Mary Rose*. She'll be deep in it, perfectly preserved, with probably nothing showing. Even if a little bit did show here and there, the odds are it would be camouflaged by slipper limpet beds. Visual search highly unprofitable. Core-sampling quite useless, quite apart from inflicting unnecessary damage, because she may not be the only wreck or waterlogged buried wood in the area. Once found, an air-lift would be required to obtain the necessary evidence of identity.

On the bright side, I reported that the Deanes' gunpowder charges could have had little effect in soil such as this, which was, however, a guarantee of good preservation, as shown by the state of the wood he brought up, particularly the yew longbows.

Towse's depth gauge had shown readings between 40 and 45 feet, which were correct for that time of the tide, but we had recognised no scour-marks, only a distinctly uneven sea-bed, compared to the level plain near the *Royal George*; although the conditions were such that a scour-hollow had we swum over it, would probably not have been noticeable. There was only one suspicious circumstance, erratic compass behaviour at one point of our track, confirmed by Harknett whose job was to note the progress of the surface buoy we were towing, as a check on our navigation. We had started with a circular sweep round the anchor, for acclimatisation, then set off north-east by compass. After covering 50 feet we had then, still following the same compass course, done a 90-degree turn to the left! We had carried on for a few minutes, then aware that something was wrong, had surfaced, taken a compass bearing on the boat, and dived again to intercept our original track. As Towse had swum on my right, whereas the deviation had been 90-degrees left, the error could not have been due to the mass of metal represented by his cylinder. Some other mass of metal might have been responsible, there being two basic possibilities—the iron guns, ammunition and fittings of the *Mary Rose,* which might amount to over 100 tons, or an undersea cable. But no undersea cables were shown on our charts. This odd incident gave me an idea.

In the meantime, I asked Miss Taylor if she could use her influence to obtain the loan of sub-bottom sonar ("pinger"), which I thought would be most useful, but possibly also a magnetometer, preferably of a crude type which would not pick up the many metal anchorage artefacts which I expected to find buried in the area. I stated that we did *not* want a core-sampler, and I now excluded the idea of full excavation in favour of salvage entire. I wrote boldly: "With the firm conviction that the remains of the ship will be in a good state of preservation, I would suggest the ultimate possibility of lifting her intact on a flexible cradle; raise the complete ship, rather than pick it to bits." All these points seem very obvious now, but they were far from being accepted at the time.

There was a strong Dumas-faction in C.N.A. which was pro-core and anti-pinger, based on the dictums of *Deep-Water Archaeology.* Sonar devices were supposed to be useless and it was recommended that the probing of an entire wreck-site should be carried out by taking at least scores, if not hundreds, of core-samples; leaving poles stuck in the holes. This scheme had all the impressive authority behind it of one of Cousteau's team, backed by Honor Frost and the chairman of C.N.A., but I do not know that anyone anywhere actually carried out any "soundings" on these destructive and cumbersome lines, even in the Mediterranean, where it might have provided some information. At Spithead we considered it useless, because there was so much driftwood, plus anchorage artefacts, lying on hard bottoms; we also expected to find them on a soft seabed, but buried. Hence core-samples would give an almost meaningless pattern. But where they went into the wreck, they would cause damage; and if poles were left standing afterwards, as the mapping method required, these would be destructive of fishermen's nets. The end result would be that the marker poles would be either removed or violently dis-turbed, while at the same time unsuspecting fishermen would suffer hundreds of pounds worth of damage to their equip-ment. This latter factor, that Spithead was a heavily trawled area, prevented us from putting in any dangerously sub-stantial bottom markers, which we would have liked to have done. Instead, we had to rely on establishing a very accurate "grid" from navigational transits ashore.

At any rate, those were my ideas. Margaret Rule agreed with most of what I reported and circulated in writing, al-though unfortunately she could not check my seabed observa-tions personally. I hoped that Margot Varese would soon be able to do that. John Towse also agreed, but with a tinge of pessimism, particularly regarding the results to be expected from a "pinger" and he also wanted to check the position with navigational instruments (we later did this, but it was a waste of time when carried out from a small boat in a choppy sea). Alan Bax believed only in sextants for surface positioning and seabed markers and jackstays for underwater search pro-cedures. Maurice Harknett was getting impatient with what was obviously going to be a long, boring job and was anxious to carry on with general wreck exploration, in which I was already assisting him. If the search for the *Mary Rose* be re-garded as a play, then these were the cast for Scene II, and the essential dramatic conflict came from the lines they spoke —which were the ideas basic to each character. Who was to be hero and who was to be villain, had not yet been settled (for this was the essence of the "plot", that its inevitable development would eventually reveal this), the hero would be he who was right. The villain, of course, would be in the wrong.

The immediate result of my thinking on the matter was felt directly at home, where my children fell about in fits and then rushed off to tell their mother that poor Daddy was using a compass to find his way about the house. I was in fact marching up and down outside the cupboard where I kept four aqualung cylinders and two weight-belts and noting what the compass had to say about it. The answer was nothing. The only object which stirred it at all was the car, when two feet distant. This was good news, in that the instrument (the best underwater compass then available) would not be affected by small, non-significant buried items, but would react only to a large mass of metal at close range. But it was also bad news, because the chronic shortage of money to pay for boats had prevented us from carrying out sufficient navigational exercises, and we really needed something that would detect from a distance at this stage. I decided to use as the basis for a straight-line search a "transit" made on the Southsea shore by one side of the Royal Navy war memorial forming a single straight line with a very distinctive feature on the Grosvenor Hotel behind it. The two "marks" were rather too close for a really fine line, but it was workable once I had stood in front of the hotel and memorised the details at close range. I calculated that this line should run either over the northern end of the site at best, or just off it, at worst. It would also intersect on the broadside—the approach giving the largest target. The problem of maintaining this course while dived, and while using one's underwater compass as a metal detector, was to be solved by having the underwater pair towed by a dinghy which, steered by bearing compass, would keep the correct line. This required nearly slack water, so that the divers would tamely follow the dinghy and not be pushed off to one side. We would start this run well off the site towards the Isle of Wight, because the only usable intersecting transit we had on the Gosport shore was poor, being an imprecise "open" mark—Gosport church off to one side of the submarine escape tower at Blockhouse—as well as making only a 37° angle with the Southsea mark. 90° is optimum, and anything less reduces accuracy. Still, our primary marks for a particular rock on Church Rocks, two miles out to sea, had been only 47° and that had worked well for years. As a rough guide, this would be good enough for us to be sure, not that we were "on" on the Mary Rose but that we were definitely "off" it in a definite direction. And if we then followed a definite line towards it, we could hardly fail to pass either over or very close to it.

Some big ship navigational experts regard these pro-cedures with suspicion, because of the errors involved. But this is also true of the ordinary magnetic compass, which suffers from so many errors—variation, deviation, inclination, and so on—that, logically, anyone using it should promptly get lost. They don't, because the users know that the errors exist and can allow for them. Similarly with maps and charts —all are inaccurate, but provided one knows precisely what the inaccuracy is, one is not misled. Indeed, it is even possible to use buoys, which swing with the tide, as "marks", provided the time of the tide is known. The vital point is to know, with certainty, just how reliable or unreliable any particular feature is, and plan accordingly. But this is only half the story. A great deal depends upon the ability of the boatman to keep an absolutely straight course in line with the marks, which depends in turn on wind and sea conditions and also his own familiarity with the marks.

Most of the wrecks we had found by these methods were modern, upstanding examples, up to 15 feet high. When you saw them, you were in no doubt that you had hit your target. But if the chart contours at the *Mary Rose* site were correct, all we were likely to see was a depression too wide to be grasped at a glance. It might appear merely as a slope, a local change of depth. Underwater visibility cannot be guaranteed and in the case of one modern wreck we had located and whose identity and layout was therefore unknown to us, had been right down to 18 inches; less than the length of one's own extended arm. However, assuming better visibility than that, a depth alteration would be a reasonable clue on a course to or from Southsea across the *Mary Rose* site. Going towards Southsea, the general trend of the seabed is up, so that a sudden drop might be noticeable; and similarly, coming from Southsea, the general trend of the seabed is down so that, although entry into the depression might not be remarked, the sudden rise of seabed on the opposite site probably would be. Detection of the site by contour change was therefore second string to the compass as metal detector, and Margot Varese would provide an invaluable check on my own observations.

Putting her down at Spithead so early in her diving career was something of a risk, but I suspected that her mild and gentle manner was deceptive; certainly, her unflinching acceptance of the wreck dive in the blizzard back in April hinted at determination. I thought she would be unlikely to panic, whatever happened. Panic in a diver is equivalent to suicide, being closely followed in this respect only by bold recklessness. Because of Margot's inexperience, I decided not to tow a marker buoy on the surface, but merely to hang on to the dinghy's anchor all the time, and never leave it. Margaret Rule was to sit in it with a bearing compass and Peter Cope and a pair of oars were the motive power. As Margot and I put on our equipment, the next Isle of Wight "boat" hove into view from the direction of Ryde. They are really small, fast ships of about 1,000 tons, carrying the passenger traffic from the Wight to the mainland and back. At around high water they use the short cut of the Swashway, but at low tide take the longer route over the *Mary Rose* site. We watched this one come straight at us and let it roar past before jumping overboard. We swam down the dinghy's anchor rope in excellent visibility which reduced to 7 or 8 feet on the bottom, where we took up station. I was ahead and low, with compass and camera, Margot to my right, slightly behind and above, in a deliberate imitation of the Luftwaffe formation for single-seat fighters, designed to give both people the best possible view. Margot held a 4-foot hand-spear for probing. Nearly 50 feet above, Margaret Rule had the other end of the anchor rope in her hand, and when I lifted the anchor and tugged the rope, Peter Cope started rowing. We tried to assist by swimming gently.

At this speed we went north-east for some 20 minutes, with ample time to note and probe. Twice my compass needle swung wildly off course, but the first deviation was accompanied by violent twitchings of the dinghy anchor rope and the second by rapid signals from Margot, who was trying to tell me in sign language that she could hear noises, principally a high-pitched whine with a background roar. Then our course went back to N.E. again. All this time we were passing over a seabed of uniform pattern. It was basically mud and clay with narrow bands of slipper limpet beds some 18 inches across and 4–6 inches high, divided from each other by bands of bare seabed of greater width. They were aligned roughly north-south, at an angle to the current and to our own course. In principle, they were the same as the beds we had seen in shallower water near Spit Sand, which were, however, much broader and higher—15 feet across and up to 18 inches high, with the bare bands fully 25 feet across. These limpets have no means of propulsion and I therefore assumed that the pattern was most probably due to wave action; certainly, marine biologists with whom I had discussed the matter also held this opinion.

Then the pattern changed. Mud and clay gave way to sand and the narrow strips of slipper limpet gave way to a wide blob of the creatures, irregular in shape. And within a minute the anchor had lifted clear of the seabed to a height of some three or four feet, clear indication that there was a depression in the seabed at this point. I would have liked to have let go of the anchor and made a close search, but that would have meant surfacing free when our air ran out, right in the path of what was obviously a procession of Isle of Wight boats doing 15 knots over our heads. I chose the safe way and we both surfaced up the dinghy's anchor line. The compass deviations had indeed been caused by Margaret Rule urging Peter Cope to row frantically out of the way of approaching ships. There could be no second chance this day because Harknett and Cope had been doing us a favour by coming to Spithead at all, and they were anxious to use the excellent weather conditions, with clear surface visibility, to find two wrecks three miles out to sea, but in shallow water on the Horse Tail, which had baffled a great many people for a long time.

According to my research, they were the UB-21, a First World War German submarine, and the British destroyer H.M.S. *Undine*, sunk in 1928. They were difficult to find by the transit method, as most of the possible landmarks were many miles away and therefore often obscured or made unclear by haze. Spithead, only a mile or so from the heavily built-up Portsmouth and Gosport shores, forming a right-angle, was a much easier proposition. We anchored to the north of the Horse Tail and then carried out underwater searches up towards the crest of it. Visibility was something like 25 feet, far better than at Spithead, and both Harknett and I found scattered metal remains, but not the wreck itself. Had we pushed on a little further, we would have bumped into UB-21, which was not to be properly discovered until 1970. I still kick myself for this, but we were short of air, and I wanted Margot to be sure of a real wreck dive, so we up-anchored and headed along the Horse for the buoyed remains of the armed trawler *Cambrian,* sunk by magnetic mine in 1940. In the wonderful warm visibility of June, we could sit on the bottom and see the surface of the water 25 feet above.

Although we were able to give Margot a lot more diving experience during the next two months, including a most instructive inspection of the remains of building foundations on Church Rocks, I could not lure Harknett back to Spithead until mid-August. By now, the Hydrographer had given us a transfer position for the *Mary Rose* from Sheringham's old chart, which associated the wreck with the northern scour-like depression marked on the modern chart. Margot and I did a tide-ride, towing a surface buoy, from the opposite direction to our previous dinghy-ride, starting off the depression in patchy visibility of 4 to 6 feet, with the natural slope being gently downwards. We both carried probes, and used them. Initially, wrote Margot in her report, "No irregularities noticed and nothing at all of note." Further on, "The seabed was cratered with small, shallow depressions, similar but not uniform (about 3–5 feet in diameter, 6–10 inches deep). On the right of the craters there were traces of a low, broken bank (only about 8 in. high), with an irregular edge." Finally, she noted a "continuous and deeper depression with a higher and more regular bank on its right (about $1\frac{1}{2}$–2 ft. high). By following this bank, our course changed to southerly/south-easterly."

My own report of this final feature recorded: "Towards the end, a real rise of seabed to a marked crest, coupled with a depth reduction of an indicated 5 to 6 feet within a short distance; the crest curved round and then led away to S. or S.E." This was highly unnatural and without the need for signals we turned left and swam south along it, probing. And, once more, hardly had we seen the feature we were looking for, than trouble developed. Margot's demand valve ceased to supply her with air. The air did not run out gradually, it just stopped coming. She had to go for the surface and I had to go with her. This is a deadly dangerous proceeding for the diver in trouble, because the natural tendency is to hold the breath, but the air remaining in the lungs expands rapidly when nearing the surface and can cause an embolism. As my demand valve was still functioning, I had to breathe out hard all the way to the top during our rapid ascent. However, our training worked and we surfaced without damage.

I felt sure that this depression, with its flanking ridges of unequal height, was the scour-mark caused by the wreck of the *Mary Rose* when she was still visible. But where, underneath, did the wreck lie in relation to the depression? Not all wrecks scour all round like a dish. Some scour on one side only, or more on one side than the other. The depression was not necessarily the outline of the ship, it could represent merely some of the "disturbance area" around it. Our probes had revealed nothing, although they had once or twice got stuck in the underlying clay, and I reported: "It was finally, and regretfully, decided that the chance of any of the wreck showing even a few inches is remote, and the chance of seeing it, if it did, remoter."

What we needed was an instrument which could pin-point the wreck, or part of it, so that we could first probe and then dig, in the right place. George Cooke, inventor of his own one-man submarine and a member of the B.S.-A.C.'s Scientific and Technical Group (which had assisted Alan Bax in his searches), currently had a proton magnetometer on loan from the makers, Wardle & Davenport. But he had it for only a short time, and the various people we would need already had commitments, so that we had to settle for a spring tide and unsettled weather, with a full gale forecast for the evening of the day we had chosen. We hoped to complete the work before the worst of the weather arrived, but when Margaret Rule, George Cooke and myself rendezvoused with Maurice Harknett at Langstone Harbour in the morning, it was already Force 6, gusting 7, with Force 8 (full gale) "imminent". With sonar gear, which is adversely affected by wave action and noise, the operation would have been impossible, but magnetometers are not bothered by weather as long as the small "box-of-tricks" can be kept out of the wet. This proved rather difficult, because sheets of rain were sweeping along the wave tops of a violently agitated sea, as Harknett's 26-ft. cabin cruiser ploughed into it. The very shallow water over much of the area exaggerates the effect of any gale, and no ordinary navigational instrument could possibly work in these

Fig. 11. A large skate with about a 2½ ft. "wingspan" lying on undisturbed seabed just clear of the trench, and apparently waiting to get in and grub for newly-exposed morsels of food.

Fig. 12. Mr. S. J. Utley, a Portsmouth Dockyard diver, about to go down to the *Mary Rose* site in 1969. He was the first helmet diver to do so since John Deane finished work on the wreck in 1840. Talking to him at the top of the ladder are George Clark and Alexander McKee.

Photo: Percy Ackland

Photo: Alexander McKee

Fig. 13. The Royal Engineers came again to Spithead in 1969, but with aqualungs instead of the diving helmets they had worn in 1839, when Colonel Pasley began work on the *Royal George*. The door of their landing craft is about to be lowered to allow the launching of the metal assault boat (*left*). The big compressor on the right is for powering their 8-inch air-lift.

Fig. 14. Part of the organisation required for methodical excavation—the diving boat and the compressor-carrying catamaran Roger Grenville positioned between two permanent mooring buoys and circled by the inflatable rescue boat.

Photo: Atlas-Copce

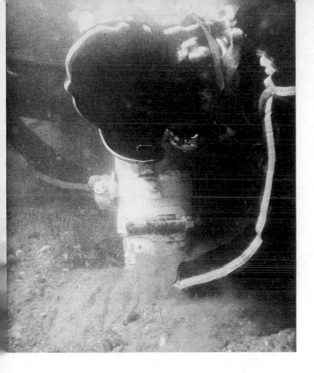

Fig. 15. Careful excavation with
the 6-inch airlift. While one diver
(seen dimly, left) holds the tube in
position, the diver in the foreground
is using his left hand to move soil towards the mouth of the tube, which
will take it away, much as a hand-
cart would do in a land excavation.

Photo: Alexander McKee

Fig. 16. Start of the South Trench Excavation: following the line of the inner skin planking two eroded
frames are exposed (*top*) and then a massive composite timber appears (*left*) with the inner skin ending
here in a butt joint.

Photo: Alexander McKee

French Battle Fleet off Bembridge I.O.W.

Encampment of the English Army

Galley Vanguard
"*MARY ROSE*"
SOUTHSEA CA

(Henr

Fig. 17. The Cowdray Engraving (above).

Fig. 18. Between the compressor-barge and the Naval pinnace, the water is heaving from the working of a 4-inch airlift. In the foreground, the next pair of divers prepare to take over the shift from the divers down below, who are nearly at the end of their time.

Photo: Alexander McKee

English Fleet at Spitsand

PORTSMOUTH   SQUARE TOWER   BLOCK HOUSE
CATHEDRAL   ROUNDTOWER
CAMBER

(...se back)   (Fishing harbour)

Fig. 19. View of the carrack *Grace Dieu*, exposed on the mud of the Hamble River at an exceptionally low tide.

Photo: Alexander McKec

Photo: The News, Portsmouth

Fig. 20. Donation of loaned equipment to the *Mary Rose* project at the start of the 1971 season. On right, the van, background the inflatable boat, foreground the gun which attracted all the support. Talking to divers Reginald Cloudsdale and Andy Gallagher are Sir Alec Rose, the round-the-world yachtsman who lives in Southsea, and Mrs. Gwen Holder, a descendant of Roger Grenville, the captain of the *Mary Rose*, who lives in Hampshire.

Fig. 21. Margaret Rule examining finds from one day's excavation of the "overburden" layer. The shape of the shoe is right, but it has been machine-stitched and is probably 19th century, not 16th. All the other items found in the upper 5 feet of sediments with it are less than a century old, but the piece of elmwood planking found lower down is probably detached wreckage from the *Mary Rose*.

Photo: Alexander McKee

Fig. 22. Percy Ackland making notes underwater.

Photo: Alexander McKee

Fig. 23. In 1972 two senior members of
the *Vasa* project came to Portsmouth to
assist with the *Mary Rose*. Alexander
McKee (centre) with the project's director, Dr. Lars Ake Kvarning (*left*) and
Captain Bengt Ohrelius, author of
"Vasa: The King's Ship" (*right*). He is
showing them two of the *Mary Rose* guns
on view at Southsea Castle.

Photo: The News, Portsmouth

Photo: Alexander McKee

Fig. 25. Ken Barton, director of Portsmouth City
Museums, and Margaret Rule, Curator of the
Fishbourne Roman Palace, about to make an in-
spection dive on the *Mary Rose*.

Fig. 26. Part of the encrusted barrel of the Sling-type gun 3 minutes after it had been raised from the
seabed in 1970. The right hand end of the ruler marks where a wrought-iron ring has been completely
exposed and is still a grey colour, minutes before it rusted over.

Photo: Alexander McKee

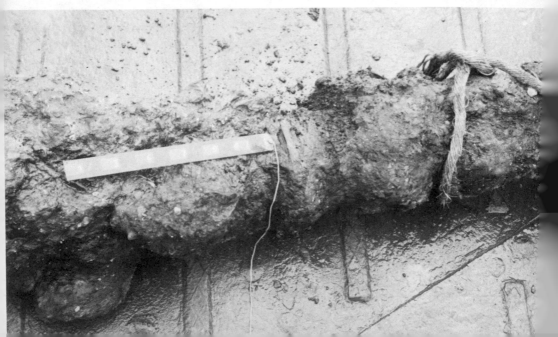

conditions. But as long as we could see our "marks" on shore, we would be all right.

There was no time to calibrate the instrument on known metal wrecks in the harbour; we had to go straight out and get it over with as soon as possible. This type of magnetometer is designed to detect anomalies in the earth's magnetic field and was beginning to be used in land archaeology for finding kilns, fireplaces and sites of that sort which were now lying invisible under the soil in open country. Buildings would baffle it, as would metal ships, so we rigged the working parts in Harknet's dinghy (first removing the metal rowlocks) and towed it astern of his boat (which had an iron keel and a lot of chain in the forepeak). The reactions of the instrument to the seabed were shown by a needle on a small dial.

We carried out two quick tests, in order to get an idea of what a "positive" reading was. The first was near Spit Fort, where the seabed is littered with metal "gash". That was clear enough. Then we moved to the *Boyne,* which gave several small indications and a mad one when we were off it—possibly from a submarine cable charted there. Then we turned for a run from Southsea towards the *Mary Rose* site. We were nearly there when the needle became violently agitated, and continued to be affected for a surprisingly long distance. We dropped a marker buoy on a second run at the point of maximum agitation. There certainly was a distinct magnetic anomaly in that area. Harknett dropped the anchor near the buoy, and I went down the anchor line, towing another marker buoy so that when I surfaced Harknett would be able to see me and do a pick-up. The waves were quite steep by then, and would hide a diver's head most of the time.

I swam down slowly, unreeling my own buoy-line, with the anchor rope pulling and plucking violently in my hand all the way. The green peasoup around me turned to black, giving the impression of forcing one's head into a black velvet cushion inside a darkened room. As I went on into it the anchor line gave way to the anchor chain and a tinge of grey spread in the darkness. I was on the bottom and could see part of one fluke of the anchor. Clearly, it was dragging, so I nosed right down into the straight furrow it had drawn across the seabed from its original position, which was that of the maximum magnetometer reading, and breathing very hard from the physical effort of trying to swim against a strong tidal stream, bored on up-current. The boat continued dragging away from me, mainly because of the wind, which was now about Force 7. Had it been almost anyone other than Harknett in charge, I would not have dared to leave safety in these conditions, but we had worked together for some years and I knew his reliability and skill. And once I had left the cloud of muck disturbed by the dragging anchor, I could see for nearly three feet, although there was little light. The anchor's track led through several small depressions and then up and over a marked ridge about 8–10 inches high. I prodded at various likely lumps, which promptly dissolved in clay, and then found one which did not dissolve. I hooked my prodder under it and it held me. Thankfully, I relaxed and let my breathing rate slow down to normal, just letting the current stream me out like a flag while I felt around the solid with my hand. It was rough, buried, linear and immovable. After I had dug a trench on both sides, I found I could get my hand under it and when the disturbed sediments were taken away by the current, I could actually see part of it. Undoubtedly, it was a buried cable about 4 inches in diameter. I left it and carried on ahead until my air ran out without finding anything else. Reaching the surface, all I could see was sky, the waves were so steep, but from the top of one of them I momentarily caught a glimpse of the cabin-top of Harknett's boat moving in for the pick-up.

Once I was back on board, Harknett turned and ran for Langstone with the wind almost directly behind him, the waves lifting up the boat on their crests and shoving it forward. We were literally surfing with a 26-ft. motor boat! This made the passage of the boom rather perilous, but Harknett managed, and we got back into Langstone. Here, at last, we were able to calibrate the magnetometer on two wreck sites well known to us. The first was the tug *Irishman* sunk with the dumb crane barge *Percy* by magnetic mine in 1941. This represented a fair mass of metal surrounded by an outlying area of scattered metal wreckage. The magnetometer showed no indication over the outlying area, but only when over the hull of the tug. This site was buoyed and had been used for training dives for the previous ten years, but the next was a "new" wreck deliberately discovered by Harknett from chart markings in 1965, when I was assisting him. The remains stood 15 feet off the bottom and were of the bucket dredger *Withern* which capsized in 1909. She was relatively intact and had given us information on the survival of wood (good condition) and the formation of concretions on ironwork (well developed) after some 55 years. Again, the magnetometer did not detect this great mass of metal from a distance, but only when actually over the wreck.

This made the "long" reading on the *Mary Rose* very puzzling, except in terms of an uncharted undersea cable. We re-checked, but there was no record of a cable in the area, and if there had, it would have been surprising because it was in No. 3 Berth of the Spithead Anchorage. Cable areas are normally marked "Anchoring and Trawling Prohibited", for obvious reasons. But a week later, on 7 September, we were able to get the magnetometer again for a second try. On this occasion, as Peter Throckmorton was in England, he came out with us, as also did Joan du Plat Taylor; it was almost a Cape Gelidonya reunion. Peter had moved on from the Bronze Age wreck excavation with George Bass to Greek and Italian sites. The work he had done on Mediterranean wreck formations was really illuminating and he was able to reconstruct the various stages of collapse of wooden ships which had subsequently become almost buried. His studies, and those of Professor van der Heide concerning similar wrecks under the dry bed of the reclaimed Zuyder Zee, were at my elbow for several years during our work on the *Mary Rose*. These ships were generally smaller and more lightly built than the Tudor battleship must have been, but nevertheless there was much to be learned from other people's careful excavation of them.

The day was warm and sunny, the sea flat calm, and we repeated the run of the previous week with greater accuracy of line than had been possible in Force 7. Once again, the magnetometer reacted before we reached the critical area, but a dive by George Cooke was negative for any surface indication of a probably buried metal object. We then carried out a second run from Southsea, and when the Gosport marks came "on" simultaneously the magnetometer became excited and we buoyed the position. We then circled slowly round the buoy and obtained slight positive readings over a fairly large area. Both Margaret and George were rather doubtful about these, but I noticed that their centre produced a much better transit—a chimney and a gasometer—than our existing Gosport "marks", and I noted this. It subsequently became standard, being replaced by the original marks only on those rare occasions when some thoughtless person deflated the gasometer. The angle was wider and the image was crisply "in line", instead of "open".

Peter Throckmorton got dressed in an old "wet" suit of mine which was fairly far gone, although some of the patches were still in good condition. However, to be effective, a wetsuit has to be a tight fit, so that only a thin film of water seeps in, to be heated up by the diver's body. As soon as Peter put it on, the suit split down the back, down both legs, and in sundry other places, to become the wettest wet-suit in the business. Then, fresh from the Gulf of Taranto, he fell virtually naked into Spithead, with visibility down to 2 feet and black with it; and I followed him. On the bottom, by staying close, I could see most of his right shoulder as he carried out a detailed inspection of the sediments. After ten minutes he began signalling, but as we had no common code he hammed it up like a star of the silent movies, leaving me to guess at his meaning.

First, he hunched his shoulders. ("I'm cold.").

Then he jabbed one finger towards the surface. ("How about getting the hell out of here, we're not doing any good.").

Finally, a crablike contraction of the fingers. ("Goodbye.").

I gave him the all-purpose British signal of the two closed fingers, meaning: "I'm all right, Jack, and I hope this finds you as it leaves me."

Still warm, in my number one suit, I carried on trying to find the contact. In fact, it was the first time I had been able to carry out a leisurely browse around, and it proved well worth while. Firstly, I learned that there was an underlying layer of hard clay, about 3 feet down, which momentarily gave the impression of firm resistance; but that a strong push on the probe invariably broke through the consolidated interface. Secondly, I came again on a number of small depressions, less than a foot deep, filled with weed, and perhaps 3 feet long; and it occurred to me that these might be the marks of anchors. Thirdly, my depth gauge indicated a rise of seabed where pools of sand appeared, and finally I noted "a well-defined ridge, 2 feet high or thereabouts and aligned more or less north-south (magnetic)". So the magnetometer contact *was* associated with the depression and the high-angled mound on its Isle of Wight side. There was a fourth, and very odd, point, a high-pitched whine which seemed to stay overhead for several minutes; this proved to be a hovercraft on the normal run from Portsmouth to Ryde more than a mile away; it was a very busy service, but I had never actually heard one before while submerged, although propeller noises were frequent.

George Cooke then dived in the same area and reported finding a cable which, in places, was clear of the seabed. We were really baffled and carried out non-diving tests on known objects, getting small, positive readings, and when the object was a charted but disused telephone cable near the *Boyne*, obtained a long, continuous, positive reading. With a magnetometer, you could obviously navigate by following the cables. It was not until much later, in really good visibility, that the mystery of the *Mary Rose* cable was solved. I could then see at once that it was not a submarine communications cable, but a very long length of heavy wire hawser, a really formidable piece of anchorage "gash". I had it lifted and moved well off the site, as by that time much greater resources were available. That was a logical solution to one question: why should there be a cable where no cable should be? But it did not tell us what it was that the magnetometer had detected: the hawser on top, or the *Mary Rose* underneath?

This was a minor irritation pushed into the background by the good news of the day, which was provided by Peter Throckmorton. Peter was one of the very few people who had dug underwater at all, let alone with care and method; he knew what results could be obtained and that the sea was potentially a good place for the preservation of man's handiwork. His most spectacular experience had been the recovery of a wicker basket in good condition from a Bronze Age wreck after 3,000 years under the sea. The smash-and-grab methods of previous Mediterranean workers (including four professionally trained men trying to direct from the surface alone, without diving), had obscured the real potentials of underwater archaeology. He was most enthusiastic about the *Mary*

Rose in that respect. He thought her likely to be well buried to some height up the hull, well preserved, and with the artefacts in good condition. Possibly, even documents might have survived inside her. This latter was an appreciation even more optimistic than our own. The depth of water and the type of soil would make digging with an air-lift cheap and easy, he thought. The existence of a great dockyard only a few miles away should make the logistics simple, while the nearby and derelict Spit Fort would make an admirable expedition base, with an old L.C.T. moored permanently over the actual site. These resources were miles beyond us at that time, but they did not loom so large after talking to Peter, with his experiences of excavating off a barren Turkish shore with an expedition organised from Pennsylvania.

But we were not yet excavators, merely the reconnaissance party. We had to find an invisible wreck and then fully identify it before anyone would dream of launching a national scheme to raise the Mary Rose. For this, I felt we needed a proper sonar survey of the whole site, although it was true that no such investigation of an archaeological area had ever been carried out before. What I believed to be the right instruments were very rare and expensive, but with Miss Taylor's help I hoped to get them. In the next stage, perhaps the most interesting of all, the few who thought the potentials of the new equipment worth testing—that is, George Bass off Turkey, Robert Marx off Jamaica, Peter Throckmorton off Greece, and myself at Spithead—were to be in a kind of competition to obtain and use what in many cases was to be the same instrument, with the same operator. This was to simplify a comparison of the results.

CHAPTER ELEVEN

THE "W" FEATURE

Overnight, snow had fallen and the five days of flat-calm winter seas, clear of plankton, were over. The forecast had been for light winds of Force 3 from the north-west; that is, blowing overland. Now, down by the Ferryboat Inn on Langstone Harbour, the wind was Force 4 to 5 from the south-east; that is, blowing across hundreds of miles of water directly in to Spithead, the worse possible direction. It was 7 January 1967, and we had at last obtained the loan of a sub-bottom sonar instrument. The day before, it had been at Hull after a spell of geological exploration work in the North Sea, where the oil companies were prospecting for natural gas. On Monday the 9th, the operating team and their instruments began another round of commercial commitments. It was Saturday the 7th, or nothing; and from the 2nd to the 6th the sea had been like glass.

We might still have made it, had not the vehicle John Mills was driving down from Hull suffered a flat tyre and delayed him slightly; if the ferryman had not argued about our right to use the pier (although we had special permission from the harbour master); and had there not been so many heavy items of equipment to be lugged a hundred yards from the vehicles to the boat. Had we got away by 10:30, as planned, the tide would have been slack, but these delays added up to a departure at 11:30, with the tide now running strongly out of harbour and the wind driving the seas against it at an angle. Inside the harbour the effect was hardly noticeable, but on the bar and outside, matters would be very different.

John Mills and Dr. Paul Marke rigged the instrument and started it going while we were still in the entrance channel, with Maurice Harknett and I looking on. Although it was called a "boomer", it made a tapping noise, unlike the "pinger" which really does "ping". Both instruments produce sound waves which are intended to penetrate the seabed and reflect the images they meet, which are then shown on a long sheet of graph paper as a permanent record of the contours of the seabed and, with luck, indications of the underlying strata. All the way from the ferry pontoon to the bar, the graph paper steadily unrolled, showing the fairly level part of the channel, then one of the mysterious "deep holes", and finally the gradual rise of seabed level to its end on the bar, where Bert Knight spun the wheel violently to meet head on a monstrous freak wave which rose up suddenly at us.

Normally, as the owner of an underwater camera impervious to spray and rain, I like to catch such moments, but I had no chance here. Both hands were required for hanging on. The wave burst over the bows and cabin and part of it swept across the rolling stern where the generator supplying the power to the sonar had been put. In clouds of steam, it stopped and so too did the unrolling of the graph paper. John Mills and his team set to work to repair the damage and, as we approached Spithead, the generator fired again. We picked up the Southsea "marks", turned and lined up for the first run. As the Gosport "marks" began to move towards the "closed" position and the engine was put to dead slow for the run across the site, the generator died; and nothing John and his team could do that day was of any use, although they spent hours stripping the machine. It was impossible even to dive the site. Two ships of over 1,000 tons, anchored nearby, were rolling heavily and our own small boat would not lie head to sea, but hung along the crest of the waves if we tried to anchor, and nearly rolled its gunwales under. The waves were about 6 feet high and vicious, because wind and sea were directly opposed. The actual wind strength was not more than Force 5, compared to the Force 7–8 which had not stopped us with the first magnetometer run. But that gale had been westerly, and the tide had been flowing from the same direction. There was protection from the land mass of the Isle of Wight and Dorset beyond and no opposition of the two basic elements acting on a boat. But with the wind south-east, the nearest land mass to slow it down was France; it could take a grip of hundreds of miles of surface water and drive it up into the shallows of the Solent area, where it fought with the outgoing tidal stream. These were facts basic to Spithead and to all work we planned to do there, and it was no good complaining, although that did not stop us from arriving back at Langstone in a state of semi-frozen fury in time for the next snowstorm.

I had first met John Mills after a lecture he had given to a C.N.A. conference at London University in March 1966. He was the British representative of E.G. & G., an American company set up by Professor Harold Edgerton of M.I.T., Boston, the pioneer of underwater flash photography at great depths who had entered the sonar field via the problem of positioning accurately a camera 10 feet off the seabed in a mile or so of water. He had worked for many years with Cousteau and was interested in all aspects of "inner space", regarding the sea as the last field left open still for true exploration. As I was to find when I met him, he thought little of the exploration of outer space, because there was "nothing there". Archaeology was one of his many interests, and therefore he had carried out with John Mills what was probably the first study of an underwater archaeological site by sub-bottom sonar, the famous Tobermory "Galleon" off the island of Mull in Scotland. This was a protected site, close to shore, its position well established by the efforts of innumerable treasure-seeking expeditions, the last of which had included Commander Lionel Crabb, a legendary figure from the days of the wartime "frogmen", who disappeared in Portsmouth Harbour in mysterious, and highly publicised circumstances during Krushchev's visit in the cruiser *Ordzhonikidze* in 1956. That last expedition had employed a crane-grab to do the digging for them, and the sonar had clearly picked up these trenches and shown, very vaguely, some unknown objects lying 8 to 10 feet below them. No one had yet dug down to see what they were, but they were certainly not treasure. I had already written a book on the Spanish Armada and I knew very well that there had been no "treasure ship", that the fleet money had been where one would expect it to be, with the pay-masters in the squadron flagships, and that all these ships were acounted for. The "galleon" was probably the *San Juan Bautista,* a hired merchant vessel, potentially interesting because sunk in an area of soft mud, but now of reduced value from the activities of the treasure hunters.

Mills had explained in his lecture that there were technical problems to be overcome with the "pinger". Low frequencies gave good penetration of the sub-bottom sediments, but at best did not show detail of small objects, such as ship ribs, and at the worst showed nothing of them at all. High frequencies gave good detail of objects on the bottom, but would not penetrate the sediments. And where the seabed sediments had a high organic content, this served as a reflector to the sonar—and nothing underneath it was shown. But the slides he displayed were most intriguing, and although, of course, I could have no idea how the *Mary Rose* would look on sonar, I was sure that it would give some indication, at the very worst, and at the best would provide a pattern of rapidly created, invisible, non-destructive trenches across the site. To anyone who had seen that dismal, depressing mud plain and had calculated the man-hours and the machinery and the money that would be needed to dig trial trenches in a conventional manner, as in land archaeology, those slides with their, at first sight, unreadable complexities, were a comparative promise of paradise.

The "Dumas-faction" were present at the conference, but they were to continue for many years to urge core-sampling. The difference of opinion as to method did not arise from any ignorance on their part, but purely from differing appreciations as to the potentials of the rival schemes. It was at this conference that I had also been introduced to Margot and agreed to take part in Miss Taylor's plan to introduce student archaeologists to practical work in British waters. But by 1967 Margot had left the university for a job which allowed her no freedom at weekends, and the students were either working very hard during term or away in the Mediterranean during vacation. Helena Wylde and Stuart Sweeny were able to come down once in February, when diving conditions were impossible, but the general response was disappointing.

On the other hand the general study of Solent area wrecks was producing results and the historical research was almost concluded. A number of dated wrecks of wooden sailing ships could now be cited as evidence that timber lasted a very long time in local conditions, even where it was freely exposed to the sea; that the tiny gribble was present, but that there was no evidence yet for Teredo attack. Bearing in mind that the life of timber in some other seas was as little as between 3 and 10 years, the contrast was striking. I dived from the shore on

two French ships driven aground in the shallows of Bracklesham Bay, Sussex. They were the *Monte Grand*, wrecked in
1920, and the *Blanche*, wrecked in 1910. Attempts had been
made to demolish the former with explosives, but the latter
was still "shipshape" in the sand. The oldest which I could
positively identify was the British barque *Caduceus*, 405 tons,
driven ashore in Hayling Bay in 1881, 84 years before Harknett and I found her as a result of a request to clear a fisherman's net which had snagged on an obstruction. She was on a
fairly hard sand and shingle bottom and was badly broken
up, but we found her ship's bell buried in the sand, which
aided rapid identification. The wood exposed to the sea was
eaten back about an inch, but a test dig showed that below the
sand the timber was perfect. What this implied was that, on
a soft and favourable seabed, a wreck would have plenty of
time to dig itself in, before the ravages of marine borers became serious. The experience of clearing the net was helpful
in understanding John Deane's psychology with the *Mary
Rose* and the Gosport fishermen. Knowing the bottom of Hayling Bay quite well, we were in no doubt that the obstruction
would prove to be a wreck. But there was no bargaining. We
got the wreck and the contents of the net; and the fisherman
got the net. We did not have to tell him that it was dangerous.
And yet the degree of hazard was much less than it had been
for John Deane, who went down alone, encumbered already
with lines and pipes, and with apparatus which prevented him
from lying down. Although we had only 3 feet visibility,
which reduced to nil as the work went on, the drill Harknett
had worked out went well. He actually cleared the net, bit
by bit (which meant that with the current it began to lie over
our heads) while I lay flat on the seabed, holding on to an
iron deck beam, ready to clear him if the net should tangle
round his bottle tap and demand valve, the one vulnerable
point of an aqualung for this work. All went well and we
finished in 10 minutes.

After that, the wreck was ours to explore. Four days later,
we knew that it had no historic importance, being of well-
known "composite" construction—an iron frame with a
wooden skin and thin brass sheathing—which enjoyed a brief
vogue in the mid-nineteenth century, when the ship had been
built. We decided to turn her into a lobster farm. This deci-

sion was to have important consequences for the *Mary Rose*
site only a year later. I was at this time carrying out the
research for a book to be called *Farming the Sea,* and a practical experiment would be interesting. But it also emphasised
the question of legal rights to areas intermediate between the
traditional shallows where much ancient precedent existed
for the cultivation of shellfish such as oysters and, on the other
hand, the recent division of the bed of the North Sea between,
in the first place, nations and, in the second, smaller blocks
to be bid for by the oil and gas companies. There was no
protection for the *Mary Rose* from the current salvage laws,
but the old precedents for farming and the new laws for gas
and oil were to suggest a different approach: to obtain rights,
not to the wreck but to the seabed surrounding and covering
the wreck. The need for this was made quite clear by the
"pirating" of a "farm" similar to the *Caduceus* set up by
Harknett near the Isle of Wight. As soon as we had "proved"
the *Mary Rose* site, the raiders would swarm in; or so we
thought. C.N.A., of course, were unable to see the attraction
of bronze guns to local divers and pooh-poohed the risk, continuing their long and unavailing efforts to alter the salvage
laws in a general way, but with no feeling of urgency. Indeed,
they had taken what Margaret Rule and I thought was most
ill-advised action in backing one team out of several which
were to engage in the rival and almost simultaneous salvage
of guns and coins from a "treasure ship". This was to become
a notorious case, archaeologically, the underwater world
scandal of 1967, and the first in British waters; but was to
be of great help to us shortly because we could cite it as an
awful warning of what might happen to more important sites.

The ship itself was not important, being from a period
where everything starts to be very well known, and anyway
the remains represented what I called a "humpty-dumpty"
wreck—lying on rock in an area of violent wave action and
therefore broken up and scattered. Its potential would not
have been great in any case. The real damage lay in the publicity for underwater treasure seeking which resulted and in
its connection, however loose, with the Committee for Nautical Archaeology. This was not the first time they had allowed
themselves to become involved with what was to become a
treasure hunt, but on the previous occasion there had been

much less treasure and therefore fewer column-inches coverage in the newspapers and the weekend glossies. Not all the people involved were treasure hunters, but those with historical motives were very much in the minority and, unfortunately, could influence matters very little. The effect on orthodox land archaeologists must have been appalling, particularly in England, where they had a bad conscience; their own "discipline" had been conceived in sin by antiquarians back in the nineteenth century. The affair also had an adverse effect on press and television, the representatives of the media becoming conditioned to think of wrecks only in terms of ever more spectacular finds. Our own investigation now became almost meaningless to most of them.

Both the "treasure ship" sites, which were on rock, and that of the *Caduceus* on hard-packed sand and shingle, appeared to bear out the Dumas-dictum: "in shallow water the sea breaks everything and the dislocation of a wreck decreases its interest". Dumas immediately listed Mediterranean exceptions to this rule, but it was the more pessimistic general statement which was remembered and quoted. There were many sites in the rocky West Country which showed its application beyond the Mediterranean, but the gentle, sandy slopes of Hampshire and Sussex, which break the force of the waves gradually, showed here and there more optimistic results. The *Blanche* was one where the water was exceedingly shallow but the lower part of the ship was still articulated. Another was an unknown wooden wreck, locally supposed to be a "convict ship", which was in exceedingly soft sand not 100 yards from where we usually embarked near the Ferryboat Inn on Hayling Island. Peter Cope had discovered this originally and although not much was showing, I located what looked like part of a bulwark and finally recognised a projection from it as a badly-worn cleat still *in situ*. So this small ship, whatever she was, must be buried almost entire. Yet on an ordinary low tide the upper part of the visible wreckage, which lay on a steep slope, was barely 6 feet under water. The implications for the preservation of a small proportion of historic wrecks dating back to Roman times and beyond were enormous.

1967 also provided wrecks for study towards both ends of the time-scale. The most interesting at the modern end was the

500-ton Danish freighter *Bettann*, which heeled over and sank on the Horse Sand on 19 January. She was lying on her port side, heeled about 110° from the vertical, when I saw her for the first time on 4 April, two and a half months after the sinking. That part of her which now lay upward towards the light in the southern arc of the sky was already covered with a thin film of brownish algae, but the planes which now lay always in shadow or semi-darkness were quite free of growth, although a few small spider crabs had taken up residence there. I saw no other living thing, no fish at all, and in the dim underwater light of late afternoon could see nothing through the window of the captain's cabin except a grey, ribbed mass of motionless curtain lying underneath me. The tip of the mast lay in a tangle of fallen rigging and blocks on hard-packed shingle and had not dug in much. Only 50 years before, as evidenced by the wrecks of the *Blanche* and the *Monte Grand,* this ship might have been a wooden sailing vessel instead of a radar-equipped steel coaster. It was only so recently that the age of sail had passed away.

Towards the other end of the time-scale was the wreck of Henry V's *Grace Dieu,* built at Southampton in 1416–18, 550 years before, and burnt-out in the Hamble River in 1439. As she was the only known carrack wreck in the world, and a direct ancestor of the *Mary Rose,* I felt it was time I studied the remains in relation to their environment, leaving constructional questions to Morrie Young and his team from Southampton. Unlike them, I did not dive but made my inspection on foot, when some of the remains exposed at low water of the equinoctal spring tides in May and September that year, and from the air the following year. Contrary to a statement made by a protagonist of "Sweyn's Longship" theory, this wreck had certainly been destroyed by fire; and when seen from the air she showed no Viking ship outline, but rather that of some enormous flatfish lying stranded on the mud. Morrie Young's trial digs showed that these remains were of the bottom part of the ship, low down the hull, which accounted for the double-ended "pinched" look of the bow and stern areas. This was a very good trial run for when we would eventually have to determine, from similar evidence, how high up the hull the *Mary Rose* was preserved. There was less of the *Grace Dieu* than there was of the *Blanche,* and

this was due, not merely to the fire which must have burnt
her to the water-line when she was riding high in an unloaded
state but also to the activities of a damnable nineteenth
century antiquarian who had carried out his "excavations"
with explosives.

The site was a mixture of salt and fresh water contaminated by much modern metal "gash", but there were seasquirts
on the tops of the timbers as well as *Jassa*, a shrimp-like
creature which brings its own mud to build homes on solid
surfaces, so the preservation of these timbers was not due to
mud burial. Mr. R. V. Wells, the marine naturalist advising
us, thought it more likely that the burning of the wood had
helped to preserve it. He found vague hints of gribble attack
and at one point some evidence for the activities at some time
long past of an actual boring worm which could have been
a Teredo. The most surprising discovery was of two large
molluscs just under the mud, which proved to be specimens
of *Venus mercenaria,* an appetising clam from American
waters which had been first reported in the Solent ten years
earlier but never from the Hamble River. During the period
of our investigations the whole Solent area was in fact under-
going drastic changes as a result of the severe "Ice Age" winter
of 1962–63, which had killed off much local life and left the
area open to colonisation on a first-come first-served basis.
Immigrants, such as the Japanese seasquirt, *Styela clava,* probably brought back on the hulls of warships returning from
Korea, and this American shellfish whose ancestors had perhaps been prematurely discarded, alive, from the galley of
some liner going up Southampton Water, had started on
equal terms with the native inhabitants in occupying the now
empty spaces on the underwater map. Further, there had been
a recent shift of the Gulf Stream at the western entrance to
the English Channel; and no one could tell what changes in
the underwater environment had taken place in the past,
because records of marine life had not been kept until modern
times. The wrecks might speak, but it was certain that nothing would be found in books. Well, almost certain.

The records of the early divers did give some information.
The Royal Engineers Historical Society at Chatham in Kent
had a great deal of evidence in their library, some of it un-
published, and this produced an eye-witness account by the

diver who found her, of the *Edgar* standing two gundecks
high above the seabed 133 years after she had blown up and
sunk at Spithead, the guns deformed with encrustations, the
timber ready to collapse at a touch. A clue I found there sent
me to the Public Record Office to search the files of the Board
of Ordnance for more information on early diving gear. This
quickly produced a further mass of evidence, including Pasley's technical appraisals of contemporary equipment, and
then, by chance, occurred a stroke of luck equalling that early
discovery of the chart position at the Hydrographer's. Now,
as I leafed through the red-taped bundles of old, hand-written
documents, I found a thick sheaf of letters boldly headed
"Mary Rose", sub-titled an *Account of the Ordnance recovered from the Mary Rose lost off Spithead in 1545*. This
file contained John Deane's correspondence with the Board
of Ordnance from 1836 to 1841, giving the circumstances of
the discovery and of the guns found, in great detail, with
similarly detailed reports from the Board.

Next, occurred another stroke of luck, equally as great.
I had been to the Science Museum at South Kensington in
search of official drawings made by artists of the Royal Engineers of some of the recoveries from the *Royal George* and
the *Edgar*, and also to see if they had any trace of the manuscript or illustrations for John Deane's book, his *Cabinet of
Submarine Recoveries, Relics and Antiquities*, which was
referred to in the Board of Ordnance file as being in preparation, complete with an impressive list of subscribers. They
possessed the Royal Engineers' material but not Deane's.
However, they were then mounting an exhibition to illus-
trate the development of diving gear, and very shortly received
a letter from a Miss Muriel Pettman Pout, enclosing a copy of
a booklet, *Method of Using Deane's Patent Diving Apparatus*.
Miss Pettman Pout was a relative of John Deane. I wrote to
her at once, enquiring about the missing MSS, which she did
not have. But she had possessed some watercolour sketches of
guns and artefacts which Deane had raised from many ships,
including the *Mary Rose*. These had been loaned to an antiquarian who had recently died, but she eventually recovered
them. They showed a brilliant fidelity to life and had
obviously been done almost as soon as the objects had been
raised from the sea. The concretions, the algae, the sea growth,

Photo: Portsmouth City Museums

Fig. 27. The breach-end of the Sling-class gun after the concretion had been chipped off to reveal a shiny cast-iron shot in "mint" condition, with part of the wadding still visible (*right*). The last hand to touch the shot before this was that of the Tudor seaman who loaded the gun for action against the French in 1545.

Fig. 28. The 1971 gun at Southsea Castle, as the last of the concretion is chipped off. The position of the hammer marks the end of the barrel (where the stone shot was) and the start of the gunpowder chamber. This is a short, stubby gun of short range and heavy calibre, now identified as a "Port Piece".

Photo: Alexander McKee

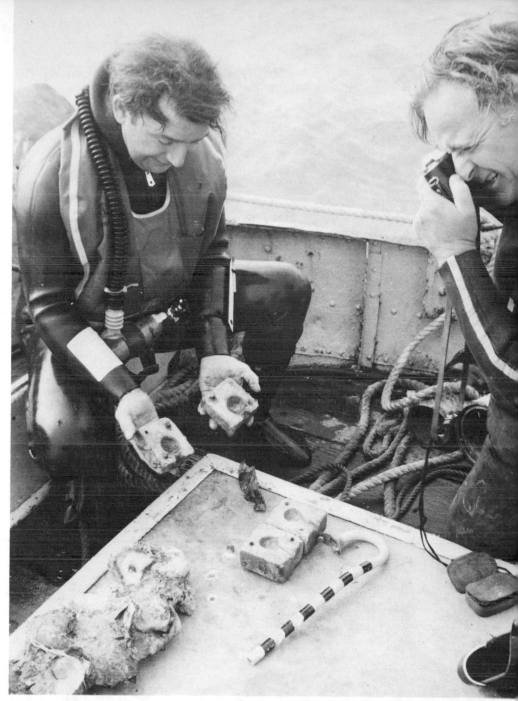

Photo: Alexander McKee
Fig. 29. Maurice Young photographing two stone
moulds for making lead shot which have just been
excavated by Reginald Cloudsdale. Bottom left is an
oyster-encrusted concretion covering some metal
object: what it is will not be known until it has been
X-rayed at Southsea Castle.

Photo: BP Chemicals International Ltd.

Fig. 30. The jug found by Percy Ackland in the South Trench in 1972. It is the oldest specimen of English pewter to be discovered anywhere.

Fig. 31. Some of the items in the "group find": one of the two combs, a thimble, an awl handle, two bobbins, and the bottom of a round box. They were part of the personal kit of one man, whether sailor or soldier is not known.

Photo: BP Chemicals International Ltd.

the encrusting oyster shells—even Teredo tunnels in wood
from a West Country wreck—were most faithfully rendered.
For the iron "built-up" guns this was most important, for it
showed them in their original state. I had located the present
whereabouts of a good many of these guns, and both the iron
and the wood were in poor condition, owing to lack of knowledge of conservation techniques at the time they were
recovered.

This fortunate discovery of the "Pettman Pout Portfolio"
complemented what was known as the "Harle Portfolio" held
by Southsea Castle Museum. This consisted of a smaller number of watercolour sketches, one being of artefacts raised from
the *Mary Rose,* which had previously been thought to have
something to do with Deane's auctioning of timber and relics
at Portsmouth in 1840. It was now clear that these also were
illustrations intended for Deane's book, and that the collection had been split up among relatives. Apart from the missing MSS, which is still lost, that virtually concluded the research into the story of John Deane, the discovery of the *Mary
Rose*, the development of early diving gear, and the history
of what had actually been done to her and recovered from her.
I was too unworldly to realise then, in my excitement, what
offence I might have given to C.N.A., for on that Committee
sat the representatives of a number of museums which should
have known all about all these documents anyway, but had
had to be told by an outsider not even resident in London.
The fact that I also insisted that the *Mary Rose* was where
they thought she was not, and that she had not been seriously
damaged by gunpowder, whereas they were convinced that
she had, only added insult to injury. But worse was to follow.

In one matter only was I perhaps less than naive. I knew
that they had no evidence for their deep conviction that the
Mary Rose had been blown to pieces by Colonel Pasley, for
they could never produce any. Whereas in the Ordnance
Board file I actually had John Deane's indent for 13-inch
"bomb shells", plus the order to issue him with six of them.
This I regarded as being more like evidence, because it was
sufficiently detailed to enable some calculation of the theoretical damage to be made; and it was also, but a small point
perhaps, authentic.

However, in two books in the Royal Engineers' library

there were one-line references to Pasley having blown up the *Mary Rose* in 1844. The first read: "In addition to the *Edgar,* the wreck of the *Mary Rose* was also dealt with"; and the second: "Later in the year, the wreck of the *Mary Rose* was also destroyed under Pasley's directions". Fortunately, these lines seemed to have escaped the academics, otherwise such solidly based attacks might have withered my chances of getting the support I badly needed. The scholars made great play with Pasley because he had used giant one-ton charges of gunpowder on the *Royal George* and they were arguing that he would have used them also on the *Mary Rose.* These would be very different to 13-inch bomb shells. In fact, I knew that the giant charges had been used sparingly, often with no success, and only then against the hull when the wreck was still proud of the bottom; and that it had taken five years to turn the *Royal George* into a compost heap. I simply did not believe the simple one-line references, with their implication that the *Mary Rose* was dealt with casually, almost in passing, at the end of the 1844 season. Nor was I wrong. I went first to the *Hampshire Telegraph,* which recorded that Pasley's divers had worked on the *Edgar* until the first week of November and then packed up for the season, as everyone did then and as we usually do now (for the same good reasons). I then went to the British Museum to read through Pasley's own handwritten diaries of the Spithead operations. They were entirely concerned with work on the *Edgar,* which was proving obstinate and inflicting casualties on his divers. I learnt that the wood of this ship was "rotten . . . like peat". His last visit to Spithead was on 28 October, with work still proceeding on the *Edgar.* On 5 November Lieutenant Barlow visited him to report on the season's work, now concluded. And this was the last season of all. No mention of the *Mary Rose,* let alone an attempt to blow her up. That he could have done so, and failed to mention it in his record of work done was inconceivable. In any case, his men had been working flat out on an obstinate *Edgar* right up to the end of the season. There simply was no time for them to have demolished the *Mary Rose.* Therefore, I could exclude Pasley and take into my calculations as the agents of destruction only the Venetian salvage operators of 1545–9, the organic life present in that undersea environment from that time until

1836, the small explosions caused by Deane, and the anchors and trawls of countless ships over many centuries. That was enough, without adding imaginary one-ton charges of gunpowder.

Although this was my own appreciation, I kept fairly quiet about the two single-line references to Pasley and the *Mary Rose*. For, although I had satisfied myself that the statements were wrong, it needed little imagination to see what could be made of them. Academics have a built-in tendency to pessimism, based on fear of ridicule by rival scholars. If two possible theories present themselves, the one only moderately boring, the other infinitely dreary and depressing, then it is the latter invariably which they will favour, because this establishes them as serious scholars in the eyes of other scholars. Conversely, dramatic discoveries are of their nature basically wild and foolish. This is excellent practice for academics, but hopeless for an explorer, since the world is still full of surprises and the serious pessimist is bound to be wrong quite often. And while, if an academic is wrong, it is only ink that is spilt after all, an explorer is tying up time, money and other people's effort on his own judgement. And since he is exploring, he cannot always be sure of what he is going to find. Margaret Rule and I made this point quite often, that the work we were doing was pure research in a new and promising field, and therefore well worth while even if there were no dramatic discoveries, but only the amassing of many small facts.

Fortunately there were at least as many positivists as there were professional defeatists, the interminable "nein-sagers" of London. Prominent among the former were Professor Edgerton and his British representative, John Mills. John was planning a technically spectacular demonstration of E.G. & G. equipment to potential customers, which was to consist of two days of private trials (the set-up was *that* new), followed by two days of customer-evaluation. He chose the Solent area as the scene, in order to be able to try out the new arrangement on the *Mary Rose* if the weather was favourable, and Southampton as the base, in order to have the protected stretch of Southampton Water to operate in if the weather should prove bad. And he invited me to be present on all four days, if I wished. I accepted with alacrity, as this would teach

me the A to B of the business. The weather *was* bad, Force 5
to 8 for the first three days, with gusts to 70 m.p.h., on top of a
big spring tide in October. John had hired a small ship, the
Solent Queen, which should be reasonably steady, so this time
I borrowed a sextant.

The set-up was a common-sense but then novel combination of two different types of sonar instrument designed to
investigate the nature of the seabed and to record it on graph
paper. Both worked by sending out sound pulses into the
water and then recording them when they returned as echoes.
Parts of both systems were towed astern underwater, one in
an oil-filled length of hose, the other in a torpedo-shaped
"fish". The controls and the graph paper were housed in flat
boxes, one about the size of a record player, the other larger.
Although they worked on the same principles as A.S.D.I.C. and
indeed the ordinary echo-sounder, and would do their jobs as
well, they were designed specifically for exploration.

One was a sideways-looking sonar, called a sidescanner for
short. This was designed to show the shapes and patterns of
the seabed. It could be set for three ranges—250 feet, 500 feet,
1,000 feet. But the longer the range, the larger the object had
to be before it would show on the graph paper. Theoretically,
at a range of ten miles an object would have to be 500 feet
long in order to be detected. Unlike most previous models,
which were one-eyed, this instrument was a dual-channel one;
that is, it looked both ways to the range set, which could be
1,000 feet. So, with the scanner searching on both sides of
the beat to extreme effective range, a 2,000-ft.-wide stretch of
seabed was recorded on graph paper. Considering that underwater visibility at this time in this area was about 2 feet or
less, the advantages it gave over visual search by divers (or, for
that matter, underwater television) was obvious. So obvious,
that I was not able to understand the aversion to sonar of the
Mediterranean divers and their English sympathisers. This
scepticism did not taint the American archaeological divers
in the Mediterranean, who had first used a sidescanner in
August, two months earlier. With it, Dr. George Bass had
scored the first archaeological success using a sidescanner,
almost immediately. But he did not have, linked with it, the
additional instrument John Mills was trying out.

This was a sub-bottom sonar, or "pinger", for continuous

seismic profiling. The instrument works very much like an ordinary recording echo-sounder, tracing on graph paper the ups and downs of the seabed in profile, but to a larger scale and in much finer detail than the comparatively crude machines adequate for ordinary boatwork. But in addition to showing the seafloor directly below the boat, the sounds penetrate the sediments of the seabed and depict the underlying layers. So, while the sidescanner looks sideways for a considerable distance to show the shapes and patterns of the seabed, the pinger looks downwards to and through the seafloor in a narrow band to reveal its composition, rather like slicing a cake to see how it has been made. Neither instrument names the ingredients, but records only the patterns, the shapes, the layers; and these have to be interpreted. This demands experienced operators and although a number of people had acquired great knowledge in the interpretation of the graphs for geological surveys, there existed in October 1967 virtually no comparative information on what archaeological objects would look like if recorded by these machines. I understand that Professor Edgerton's experiments with a pinger at Tobermory, and Doctor Bass's work with a side scanner off Turkey (but on a visible wreck, not a buried one), then represented the sum total of human knowledge on the subject.

As the ship moved down Southampton Water, I watched very closely what the sidescan showed, not only of the bottom but of the surrounding scene. Off Netley, there were some very intricate mud ripples on the bottom, like a spine with ribs; and then the marks of dredging. Channel buoys showed and the piers on the bank, and the operator, without turning his head to look, could always tell when a ship was coming, for the sidescan showed that too. But not as a photograph would, for the representations were made by sound waves, not light waves. What it really picked up initially was the wake of the ship—a pattern of water disturbance—an anomaly in the sea. Picked it up and then pictured it in terms of shadows on graph paper. As we came to the oil refinery at Fawley, so the pierheads were drawn on the graph paper and then an immense curving object. The sound waves were reflecting off the hull of the tanker *Esso London*, 90,000 deadweight tons; and they picked up a tiny object hanging from her bows on a line, as well as the curve of her side. In the Needles Channel, a charted pipeline did not show, perhaps because it was buried, but some cables showed where they should have done; and then a really big wreck, about 300 feet long, appeared unexpectedly, as a large, white, measured shadow. The sunken hull was stopping the sonar and thereby outlining itself by the space behind it, which showed white. I looked quickly at the chart and there was indeed a wreck marked at that point.

These tests and demonstrations went on for three days, with the weather too bad to attempt Spithead, and on the second day occurred a disaster to the pinger. The oil-filled hydrophone hose was being towed to one side, clear of the ship's wake, but during a turn in rough seas with wind strength Force 7 to 8, the hose crossed into the wake and became entangled with the screw. Had there not been a mooring buoy nearby, the ship would have begun to drift helplessly, with its propeller seized up, in the fast-ebbing tidal stream. As my suit and cylinder represented the only diving gear aboard (kept, hopefully, for the *Mary Rose*), I had to attempt to clear the mess. But because we were moored this meant hanging on to the screw and rudder with one hand in a tearing 3-knot current which kept trying to pull my mask off my face. A younger man would have had no trouble, but in middle-age it took me 25 minutes to cut through the multiple strands of thick nylon rope wrapped round the propeller shaft and the screw, detach the hose tied to it (hydrophone miraculously still intact), and yet, when loose, prevent it from being swept away in the current which was buffeting me like a straw, and get it back to those on deck. Fortunately, I just managed it, so that the "pinger" was still operative, although the graphs were of much reduced quality.

On the fourth and final day the wind dropped to a mere Force 3, but naturally the potential customers had to come first. This time we took the route to Spithead and went on past the anchorage out to the rock ledges off Bembridge, hard ground instead of generally muddy, and interesting geologically. On the way back, with all work completed, John Mills said there was just time for a quick ten-minute try for the *Mary Rose*. I had intended to go first across the site, to let the "pinger" see the rabbit to begin with, but the helms-

man was not familiar with the "marks" and I was not practised in turning a ship, and we ran 200 feet ahead of the site
on the way in. As we did so, the scanner began to delineate
an anomaly about 200 feet away, which took us all by surprise.
Then, turning, I did a run along the Southsea "marks" and
as the Gosport "marks" began to close, shouted stand by to
the two operators, John Mills on the pinger and Robert
Henderson on the sidescanner. A moment later, both pinger
and scanner simultaneously showed an anomaly, and the
customers, who included Dutch geologists on the one hand
and representatives of the Home Office on the other, were
almost climbing up the operators' backs to get a better look
at the graphs.

I turned, came back to the same spot, and once again both
instruments recorded an anomaly. I did not see the graphs
until later and at this time they did not mean very much to
me. I was still mentally thrown by what appeared to be the
capability of the sidescanner to pick up a buried object. I
should have realised sooner that what the scanner had done
was to pick up a seabed anomaly—the pattern of mounds and
depressions seen by Margot and myself the previous year
and that only the pinger had shown a buried anomaly 20 feet
below one of these mounds. However, the operators were in
little doubt that an anomaly unique to the area, recorded by
both instruments, must mean an artificial disturbance of the
seabed at that point, rather than, say, a rock formation. What
was to prove the most useful of the three scanner pictures was
the first, taken from 200 feet ahead of the site. In effect, this
was an almost instantaneous map of the anomaly, for the
graph paper recorded its measurements, which were 200 feet
long by 75 feet wide. This was larger than I expected the
Mary Rose to be, but not at all excessive for a disturbance
area which might contain much scattered wreckage. When the
boat was directly overhead, with both Southsea and Gosport
"marks" bearing correctly, the scanner showed a mound with
scouring on each side, while the pinger gave the height of the
mound (4 to 5 feet), showed an object possibly several feet
thick 20 feet below the mound, and recorded a geological
layer at between 35 and 40 feet below the seabed. I could not
read the poor quality pinger graphs, but John Mills pointed
out that the deep layer was continuous throughout the area,

while the object at 20 feet was limited in extent and associated with the mound. The alignment of the mound pattern appeared to be about south-east, very approximately, which was near enough to the heading of the *Mary Rose* and of the "crested mound" noted by Margot and I; and the Southsea "transit" went across the back end of the site—that is, it was the stern area, if she had sunk on her original heading.

A brief exploration by sonar had provided a good deal of information in under 20 minutes, and I was enthusiastic about the possibilities of running methodical patterns around and across the area; in effect, "invisible trenching". I went rather too far, and thought we might be able to obtain complete proof of identity "without ever touching the wreck at all: the perfect solution". I thought we had about 85 per cent of the proof already, in that the anomaly checked for shape, size, alignment and chart position with the wreck of the *Mary Rose*; and neither Margaret Rule nor I believed in identification by the first artefacts you found, because of the layers of anchorage "gash".

I wrote to George Bass, who replied:

> Sidescanning and mud-pentrating sonar are obviously the answer to the underwater archaeologist's prayers. We searched for over a month for a 300-foot-deep wreck off Turkey in 1965, using both underwater television and a one-man-towed observation capsule. We never even saw an amphora. This past summer we searched the area for only *two mornings* with a sidescanner, and picked up a target! Our two-man submarine went down for a look and landed on top of a huge Roman shipwreck!

This wreck was "proud" of the bottom and known because of objects which had come up in sponge draggers' nets from somewhere in a four-mile area. The *Mary Rose* was a different problem because although the position was known, the hull was buried. Sonar was the answer in both cases, but a buried wreck was more difficult of proof. And the drawback to proof by the orthodox method of excavation was that so cumbersome and public an undertaking must inevitably give away the location of the site, not merely to the many small-time local pirates but to legal salvagers also.

The law then was, and still is, that contracts to salvage

sunken ships are sold on a commercial basis to the highest bidder. The premise on which the law is based assumes a modern wreck, which may be raised entire, or, as is more usual, stripped of valuable metals or cargo. If no salvage contract has been issued, then it is open to anyone to take what he likes from the wreck, provided that he hands the items to the Receiver of Wreck, an official of H.M. Customs. They are kept for 12 months by the Receiver and then put up for auction, the finder receiving a proportion of the proceeds. In October 1967 the *Mary Rose* could be plundered, ripped open, blown apart by anyone who cared to do it. And it would be perfectly legal. Items which were handed to the Receiver, and might fall to pieces if not treated, had to be kept by the Receiver for the statutory time; and if they had disintegrated at the end of twelve months, that was perfectly legal too.

In this very year, 1967, official contracts to salvage items from a single vessel, H.M.S. *Association* in the Scilly Isles, were in possession of three different parties (one of them actually backed by the Committee for Nautical Archaeology!); and the resulting pressure on the competitors had ruined any good intentions any of them may have had. But it was all perfectly legal (although some pirates were believed to have been at work also). C.N.A. had been trying for more than two years to get the law changed, but without result, and on 11 October I wrote to Joan du Plat Taylor to find how matters stood, and whether they thought they might be able to obtain site protection for the *Mary Rose*. Miss Taylor replied that an application "should come really from you and Mrs. Rule". We took this to mean that C.N.A. had failed, which was correct. This was the decisive moment in our relations with London. Up to now we had thought that all we had to do was find the wreck and prove identity. Then, as with the *Vasa*, the State would take over.

In November we formed a Mary Rose (1967) Committee to try to obtain the legal protection which the London academics could not offer. We kept it to four people: Margaret Rule representing the two-county Joint Archaeological Committee, Lt.-Cdr. Alan Bax representing the Royal Navy, Mr. W. O. B. Majer representing the Society for Nautical Research, and myself, originator of the project, representing the local Sub-Aqua Clubs, and in a sense the army also, for the

Mary Rose was a soldier's ship and I was a military historian. We did write to the Ministry of Defence, brashly suggesting that they amend their standard salvage contract specifically to cover an archaeological investigation, but we had no high hopes there.

Our main move was based on the fact that quite large areas of seabed and foreshore have owners, with the same rights as the owners of an ordinary land holding. The old laws had been used to protect the rights of oyster-cultivators and there were new ones to take account of exploration for gas and oil. The owner of the seabed at Spithead was Her Majesty the Queen and it was administered for her by a body called the Crown Estate Commissioners. They advised us that we might apply for a lease to an area containing the wreck of the *Mary Rose*, which we did, stating that our object was archaeological investigation of the seabed. We applied on 3 January 1968 and received a favourable reply on 11 March. The lease, at an annual rent of £1, came into effect on 1 April. The Board of Trade were similarly swift in agreeing to an arrangement I suggested, based on the divorce laws, that the Receiver retain "legal custody" of the sample artefacts we must raise, but that their physical control should lie with the conservation laboratory to which they were sent. Whatever the shortcomings of London academics, it was clear that Whitehall could move fast and effectively, and we were very grateful. Now that we were the "owners" of the seabed around and above the *Mary Rose*, we could prosecute any intruders for trespass. Further, the site was under close naval observation and they had policing facilities already. What C.N.A. had done was to try to get a law changed. What we had done, was to make use of an existing law in an unusual but perfectly valid context. They had thought of the ship, we had thought of the site.

But now we needed money for a further sonar survey and for constructing an air-lift for a trial dig. Mr. Majer asked the Society for Nautical Research for (considering this was the *Mary Rose*) the comparatively modest sum of £250. However, the very same people of the Dumas-faction who sat on C.N.A. also sat on S.N.R., and they got it turned down on the grounds that sonar was useless, an air-lift excavation would fill in, and that we must take hundreds of core-samples to prove we had a wreck there. The Oracle of the Mediterranean had spoken and no one else on either of these two bodies knew enough to contradict. Eventually, a Sunday newspaper agreed to pay the boat costs for a full pinger survey which Professor Edgerton was prepared to carry out for us free of charge.

Before coming to England in July, Professor Edgerton carried out a survey of a barren seabed off Jamaica where the two scuttled caravels of Columbus were supposed to lie. The results showed two distinct anomalies in a simple sub-bottom strata. When Robert Marx dug them later he found wooden ship remains. Arriving in Britain, the Professor went to Tobermory for another attempt at the "galleon", which was again inconclusive. There was something about 8 or 9 feet down under clay which could be a layer of shingle. In the known area of the wreck—and there only—the pinger was being baffled for some unknown reason. Outside the area of the wreck it gave a very clear sub-bottom picture and when some recorded anomalies nearer to shore were later dug, they proved to be large boulders about 20 feet down. Professor Edgerton and John Mills then came down to Portsmouth to attempt the *Mary Rose* with two pingers, a 12 K/c instrument which did not penetrate deep but gave finer detail and a 5 K/c instrument which gave deeper penetration with some loss of detail. They were with us for five days but on only two days did the weather allow work to be done.

We had a big boat and we needed it, as navigation and logging was all important. In a group forward we had four people—the boatman, myself to concentrate primarily on the Southsea marks and keep a record, Margaret Rule to attend to the Gosport marks and keep a record, and the Professor with his pingers, who entered on the graph paper our remarks. We, of course, also logged his remarks. Just behind us was John Mills with a sextant, and in the stern two buoymen, Peter Cope and Bill Majer, to mark significant anomalies. There was also an E.G. & G. diver with a high-pressure air-lance for probing contacts; and, of course, the press.

We planned to run the Southsea mark first, and drop two buoys, one to mark the start of the anomaly, the other where it ended; and then to run lines 50 feet apart parallel to those two buoys, dropping further buoys. This should mark out the anomaly on the surface. The runs would be long ones, so as to delimit the area. But we were in trouble almost at once. This was not a simple seabed as off Jamaica, or a blurred one as at Tobermory. On our first run, everything seemed to be going according to plan. Just before the Gosport marks closed, up came an anomaly, which was buoyed both sides, but as we ploughed on, up came another anomaly—and we had to buoy that too. When we looked closer, we found we had three anomalies on that line, two grouped on the marks and a smaller one beyond. There was nothing to do but carry on methodically, running parallel lines.

After a bit, things began to settle down. Running from Southsea, a mound appeared just before the marks closed, and then a depression with a sub-bottom feature like a curved "tongue" underlying them 10 feet down. As the marks closed, a very high crested ridge showed on the seabed and here began a sub-bottom anomaly which looked like a flattened letter "W". Each run now showed the same familiar pattern and it became clear that the third sub-mud feature of the first run, which was 20 feet down, was too small to be a ship. The Professor noted a discontinuity of the seabed when just south-west of the Gosport marks, and now began to mark up the "W" feature with red arrows, as this appeared to be the most significant to him. We, of course, were in the dark as to his interpretations and the matter was far too technical for him to explain quickly. He decided to anchor and send down the diver with the 12-ft.-long air-lance to probe both the "tongue" and the "W". The tongue resisted at first, but then the compressed air broke through it silently. So it was not a rock, not a wreck, and not shingle, either, for shingle rattles. He assumed probably a consolidated clay layer. But the tide began to run fast and he could not drag the airhose and lance over to the "W" feature. Time was precious, so we recovered him and carried on with the sonar survey, on new marks which I improvised steadily southwards.

A delay caused by a gale enabled me to study the graphs and also to work out a "fan" pattern of marks to cover the site and delimit it. In fact, there were three groups of marks which gave three different "fans", of very great accuracy. In effect, this was to lay fixed lines across the site, with each line given a code number. Provided that these lines were run exactly, on a dead straight course, with the bearing of the

Gosport marks taken at various times, then the graphs could be studied at leisure later and compared line by line. But here we hit unexpected trouble. The boat would run straight while going away from Southsea towards the Isle of Wight, but it veered and "hunted" awkwardly when steering back to Southsea. As a line like an intoxicated snake was of no use to us, we decided to use the pinger only when running slowly from Southsea, then turn and came back fast for another run. Just before rising seas caused us to pack up, and while de-limiting well over towards the Isle of Wight, the pinger picked up what the Professor was sure, for the first time, was a wreck, because of what he took to be a scour-mark in association with a sub-bottom feature which reached up almost to the seabed. I took the marks of this, although I thought the scour might really be the drop off towards the navigational channel for Southampton.

Afterwards, we held a gloomy conference in a dingy cafe at Eastney. Professor Edgerton thought the scour feature was the *Mary Rose*, while I disagreed because it was too far from the chart position; he also now dismissed the "W" feature as being geology, not a wreck, but here Margaret Rule disagreed because it did not fit the geological history of the area. And our newspaper friends had no story, because everything was still unsure.

It took me three weeks work to compute the results of the survey, because many of the improvised marks had to be identified on the ground and then put on the chart. I gave local offence by asking for the whereabouts of the "smoking" red chimney, the owners denying that it did so. The "W" feature was very much in the running, but the "scoured wreck" was 900 feet from the chart position. However, I im-plored Harknett to look at it, in case it was another wreck, and we dived it. At first sight, it did look like a wreck lying on a beach, with a piece of timber sticking out of a sand slope, and pottery lying around. But the timber was loose driftwood, the artefacts of different dates, the sub-mud feature was simply clay with a hard interface 18 inches down, and the scour was in fact the drop off to the navigational channel.

But the more I studied the "W" feature, the more certain I became. When I compared the sidescan graph of the seabed anomaly, I could now see just how the pinger anomalies tied up with it. The sidescanner was really showing two mounds, with a depression in between. This depression was a scour-mark, and the mound nearest to Southsea I called the "counter-mound", for the "W" feature began under the other, high-ridged, mound. I now thought of this as the "port side mound". The pinger, but not the scanner, did show a "star-board side mound", but it was so small that I doubted that a diver would see it among the pattern of small natural ridges. What had happened, I thought, was that the *Mary Rose* had scoured much more on one side than on the other. Indeed, what I was looking at was very similar to a famous echo-sounder graph of the *Lusitania*, with its one-sided scour and counter-mound. I now began, tentatively, to try to link the lines showing the "W" feature with a blow-up of the scanner graph, so as to produce a three-dimensional plan of the site. This was bold, as I now realise, but in fact I had missed a significant anomaly, which had also escaped everyone else, because at the time there was so little comparative informa-tion on what a wreck would really look like on a sub-mud sonar graph. All I was sure of was that this scoured feature, the most prominent object for a mile on what was a basically flat plain, represented an artificial disturbance of the seabed and that, somehow, the "W" feature in some way represented the remains of the ship itself.

It had been a fascinating exercise, watching the shapes of former plains and buried hilltops and one-time lakes appear deep below the present seabed, as shown by sonar. There was no trouble in identifying these, because Professor Edgerton had had so much experience with geological interpretation. There was a geological layer about 35–40 feet down which showed a marked discontinuity under the *Mary Rose* site, and which rose into a steep hill deep below Spit Bank. This was a former land surface on which marine sediments had later been deposited, and the Professor who had discovered this new "mountain", was kind enough to call it after me! It was just possible, I thought, that the break in the strata had been caused by the weight of the wreck and that the lowest part of it might be perhaps 35 feet down. But that would be incredibly optimistic.

CHAPTER TWELVE

FIRE BRIGADE
BELOW FIVE FATHOMS

Overnight, the fog had come down. A clammy grey mist clung to the grey October sea, where yesterday had been the bright sunshine of a late "St. Martin's summer". The passing *Queen Elizabeth* went by like a dim ghost. Spit Fort was visible, but the shorelines of Portsmouth and Gosport were featureless. None of the forward "marks" could be seen, let alone the back markers several miles inland with which they had to be aligned. I had insisted on a recording echo-sounder because, with so many "pinger" graphs now available, it was possible to check navigation by the known bottom contours; but the echo-sounder had just broken down.

We were out at Spithead in a proper salvage vessel fully equipped for a trial excavation to prove whether the "W" feature was wood or geology, and at a cost far greater than any we had had to meet before; with an excellent diving team including a shipwright, two experienced student archeologists, a marine biologist, a marine zoologist and a non-diving conservation expert; the sea was smooth and un-ruffled; and although we knew we were somewhere near the *Mary Rose* site, effectively we were lost. And there was nothing I could do about it. I felt like an amateur musician who had brought a complete lorryload of harps to the party. The fact that it was hardly my fault did not make the humiliation less.

It was not that the fog was unpredictable, but that it was, and that I had predicted it. In July 1968, when we had completed the "pinger" survey and I had arrived at positive and optimistic conclusions, I had pressed our newspaper friends for further financial backing immediately in order to prove the matter one way or the other. But they were going away to Italy for six weeks, followed by a visit to America for a further six weeks, and would not return until the second week in October. We would have to defer the dig until then. Now October is a month for gales and fogs. In gales, one can see the "marks" but cannot work; in fogs, the sea is calm but one cannot see the "marks"; and an October fog tends to cling, whereas summer fog, mist or haze is usually soon blown away by a rising breeze or burnt away by the mid-day sun. I warned them in writing that: "Fog or mist would ruin everything, as we would be unable to carry out the navigational plan for picking up the site." I suggested that we risk the venture only if a "St. Martin's summer", also common in October, arrived. So we stood by, as did the Southampton salvage company, and the salvage people rang me on 21 October, suggesting that we go next day, as all indications were good. I agreed, but the 21st was a Monday, when many Sunday newspaper people are not in their offices. We rang their home, and they were not there either, nor had they left any address. In fact, they were away from London altogether, and were then at— Southampton! The 22nd, when we contacted them too late, was a perfect day—calm, warm, sunny, with excellent air visibility. Nevertheless, the forecast for the 23rd gave some hope that these conditions would continue: early fog was mentioned, but it was supposed to clear later. In fact, it got worse.

The salvage vessel held a complete range of equipment. There was a giant compressor to work a really powerful air-lift, a small pump to supply a water-jet, an air-lance for probing and a professional diver to operate them. I decided to get them to try out the water-jet, because this was a small, cheap, light, simple affair which might not be beyond our own resources in the immediate future, whereas the big air-lift compressor would require a very big and very expensive boat, apart from all the legendary difficulties of rigging such things. The water-jet was only a simple Fire Service nozzle and hose of 2-inch diameter, powered by a little pump on two wheels, fully portable in a 25–30 ft. motor boat. The diver operated it for 20 minutes and in this time was able to dig five or six holes each one 4 or 5 feet deep and about 18 inches in diameter. He pointed the jet vertically downwards into the seabed, building up the water pressure underneath and creating a cavity, which collapsed, leaving a small, round hole. He could not stay in one place, however, because the tide was running and the boat was swinging, and so he and the hose were literally pulled out of the hole. He stated that in this seabed multiple jets could trench both deeply and easily.

What I wanted to do was not to dig a hole but to trench through the "port side mound" so as to get down close to the suspect feature. As this was a "W", some parts were much deeper than others, 12 to 15 feet below the seabed and out of our reach, but at three points it appeared to be only some 5 to 6 feet down. To trench and then to probe in the trench for a shallow "contact" seemed to be the method most suited to our meagre resources. The drawback was obviously going to be the way the boat swung with wind and tide, pulling the digging machinery with it. The currents at the site were complicated, an "X" pattern and by no means a simple to-and-fro; and winds were variable in direction, also, from hour to hour, sometimes from minute to minute. Obviously, there was a mooring problem which only money could really solve.

The day had been expensive, but not quite a waste of time, because we were to use water-jets as the main excavation tool for two years, and after that for the reverse job of "back-filling" excavations. The lessons we learned from the professional diver were basic. He had also reported that there was no cave-in of the holes, the sides were hard enough to hold firm; this was something I had suspected before from noting the clean, vertical sides of anchor-furrows on the site. Most people, thinking of a sand seabed, imagine an almost immediate fill, but this is not so with clay. We should be able to dig almost professionally "clean" trenches, with the stratification preserved in the sides.

The only thing which worried me (and still does) was the tidal stream, very fast on springs. I was developing an idea for an underwater "house" (more the size of a warehouse) with the still water inside it clarified to give 100 ft. visibility, as had already been done by an American team in a muddy Aztec well. My idea was, in effect, a submerged coffer dam, but the Queen's Harbour Master, who was very interested in the project, suggested an improvement—a concrete structure, hollow inside like a Mulberry harbour component, but with an open bottom, to be towed into position and then sunk, as the Nab Tower had been. Like the Nab Tower, the upper parts of the walls would be well above water, creating a kind of swimming bath at Spithead inside which work could go on in an orderly and tidy fashion. I did not like the idea of doing any really delicate excavation when the whole thing was exposed to immensely powerful and uncontrollable natural forces.

However, this was very much in the far future, because at the moment we were concerned, not so much with wreckage as a mass of "overburden" lying on top of a sub-mud feature which we had to establish as the *Mary Rose*. Probably some parts of this came closer to the surface than the 5–6 ft. shown by the "pinger", and in desperation I had planned mass digs by 22 divers using their hands only; indeed, during October and November I had organised no fewer than six operations, five of which were cancelled by bad weather, and the sixth, the expensive one, proving abortive because of fog. This was a most frustrating stop-go period, but we were desperate to get hard evidence soon, so as to be able to fight what I called the "Battle of the Winter". That is, to convince sufficient people to get enough support to plan a proper excavation programme for 1969, and not the hand-to-mouth expedients we had been compelled to devise to date. So we planned one final forlorn hope for 28 November, without any digging machinery, for we could not afford it.

And it proved an exact repetition of 23 October. The morning was calm and misty. But we went all the same. Then the pattern began to change, very slightly. This time the recording echo-sounder worked. Some marks were visible at the beginning of the run, near to Southsea, but they vanished in the mist after a few minutes; as they did so I went on to the sounder, and checked the bottom contours. On the third run I was satisfied that we were somewhere over the site, and anchored. And then we sat down and waited for the sun to break through. And waited, and waited, and waited. We waited all morning, in fact. No one complained, no eager beaver urged action, no pessimist said call it off. No one even suggested diving, although the water was obviously very clear, because if you have divers down you are crippled and dare not move. If the sun did come through, it might be only briefly. People were munching sandwiches when, just after one o'clock, a slight breeze sprang up from seaward and began to roll back the mist, first from Southsea, then from Gosport. I ordered anchor up and engine started.

I took a snap decision to use the original Southsea marks, which led over a low, widespread mound which was at the back end of the site, rather than the new marks which cut across the extremely conspicuous "port side mound". The latter was the place I really wanted, but the actual buildings were further away and much further from each other, which made them more accurate, but also required 5 to 6 miles air visibility. I thought we might not get that much, and we didn't. Nor did we have long, only some six minutes or so. But, as we were so near, it was sufficient to line up with the Southsea marks and then anchor when the Gosport marks closed. I knew now, from the Edgerton survey, that on that intersecting line we were over the counter-mound, not the "stern mound".

So everything depended on the underwater navigators, already fully briefed. They were Morrie Young, the Southampton shipwright, and Percy Ackland, also from Southampton. Morrie was fully in the picture as to what we had done to date, Percy I did not know very well then, but he was soon to become our crack underwater navigator, the "gun dog" we always sent down first. Until I met him, I thought I was competent; but Percy was more than competent, he was uncanny. I could always explain what I did and why I did it, but Percy was in a class beyond that. In this case, I had to do the explaining. I gave them a 100 ft. tape (originally used for surveying the Roman "Palace" at Fishbourne and now a little the worse for wear), and told them to attach one end to the anchor, then swim out on a compass heading of south-west. The first 50 feet would definitely be "cold", but at about the extreme length of the tape there should be a low, wide mound. There were many slight mounds all over the area, made by wave action, and all on the same alignment. This mound was unnatural, and would tell them so because it was aligned across the natural pattern, was rather higher, and very much wider. They were to take a buoy with them and mark up the mound.

When Morrie and Percy returned, without the buoy, they reported that it was on the mound, which was 6 feet beyond the extremity of the tape; that is, 106 feet from the anchor.

Up to this point, they had seen many mounds, aligned almost at right-angles to their line of swim, but this one trended at a distinct angle to the natural topographical pattern and beyond it was a steep depression.

I sent in the next team to probe along the crest of this mound, for I reasoned that this was where the wreckage might come closest to the surface. They were three members of Southsea branch, who habitually worked together on semi-professional jobs involving the use of air-lifts and water-jets. Two were in the Fire Service—Station Office George Clark and Leading Fireman Tom Smith. Don Bullivant worked at an Admiralty shore station. They were to re-lay the tape along the crest of the mound, and, with one 12 ft. and two 8 ft. probes, thoroughly investigate it. And they did, obtaining resistance on the crest, but no bottom a foot away on the slope. They did not just casually thrust in the probes, but made a close grouping; because if the side of a ship was under the crest, one could get a negative by moving only a very short distance either side.

In my usual optimistic fashion, I went down to join them, carrying a really solid steel hand-spear only 4 feet long. At first, I could see only 9 inches, because the others were up-stream to the north of me, and their efforts were stirring up the sediment. I began probing across the marked crest on a line at 1-foot intervals. No resistance at all at the first and second spots. The third time, the spear went down 3 feet and then stopped. A clay interface can have this effect, so I pushed. No result. I put all my force into it. Still no result. I tried to move the spear sideways. Impossible. The spear had made no sound when it met resistance, so the object was not rock, not shingle, not metal. Convinced now that I was into timber, I began to dig like a dog at a bone with an entrenching tool around the spear. When I was down two feet, up came the firemen, beckoning at me imperatively to follow them along the tape. I therefore tried to extricate the spear. I pulled up, I pulled sideways, forwards and backwards, and could not free it. After three minutes working at it, I freed the spear point from whatever it had stuck into and followed the others along the tape to the north.

About 30 feet away along the crest of the mound they had two probes in. The 8 ft. iron probe was sticking well out, having met solid resistance early. The 12 ft. probe, made of lighter metal, was bent into a "V", having folded in the middle from the force applied to it when it had hit resistance. I checked both these contacts with my steel hand-spear, and met the same solid resistance about 3 feet down. Again, there was no noise whatever when the spear stopped sliding downwards into the clay. That made three contacts within 30 feet, all along the crest of the mound. Had we not been delayed all morning, we could have dug down there and then to expose the contacts; but it was now late afternoon on a winter's day and our daylight was running out.

To leave matters for a whole winter was almost unbearable, so we were most grateful when Lieutenant Andrew Linsley of the Naval Air Command Sub-Aqua Club offered to arrange for us to have the use of a 112-ft. minesweeper, H.M.S. *Portisham*, for a day. Quite apart from transporting most of the divers, I thought we could use her to solve the winter weather problems, both of them. If the trouble was strong winds and a heavy sea, the minesweeper could be anchored bow and stern across the sea and the boat we would have to hire for the digging machinery could anchor in the shelter of this 112-ft. long artificial breakwater. But if the trouble was fog, then I thought the ship's radar and sonar would cope. Some of the new Southsea and Gosport transits would make excellent radar targets, I thought, and a sonar trace of the bottom contours would give the check. But I had only 36 hours in which to make arrangements, because the minesweeper was free only on 8 December, and I heard about it on the 6th. In this time Station Officer Clark organised the loan of a Portsmouth City Fire Brigade pump, hoses and branch, plus a small team of Brigade divers. Morrie Young and I agreed to split the cost of the boat to carry this equipment, but neither he nor I could dive because of the after-effects of the last weekend; and Percy was not free. I hurriedly recruited two experienced divers from Southsea, Dick Millerchip and John Bevan, but they did not know the site at all.*

The 8th was another calm, rather misty day, but good enough to see the old Southsea marks for the back end of the

---

* Bevan was later to be one of the first two divers in the world to reach a simulated depth of 1,500 feet in a chamber at the Royal Naval Physiological Laboratory at Alverstoke, near Gosport.

site, with the water so unruffled that we could make a perfectly straight run. This time we were going to do things
differently, in what was to become standard procedure: we
were going to "bomb", that is, make up a small buoy with a
very heavy weight and only just enough line to reach the surface. It is an old trick when you want to mark a precise spot and
keep it marked, when your boat is liable to drag its anchor.
The type of buoy described will not drag, and gives an almost
vertical line to the marked place. The latter was necessary,
because once the spot was found, a heavily weighted branch
and hose had to be taken down to it and positioned exactly.
The weight needed varies between 50 and 100 lb., and no diver
can swim far with that—except downwards. Therefore the
drill is: mark the approximate position with a "bomb buoy",
then use the bomb sinker as datum for a seabed search for the
exact position, then move the sinker to that position, then re-
anchor the boat—this is the catch–so that the boat is near
enough to the buoy to make the lowering of the weighted hose
easy. A four-point mooring would make the final positioning
simple, but this was out of the question at that time.

The navigational procedure was also to become standard
for every occasion on which we had a recording echo-sounder.
On a "bombing run" the boatman looked over his shoulder
at the Southsea marks, someone else called out how the Gosport marks bore, I kept my eyes on the echo-sounder graph
unrolling its picture of a very familiar seabed pattern, and
two "buoymen" stood by the line to the sounder's transducer;
that is, the exact point being recorded, and while one unrolled the buoy and its line so that no hang-up should occur,
the other stood by to chuck over the weight. The idea was
that it should fall vertically through the water at the exact
moment the Ferrograph recorded the desired seabed feature
directly underneath it. Many recorded "pinger" runs had
given a variety of targets which could be hit by this method,
provided that the marks could be seen and that the procedure
was accurately and slickly carried out. But this was the first
time we had tried it and on Gosport transits which did not
mark the "stern mound" but merely gave final warning of its
approach. The early warning was the appearance of the
"counter-mound" on the graph. So the familiar picture began
to unroll. The steep slope of Spit Bank . . . flattening out . . .

the first upward curve of the ink, the "counter-mound" . . .
down again into the depression. . . . The watcher called:
"Gosport closing—Gosport on!" The two buoymen got ready
and the boatman slowed the engine. Then the ink line on the
graph began to climb again, and I shouted: "Go! Go! Go!"
With a splash the buoy-sinker hit the water and vanished
instantly. We carried on for a minute more, letting the Ferrograph complete its picture of the "stern mound", and then
we turned and came back to where we had dropped the buoy.
There was no sign of it. The boatman swore. The line he had
made up must have been a little *too* short.

Not to worry, we still had the anchor. So we ran back
towards Southsea, turned again, and lined up for another run.
But instead of letting the anchor go from the bow, where it
would have been some 15 feet forward of the transducer, it
was led back to a winch only a few feet away. To drop from
different positions on a 40 ft. boat is to introduce needless
errors. Exactly the same procedure was carried out, only this
time it was the anchor which was dropped instead of the buoy-
sinker. And as the anchor roared out, with the boat still in
the dropping position, up popped the bomb buoy to the surface—6 feet away on the port side! I promptly apologised for
not anchoring directly over it, and the boatman said it was his
fault, because he had not lined up the marks exactly, otherwise we *would* have been over it. It was no fluke, we were
to use the method for the next two years, with an average
error of about 10 feet (and that error in a *known* direction).
It was a heartening result for a first try.

The two search divers then went down with the 100 ft.
Fishbourne tape, tied one end to the anchor and carried out
a circular sweep search from it, hoping that the tape would
snag on one of the two probes we had left down ten days
before, provided that they were still there and still upright.
Several trawlers were at work nearby at that moment, and
their gear could have flattened the rods or removed them
completely. In case this had happened, the divers were also
to look for the crest of a prominent mound. But the tape did
not snag on anything and the visibility and light were so
poor that they reported being unable to make out any bottom
contours at all, not even the small, natural mounds.

This was when we needed the main body of divers to carry

on the search, but the minesweeper had been delayed. So
Bevan and Millerchip had to go down again, suffering badly
from cold, because I wanted to reserve the firemen's energies
for the strenuous work of rigging and operating the water-jet.
We had shot our bolt without success when the *Portisham*
arrived, sending over a very eager beaver, already kitted up,
and raring to go. I was all in favour of cooling him off, for
I distrust vast enthusiasm. But he was a prominent sextant-
man, sonar-doubter and a constant critic of "marks", in fact
a navigation expert in big ships. So I gave him a navigation
job, to take out the tape for 40 feet due south of our boat's
anchor, as the start of a probe-on-fixed-lines search. He had
an underwater camera, a bag of tools suitable for a wrecking
job on a copper-encrusted modern wreck, but no compass. So
I lent him mine. He dived, losing the wrecking tools in the
process, but still holding on to the tape and a marker buoy.
As he swam out from the anchor, we saw with astonishment
his buoy moving steadily in the direction of Portsmouth
Harbour. Due north. After fifteen minutes, he returned,
minus the toolbag, and as he reached the top of the ladder,
was heard to ask me: "Does your compass have a north-seeking
needle?" I replied that the needle did indeed indicate
magnetic north.

He dived again and by now the whole boat were watching
his marker buoy with intense interest. It proceeded erratically
east for a time, then veered round to south at last, and then
lost it. When he surfaced again, he stated that he had swum
out due south for the full 100 feet of the tape, and appeared
annoyed when I reminded him that the distance was to be
40 feet. He then produced a most interesting historical artefact which he thought extremely significant because he had
found it buried under the mud. If it had indeed come from
the *Mary Rose,* it proved beyond doubt that she was badly in
need of a boiler clean when she heeled over and sank.

I then sent Hugh Ainsley, an experienced underwater
archaeologist, and a Naval diver, Petty Officer Hollomby, to
probe 40 ft. due south along the marked tape. When they
returned (with the lost toolbag) they reported that they had
had initial difficulty in doing this, as the tape had been laid in
a circle, and had brought them back near to their start point.
They had straightened out the mess as far as they could, for

there were many bends and twists in it, and had done a little probing, but had found resistance at one point only, about 5 feet down, but could not swear it was not a clay interface. The owner of the toolbag interrupted hotly to deny that he had done anything but lay out the tape in a perfectly straight line due south. He then told me that my methods were all wrong, that the sonar interpretations were all in the mind, and that we should use wooden stakes as bottom markers (although a trawler was visibly at work only a short distance away), and that he had had very great experience of these matters. I dare say he had, but it did not prevent him from being designated, from then on, as the Navigating Officer (North and South).

As the *Portisham* had to leave early and darkness was not too far away, together with a fast current-run, I decided to invest in the future rather than a somewhat unsatisfactory present, and get the water-jet down for an operational test by the men who would be using it next year. George Clark gave it a thorough trial with trenching rather than hole-digging in mind. He found that as set, it would hardly dig at all; it merely blasted off the top one foot of seabed. When directed downwards it was like a needle, it bored thin holes; not at all what we wanted. There was a lot of excess power, too, which could be used if the branch was more heavily weighted. All that was required to make it dig powerfully but gently was to make a modification which would produce not a thin, hard jet of water but a wide, gentle spray like a watering-can. He thought he could do this quite easily over the winter.

Overnight, the light westerly wind of Force 2 to 3 had gone round to south-west and increased to Force 6. A heavy sea was running on the Winner Banks outside. Even inside Langstone Harbour, the waves were streaked with foam. It was 26 May 1969, and we had at last got sufficient finance to make just one boat trip with the modified nozzle to the water-jet. The Fire Brigade team were there in full force, Morrie Young and Percy Ackland had come over from Southampton, and three Southsea divers were ready to lend a hand with the digging of the first trial trench. The two London divers, Hugh Ainsley and Robin Piercy, who had read archaeology and

had considerable practical experience in the Mediterranean,
were not with us; but otherwise it was a well-balanced team.

For a diversionary target, in this eventuality, I had picked
Pete Cope's "Convict Ship" just off the Ferryboat Inn on the
Hayling shore. It is a soft, steeply sloping seabed in which
anchors find it hard to bite, and with a fast, swinging current.
We anchored a little distance from where I judged the wreck
to be, with the boat veering to within 20 feet of the beach
and then swinging out to 40 feet. The Solent scene had
changed in the past few years and boating had become a
popular sport. This tiny, uncertain gap into which we had to
dive proved an irresistible magnet to powerboat and sailing
enthusiasts alike, all of them learner-drivers. Powerboats came
bouncing through it at 20 knots, skidding wildly (defying the
harbour speed limit of 10 knots), while the real sailors showed
off their skill, the first by nearly ramming us and then reeling
past our bows so violently that his rudder dropped off, the
next making an equal misjudgement and an equally violent
correction, which resulted in a capsize. We had an enormous
diving flag flying from the mast, a crowd of fully kitted divers
standing on deck and a red-painted Portsmouth Fire Brigade
pump mounted in a prominent position. But it made no difference to the joyous fun and games the holidaymakers were
having with us. Their emotional release from traffic jams
made them innocent of all danger they might create for others.
In over twelve years the amateur divers of Southsea had
suffered only two casualties, one fatal, one injured, and both
of them from this cause.

I had to dive, find the wreck, and put a marker buoy on
it, without being chopped by the screws, which are like
butchers' high-speed knives, more savage than any shark. Once
I had the buoy in position, however, between boat and shore,
it created a hazard to their propellers which kept all but the
most daring away. We had only a short period of slack water,
but George Clark got the weighted nozzle and hose down
quickly and began to dig around the bit of bulwark timber,
less than 6 feet long, sticking about a foot out of the ground,
which was all that showed of the wreck. I had taken Margot
Varese and Bob Hurst to this ship two years before, to show
them what a real wooden shipwreck looked like; and they
had found it difficult to believe (which was the point of the

exercise). After less than ten minutes' jetting, George Clark surfaced to invite the rest of us down to see the results. I logged them as "incredible". A ship's deck and its framing had been exposed to a depth of 2 feet over an area 12 feet long by 4 feet wide. Most of the timber was free from the attack of marine borers, and although the frames had a slightly weathered appearance, the beams appeared virgin. Morrie Young was at work with a saw, taking three samples and timing his cuts. The timber proved to be American and English elm, the frames 2 × 2s and 3 × 3s, the planks 8 inches, and the time to cut out a section of plank 90 seconds. Timber from the Tudor period can be dated fairly accurately, and we intended in due course to "prove" *Mary Rose* by taking deliberate samples of large timbers and then having them dated by the tree-ring method. Morrie now estimated that, for the *Mary Rose,* the task might take 30 minutes, because her framing would be much heavier, in the nature of 9 × 9s and 12 × 12s, he thought (and he was absolutely right).

Of course this had been a professional job both ways, with a senior fireman on the jet and a real shipwright to examine what he exposed. But it was also much too easy. The sloping sand and shingle seabed was not hard to undercut with the jet—the increasingly fast current immediately swept away the disturbed sediments and kept the water clear—and there was no orientation problem of keeping the jet on target all the time, because part of the wreck had been visible to start with. It was merely a question of directing the nozzle along a visible structure. But the *Mary Rose* was not like that, she had many, many feet of "overburden" on top of her. So I asked Bert Knight, our boatman, who was also an experienced diver, to find us some nice mud and clay somewhere in Langstone, and we tried out my "start line" procedure, based on a military night attack. This consisted of 15 feet of yellow tape pegged out on the ground in a straight line by a hand-spear at either end. The distance of 15 feet was to allow two water-jets to operate together, both "firing" in the same direction. For the original positioning of the jet it worked, but not when the pressure was turned on. Visibility disappeared completely into total darkness. George Clark only knew where he was by keeping one flipper pressed down hard on one spear, but he had no idea of direction, only that the nozzle was pointing downwards. It was in fact working well and undercutting the sea-bed, causing it to collapse, as his companion, Morrie Young, survived to testify. One moment he was lying down on mud, and then he was on water, as the ground was blasted from under him by the invisible jet! The result was a crater 4 feet deep by about 2 feet wide, after 10 minutes; and what we wanted was a trench on a fixed alignment. But now that we knew the nature of the real problems on a site similar to the *Mary Rose,* George Clark was able to work out a simple solution based on weighted guide ropes. The divers would keep sense of direction by touch.

The amazing armada sailed on 5 July. Overnight, Barbara Andrews had taken the two freely loaned boats off their mud-mooring at high water and put them alongside Harknett's boat on its deep-water mooring, so that they would be ready first thing in the morning. The forecast for light winds from a favourable direction was correct, the sea was almost flat calm, the morning warm and sunny, the underwater visibility marvellous. But the motors and petrol tanks for the loaned boats had to be rowed out to them slowly and precariously in a tiny dinghy, and time pased. A mass of heavy equipment, dozens of cylinders, weight-belts, kit-bags, the Fire Brigade pump, the 56 lb. weights for the hoses and the jackstay, the inter-com system, a truly giant bottle for surface demand use—all this had to be unloaded from vehicles and man-handled over a hundred yards down to the pontoon, and more time passed. And when the boats were alongside, and their engines and tanks had been fitted, they then had to be properly and carefully loaded, for they were eminently un-suitable craft, and more time passed. And then this part of the armada sailed down the Langstone channel against the tide, at about walking speed, and more time passed, about two hours of it, before we reached Spithead. Here the rest of the fleet rendezvoused with us, a small three-diver motor boat and a one-diver sailing dinghy. Then the "port side mound" had to be located at its most prominent point and marked up, the boats had to be re-anchored nearby, for the current was now fast, the ropes and the weights and the hoses had to be placed in position, and a good deal more time passed.

Had a time-and-motion study expert been present, he

would have been cast overboard, together with his findings,
for we all knew them already. We also knew the answer—
£25,000. For big machinery, which would require a big boat
(or a small ship), which in turn would demand big, semi-
permanent moorings. I had begun to charge for the little local
lectures I gave, and this had now brought in £3, a well-wisher
had donated £1, so we had already £4 of the £25,000. And
today was costing us nothing, apart from petrol. Southsea
B.S.-A.C. had loaned their stormboat, a wooden river-assault
craft which made a good diving platform for us, but was dead
slow; the Portsmouth College of Technology had loaned a
small wooden pontoon with an equally weak motor, and on
this, dangerously high up, we had had to mount the pump
and hoses loaned by Portsmouth City Fire Brigade. And we
were exceptionally grateful to them all, for they were early
supporters, vital to any such enterprise, when most people
doubted. At this time, we could never tire of Margaret Rule
telling us the lessons of the Fishbourne Roman "Palace"
excavation, which was that the first £10 to "prove" a site is
always the most difficult sum to raise, because until you have
carried out your trial dig, no one knows what is there or what
it is likely to be worth. The first £100 is much easier than the
first ten, and when this shows promising results, diffident
donors beg you to accept a couple of thousand, if you think
it will be any help, while the media—and other parties also—
scent a rich and development-worthy "property" ripe for ex-
ploitation or take-over, which brings it own problems in due
course. But we were far away from that stage, and would never
reach it, ever, unless with totally inadequate equipment and
on a shoestring budget we could tackle a huge job successfully.
At least, the weather was on our side.

   And the team was an excellent one, with George Clark;
Tom Smith and Don Bullivant to lead the digging team,
Morrie Young and Percy Ackland assessing the results, and
Barbara Andrews, the very competent diving officer of Southsea B.S.-A.C., to co-ordinate the efforts of the less experienced
divers from Southsea. Very few girls take up diving, but those
who do tend to be very, very good; Barbara was exceptionally
so. The Fire Brigade team had brought the equipment they
often used on semi-pro jobs, including a boat-to-diver inter-
com set and surface demand gear. With this, the diver does

not wear a small cylinder on his back, but is supplied via a high-pressure line with compressed air from a huge cylinder in the boat above, his demand valve allowing him to breathe air at the right pressure automatically. This is not the same as with a helmet diver, who is supplied with a continuous stream of air into a helmet, any excess being valved off; but it does enable a diver with fins to work underwater for a hour or more at a stretch, without having to come up and change cylinders. The modern aqualung is a poor piece of equipment, as Cousteau was long ago the first to point out.

Once the "port side mound" had been located and buoyed at the "midships" position (not the "stern area"), it was probed and resistance felt between 6 and 8 feet down at several points. Then two jets were set up, with two teams to run them simultaneously. On the second shift, George Clark was operating one jet, helped by Eric Sivyer, a novice diver from the archaeological training programme I had launched the previous year, and George Parr, an ex-professional helmet diver who now aqualunged for a hobby. They were trenching along the mound rather than through it, as I had wanted, because this gave them direction, and after digging to a depth of 6 feet, Clark uncovered at that depth a piece of timber. He gave it to Parr to hold, but in total, swirling darkness, with the wood being slippery, and having virtually no weight in water, it eased out of Parr's grasp without his noticing it and vanished in the total blackness which enveloped them both at that moment, down in the trench, inside the seabed. When Clark reported this over the intercom to the boat, I decided to make my next dive at once.

The visibility was now about 8 or 10 feet, with mud clouds welling up to obscure it. I followed the three lines which led to George Clark, somewhere in the slowly boiling circles of mud—the intercom line (orange), the surface-demand line (black) and the hose (greyish-white canvas). When I found him, he appeared to be swimming forward with a heaving motion through the seabed, most of the mud not rising at once, but welling up from around his shoulders and streaming backwards in the current. I noted:

It was like looking down from an aeroplane on a man walking jerkily through the clouds, with his head and shoulders only visible. The mud was like convolvulus flowers. A kind of off-grey slow-swirling pattern of convoluted circles, evolving in slow motion from around George's head and shoulders as he dug the trench forward. He had a peculiar kind of bounding motion, half-swimming, half-walking, with this immense, intricately convoluted mud pattern evolving around him. It was extraordinarily beautiful, particularly when silver bubbles burst up through the slow-motion patterns of the welling mud.

What I was looking at was a real expert digging a trench underwater; no novice could possibly obtain that standard without long practice, but novices we must necessarily use. It was to be a test of nerve, as well as skill, for as the trench went lower, then so the jet operator entered total darkness inside the bottom of the sea, with the ever-present danger of a cave-in.

At the end of the day, when Morrie Young went down to inspect the results, he found that the trench was 15 feet long, 6 feet wide and 6 feet deep, and had been cut precisely along the line of the mound, as the semi curved section of seabed showed at either end. He probed both sideways and downwards in it, but got no contact with a hull. At one point in the very deepest level of the trench what appeared to be stratification showed—a layer of light shell and grit, much smaller than beach shingle. This suggested an old seabed, as did the piece of timber found at that depth, with more recent depositions of mud and clay on top. But it could also be interpreted as the "disturbance area" around a wreck.

For a year or so Morrie and I had been considering the sonar surveys, in conjunction with precedents already studied, of which the two most important were Peter Throckmorton's trial trenches through the lightly built wrecks at Methone, which had collapsed in a sequence he was able to reconstruct, and Professor van der Heide's many land excavations of wrecks on the former bed of the Zuyder Zee. The latter had not collapsed, but they had been cut off at the level of the seabed contemporary with their sinking, which had then been overlaid with later sedimentation layers. But the most interesting point had emerged from the fact that Van der Heide's careful excavations had methodically covered the entire wreck site,

and were not confined merely to the actual hulls. And these
had clearly showed the creation of scour-pits on either side
of the sunken ships, which had later been filled in with a
"mix" of soil. They were very noticeable, and he called them
the "disturbance areas". It was also noticeable that the sides.
of the ship produced small port and starboard side mounds
on the new seabed many feet above, with a shallow depression
between them. Throckmorton's drawings depicted very
similar sections from the Mediterranean.

As fields of Solent area study I had taken the result of
Towse's work on the "Norman Castle" wreck off the Isle of
Wight, plus four old wooden ships, and innumerable modern
wrecks showing the action of scour; and to this I had added
the "mix" which must result from the anchorage artefacts
of Spithead, both those so heavy they would go straight down
and those which could be carried, like the slipper limpet
shells and the light shingle, continually across the seabed.
Now, a particular study of Morrie Young's provided the lynch-
pin, tying all this together in a new, complete and satisfying
theory. His subject had been a cabin cruiser sunk on mud
some 11 weeks before. She had already disappeared into the
seabed to her water-line and had created two scour-pits, one
on each side, which were prominently "lipped", or mounded,
on the sides away from the wreck. And at the bottom of these
scour-pits, against the hull and even partly underneath it,
were man-made objects which had nothing but an accidental
relationship with the wreck. They had not come from it, they
had never been on it or a part of it; they were merely "drift
artefacts", single items in a mass of light material both natural
and artificial which is continually in motion across the seabed
of the English Channel, with a general movement direction of
west to east. A can of beer dropped off Cornwall from a
sharkboat could end up in the scour-pit of a cabin cruiser off
the Isle of Wight. They would both be contemporary, and
who could tell the difference 400 years from now? And this
process had been going on since the first ship sank, so many
scour-pits must contain artefacts of widely differing dates,
many of them later than the date of the sinking.

This theory was injurious to the dictum widely propagated
in underwater circles, and also by trusting academics, that
a wreck was a "capsule in time", a "closed find" not interfered

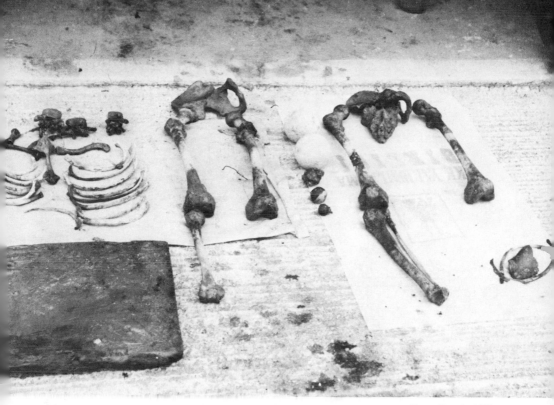

Photo: Alexander McKee

Fig. 32. Human remains were found at a fairly high level in the collapsed castle structure. Left is part of a stout plank some of the bones were lying on and top centre two stone shot and three lead shot from the same area.

Fig. 33. Gamma-ray picture through the breech-end of the "Sling-class gun", showing the thin line of the rough-weld down the barrel. Until this picture was taken, it was thought that the barrel had been "built-up" in the conventional manner with a number of staves bound together by iron hoops.

Photo: H. M. Dockyard

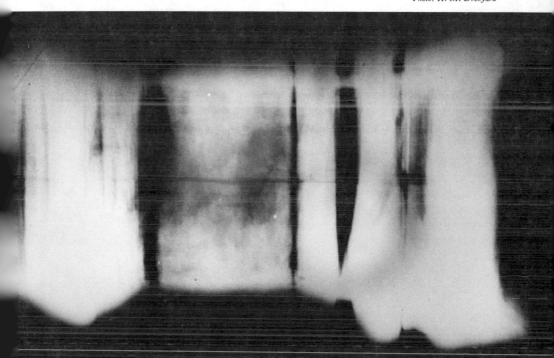

Fig. 34. A pile of stone shot excavated from the South Trench. They are of two different sizes, 6½-inch and 4-inch, and are ammunition for Port Pieces and Fowlers respectively. A Fowler has not yet been found and is still an unknown type of gun.

Fig. 35. Airlift lying in the North Trench after a digging shift down through about 5 feet of "overburden". The tops of newly exposed frames are down out of sight in the darkness at the bottom of the trench and all the excavated soil was deposited long after the ship sank.

with by later generations, with everything in and around the wreck indubitably belonging to it, particularly when it was completely buried. For Morrie then went on to show how, as the wreck collapsed or decayed, the scour-pits would fill in to a greater or lesser extent, with the port and starboard side mounds moving in towards the ship. Eventually, all would be covered, perhaps many, many feet deep. This was why we thought that the wood found by Clark and lost by Parr was probably detached wreckage from the *Mary Rose,* but not necessarily so—it might have been a piece of waterlogged driftwood which had dropped into her port side scour-pit when this was much deeper than it was now. We concluded that every detached object would have to be considered with at least these two alternative possibilities in mind.

We had then set to work to produce alternative solutions to the riddle presented by the "W" feature. Broadly, there were two possible alternatives. Either the "W" was a true cross-section through all the remaining wreckage—in which case the *Mary Rose* had collapsed and would have to be excavated, not raised; or the "W" was merely the "interface" between the upper part of the wreckage and the later sedimentation layers, and that, in effect, the sonar pulses had bounced off it. This latter was optimistic and could mean that the wreck of the *Mary Rose* might stand 30 feet high under the mud. Morrie took the pessimistic alternative and tried to work out a collapse sequence for a heavily built ship which could result in the wreckage forming into a "W" shape, while I explored the optimistic possibilities, finding a solution which presumed that her 40 degree angle of heel still remained. This was not necessarily true, as she might have rolled more nearly upright from the scouring action, but the object was to keep our brains lively as we excavated and to be able to assess evidence from several standpoints.

At the same time, I produced the first site plan from the sonar indications, which was modified for alignment as we learned more. Its principal area of error, however, lay in that the fixed lines made by the different "transits" could be placed on the mound shown by the sidescanner only in the most approximate way. Fifteen minutes' worth of scanner had been enough merely to run a single line across the mound pattern, and although this was clearly at the "back end" of the site, it could not be tied in precisely. The placing of the other lines was just guesswork. However, these lines were fixed geographically and what lay below them was known; it was just where they cut the pattern shown by scanner that was imprecise. For convenience in running them, they had been coded; they were really fans, based on variations on a basic transit. There was the MG group for the back end of the site, the QF group a little further forward and the JM group, which consisted of no fewer than six lines, running from aft of amidships to the bow. These were all lines running out from Southsea roughly across the broadside. For the intersecting Gosport marks, there was only the GCG group. We had not run the original and inferior Gosport marks with sonar, nor had we used another mark, which was best of all but either difficult or impossible to see. But for all the coded lines we had corresponding "pinger" traces, with up to four runs on any one line.

Thus, with the fan lines of the sub-mud investigations laid aproximately in position over the scanner picture of the seabed surface, we had a crude three-dimensional map of our site. Primitive though it was, it represented almost certainly the first of its kind in archaeology, and I felt that many a land archaeologist would be happy to have so much information in advance of excavation.

The principal decision taken as a result was to dig the first trial trench across what seemed to be the middle of the site, represented by the most accurate "transit" of all, coded as JM3. The "W" lay deepest of all at this point, which made us think it might be the waist of the ship. It made our task harder, but would reduce the risk of damage to any exposed wreckage from anchors and trawls very considerably. The back and front ends were shown by pinger to be nearer to the surface, but if these represented the castles, their wreckage was likely to be both fragile and complicated; also, their shallow burial meant possibly ruinous exposure to the anchor and trawl hazards. This decision loaded the odds against us, but we thought that loss of time meant little when put in the balance against the possibility of damage to such an important site. But the decision had been taken after a London newspaper had promised us £100 for boat costs, so that we could plan a proper programme of work for the good months

of June and July, in what was proving to be the best summer
for 10 years with incredible visibility of up to 25 feet at
Spithead; but the money did not come through until all that
was over, and we were facing the autumn and winter. So
once again the odds were loaded against us.

When we returned to the trench along the port side
mound on the JM3 line, it had to be with the cheap-and-
cheerful set-up of loaned boats. To load them and reach the
site took three hours, as against the forty minutes with one big,
fast, commercially hired boat. So six hours of every working
day were lost, plus an hour or more trying to position the
jets from craft which swung and veered because they had no
moorings. And we were limited to Saturdays only, because
their owners required the boats for themselves on Sundays.
As if that were not enough, fate had three surprises for us,
one after the other. But at first all went excellently well, although the comparison between our plodding progress out
to Spithead and the shattering speeds of the forty-two competitors in the *Daily Telegraph* and B.P. Round Britain
Powerboat Race who had just passed over the *Mary Rose* in
their massed start, made us feel like the poor relatives at the
rich man's feast. The price of just one of those boats would
have let us complete our task that summer.

The ultimate intention was to turn George Clark's 15-ft.-
long trench along the mound into a 15-ft. wide trench across
the site, overlapping slightly on both the Southsea and Isle
of Wight sides. This width would be necessary in order to
avoid a cave-in. We had no echo-sounder, so I simply
"bombed" on the marks and let the boat carry on beyond
while it laid out a 100-ft. line attached to the "bomb" sinker
as a guide to the alignment and length of the intended JM3
trench, which would then be exactly along a really accurate
transit for a fixed distance. I was aiming the bomb for George
Clarks' trench but expected to have to carry out a short semi-
circular sweep search to find it, even in good visibility. But
when I reached the 56-lb. sinker of the bomb buoy, 45 feet
down, conditions were terrible. The seabed appeared to be
in a state of semi-suspension. All I could do was follow the
jackstay we had laid from the surface across the site. A
measured 17 feet beyond the bomb sinker I found myself on
top of a dense, dark mass of slubweed, with an upheaval in

the clay by my right shoulder. It was George Clark's trench full to the brim with weed, and the jackstay leading right across it! Admittedly, sea and air conditions had been perfect, but nevertheless the error produced by the Gosport intersecting transits had been only 17 ft., and the error for the JM3 line was nil. The best a sextant can achieve is a 50 ft. error all round a central point.

I marked up George's trench with a spear, tying the guide line to it, so that the workers would find their position clearly marked, and then went beyond along the guide line for a recce. My fins stirred up unusually large amounts of sediment, and then, gradually, I became disoriented. I dropped my specimen-bag, took two minutes to realise it had gone, came back along the line and found it, tried to do a job I had set myself and failed, became disheartened by the immense clouds of muck, and was losing concentration and will. Vaguely alarmed, I "washed out" the dive, and surfaced, thinking I was ill. And so I was in a way. But it was not until some days later, comparing notes with Harknett, who had had a similar experience that day on a quite different site, that we tracked down the cause to cylinders filled at a particular time by a certain compressor. Somehow, it had become contaminated by oil. We had been breathing an air–oil mixture under pressure! He said it felt as though his throat was being cut, whereas I merely felt generally unwell. The muck-clouds at Spithead may have been the result of the screws of those forty-two powerboats passing over generally, or their particular effect on the open trench. That the trench had not filled in appreciably with sediment was a favourable factor, but the weed was going to be a problem. It was passing across the site, current-borne, at such a rate that it wrapped itself round all lines and tapes, so that they became immensely heavy and tended to bow out. More serious was the fact that as yet only the Fire Brigade team could dig effectively—although one novice was getting the hang of it quickly, surfacing with his face, under his mask, as black as a miner's—and that we were unable to give anyone much experience. Between 26 May and 26 July we were able to plan only five operations, three of which were carried out in perfect conditions, the remaining two being diverted to training inside Langstone Harbour because of adverse weather. Conditions did not have to be very bad to make the pontoon and fire pump an unseaworthy proposition, and on one occasion a sudden squall had had my heart in my mouth for 20 minutes, trying to decide whether to jettison everything and look a fool if the wind died down as quickly as it had blown up, or hang on hoping for the best and look an ass if the pontoon capsized and deposited the Fire Brigade's pump on to the bottom of Spithead. By carefully watching how, in the far distance, the sails of yachts were beginning to come upright, I made the correct decision—hang on. But it was a near thing and I did not want many more like that.

The worst of it was, that this stage was strictly speaking not archaeology at all. The top five feet of sediment at least was mere "overburden", recently deposited and having nothing to do with the curious "W" feature which on the JM3 line was never nearer the seabed than 6 feet and at most points was considerably deeper. What we needed was a mechanical excavator to shift large amounts of "overburden" in a careful and controlled manner. I had had an offer, which I had at first rejected because I thought the machine might be too brutal, but now I had to consider it closely. It looked to have possibilities, in view of what we had found out by actual digging. But the date of the loan was not for me to decide. When it was available, we would have to go, regardless.

CHAPTER THIRTEEN

ROYAL ENGINEERS
AT SPITHEAD

The wind was rising (tomorrow it would be Force 6), and the strong currents of a really big spring tide were boiling over Spit Bank. The hired diving boat, 40 feet long, was pitching and rolling crazily. We had £50 to spend and that gave us four operations. This one, on 2 September, was the first. But the divers had merely to mark, check and report progress. The mechanical excavator was mounted in a ship 180 feet long, and although she swung and veered on her bow and stern anchors, her deck hardly moved. The excavator was operated by remote control, but was far more sensitive than one would imagine by looking at it. The depth of dig could be pre-set and there was a choice of sensitivities. At utmost sensitivity the machine would not penetrate consolidated clay or a hard grit layer, such as that in which the timber had been found in the JM 3 trench, where all probe contacts were two or three feet further down than they were in the "stern area".

What I intended was to dig a wide, shallow trench down to, but not through, what I thought was that older seabed some 5 to 6 feet down. But because of the strong winds and stronger tides on both 2nd and 3rd September, the excavation was not so neat as I had planned for. The ship shifted position slightly from time to time, and consequently a number of short trenches were dug, on and adjacent to the JM3 line. But in those two days some 480 cubic yards of "overburden" was removed, easing the future task of the jets considerably. The dig revealed very quickly an interesting, if expected, pattern. From the top layer up came slipper limpet, indignant hermit crabs and unspeakable sponges. There were but few artefacts in the first 5 feet, but between 5 and 6 feet there was a distinct layer of anchorage "gash", similiar to that lying exposed on the modern seabed at the *Royal George* site. These included a strip of lead, a concreted stanchion, clay pipes, pottery, animal bones and an enormous glass jug covered in new-looking barnacles. Everything which could be dated was nineteenth or twentieth century and the principle of burial appeared to be that heavy objects which were small in area sank through the light upper sediments faster than light or flat objects. At one point I decided to risk a penetration through the consolidated layer at around 6 feet and this immediately uncovered part of an old elm plank, attacked by gribble, and studded with holes for iron nails which had vanished. Morrie Young thought this might be either outer hull sheathing or a detached fragment of collapsed castlework. It was too thin to get a tree-ring dating from it. Underwater visibility was only 18 inches on the seabed and less than that in the excavations, which rapidly filled with weed.

Three days later, on 6 September, we set out on the first stage of making one continuous trench out of the rather untidy excavations. But first the "bomb" went down and then the running jackstay to indicate the line. The bomb hit 8 feet from the Southsea end of the trench, instead of 17 feet as on the previous occasion. This was because the trench now extended some 10 feet further towards Southsea. After the recce teams had made their report, I went down with Eric Sivyer to inspect and mark up the digging line, and swam straight down into clouds of "smoke". I put my head into it until I could feel some sort of seabed in my fingers just under my face, but I could see only about as much as a cat might in a darkened room with its head stuffed inside a wet, black blanket. First, I unjustly blamed the four recce divers for stirring up the sediment with their fins, and then I blamed the innocent Sivyer for carelessness. But I had to report later:

Trenching began at the S.W. face. Impossible to measure results, as the seabed appeared to be on fire when we first saw it, and this became worse once trenching started. Extraordinary, and for us, unprecedented. The trenches were pouring forth white sediment in clouds resembling those from a bonfire, three days after they had been dug. Looked like the bottom of a volcano. Assume this will result in the trenches losing their separate identity, which is what we wanted.

It was fortunate for us that we had got on with the time-and-motion study, or no work would have been done. The "bomb" buoy and running jackstay technique cut the search time to nearly nil, because when the first team arrived at the sinker and faced south-west along the jackstay, they found themselves actually looking at the south-west end of the trench, if the visibility was good, and if it was not, then a couple of flipper strokes took them to the trench at one precise point. There was no swimming round in circles or navigating with a possibly erratic compass. Similarly, we had decided to cut out the time-wasting procedure of laying out a thick rope guide line, heavily weighted both ends, to help the jetters to keep direction. Instead, the Southampton team had made up a 38-foot-long guiderail formed from three sections of heavy piping screwed together. We had intended to do this on the seabed, which was now impossible, so instead it was assembled on the surface and then held between two boats which manœuvred until the "rail" was aligned exactly to JM3. And then we let it go.

It arrived exactly where intended, with one end a few feet from the Southsea end of the JM3 trench. As it would undoubtedly sink into the mud, a small plastic sub-surface buoy was attached to it by a short length of line. We judged this to be an almost net-proof method of seabed marking, which would not damage the nets. But several other similar markers were put down, in case we lost one to the otter-board of a trawl. With this solid guiderail to hold on to, the divers were able to jet in total darkness in the right direction, although many were new to the work, including a team from Plessey Radar Sub-Aqua Club who had come out from the Isle of Wight in their own boat to join us for the first time.

From lack of finance we could not mount another operation for a complete month, and at this time the pressure was always on to obtain decisive results with a one-day, one-shot, regardless-of-weather attempt; which is not the way one would choose to do it. For 5 October, I built up a really tremendous effort (considering it was financed with less than £20). Local enthusiasm helped me put on a show worth ten times that amount, with five boats and three dozen divers. As usual, I put my "Intentions" in writing and circulated them: "To jet a main trench along the existing guiderail through the present maze of excavations. Desired dimensions: length 25 ft., width 5–6 ft., depth 4–5 ft. Then to probe along this trench for parts of the wreck nearest to the surface; and if possible to expose a portion of it by further use of the jets." The reason for always recording intention, method, weather, forces available and result was as a ruthless check on what I hoped would be our progress from amateur to semi-pro. On this occasion I had ample grounds for confidence, because a substantial part of the team—the "storm troops"—were professionals; all I had to do was deploy effectively, and then let them go.

It was the deployment which had me worried because, for guaranteed effectiveness, two 4-point moorings were required, one for each of the two main boats which must not drag or swing. We had no moorings at all, so would have to rely on two anchors per boat, and, without moorings, how a boat will lie to the prevailing sea and wind cannot be known until you have tried it. In the hired M.F.V. *Silvest* was the Fire Brigade pump. This had to be positioned almost exactly over the guiderail some 50 feet below, so that the weighted nozzles and hoses could be taken directly to the face to be dug. There was a good team in that boat, led by George Clark, and with two visiting professional divers—Bob Lusty from the famous R.N. diving experimental ship *Reclaim,* and a civilian diver, Mr. Wright from the dockyard salvage ship *Goldeneye.* In the naval pinnace *Orca* was a large compressor and Mr. S. J. Utley with four other helmet divers from Portsmouth Dockyard. They were eager to help because they thought, and I agreed with them, that for this sort of digging task a helmet diver was more suitable than an aqualunger. With aqualungs we had to change over shifts of two men every twenty minutes, and it took some time for the new team, in near zero visibility, to pick up where the others had left off. Whereas one helmet diver only was required on a jet, and he could stay one or two hours at a time if necessary. He could also make himself heavy (a great advantage), he was in telephone communication with the surface and he would almost certainly survive a cave-in of the trench, whereas an aqualung diver almost certainly would not. Apart from that, these helmet divers were experienced underwater diggers and possessed moreover a reaction jet which was a balanced instrument easy to operate. The only trouble was, that their boat must not drag its anchors, or the helmet diver might be dead. And their boat had to be positioned close to the pump boat, and with a line rigged to guide the helmet divers down to the right place in the trench where the jet attached to the pump boat should be waiting for them. Any connection with the organisation of land archaeology was purely fortituous. The nearest equivalent would be, while sitting above cloud, to drop plumb lines on exact spots on the earth below from a couple of barrage balloons kiting about in a gusty wind, when attached to insecurely fixed winches. I also had to try to communicate by shouting over the waves above the sound of a fire pump blasting away in one boat and a compressor hammering its heart out in another.

As there were so many professionals present, I was very keen to scent out their reactions to our operation, in order to tighten it up. The first mishap occurred on the "bombing" run, the buoyline becoming slightly tangled and delaying the drop through the water of the 56-lb. sinker by a few seconds. Instead of hitting near the Southsea end of the guide-rail it landed alongside the other end, about five feet to one side of it. But none of the professionals noticed, because within five minutes of the Southampton team going down, surface buoys were flying on either end of the guiderail, as planned. But now we had to anchor the two main boats, one on either side of the alignment of the buoys, and that was up to the professional boatmen. Then down went the two jets and hoses from *Silvest*, and out went a "strayline" from *Orca* to lead the helmet divers to their work. I went aboard *Orca* at this point, to see that Mr. Utley was happy, as indeed he was, because the strayline took him directly from his shot line to the trench. I saw Mr. Utley's helmet disappear into the green water, as he went down to the *Mary Rose*, the first helmet diver to visit the site since John Deane in October 1840, almost 130 years before. With the big compressor roaring away by my ear, I watched a continuous stream of air boiling to the surface to mark his progress, so different to the bursts of bubbles which mark the breathing rhythm of an aqualung diver. With five helmet divers, each doing shifts of an hour and a half or more, they would probably be able to do the job by themselves, without assistance from the lung divers.

The weather was perfect, sunny and very warm, with only a slight swell on the sea. The compressor was roaring away happily and shortly the fire pump would start to hammer out the good news of work in progress. Then, by my left ear, there was a tremendous bang. I saw rubber rings fly out of the compressor, and it died. For good, obviously. And Utley was 50 feet down without air. In Pasley's day, he would probably have been dead. Even as it was, I was immensely relieved to see him rise slowly to the surface, and be rapidly hauled in to the side of the boat by his safety line. The irony of the accident was, that he had obtained a newly overhauled compressor for this job, instead of the old one his team normally used in the dockyard. It should not have sheared. But it had. And now all the helmet divers were out of action.

I was left with the aqualungers. Most of the experienced men had already dived once, and the professionals had only a single cylinder with them. There were four or five Navy divers in *Orca,* as well as the helmet men, but these were all SDs—"Ships' Divers"—with little training or experience. Besides, most of them were now seasick from the swell. The difference between "SD" and "CD"—a Clearance Diver, such as Bob Lusty was—is immense. The latter is a fully trained full-time professional of great experience. There was a whole boatload of civilian amateurs from Southsea, but, apart from Eric Sivyer, they were all new enthusiasts with not much experience. I had intended to let them learn by watching what the professionals did, but it was out of the question to send them down to dig in total darkness in what was now quite a deep trench. But Plessey Radar had fielded a team of seven and as divers most were experienced; I thought I could risk them, provided they were led by people with digging experience from the pump boat, and organised by George Clark.

George took over, briefed them on the jets, divided them into pairs with one experienced man leading a novice "digger", and got the whole thing moving again. Shortly after, I did an inspection dive and experienced at first hand the difficulty of the team change-overs. When you go down first, you know where you are, that there is no one else down there, and the disappearance of all visibility makes no difference. But this was different. I swam down the "bomb" buoyline in

8 feet visibility until I arrived at the cloud of up-welling muck from the jetting, stuck my head inside it and could see nothing, carried on down until my fingers touched the unmistakable iron weight, and then felt around for the guiderail, without success. Not only was there no visibility, but everything was very dark, because the sinker had been moved into the trench and I was not on the seabed at all, but in the bottom of a great pit 4 to 6 feet below it, with its sides rising above me. I could easily have blundered into someone, and we might both have got entangled in a line. So I surfaced, swam over to a white buoy marking the Southsea end of the guiderail, and found visibility right down to the bottom. Indeed, I had arrived in the middle of a change-over of shiftworkers. The end of the guiderail, buoyed up, was sticking out of the mud and easy to see or feel, with one diver hanging on to it, doing nothing; while along the rail was a jet, unattended, blasting away gently and anchored by a weight. The diver was a No. 2, waiting for his No. 1, and meanwhile getting himself acclimatised to a slightly nightmarish landscape.

With my own start point now clear, I finned gently along to find the second jet, which was being worked. That is to say, a continuous cloud of sediment was obscuring everything at that point, but out of it was sticking a few inches of a red-banded snorkel. The diver operating it was clearly right down inside the new seabed at the bottom of the trench inside the old seabed, and working his jet to maximum effect. That snorkel belonged to Andy Gallagher, an impetuous young fireman from Chichester. Of his No. 2 I could see no sign, which was hardly surprising, for while No. 1 holds the hose over his shoulder with one hand, keeping the other one on the guiderail, the No. 2 keeps his hands on the weighted rope to the nozzle and moves this steadily forward, so he was probably a trifle below Gallagher.

I carried out my usual natural history tour of the excavation complex and got a shock when I bumped into what looked like a tree trunk soaring vertically upwards. It was in fact an enormously thick collection of seaweed, with little crabs climbing up and down it. Swimming up it, I came to a solid plastic marker buoy about 10 feet from its base. The core of the trunk, which had collected so much slubweed, was a thin line leading to a really heavy weight buried under the mud, which we called "Morrie's Massive Marker", after its inventor. Our excavation, I noticed, was already being occupied and colonised. There were lots of little trenches in our trenches, made by bottom-living fish of the blenny or goby type, which were hopping about. And the shoals of whiting pout, which I had first noticed on 6 September, after the work done three days before, were still there. These fish, which are normally prettily striped in black and silver, are to be found on most wrecks and rocks areas locally, but never on barren seabeds like Spithead. They had obviously been attracted by the trenches, which may have offered them food and also, perhaps, protection from the full force of the currents; because, even when the tidal streams were running, the water in the excavations was almost still. They proved to be permanent residents, remaining on the site all the year round, year after year.

On my final inspection dive, at sunset, the pout surrounded me so close and solidly packed that I couldn't even see water, let alone seabed or trench. They were the usual size, between 8 and 10 inches long (although a torpedo boat destroyer, H.M.S. *Velox*, which I had seen earlier that year, could boast some really giant pout at least 2 feet long). Freeing myself of them. I found myself 4 feet below the seabed with the side of the excavation above me, like a moon landscape without shadow. In the bottom of the trench was a light sprinkling of slipper limpet shells, newly drifted in by the current, and the first site proof of the "collection" theory. There was now a continuous trench for the full 38 feet of the guiderail—6 feet deep at the Wight end, 3 feet deep at the Southsea end and about 4 or 5 feet wide. The aqualungers had done the impossible and succeeded on their own. It put up morale 100 per cent. Before, we had all suffered from some form of the insidious "clay psychosis", the deep conviction that nothing would shift sufficient of this seabed this side of Christmas. It had been disheartening because it was all "overburden", recently deposited sediments of interest to oceanographers but having no archaeological significance.

There was one more big card to play in 1969. This resulted from contact with the Royal Engineers' Diving School at Marchwood, near Southampton. From time to time they held advanced courses for Diving Supervisors at Spithead and they were looking for a real project which they could usefully carry out, rather than put their men through dummy exercises. And they decided that the *Mary Rose*, being an historically important wreck and not a treasure ship, was just such a project. Not for the first time, nor for the last, were we to be grateful for the fact that King Henry VIII's battleship had carried guns and fighting men, but no treasure. The scheme, as the Royal Engineers planned it, was perfect from our point of view. Firstly, it would give five days' continuous working from a proper base, instead of hit-or-miss one-shot operations on a shoestring. Their plan was to use a low-profile "Z" Craft to carry a Coles crane which could move about the deck so as to position exactly the massive one-ton 8-inch air-lift which would do the digging. The landing craft itself would be held by temporary moorings. With sufficient advanced warning, many of our own divers would be able to join them in the inspection role, although the dates were all weekdays. Because of the risk of fog in October, I would mark up the site with a surface buoy one week previously. On a commercial costing, the resources to be employed were worth tens of thousands of pounds, and we still do not have anything as good as this. But inexorably, piece by piece, their excellent plan began to come apart at the seams.

The low-profile landing craft was taken out of service at short notice, and with it the chance of using a crane. Now, there was only an "RPL" available. This was a high-profile slab-sided landing craft which had tremendous windage and would therefore tend to drag at her moorings. A crane could not be used from it, and instead an immobile beam had to be rigged for the suspension of the one-ton air-lift. Then it proved impossible for the navy to supply the army with moorings, because they might create a navigational hazard when not in use. Although very willing to help, all the navy could do was loan a large can buoy to mark up the site in case of fog. And then the army had to bring their dates forward by one week, at the last moment, which ruined the leave-of-absence arrangements that our civilian divers had made, and cut to nil any chance I had of laying the can buoy well in advance in order to counter the risk of a cancellation or two from fog. Instead it had to be laid on the same morning as the RPL left Southampton, and that morning there rolled up a fog so dense that visibility came down to 150 feet and, because of the danger of being run down by shipping, we had to tie up to Spit Fort and wait for it to lift. When the sun eventually broke through the RPL *Eden*, steering on radar, had arrived before we had been able to lay the can buoy. As its sinker weighed 5 cwt., not including the chain, and there were only three of us in the boat, there was a delay before we sent it overboard to land 10 feet from the Southsea end of the JM3 trench. Meanwhile, the Royal Engineers tried out the one-ton air-lift, which was on loan to them, and the compressed air line split. By then, it was tea-time.

From now on, we were to operate from the *Eden*, which was moored at the Gunwharf by H.M.S. *Vernon*, the navy diving school. The Gunwharf was where John Deane had landed his guns from the *Mary Rose*, when the office of the Board of Ordnance had been situated there. Our first day out of there was also 21 October, Trafalgar Day, so if one was looking for omens, they were good. But apart from myself, I had only one diver; luckily, it was Pete Powell, one of the very best of Morrie Young's excellent Southampton team. And although there was a thick mist, the can buoy marked the site. I went up on the bridge to help navigate to it, with the 42-ft. hold of the 74-ft.-long landing craft lying in front and below me. This ample working area held a giant compressor, the heavy steel air-lift, a metal stormboat with outboard engine and the diving gear, and still had a lot of space left over. When the bow doors went down, the assault boat was launched out of it to take out some of the three anchors which, in lieu of moorings, would have to hold the landing craft in position. The doors, when down, made quite the best diving platform I had ever seen; except for its high sides with their excessive windage, this was an ideal craft for the job. The air-lift was rigged outboard on the starboard side from a heavy beam running across the top of the doors. Basically, it was a one-ton steel tube of 8-inch diameter fed at the lower end with compressed air via a rubber hose. The compressed air, expanding as it rose up the tube towards the surface, would exert a powerful suction effect on the seabed. But it had to be dropped plumb, which meant that the entire vessel had to be positioned so that the starboard end of the beam was directly above the particular part of the seabed it was desired to dig. And in the morning the *Eden* would not hold any position, let alone the one I wanted; she moved all the time with the tug of the currents.

But after the mealbreak, the R.E.s had her just right, lying along the JM3 trench, with the can buoy aft and the air-lift beam hanging, by my calculation, just clear of the wreck on the Isle of Wight side. The known length of the *Eden's* hold made a good measuring stick. Now, all we had to do was dig a quick hole to delimit the wreck area on the Wight side, then drop back 10 feet by paying out more anchor cable, for another dig which would be a "possible", then another 10 feet for a "probable", and so on. The current was now ebbing from Southampton Water, so it would automatically push us towards Southsea when we wanted it to, and the Southsea "marks" were now showing loud and clear in bright sunshine. I tried to explain this procedure to Mr. Stanley, the R.E.s' civilian diving instructor, an ex-navy man, and was highly gratified to be cut short. Normally, my explanations of the "W" feature and its navigational tie-ins produced dazed or incredulous expressions, particularly from academics. But Mr. Stanley took one look at the JM3 mark, and said, "Good one". The idea of dropping back along this fixed line took him about one-tenth of a second to grasp, and we were away, with Warrant Officer Dineen organising the teams of R.E. divers.

The air-lift began to fountain mud-stained water up to the surface, quickly producing a cavity 5 feet wide and 5 feet deep. After that, it dug itself down into the seabed for a depth of 17 feet, a firm negative and also an indication of the soft nature of the sediments to that depth. It was not stopped by an obstruction, it was turned off to avoid blockage. Bearing the "pinger" records in mind, I noted: "We could very well have a hull 25 feet deep." Then the air-lift was raised and we dropped back 10 ft. to the "possible" area for scattered wreckage or perhaps main structure, if the "W" was the wreck. Sergeant Ferguson, the R.E. diver, got down to about 8 feet here, producing a broad cavity at the top with a narrow hole at the bottom, like a funnel for pouring petrol. At this point, he stopped and came up to report trouble. From what he said, Pete Powell guessed that the air-lift had been stopped by something, and went down himself with a manual corer made by Morrie Young. This was a probe with a small coring head, designed to take tiny samples of an obstruction. By lying head down in the cavity, he could put the corer right down to 8 ft. where it hit a solid. This, he was sure, was wood, a judgement based on great experience in the building trade. In the core head were parts of tiny shellfish mixed with a few splinters of dark wood. He also probed around widely with a spear and met resistance about 9 feet down, which could not be penetrated more than a quarter of an inch. Very hard wood, he thought.

Lance-Corporal Flannigan then re-started the air-lift, with orders to widen the hole so that the solid could be inspected and was given a spear to probe with. Meanwhile, Powell sharpened up the metal lips of the corer, which had been bent by the timber of which it had taken a small outer sample. The tiny sea shells which had come up with the weed fragments suggested that the timber might have acted as a settling sur-face for spat, which would mean that it had been exposed to seawater at that time. But given another thirty minutes, all speculation would be over. We should know.

But after Flannigan had been working only a short time, the *Eden* began to drag off JM3 towards the Gosport mark, pulling the air-lift out of the cavity and towing it away across the seabed, digging a shallow trench all on its own, with Flannigan following it. Without moorings to haul in on, the Engineers were powerless to correct the swing in the short time left. Flannigan had begun by using the spear: "I probed around in a circle at the bottom of the hole and got solid—solid—solid every time." His interpretation was, " The air-lift made a hole as deep as it would go, till it hit something. Not a plank, but definitely solid timber."

There were still three days ahead of us, however, and on the first of them there was almost no wind, only a dense fog lying heavily on the water. But site location was no problem now; the *Eden* simply picked up the can buoy on her radar and we steered straight to it. This was a most frustrating day for Percy Ackland and myself. The *Eden* veered badly off site on several occasions, mostly from tide but once from a sudden breeze as well, but for one period of nearly three hours she lay perfectly positioned—and during this time the air-lift broke down three times and was three times repaired. This was unique in the experience of the Engineers. Only one useful cavity was dug, ten feet from the "port side mound" and definitely on top of the "W" feature, which immediately produced a solid obstruction eight feet down. Ackland used a hammer to drive home a probe into it and concluded it was a soft solid, possibly an iron concretion. And that was the sum total of the day's work.

For Thursday, 23 October I had managed to get a team together, instead of single divers, because I had thought that by this day we would be getting somewhere. We had two from Southsea, two from Southampton and two from Brighton B.S.-A.C. The forecast was for light winds Force 1 to 3 S.W. The direction was right, but the reality was Force 4 to 5, producing waves just a trifle too high for the landing craft to get her bow doors down without damage. We waited for the tide to turn and run with the wind, but there was no improvement, as the wind was rising and we were obviously in for a blow. So the last day was cancelled, leaving us all in an optimistic frame of mind. The dreaded "clay phychosis" resulting from digging with the relatively weak jets, which had made everyone think, "Maybe there's nothing there", had now given way, after powerful air-lift experience, to: "There's something there all right." Correspondence with George Bass and the Throckmortons had inured me to hair-raising tales of what happened with old, loaned machinery, and for light reading I could always browse through books on professional salvage where, on a bigger scale, the elements could always make or break the best-laid plans.

But the can buoy was still there, marking up the site, and I decided to risk just one more operation while we had this safeguard against the fog hazard still in position. The day before it was to be removed, Sunday, 2 November, provided an excellent tide, so I chose that date; I managed to squeeze a little more money out of our press friends to finance a second boat to take the helmet divers; and Dick Millerchip came along with Leslie Lemin in an inflatable, not just to dive but to act as safety boat and communicator between the two big boats, for I still had not learned how to walk on the water. In the pinnace *Gyron* was mounted the battered old compressor the helmet divers normally used (which ran without fault) with four helmet divers, S. J. Utley, Joe Davidson, Roy Mudey and Norman Coleborn. In Tony Glover's *M.F.V. Julie-Anne* (converted from a *Queen Elizabeth* lifeboat) was a Fire Brigade pump (and in four years' work no Fire Brigade machinery ever went unserviceable on us). George Clark and Andy Gallagher represented the Fire Brigade, I and Eric Sivyer represented Southsea branch, while Southampton fielded three of their best, Percy Ackland, Reginald Clouds-dale and Peter Powell. The teams were good—and they had to be. The early forecast of Force 3 to 4 westerly changed very late to Force 5–6, increasing to 8. That would have blown an inexperienced team to pieces, particularly in November, in view of what they had to do. It is no trick just to dive in this weather; carrying out, without moorings, a job for which moorings are required, is quite another matter.

With this the final operation of the year, and a short winter day as well, I had lowered my sights on the target. Probe contacts over 6 feet down were to be ignored, because there would be no time to uncover them. I had worked out a safe procedure with "stepped" trenches, to produce sufficient space at the bottom for a diver to lie down and saw off a sample of timber substantial enough to be dated by dendro-chronology. And the width at the top to do this 10 feet down was 20 feet at a minimum and 25 feet to be absolutely safe. A contact 8 feet down was still an impossible proposition: 6 feet was the absolute maximum. So I decided to swamp the area with oversize probe teams of aqualungers and keep the helmet divers for the static digging. But it was still a long chance, even probing in the bottom of excavations. The first probe team consisted of myself with a 5-ft. probe, Ackland with a 6-ft. probe and Powell with a 10-ft. probe.

Because wind and tide were both coming from the west, the boats were not rolling much, but they were pitching heavily and showing a lot of keel. I logged that: "The buoy was bucking and smashing and throwing up white water, the chain was shaking and jerking all the way down. Visibility on bottom a very clear 12 feet. Water warm for November." The 5-cwt. sinker was invisible under the mud, so Percy tied the end of his distance line to the chain; he would unreel this behind us as we flew forward on a three-man front. And here was a little navigation problem, for on the last day of the

Eden the bad weather had brought her into contact with the can buoy and she had dragged it out of position. I steered S.W., decided the current was running at a slight angle, and drifting me a little left, so steered a bit to the right—and there was the port side mound, large as life and intact (which it was no longer on JM3), so I was probably nearer to JM4. I carried on past the mound towards the starboard side and, fairly far over, came to a decently wide crater about 3 or 4 feet deep, representing the more untidy part of the dig by the mechanical excavator. I probed once into the accumulated sand layer in the bottom, and the blunt probe slid in easily to its full length. I moved left a few feet and probed again —solid. Only about 2 or 3 feet down. I could hardly believe my luck, and suspected a clay interface, but hammering on the probe with a knife failed to drive it in further. I beckoned Percy over, holding up, optimistically, only two fingers; he checked with a pointed probe, which stopped, and then he held up three fingers, a pessimistic 3 feet. I then beckoned Pete Powell, who had the 10-ft. probe and got him to test around—but he got no contacts at all down to 7 or 8 feet.

So we had a limited area solid, which could be a single piece of wreckage, the side of a wreck, or the ruins of the spar deck; or, indeed, almost anything, for a wreck rarely presents a flat surface. To find out what it was would take a helmet diver five minutes, using a jet for digging. At a pinch, it could have been done by hand-digging in a few hours. I was to wish I had given the order to hand-dig. But instead, I got Percy to mark it up by tying his distance line to a probe; so we now had a line from the can buoy chain to the "contact" along the bottom. I used the last of my air for a continuation of the original swim line, which revealed a short distance beyond a virgin seabed with a skate sitting on it. I grabbed the skate by the tail, then let it go again, reflecting that this was not the occasion to waste time in search of supper. As the skate rose up like a jetliner on take-off, Pete came down on it for the kill with his 10 ft. probe, then he too recollected that we had urgent business on hand.

The next stage was to mark the contact on the surface by attaching the line of a light buoy to the bottom probe. We now had two markers on it, one along the seabed, the other to the surface. Now it was George Clark's turn to run things and rig the water-jet. He had a strong line attached to the 56-lb. weight required to anchor the jet, then he had it suspended under a buoy with its tap open, swum by two divers in very heavy seas and a strongish current on the surface to the marker buoy, and then down the marker buoy line to the contact. The contact was now marked up three ways and while they were down there, Gallagher and Sivyer also forcibly probed around the contact, finding solid resistance in their turn. Then they returned to us, and Andy took the hose down along the heavy line leading to the 56-lb. weight, to which he would tie it. Once that was done, the pump could be started and we could begin.

The helmet divers' boat was riding easily and steadily in just the right position, in spite of a Force 6 wind and high waves with white horses. Our pump boat was riding easily and steadily just off her starboard side, near enough to make a single length of hose reach the contact and so prevent the twisting and turning of a long hose which occurred before when the boat had veered and shifted with shifts of wind and tide. All was still 100 per cent, and better than on many occasions in summer, for we all had that much more experience now. All was still well, even when the hose was fully out, lying on the surface and bowed in a half-circle with the push of the tidal stream. But as Andy swam with the nozzle further down the line to the weight, so the hose began to straighten. Probably this caused extra drag on our port side, possibly also the veering Force 6 wind may have had something to do with what happened next. Like a nervous horse, the pump boat went right out of control, dragging her anchor over to port and apparently about to collide with the helmet divers' boat. Tony Glover had the wheel hard over to correct, and his engine going, but it had absolutely no observable effect. This was disaster, pure and simple, for not only was the pump likely to be dragged bodily overboard by the hose but Andy Gallagher was down there in a tangle of dragging, moving lines.

Instantly, George Clark uncoupled the hose from the pump and some of the divers snatched the yellow line leading to the 56-lb. weight at the contact, and as we went reeling across the bows of the helmet divers' pinnace, threw it over to them and they caught it. We were still marked up, we still had a firm line to the contact, as well as two lighter lines. What we did not know for some minutes was that the anchor of the pump boat now dragged, perversely, on a line right across the contact, ripping up the yellow line, the distance line, the marker buoy line and dragging them in a crazy tangle together with the 56-lb. weight for some distance over the seabed. By quick thinking, from this crazy confusion at 45 feet, Andy Gallagher escaped and made for the stormy surface of the sea. We roared out to him to swim down tide to the can buoy and hold on to it. Then Millerchip went racing by in his inflatable and with Lemin leaning right over the side they picked Andy out of the water, very flushed, excited and pleased with himself.

Mr. Utley at once sent down one of his divers to inspect the damage, while we in the pump boat sorted ourselves out for another try. This time we moored to the can buoy, hoping it would not drag, and George intended to have the hose swum forward from there. I jumped—you could not step— into the inflatable and was carried across to the pinnace where again I had to take a flying leap over the water, making a splendid entrance on all fours, but undamaged. Then I listened with Utley to the crackling telephone as his diver reported the situation on the seabed: all lines carried away, contact no longer marked. Utley decided to let two of his divers probe around thoroughly on their own, while I went back to the pump boat to organise another aqualung probe team to relocate the contact. I put in Percy Ackland to lead this and, against all odds, he succeeded. Taking out a new distance line from the can buoy chain, he found the drag mark made by the 56-lb. weight, and followed it into the crater where we had found the contact. And then his air ran out. So, assuming his companion must have seen the drag mark he had been following, he handed over the distance line, expecting him to mark up as before. But his companion, perhaps following the beat of his flippers too closely, had not seen the drag mark and merely assumed that he was to carry on with the search. Finding nothing, he came up, bringing the unused distance line back with him. And that, I thought, really was that for 1969.

So I suggested a final survey of the excavations, in this really excellent visibility, so that we could note in 1970 what changes had taken place over the winter. With a sigh of relief, George Clark abandoned his onerous job as pump controller and began to suit up. He took a really solid, long probe which produced one contact only—a quite enormous turbot so fat it would feed a whole family. I took a probe and a camera and went over the whole trench system, but first heading out for JM4 to see the helmet diver at work. He was busy probing, surrounded by a cloud of muck raised by his own feet. All helmet divers reported 4 feet visibility, all aqualung divers reported 12 feet visibility—and here was the reason. But whereas, once the helmet divers were down they stayed down, the aqualungers were up and down all the time because of frequent bottle changes. Then I altered course to pick up the JM3 trench and for the first time saw it in good visibility and unobscured by the clouds raised by jetting: "It was long, straight, wide, continuous, exactly aligned and in one place 5 feet deep." The sub-surface buoy was still holding up out of the mud the Southsea end of the guiderail. There was a light fill of sand and some pockets of dead weed, but what most noticeably had collected in the trench were modern anchorage artefacts, mostly plastic cups, polythene bags, and so on. The principle of collection made me believe that light artefacts would drift inside a wreck, as well as collecting in the scour-pits.

The opposite principle to drift, that of direct descent, was illustrated best by a cup half-protruding from the nearly vertical clay wall of the trench. It was Woolworth's, circa 1920, and it had sunk nearly 18 inches below the seabed in what could have been but a few short years only. Although the light was now poor, I managed to photograph this and other relevant items. However, the most interesting of the deposited artefacts was my own snorkel, lost in a tide struggle earlier in the year, and now picked up by Leslie Lemin. The trench area was generally tidied up of stray lines, and so on, and indeed a certain rivalry had set in between the helmet divers and the aqualungers; no one was going to give up first while some useful work still remained to be done. We therefore remained on site until sunset, with a full Force 8 gale about to set in. The aqualungers packed up ten minutes before the helmet divers did, and then both boats ran for Portsmouth Harbour, although we in the pump boat had left our cars at Langstone. No one was going to get in over the bar now. It was a defiant touch to the end of the year, for we knew that we had again lost the battle of the winter even before it had begun.

Although there was clearly a lot of deeply buried wreckage in the area, we had nothing like enough evidence to expect support from London where, as we knew, they were still saying, not only that we were in the wrong place but that we were wandering wildly all over Spithead without a clue as to where we were. They had already turned down our application for money to build an air-lift of our own, and we could expect no help whatever from anyone but ourselves. From this, and from a close analysis of what was wrong with our operation, the plan for 1970 evolved.

CHAPTER FOURTEEN

THE
MARY ROSE ASSOCIATION

We made a detailed technical analysis of the shortcomings of 1969 and, ignoring technicalities, what it boiled down to was lack of moorings and lack of money. All our major troubles were on the surface; any underwater problems which cropped up were soon solved. Our assets consisted of the hard core of the diving team which had been built up over the years and which had proved they could withstand continual disappointment, astonishing runs of bad luck, and a degree of danger not encountered in ordinary sport diving. It was on this that we decided to build.

We formed ourselves into the *Mary Rose* Association, a group confined to those actually doing the work at Spithead. Each man paid a one pound subscription to start with, and agreed to pay an equal share of the costs of boat hire. Tony Glover, who had become very interested in the project and was to be an important member from now on, made the thing possible by offering the use of his boat at a much reduced rate. We would therefore have a big, fast, beamy boat with a sheltered cabin at one end and a large working area at the other. The latter catered for the machinery we would have to mount, the former allowed cold, wet divers to warm up a trifle before their next dive. This boat was based on Flathouse Quay, just north of Portsmouth Naval Dockyard, and no longer would there be the long trips from Langstone, the doubt about getting back in bad weather, and the exhausting struggles from the car park to the pontoon with heavy equipment. We would have to restrict ourselves to neap tides giving the best possible chance of success, but now we could plan a proper working programme in advance to utilise the best months of the year, instead of trying to cater to the whims of city-insulated people who did not realise that, on the coast, there was a difference between July and November.

But moorings also we must have, or all this might be thrown away to no purpose, as before. Proper, buoyed moorings, secure and easy to pick up, were then out of the question. Instead, with a good deal of advice from Bob Lusty, a form of cheap-and-cheerful ground mooring was devised. The Southampton divers were able to get hold of ten 1-cwt. concrete blocks, to which they attached ring-bolts. From a most helpful local source we obtained two 100-ft. lengths of wire hawser. A single mooring then consisted of five 1-cwt. blocks strung on a 100 ft. hawser at about 15 ft. intervals. From another keenly interested local source we obtained two long lengths of manila rope. One was to be attached to each 5-block mooring, as the actual connection between the mooring and the boat. After use, the free ends would be left in the trench, ready for picking up next time. Such moorings would have a damping effect, Bob told us, because when heavy seas brought the strain on the manila line, then the first block would lift off the bottom, and possibly the next one also, giving a certain flexibility to counter the lack of any real weight, because concrete is light in water. On Tony's advice, one mooring would be laid east of the site, and one west, a trifle north of centre so that in average conditions of wind and tide, the boat would be held bow-and-stern close to the JM3 trench. Bob Lusty could not be with us, but he told us how to lay them, so that each string of blocks fell to the bottom in the right place, in a dead-straight line, and with the wire taut. With more advice from Tony, we novices did it first go, and I was able to report on 16 May: "Two adequate moorings smoothly and accurately laid. Luck ran with us all the way. Site proved to be exactly as predicted: trenches filled in only a little and with slight blurring of the edges. Sub-surface buoy OK." That was last year's buoy, marking the Southsea end of the guiderail.

Weed had gathered thickly on the short line of this buoy, and was streaming out in the current, together with a long length of unexposed 35 mm. film. Morrie Young, diving initially to find this buoy, had reported failure, but had noticed a length of 35 mm. film on the ground. Visibility was poor and he had obviously been within two feet of his objective, without seeing it. A better illustration of our site-marking problems could hardly be offered. Those we intended to try to solve by driving numbered metal stakes into the bottom of the trench at 10-ft. intervals, linked by a ground tape, so that all probe "contacts" could be plotted afterwards. On this occasion we had time only for a little probing. I bumped into Percy Ackland (by following his distance line) while he was investigating a contact. He was making finger gestures to indicate depth of contact, and the number of fingers being flicked at me was incredible—I thought at least a dozen. What he had got in fact were two contacts, one at 5–6 feet, the other at 7 feet, below trench bottom.

This was the nature of our horrible problem, that enormous labour was required to investigate just one contact; and that we could work only once a fortnight. I had met George Bass in London the previous January, in connection with a chapter I was writing for a book of which he was the editor, and he put on paper a considered comparison between Mediterranean sites and ours:

> I think that my group is now very expert in mapping and digging wrecks which are in deep, clear water with little sand overburden. We have never faced a situation remotely similar to yours—open sea, thick clay, poor visibility—so our experiences would be almost meaningless. We put down 16 to 20 divers twice a day, in pairs, 6 days a week, for three months at a time. But with our little air-lifts (4″ diam. P.V.C. irrigation pipe), even three at a time, it still takes us several years to do a wreck 65 feet long and covered by from 6 inches to two feet of sand. Our methods wouldn't begin to dent your site, and as our mapping methods all depend on photography now they would be of no use (we need to get 15 to 20 feet above the wreck to take the pictures).* I would like to be helpful, but wouldn't have any better ideas than you've already thought up. I felt bad that I couldn't suggest a thing!

According to George Clark (and virtually everyone else with similar experience) the quickest method of shifting clay and mud was to break it up with a hard, pencil-like water-jet and

---

* For optimum picture quality, with minimum distortion, photographs taken 15 feet from an underwater object require a visibility of 150 feet. For a totally blank result, focus on 15 feet in 15 feet visibility. —*Author's note.*

then suck up the sediments with a big air-lift. We had had
plans for a P.V.C. air-lift (copied from Bass and Throckmorton models) on the drawing board since 1968, had applied
three times for finance to a body supposedly interested in
nautical research, and been three times turned down. We
found this odd, because it was only London academics who
brushed aside the evidence; the Research Laboratory for
Archaeology and the History of Art at the University of
Oxford had earlier in the year invited me to lecture on the
sonar investigation we had carried out. But in May 1970 we
did not at first even have water-jets, because George Clark
was away on a long course. Mr. Utley had gone to Gibraltar
and, in any event, with only a one-boat mooring, and the
memory of what had happened last November to a boat without moorings, I did not feel like risking the helmet divers.
Bob Lusty, who had just been appointed diving officer of
H.M.S. *Reclaim*, to replace an officer who had had an accident
at 450 feet, would only be with us from time to time. This
was awkward, because the effective use of these tools depends
initially on having a knowledgeable man with the capability
of organising small work teams from scratch; and George and
Bob were the only people with the appropriate experience.

On 30 May, for the second of what I called *Mary Rose*
"self-floating" (i.e. diver-financed) operations, we had no fire
pump, but we did have Bob Lusty. The intention was simply
to tape out and stake out the trench, prior to probing, and
I dived first to be sure of best visibility, carrying the ex-
Fishbourne tape, accompanied by Percy Ackland towing a
surface buoy. We found the trench to be now some 90 feet
long, the 38-ft. guiderail trench jetted in 1969 probably
having funnelled the water into the untidy remainder of the
excavation and so completed our work for us. Visibility was
good and it was easy to find the Southsea end of the guiderail,
tie off the tape to it, and then swim it up to the Isle of Wight
end, unreeling as we went. On the way, we passed the "deep"
contact found by Percy two weeks before, and he left his surface buoy on it as a temporary marker, to be replaced later
with a stake marked "A". This lay about 7 feet below trench
bottom and was out of our reach at present. Morrie Young
and Ray McLaren then put in the first six numbered stakes
at 10-ft. intervals, pulling the tape taut against its tendency

to bow out in the current. The careful log now being kept by Ackland shows that this took 9 minutes, surface to surface. The first probe team, Reg Cloudsdale and Andy Gallagher, had strict instructions to start from the Wight end and probe in towards where I thought the starboard side might be, near Deep Contact "A", to ignore any other deep contacts, but to mark up anything found at the 3 to 5 ft. level. Andy surfaced after 10 minutes to report: "Found contact 87 ft. about 2 ft. down". That is, 87 feet along the tape, in the Wight end, 2 feet below trench bottom and about 7 feet below original sea-bed level. Reg struck a discouraging note; he wasn't very sure about the contact. Andy dived again and reported "contact not very large". Then Bob Lusty went down, and dug himself into the bottom of the trench, using his whole body. Seventeen minutes later he surfaced to report: "Definitely wood in blue clay". He had a small sample to prove it and had left a probe to mark the place.

An Isle of Wight team turned up, but as they had a number of novices aboard, I asked them merely to probe at a different point, not dig. They did so and delivered a negative report. Morrie Young then came up and reported: "Tape broken away". This was the tape I had laid, which actually led to the contact. It was not hard to guess that a novice had swum into it, become entangled, and tried to thrash his way free. For a full 60 seconds, indoctrinated now by years of last-minute undeserved disaster, we all flinched. Not again!

Then Morrie asked for a saw, got it, and disappeared. Even the saw was an admission that we feared an inexplicable defeat within minutes, and wanted some shred of proof before it was too late. But nothing happened, then or afterwards, except steady and ultra-cautious excavation. The moorings always held the boats above and the markers always led to the desired place on the seabed. On a shoestring, we had solved the really basic problems.

I carried out the last dive to inspect progress and mark up the contact in a trawl-proof way. There had been much speculation as to whether the timber was a beam or something else, part of the ship's structure or a scattered piece of wreck-age. After so much mere mud-shifting, it was an indescribably satisfying feeling to swim down into the trench and then over the lip of the long, narrow excavation at the bottom of it,

and even in the dim underwater light of evening, to see unmistakable timber below me—and ship timber at that. It was
not in cold fact a dramatic sight, because only 2 or 3 feet
horizontally of the timber was exposed. It was clearly a plank,
with both ends still buried; about a foot across and 2 to 3
inches thick, but so worn that these measurements were only
approximate. There were a number of regular holes in it,
between 1 and 2 inches wide. I reported: "My impression was
that this was not part of the ship structure *in situ*, but a piece
broken off or collected." The big surprise, first revealed by
Morrie's small sawn sample, was that the plank had been
massively attacked by Teredo. I had never seen, anywhere in
those parts of the Solent I knew well, any sign of Teredo at
all; but we were all convinced that we were looking at the
signs of their work now. The plank, which lay at an angle
between 7 and 8 feet below the height of the original seabed,
was embedded in the upper layer of a clay stratum, distinctly
different to the light sediments which had overlain it. The
attack must have taken place a very long time ago. This was
clearly important news for marine naturalists.

The careful excavation of the plank and its eventual lifting took four days' work spread out over six weeks. There
were no cancellations. If the weather was poor, it was either
on the day before or on the day after the date of the planned
operation. The timber itself was totally hand-dug, although
we used spades and later a jet to clear off the overburden
from above one end, which went in under the side of the
trench, so that there was a high, almost vertical wall above it.
The slow excavation was deliberate, because the detail of
what was around the plank was more important than the
plank itself; further, the entire team needed to be drilled
into looking at objects in this manner. The simple facts which
emerged were that the plank was lying inclined in the clay
layer, with the northern end broken at some time long past;
that the upper face had been more massively attacked by
marine borers than the underside; that at the southern,
unbroken end there was a concentration of small iron concretions, probably nails; and that what looked like a shoe-
buckle but was actually part of a ship's lantern circa 1700
was found under the plank. The deduction was, that the
plank had been broken off the wreck long ago and represented

only an outlying item of scattered wreckage. Other observations were that the excavation filled with a weed layer up to 3 feet deep and that the walls of the main trench were becoming honeycombed with small caves dug by fish and crabs at regular intervals at regular levels, looking rather like the windows of a block of flats. Indeed, when I came down to photograph the excavation at various stages, blenny-type fish and hermit crabs would come scuttling "into camera" as if crying "Cheese!" When the plank finally came up in a sling, I went down past it to observe and photograph the "bed" where it had lain. This was of flattened and lightly scored clay, and although I looked minutely the only significant artefact in sight was a car key belonging to the current diving officer of Southsea B.S.–A.C. He was relieved to get it back.

I also found that the divers had celebrated the occasion by playing a joke on me. Directly beside the excavation, our spade was thrust into the ground and beside it was balanced a triangular painted sign of the familiar "Men at Work" type showing a labourer with a shovel. Above, amid grins, Morrie Young was making an examination of the plank before wrapping it in the vast sheet of tough polythene I had brought along for the purpose. He thought it English oak of great age, from the main hull structure rather than the castles, although its poor condition made its original dimensions difficult to reconstruct. It had been fastened to the frames by trenails— big wooden pins of 1½-inch diameter, with oak wedges driven in to secure them. He thought the spacing of the holes indicater 12-inch frames. Although disputed, these deductions proved to be correct; and the iron-nail concretions also were significant, in that the planks were initially "hung" with small iron nails, before being "fastened" by trenails.

The plank came up at 4 p.m. and by 7 p.m. it was with Margaret Rule at Westbourne where we placed it in the mill stream which runs through the grounds of her house. This was standard "holding" treatment for some types of organic material, before going into her P.E.G. tank at the Fishbourne laboratory. The fresh water washes off the salt and keeps the material stable, whereas if left to dry out, it would shrink and crack. Next day I took some small samples to the Marine Biology Centre at Ferry Point, Hayling Island, where I learned that I had missed by two weeks one of the world's foremost experts on the Teredo, Professor Ruth Turner of Harvard University. However, Dr. Brian Morton advised me to get in touch with Patrick Board of the Central Electricity Research Laboratories at Leatherhead in Surrey, who had developed extraordinarily fine techniques for X-raying Teredo tunnels in wood so that the habits of the creature could be studied accurately. Dr. Morton could tell me only that the Teredo was always present, potentially, but that he had had difficulty in finding actual specimens. Everything had to be just right for the Teredo, otherwise it would not survive, whereas borers like the gribble were tougher. Possibly conditions, such as water temperature, had been more favourable to them hundreds of years ago than they were now; but there were no records, so no one could be certain. However, one of the burrows in our timber was a foot long; he had never seen such a heavy infestation as that.

Pat Board came down to see Margaret Rule right away and they divided the plank between them (photographs and drawings having already been made); Mr. Board was to take the bad end (with the best Teredo tunnels), Mrs. Rule was to have the good end (for wood conservation tests with P.E.G.). In short, the plank was expendable. But first it had to be sawn in two, and as the outer surface had the consistency of soft, black, flaky cheese, no trouble was expected. But as the saw bit deeper, there came an unexpectedly harsh noise—like the sound of steel cutting sound timber! And this was because the heart wood of even this really decayed piece really was sound, producing genuine sawdust! Further, some parts of actual Teredo were still present.

The X-ray pictures were excellent, confirming Mr. Board's diagnosis of the remains of one long-dead beast, that it was of the species called *Nototeredo norvagica*, not *Teredo navalis*. According to Ruth Turner's *Survey and Illustrated Catalogue of the Teredinidae*, 1966, this species had world-wide distribution in fully marine conditions, from tropical waters to cold northern seas. There were thought to be at least a score of different Teredo species in British waters and although some had probably been introduced in the bottoms of ships, many must be local in origin. The real problem now was to attempt to date our Teredo. The basic facts about the beast appeared to be that before it could get a footing in hardwoods such as oak, the timber had to be softened up for five years by the action first of bacilli and then of fungi, and that even light silting might stop matters at fungi stage. And, as I had frequently observed, wrecks did sometimes collect a light layer of silt on portions lying proud of the seabed.

Putting this through the computer of combined historical and observed fact, gave a working theory that we had the oldest Teredo in England, possibly alive when Good Queen Bess was young. (My daughters were already making fanciful drawings, based on the X-rays, of their favourite animal, he whom they called Terence, the Tudor Teredo.) The firmest part of the computation was largely Tudor, based on: 1545 —*Mary Rose* sank; 1569—William Monson born; 1623— publication of Monson's Tracts, in which he stated that he had at one time, with his own eyes, seen "part of the ribs" of the *Mary Rose*. Punching in the depth-data, and assuming he did not dive, that gave a really substantial wreck at the time he saw her, and that excluded Terence entirely, or so I thought. (Mr. Board thought she might have sunk because her timbers were rotten from Teredo.) Feeding in the collapse of the upper part of the hull from gribble at least, plus sundry rippings and tearings from the instant salvagers of 1545–9, one now had a much reduced wreck by 1600, less of an obstruction to the currents, therefore a falling off in the force of the eddies, and therefore a gradual closing up and filling in of the scour-pits round her. I did not see it at the time, but I could have deduced a possible roll of the hull into the starboard scour-pit, thus largely filling it up and correcting the heel to port. The plank could have been ripped off by the salvagers or by an anchor later, but I felt that it had settled inside the disturbance area surrounding the wreck, and then been quickly covered with sediment which would have killed off all marine borers. Inserting the fact of present burial inside a clay layer covered by some 5 feet of light overburden, I rather plumped for 1600–1700. (Margaret Rule regarded the clay more lightly and thought that the wood could have been re-exposed as late as the nineteenth century; but she had not examined that clay layer face to face.)

All that was really sure was that, at some time past, but most probably in late Tudor times, there had been a very different underwater environment at Spithead than there was today. Possibly the water temperature rose higher, and entirely without the assistance of the Central Electricity Board, whose new power station at Marchwood, near Southampton, was reputed to produce environmental changes. I was slightly sceptical, because I had experience dating back to 1958 of literally skin-diving in the warm water outflow of the Portsmouth station at Sally Port, which had an intermittent flow and a narrow funnel which bent with the prevailing current. You could submerge in the narrow, warm-water band and literally punch your arm through a warm wall into the cold water outside. The bass and mullet loved it as much as I did, but any static creature was going to find the temperature changes from hour to hour a little bit unsettling, I thought. The human body can adapt to a much wider range of warm and cold than many marine creatures, which are fairly closely keyed in to a particular temperature.

"'Terence'" was the first item of pure research to emerge that year, to be followed closely by another scientific surprise, and to their credit the local press gave him a write-up. But the national media could hardly be expected to treat one worm-eaten plank as "news", when the pattern of "underwater archaeology" had been set for them by expeditions grubbing for gold coins and bronze guns. Consequently, we were grateful that Portsmouth Corporation voted us a grant of £100 towards costs. This always was, and still is, the fundamental difficulty of obtaining backing for a serious project: that you have to be serious, and that there is no immediate bonanza for the backers.

But while Terence was still having his photograph taken, I was seriously accosted at Southsea branch clubhouse regarding the plank, news of the discovery having just leaked out, and quizzed as to whether or not I had properly recorded the timber *in situ*. The assumption was, that we had only just found it, and might not be able to find it again (Spithead being large, and a plank quite small); but as the man who had been able to return at will to the diving officer's car key at Spithead, I felt quite huffed, so I assured everyone that their suspicions were correct—we would be quite incapable of finding that plank at Spithead again. This showed how an "inside story" might well be written in the future, for in principle I never briefed all and sundry on how to find anything on the site. Newcomers were simply told to swim down a particular buoy line to do a particular job of work at a particular place. At this stage "need to know" was the essential criterion, because everyone tends to talk in the club bar, and so only the leaders had a copy of the site plan; few people knew that the first dives were always a search to pick up the mooring lines, which had to be left free instead of secured on the bottom to a ring, as one would normally do, because such an arrangement would be guaranteed to collect both anchors and trawls.

But almost immediately I made myself unpopular with quite a different section of the branch—those interested in a little light salvage. The cause was UB-21, which had now been found just beyond the position where Harknett and I had seen outlying wreckage in 1966. Harknett himself said he thought there was a torpedo in the starboard bow tube and took me out to obtain photographic evidence. The place was a photographer's paradise and it was easy to obtain pictures of the warhead, because the tube door was open. One could also nip round the back and have a look down the loading bay, for someone had cracked that submarine wide open. But I was terrified by the banging and clanging that was going on—rather like Wotan's Smithy underwater—where a team from another diving boat were hard at work obtaining souvenirs. Pausing only to pick up a lobster, I fled and hid behind the engine room. The explosion came a few nights later, at the clubhouse, where I was told to my face that it was not a torpedo in the tube; and some even doubted that it was a U-boat at all. The first group seemed to take the view that to find a torpedo in a torpedo tube was totally unexpected and that it was much more likely to contain either a double-decker bus or a ticket to the circus; while the latter group simply assumed that a U-boat was much too exotic a vessel to have been sunk anywhere near prosaic Portsmouth. This was so much like the attitude of the London academics, that the explosion took place there and then. I got on the "hot" line to Bob Lusty and explained the position, adding that up to three diving boats at any one time were working the site, so that if the thing went off the casualty list would be very high.

After that, things moved. Harknett and I met his team

from *Reclaim* on site and showed them the warhead. Lusty thought there was a good chance that the explosive had started to crystallise and therefore was unstable, likely to go up from the least cause. I gave him my list of vital statistics for UB-21, which had been launched in 1915 at Blohm & Voss, Hamburg (where I had made my early helmet dives into the River Elbe), had carried two 20-inch tubes, and had been sunk in 1920 after surrendering in 1918. The list and Bob's report went to the Flag Officer Spithead, who passed it on to *Vernon* for action. Harknett and I went out again and met the *Vernon* team on site, showed them the warhead and learned that it was so far gone that the explosive was open to the sea and could blow merely from wave action. It was a G.7 torpedo with a 200-kilogram (about 450 lbs.) explosive charge, about two-thirds of which had washed out. It made a nice bang, all the same, and killed numbers of large bass which had been nearby or actually in the hull. Solemnly, the *Vernon* lads said that they must be the first to dive afterwards, in case anything had hung fire. After 20 minutes, all the bass were Navy, and it was our turn.

The sand leading up to the U-boat had been turned black and all the sand ripples had had their tops flattened. Steel had been cut as with a knife. However, most of the boat was still there, but looking very strange because its camouflage of algae, seaweed and so on had been stripped off. Now the steel was gleaming metal instead of rusting junk and one could easily identify a bow-plane, the conning tower, and other items. The only souvenir I brought back from the wreck was a piece of silk which had encased a pipe; the material had been exposed to rusty water for fifty years and was brown-stained but otherwise in excellent condition.

There was a little technological spin-off for the *Mary Rose*, however, the loan of a small air-lift for experimental purposes. This was to open the next phase of excavation, which was basically air-lifting, with jets used only occasionally for special purposes.

CHAPTER FIFTEEN

DOWN TO THE "W" FEATURE

When I had written to Peter and Joan Throckmorton in 1968 for advice on constructing an archaeological air-lift, I had included a request for a list of the most likely faults and troubles. Joan had replied, thoughtfully: *"What can go wrong?* Oh, ho, ho, ho. Here I am on solid ground." Then followed a long, and, as we discovered, most accurate analysis of all the tantrums these air-suction tubes were liable to throw; plus the conclusion that knowing, in theory, what was wrong was of absolutely no use at all in putting things right. That was a matter of mere experience.

So I cadged for one day a miniature air-lift consisting of a 2½-inch-diameter plastic tube 10 feet long, powered by a small compressor which fed air down through a rubber line to the bottom of the tube. The air would then rise up the tube, expanding as it went, creating a suction effect at the bottom. At this size, I hoped that all our troubles would be little ones.

The main tool would be the water-jet, however, and the target was Deep Contact "A". This appeared to be limited in area and so probably represented only more scattered wreckage, but it was at an intriguing depth and in investigating it we were moving methodically along the JM3 trench from the Isle of Wight end towards Southsea so that, sooner or later, we must hit the "W" feature and find out what it really was.

While the jetting went on, Ray McLaren and I swam the air-lift tube and hose down towards the digger, intending to see if it would get rid of the sediments he was stirring up. Then Ray had ear trouble and I carried on alone, holding the air-lift tube over my shoulder like a rifle at the slope and with one hand on the fire hose leading to the jet. This was to be a very good comparison of these tools. The first sign of the jet work was a white cloud of murk "whiteout"), which meant trailing one finger along the seabed to try to feel when you

came to the trench. Then there was a colour change of the
murk from white to black ("blackout"). Occasionally, the
whirling cloud broke up and one could look down a kind of
tunnel probably about 6 feet down inside the seabed by now,
so I stopped at the trench edge for a trial of the midget air-
lift. I turned the tap on and sucked at various distances from
the seabed and found that, although it could not clear the
muck being stirred up ahead, it did improve the visibility.
That is, whereas the jet made the worker unable to see what
he was working at, the air-lift actually improved vision. At
this tiny size, it was eminently controllable and selective,
capable of really delicate work. I tried it out on the local fauna
in the trench and reported:

> I spotted a small crab among the slipper limpets and
> moved the end of the tube over his back. ZING! BLAM!
> SWOOSH! and he had gone, taking a fast ride up the
> tube, and presumably being released in something of a
> state 8 feet up and down tide. Then I started on the slipper
> limpets, and a stream of them followed the crab heaven-
> wards. WHOOSH! ZING! BLAM! OOUCH! One might
> go into business with this, charging the crustacea and
> mollusca for a quick ride up the fun-machine, sampling all
> the thrills of the seaside.

The beauty of the thing was that its power was controllable
in two ways. Basically, by turning the tap, but also by varying the height of the tube above the seabed. At a certain
height above a crab, it did not move the crustacean at all, but
just before it touched his back—ZING! BLAM! SWOOSH!
and he was gone. If one wished, one could use merely a touch
of power, so that the effect on the sediments was minute. One
could put a grid across the bottom, just in case, but the trick
was not to let the air-lift dig itself into the ground, where it
was liable to blockage, but to hold it always above the seabed
at the appropriate sucking distance. Easy at this size, we
should have to learn how to perform the feat with a much
larger and more powerful machine.

However, we hit the "W" feature on 8 August, using jets
alone. On my first inspection, I took down my hand-spear
painted as surveying pole and probe combined and took
rough measurements. The main trench was only about $3\frac{1}{2}$ feet

deep at this point, but the shaft being driven to the Deep "A" was down a further $3\frac{1}{2}$ to 4 feet. It had nearly vertical sides and was only 6 feet wide. A quick calculation showed that this was a classic cave-in situation, so the next order must be to widen, not deepen. Then I lay there and just looked, rather like Rodin's statue with an aqualung on. I reported:

> I inspected the walls for stratification. Near the top and some 4 feet from original seabed level, there was a marked black discoloration. I took a sample of this, which felt fibrous to the touch. It proved to be the remains of an old weed bed, and consisted of: weed holdfasts only (no fronds) and some part of their attachments—small fragments of glass mixed with tiny pebbles and tiny molluscs. This evidence of past organic activity and the presence of some major collection area was "locked in" under at least 4 feet of mud and clay.

And on my second inspection dive, after further digging had taken place, I noticed little puffs of sediment bursting up through the clay, and actually managed to protograph one of these as it erupted. I thought this might be caused by the decaying organic matter, building up gas which was trapped by the clay layer above until our jets removed most of it and the compressed gas was able to burst through.

On a vaster geological time-scale, this is the principle of the North Sea gas fields. But in the case of a wreck, the organic material would be laid down in response to the insertion of a man-made object into the seabed. Drift weed would collect almost at once in and around the wreck, and also around any outlying wreckage and in the scour-pits particularly. This was not theory. Only a few days before I had been looking down an open hatch in the deck of UB-21 and the interior of the submarine was a mass of dead weed; and, when excavation had restarted on the Deep "A", there had been a two-foot-deep layer of driftweed in the bottom of the shaft, actually touching that much older weed layer. But quite apart from "collected" material, a wreck provides the necessary attachment surfaces for the establishment and growth of algae, weed, shellfish and many other life forms, which are continually dying off and being renewed.

Knowing that I was sticking my neck out, I wrote down

a preliminary conclusion, that: "The 'W' feature shown by the sub-mud sonar at the known position of the *Mary Rose*, is NOT the *Mary Rose*—it is a layer of compacted laminaria holdfasts (seaweed "roots") at least 3–4 feet deep, as shown on the pinger profiles". In the light of this theory, I reviewed the old argument:

> Is the "W" feature a genuine representation of the hull *in situ* (in which case the hull has opened out like an old banana skin); or, alternatively, is it merely the "upper interface" presented by the wreck to the sub-mud scanner? I now assume, provisionally, that the "W" feature as shown is a true representation of the overlying weed layer, that the hull is below it and reasonably intact, and that the keel may well be down on the solid geological layer at 35–40 ft. sub-mud. In this case, we virtually have a *Vasa*. The above is provisional, because the number of people who have actually dug underwater in an archaeological context is small, the number of those who have dug down to a buried wreck (as distinct from uncovering more of a part-buried wreck of which the upper portion is showing proud of the seabed) is smaller still, and those who have done the latter in U.K. waters is nil, apart from ourselves. The use of sub-mud sonar for archaeological prospection is, of course, in a similarly elementary state.

As soon as I could, I tried the new theory on John Mills, and he jumped at it. He said that a layer of gaseous mud was exactly the sort of thing which would show prominently on sub-mud sonar as an anomaly. Unknown to me, Peter Throckmorton had been carrying out pinger surveys with Professor Edgerton during 1969 and 1970 on Mediterranean wrecks; and when I met him again in 1971 his evidence was interesting: some half a dozen wrecks had shown only vaguely on sub-mud sonar—none had come over as a distinct anomaly. But two others had. The *Congo*, burned in the 1880s, had shown "beautifully". She had had a cargo of raisins. The *Heraclea*, bombed in 1941, had shown "fairly well". She had carried a cargo of wheat. The implications were obvious.

As well as a Tudor Teredo, we now seemed to have Tudor (and possibly Stuart) seaweed. But, assuming the new theory was correct, there was a vital difference between Peter's wrecks and ours. His decaying organic matter was cargo, probably largely confined to the hulls, unless there had been a lot of spillage. But if our sonar interface was collected weed, not wood, then the pinger presumably could not tell the difference between dead weed lying over and inside the wreck, and dead weed which had collected around it. Therefore our Deep Contact "A", overlain by compacted weed (and containing wood also as we later found out), was not necessarily the main hull at all. It could be merely scattered wreckage. That is, the careful sonar map in three dimensions, which I had so painstakingly worked out and kept amending as new facts came in, was merely a map of the *Mary Rose* site, not of the wreck itself. This had always been true of the sidescan picture, which so clearly showed the surrounding "disturbance area", but it now looked as if the "W" feature also would have to be treated in the same way, as a rough chart of the sub-mud "disturbance" layers. In fact, although I did not suspect it then, my novel three-dimensional site map, far from being overbold, was faulty in that I had not been bold enough. There was a further indication, of actual hull, which I did not then manage to interpret, purely from my own inexperience and the lack of comparative work at the time.

The immediate impact of the new theory was deep pessimism. It was horridly possible that the wreck lay deeper than we thought; and I now knew of a case off the north-east coast where a modern steel vessel had been located under 16 feet of overburden by a suction dredger and, for a time, the salvagers had thought she simply was not there. And our digging powers were strictly limited. So far from being able to run parallel trenches, even the JM3 was not fully effective, because it was not deep enough to expose the weed strata along its whole length, which would soon have proved or disproved the new theory, let alone expose deep contacts for an analysis of actual wreckage.

We had our first full-size air-lift in operation on 15 August. It had been built on 12 August as a result of interest in the project by William Selwood Ltd., a plant-hire firm near Southampton. One of their engineers, Peter Aitcheson, put it together from materials already on the premises, based on a moderate-sized compressor capable of being manhandled into Tony Glover's boat. The suction tube was of 6-inch-diameter semi-flexible plastic material, in three sections which fitted together and totalled 33 feet. Because the tube was light, it was easy to handle in the boat and in the water, but would have to be anchored by a heavy weight on a line, and would require two divers to control it. For archaeological excavation, both Bass and Throckmorton had shown that a light plastic air-lift (theirs were rigid P.V.C.) was much superior to the solid-metal tube type used by salvagers, as this sits on the bottom of its own weight and could cause damage. Our air-lift could be held clear of the seabed and moved easily over an area dictated by the length of the rope attached to the weight. With this powerful equipment, we hoped to widen and deepen the JM3 trench in an orderly manner, so as to expose contacts in a trench rather than by digging shafts down to them.

That first day was a dream. When set to widening the sides of the JM3, the air-lift simply ate seabed in a regular manner, producing straight lines and vertical faces. Peter Throckmorton had advised against putting a spoil cage or bag on the upper end of the tube, because peculiar things were likely to happen; so I took his tip and simply searched downtide for the "spoil area", which made itself obvious from its different pattern and texture. The tube had in fact picked up a small piece of "overburden" pottery and deposited it undamaged among the sedimentary spoil, as Throckmorton had said it would. This was hardly immaculate, archaeologically, but in context did not matter; the compacted weed layer should give us ample warning of the imminence of relevant material, the exact original position of which could be important.

But the second day, a fortnight later, was totally disappointing. Somehow, the air-lift had hardly any effect. Was it the stiff clay we were now in? Or was the machine at fault? Or were the operators using it wrongly? In fact, the tube had become partially blocked with clinker from faulty operation by divers who were necessarily novices at the work. But as we were all inexperienced, we took a long time to diagnose the trouble correctly; and the only remedy was more practice, which, at the rate of one operation every two weeks, we were slow in getting. And we were down to our last few pounds, with the good weather of August almost over. Now there were only the uncertain months of September and October left. And so, once again, I played the last two major cards left open to me—two days' work with the mechanical digger in September on overburden only, and five days' work with the Royal Engineers and their air-lift in October to exploit the removal of much non-significant material.

But this time, with more experience both of the capabilities of the mechanical digger and of the actual soils to be dug, I thought I might be able to make it do more than merely clear overburden from the upper 5-ft. layer, although that must come first. Once again, bad weather and strong tides brought positioning trouble, which slowed down the work. Nevertheless, the trench was widened so as to make deep digging safe in due course and then, cautiously, I started to enter the clay layer. The results were similar to the plank excavation at the start of the season; that is, below the clay layer were some scattered ships timbers. Two were uncovered and removed. The first was a small part of a "fashion piece" just under 2 feet in length, with Teredo tunnel lining and shell on one side only. This must have come from a castle, because the purpose of the curved wood was to indicate, during construction, the intended line of the upperworks. It had no context and had clearly been broken off from the upperworks long, long ago, as indeed had the second piece of wood. This was an extremely worn staghorn, or large wooden cleat, probably some 3 feet long originally, which had been attacked by gribble only. There were no Teredo tunnels at all. It had been secured by 1½-inch-diameter wooden trenails, one of which was still in position, although the other two had fallen out. Its size indicated that it may have been used to control the ropes to the foremast rather than the mainmast. That was conjecture, but at least it disposed of the ideas of some nautical historians who thought that cleats were a modern invention and that in Tudor times they "just tied off the ropes to a rail". The recovered timber pattern now read: two pieces attacked by both gribble and Teredo, two pieces attacked by gribble only, with no trace of Teredo. And all pieces were scattered remnants, one from the side of the hull, with two certainly and one more probably, from the upperworks. There were no signs of a hull as such but only of the outlying (or overlying) wreckage.

On the last day, helped by Morrie Young and Percy Ackland, plus an accurate positioning, I decided to excavate deeply into the port side mound in the area of the concreted-iron "contact" located 8 feet down by the Royal Engineers' air-lift the previous year. What we found was an 8-ft.-long vaguely sausage-shaped concretion, thicker at one end than the other, the thick end being uppermost. There was ample power available for lifting, and the concretion was soon swayed up and lowered down on deck. Morrie later commented that I then went immediately into a state of shock and he was quite right. From the first moment I saw it in air, that grey concretion had a knobbly look—as if it concealed the multi-ringed barrel of a built-up gun. Almost from the first, I had made my own definition of the evidence required to prove that this was the wreck site of the *Mary Rose,* which I boiled down to the simple jingle: Big Tudor Battleship Headed No-man's-land. The sonar had confirmed approximate size and alignment, a built-up gun of weight would give both Tudor and battleship in one. But it was years since I had last dreamed of finding a gun or an archer to clinch the matter of identification. I had become preoccupied with the various technical phases of the operation, all of which had to be mastered from scratch. And now I was launched into another technical phase, which was part-psychological, for I had to convince almost everyone that what looked like some 14 cwt. of concrete should be treated like a basket of eggs, because if it was a built-up gun it would be weaker than a cast piece originally, quite apart from any deterioration which might have taken place.

We washed down the concretion and then examined it closely. There were seven "bumps", suggesting rings, and at the narrow end it was indented, suggesting a gun muzzle of about 4-inch bore, covered by as much concretion again. There was a small oyster valve inside and several others at the thick end, two having a markedly yellow sheen. Biologically, this was all very similar to the marine life depicted on artefacts in Deane's watercolours. Then I had another shock. At one point, and for three inches only, one of the rings was clear of concretion and covered only by clay. When this was removed by Morrie Young, we found ourselves looking at a triple-ring of grey metal bands. It was staggering because, not merely had I become accustomed to overburden only but also, from much study of the guns raised by Deane, and never properly conserved, I had somehow come to think of the *Mary Rose* as being armed with a collection of rust-brown and crumbling wrought-iron ordnance. This had overlain in my mind the contemporary paintings of siege warfare which clearly showed iron guns as being of a grey or blue-grey tone. What we were looking at, for about ten minutes, before it rusted, was part of a Tudor gun exactly as it had been on the day the *Mary Rose* heeled over and sank.

After about five minutes, the concretion started to bubble. The iron inside had eventually become stable below the sea-bed, but now it had re-entered a gaseous environment and changes were already taking place. Therefore, although we carried on digging for a little while to find a context for the concretion, I had to think of some way of getting it to a conservation laboratory before they closed for the day. I passed a message to a friend in the Ministry of Public Building and Works in the Dockyard, for transmission to Southsea Castle: "Have what appears to be a built-up iron gun from *Mary Rose* —same size as yours, or larger. Collect today at 5 p.m. Bubbling already." That alerted the laboratory, but it was the Ministry which arranged the rest. They could not find a berth for us in the Dockyard, so they arranged for us to come along-side a ship already berthed beside a crane and then the crane swung its jib out over the ship and lowered its tackle down on to our decks, where we secured it to the concretion which I had already splinted with planks to spread the load. Then the concretion rose vertically in the air for a hundred feet or so, dwindling rapidly in size, passed over the ship, and was lowered gently into a waiting lorry on the quayside. That crane was perfectly capable of picking up a modern multiple-gun turret, complete with guns, and it made light work of Henry VIII's ship ordnance.

There was a great deal to be said for having your wreck a few miles from a premier naval port. Indeed, the sole prob-lem—as with the actual excavation—was the trick of using immense power with great gentleness; but by dint of explain-ing at least twenty times that day what a built up gun was, I got it to Southsea Castle just over three hours from the time it had left the seabed at Spithead. And here another problem awaited us, for the mobile crane they had been using there only a few days before had gone and there was only manual labour left, and not much of that. Soon the stout castle walls that Henry VIII had built were ringing with my anguished cries. Getting the gun down four feet or so from the lorry to the ground was the most difficult and dangerous task of the day, but with Morrie Young's ingenuity, and a good deal of muscle-strain, the gun arrived at the door of the laboratory in one piece instead of three or four. Here it went into the hands of Chris O'Shea, Curator for Conservation at the Castle, which is basically an artillery museum and therefore equipped to deal with it. But I fancy that the old stonework is still haunted by a voice calling out in agony, "Careful, it's a built-up gun!"

Just how unique and valuable that gun was, I did not then know, but I realised that the first "political" battle had been won at a stroke—we had proved the *Mary Rose* site. Instead of being a search for what had been regarded widely as merely a myth under the mud, we had now what many people would regard as being a potentially valuable "property". We could expect substantial sympathy and support, as well as less disinterested approaches perhaps, which would enable us next year to mount an effective programme for the next phase of our plan—to establish how much of the hull was still intact. So I had good news to impart to Margaret Rule and Bill Majer at the Fishbourne Roman Palace next morning, where by coincidence we had previously arranged to hold a committee meeting.

The Palace itself was an effective illustration of what we hoped would be the final stage of the *Mary Rose* project. When I had first been shown over the site by Margaret in 1963, Barry Cunliffe's excavation was in its early stages. The site was a field near Chichester with only the season's trenches open (previous work having been backfilled), the entrance was a farm gate, the site office and conservation laboratory were in a building externally little better than a superior cowshed. But now, ten years after the first trial excavation, a large part of the great Roman state building lay permanently open but enclosed under modern brickwork and glass which followed the lines of the Roman structure and had, besides, the associated offices, lecture rooms and laboratories. Imagine a cross between this site exhibition, of which Margaret was the representative on our committee, and Nelson's *Victory* in her dry dock, which we passed every time we went out of harbour and of which Bill Majer was the representative of the organising body, and it is easy to see how the concept of a Tudor Ship Museum, with the *Mary Rose* as centre-piece, did not seem so far-fetched after all. Everything depended on the results of the next phase—to find out if there was enough left of her to be worthy of the role. I was sure there was, but we had to prove it; and that would require much greater resources than we at present possessed. Now, the decisive step forward to obtaining them had probably been made, a stroke of good fortune offsetting all the bad.

But there was no time for euphoria. Operational needs were urgent. Firstly, we could not keep the news secret very long, so, the gun having been raised on 17 September, we decided to hold up a press release until the 20th. In the meantime, I had notified the Captain of the Port, a friend of ours, Captain K. H. Martin, D.S.C., R.N., who immediately drafted a Notice to Mariners making the site of our lease a prohibited area, which would serve to protect it from anchors, trawls and pirate divers. He also alerted the naval signal stations watching Spithead, which had a police boat on call. In short, by withholding the news, we had arranged to fight the battle—if there was to be a battle—at the time and the place of our own choosing, so as to dictate the action. In fact, we were to be snooped on once by a strange diving boat whose occupants surreptitiously took our position with what might have been a sextant; but that was all. Nobody stuck his neck out for the great big chopper that was waiting.

Meanwhile, the gun (which everyone would insist on calling a "cannon") was telling its story under constant, modern interrogation which lasted well into 1972. No gun from the *Mary Rose* had ever been treated like this before. The first stage, the careful chipping off of the concretion, was orthodox; except that the chippings were retained for examination. They were in fact a layered record of the build up of sediments attracted to the ironwork since Tudor times and proved to contain many types of shellfish and also small fragments of wood, presumably part of the slide carriage or "stock", which was missing. Both the corrosion record shown by the ironwork and the biological record shown by the organisms, particularly shellfish, enclosed in the concretion, told a tale which matched in all respects. The gun had experienced two main stages underwater. The first had lasted a very long time, probably hundreds of years, during which a slow and not very serious deterioration had taken place. The second stage had lasted only a short time, perhaps as little as five years, but a rapid deterioration had taken place during this time. Other clues were the absence of a carriage, the fact that the barrel only was enclosed in the concretion (the powder chamber being missing), and that the barrel was slightly bent. The suggestion was that the gun had been buried in or soon after 1545, exposed and damaged by explosives probably in 1840, which allowed oysters, for instance, to grow to full size on the now silt-free concretion, and was then buried again and the oysters enclosed inside fresh concretion.

One other fact showed that the gun had originally entered the mud muzzle down, which fitted a "low side" gun of the *Mary Rose*. Only the first 18 inches of the muzzle contained sediment, which was inclined at a shallow angle of about 20 to 25 degrees. The rest of the barrel was hollow. The material blocking the muzzle was a blue-grey clay. At first, Chris O'Shea attempted to drill through this, but the drill would not bite. Eventually, he had to use a chisel to break up the clay and clean it out! And this was the stuff we had been trying to dig through under water. It explained a lot, particularly the way our hopes had risen as first the water-jets and then the air-lift had easily cleared the top five feet or so of light sediments, and then the way they had fallen again as we reached that underlying stiff clay layer and could produce very little impression on it in a short working day.

The clearing of the opposite end of the barrel, the concretion-covered breech, was easier. Here the layer of sediment was found to contain primed gunpowder, part of the charge from the missing chamber. As Chris carefully worked his way through the remnants of the black powder, it was his turn to be shocked. Gleaming metal appeared. Eventually, he had the "hall" of the breech cleared, and there lay a shiny cast-iron shot of $3\frac{1}{2}$-inch diameter, wadded in place with a plug of hemp, which microscopic examination in the laboratories of British Ropes Ltd., suggested was flax, now extremely brittle and degraded. But the shot was in "mint" condition, exactly as loaded, preserved to perfection by the blocking of the barrel at one end by gunpowder and at the other end by blue clay. Chris just put it on his desk for the next few weeks, still amazed at the realisation that the last hand to touch that shot before him was a gunner in the *Mary Rose,* loading for action against the French.

The barrel was long and thin, with 14 rings. It had the small bore of only $3\frac{3}{4}$ inches for a length of approximately $7\frac{1}{2}$ feet; that is, for its time, it was a high-velocity, long-range gun designed to penetrate rather than to smash. In modern times, the equivalent would be the long-barrelled anti-tank gun designed to fire a small, solid projectile at armour. And now, by turning to the Anthony Roll and looking down the list of iron guns and their ammunition in the *Mary Rose,* I could see that only the slings, demi-slings and quarter-slings fired iron shot. The port pieces and the fowlers were supplied with stone shot only, while the smaller guns shot lead or iron pellets. Up to now these ordnance titles had been simply names to historians, but as what we had could be a gun of the sling class only, one item of the unknown Tudor "gun code" had been cracked. Six more remained unidentified as yet. The *Mary Rose* gun which Southsea Castle already had (originally it had been in the Dockyard Museum) appeared to be of similar design, although many details were different. Lack of conservation in earlier times had caused such deterioration, however, that detailed comparison was difficult. The barrel had split open, revealing the wide longitudinal staves on which it had been "built-up", and although part of the stock was still attached, there was neither shot nor chamber. Still, it looked as if both these guns were of the sling class, whereas the wrought-iron guns in the various London museums were probably port pieces or fowlers, although a base or two could not be excluded.

The next main stage in the conservation of our gun was to remove the salt from the wrought-iron by placing it in an electrolytic bath for a long period. After a month or so, this removed the salt but substituted hydrogen, and therefore the next process was a short heat treatment to burn out the unwanted deposits. This required an industrial oven capable of heating a large metal object to exactly 220° Centigrade for four hours. In Deane's day, none of this technology was available, nor is every modern wreck site within easy distance of such facilities. An Armada wreck on the wild west coast of agricultural Eire, for instance, was soon to prove a problem to archaeologists, because the only adequate conservation facilities were in Belfast, over the Ulster border, where the running of guns of any sort was not then very welcome. But we had a choice of ovens and, going all parochial, chose Portsmouth Dockyard. And then, with basic conservation completed, and conventional X-rays having failed to give us a good idea of the interior construction details of the barrel, Chris O'Shea again turned to the Dockyard for an alternative method usually capable of obtaining clear images through six inches of steel. This was the gamma ray or "cobalt bomb" gambit, in which the radio-active material is passed through the barrel to obtain a negative image. The resulting pictures were the equivalent through wrought-iron of Pat Board's specialist X-ray techniques of examining Teredos through timber.

This time the shock was mine, as well as Chris O'Shea's. It was not a "built-up" gun! The rings were there all right, shown in fine detail, and shrunk on in normal fashion to the barrel to hold it together. But the barrel was *not* constructed of many separate staves. The negatives showed, unmistakably, a single white line—a weld! The barrel had been fashioned out of a single sheet of wrought-iron, rolled round a core, and then rough-welded along the seam. This resulted in a much stronger barrel than the old "built-up" hoops-and-staves method could produce—but there was no record of it. There was no mention in any document, nor did any museum we were aware of knowingly have an actual example of such a gun (although it was quite possible that some items in their collection had been constructed in this way, but had been taken for the ordinary "built-up" guns which they outwardly resembled). At the time it was found ours was a unique gun —the only one of its type known in the world. Enquiries produced only a rumour of one or two much later swivel-guns having been made in this way and found on Spanish Plate Fleet wrecks, but the basic source was unreliable. In any event, this gun was clear evidence of that bounding Tudor technology of which the design of the *Mary Rose* herself was a part, but which is merely hinted at in the documents and histories.

Taken with some of those documents, this gun did make sense. The late Mr. Carr Laughton had unearthed a payment for guns made early in the reign of Henry VIII, and this had one curious feature. The average payment for a "copper" (i.e. brass) gun was £2 per cwt., much greater than the average 12s. to 14s. paid for all types of iron gun—with one single exception: iron slings cost 4d. per lb, not far short of the £2 per cwt. of the expensive bronze pieces. Clearly, there had to be some reason for this extra costliness of the Sling (and also of a correspondingly increased performance over the ordinary iron gun), and this new, stronger method of construction, enabling an iron gun to fire iron shot instead of the much lighter stone shot, could be the explanation, coupled also with the matter of range, for by now it was clear that the sling was not a close-quarter gun, as the port pieces and fowlers almost certainly were. Possibly the new way of construction failed to get into recorded history because it was a stage which did not last very long, being soon overtaken by the ability of the foundries to cast large guns complete in iron. It also suggested, in conjunction with various documents, that the Sling was the tactical successor to the serpentine; carrying out the same job, but in a more modern and effective manner; and they may have had a faster rate of fire and been easier to work on shipboard than the early cast-bronze and cast-iron culverins which seem to have taken over their function gradually.

When the lengthy process of conservation had been completed on the barrel of the "sling" what had been lost was an uneven thickness of the outer metal averaging quarter of an inch. But the gun was "dead", completely stable. The loss, which had been predicted, was mainly the result of that unavoidable merging of a metal object with its hard sedimentary skin where, if the period of time be long enough, the metal disappears entirely into the concretion, leaving a hollow space from which a cast of the vanished artefact may be made. We were all extremely pleased with this result, for hardly any wrought-iron had survived in the *Vasa*; it had either vanished or was unrecognisable. For the *Mary Rose*, a much earlier ship in which wrought-iron was more widely used, the fact that Spithead clearly had an underwater environment far more favourable to the preservation of wrought-iron than the waters of Stockholm Harbour was important. The comparison for timber was not so favourable, but was not conclusive because thus far we had found only scattered remains mostly from high up the hull.

Attempts to locate hull structure *in situ* during the four weeks remaining to us were unsuccessful, but also maddeningly inconclusive, owing to the depth at which the contacts lay. The "gunshaft" was further dug and probed, but revealed no context. The "deep contact shaft" was taken down to 10 feet, revealing a continuation of the compacted weed layer and the fact that this contained small pieces of old timber, but we failed to make the extra two feet required to examine the contact itself. Really deep probes with an improvised high-pressure air-lance went to 14 feet around it, through immensely stiff material, but without being actually stopped. It certainly appeared to be a limited area contact, but we could not take this for fact because a wreck with its upper deck torn out or blown out by salvagers could be probed deeply in many places without giving a "positive" result. What we needed was continuous timber near enough to the surface to be fairly easily dug and examined, such as that in the "stern mound" area north of the JM3 trench or the suspiciously uneven "bow area" to the south. But about 200 feet separated the two extremities, so either or both could be merely castling which had shifted bodily or some other detached piece. During Royal Engineers Week in October, almost totally ruined by gales, I managed long, leisurely inspections in 8-feet visibility, and, zig-zagging, noted: "Over bow castle area found plenty of sand patches and mounds. Very *disturbed*. Found nylon mooring line. This led to 5 blocks in rings of mooring wire, a flatfish, an egg, a lavatory seat." This solved the riddle of what had happened to our S.W. moorings—something had picked them up and dumped them all together in a great clump of concrete and coiled wire hawser and tangled nylon. I had already located our missing N.E. moorings—one block actually in the deep contact shaft, two others just north of the JM3 trench. In spite of the Notice to Mariners, people clearly were trawling or anchoring on the site, and any timber we exposed near to the surface would be endangered.

Indeed, as far as moorings were concerned, we were back

to where we had started from in May, and no praise could be too high for the air-lifters who worked in the bottom of shafts 10 feet below the seabed in a tangle of stakes and lines, knowing that the boat above was held only by an anchor and that a sudden squall might cause chaos. Even in good seabed visibility, there was little light at the bottom of the shafts on a winter's day.

For our final dig on 24 October we were unexpectedly short of some of our best men, the Fire Brigade having been called away just seaward of the Isle of Wight, where a Channel collision between two tankers seemed about to rival in its results the wrecking of the *Torrey Canyon* off the Scillies. All day we could see the smoke coming up from behind the high downs of Culver and Bonchurch where long ago the French infantry had met King Henry's militia. By afternoon, it had grown ominously and was smeared in one long streamer for twenty miles eastwards beyond Selsey in Sussex. Over there, George Clark, shortly to be promoted Assistant Divisional Officer, was taking his turn to command the firemen working on board the flaming 42,000-ton tanker *Pacific Glory*. Their fight was far from won when we finished marking up the *Mary Rose* for next season, and ran back into harbour for the last time. It was a memorable end to a memorable year.

The interesting thing had been the use of more modern "see-through" techniques applied, so far as I know, for the first time to some aspects of underwater archaeology. The digging had provided additional evidence to appraise the original interpretations of Professor Edgerton's sub-mud sonar survey, which had "seen" some traces of the wreck invisible to the human eye, while the X-ray techniques developed by the Central Electricity Board and the "cobalt bomb" examinations by Portsmouth Dockyard had supplied evidence concerning actual wreck materials which could have been obtained in no other way. There, the primary credit belonged to the scientists and organisations concerned.

The important thing had been the building up, through years of adversity, of struggling at a vast task with woefully inadequate resources, of a really determined and, by now, extremely experienced team, who tended to "think" *Mary Rose* even in their sleep. They were totally intrigued with the ship and with the problems of uncovering and then assessing the wreckage. These were poors years for the wives, who lost their husbands every neap-tide weekend and who now tended to regard the *Mary Rose* as a deadly rival. The skill which the old hands had rapidly acquired was most obvious in the last four weeks of the season. When they were digging, even in the stiff clay, the water above boiled and turned brown, whereas with the newcomers, who were still novices with an air-lift, no matter how experienced they might be as divers, the water boiled white. They were merely aerating Spithead for the fish. But as long as the "hard core" held together, to lead, train and advise, the most determined of the newcomers would soon become expert in their turn.

It was now essential to attempt to bind them all together during the winter, in readiness for next season, because the whole project existed as an organisation only on the tele-phone. The divers came to Spithead from all over Hampshire, Sussex and the Isle of Wight, many of them arriving in their own boats at previously agreed times, so as to take over parti-cular shifts and avoid keeping too many people hanging about unnecessarily. Many of them had met only underwater, look-ing into each other's masks momentarily as one shift took over from another. I was their sole unifying contact, relying heavily on the leaders of these teams to organise their own men and resources. At the cost of enormous telephone bills we did it, but a priority for the winter was a socio-business gathering where for the first time we might all meet each other face to face, unmasked. An organisation had come into being, but what we did not realise was that other events had been set in motion which were not under our control.

CHAPTER SIXTEEN

"WE'RE WAY UP TOPSIDES!"

Once again, the gun had proved the decisive instrument of war. By the spring of 1971, the battle of the winter had been won. We had moorings, and not just lash-up ground moorings, but actual mooring buoys of modest size, with a third and much larger buoy promised shortly by British Petroleum. And we had permission to lay them on the site at Spithead. We had a giant Atlas-Copco "Silensair" compressor for the air-lift, plus compressed-air submersible pumps and submersible lamps. We had a 40-ft. catamaran converted by John Barber as a "work barge" in which this equipment could be mounted, and although it had no engines, we had enough money to hire an M.F.V. to tow it out to the site and bring it back. We had a large Avon sportsboat driven by a 20 h.p. Chrysler as rescue boat and tender. We had a 17 cwt. Bedford van for carrying engines, diving gear and fuel drums for the compressor—and for taking large timbers to the laboratories for conservation. We had cameras and film. We had ten Chesterfield aqualung cylinders. The original members of the association even had masks, fine and weight-belts donated by a firm in Guernsey—a pleasant recompense for expensive wet-suits worn out while working jets and air-lifts. All these were gifts or loans from organisations or individuals who believed that we had a viable and important project in hand.

And it was to be very nearly wrecked by others who came forward to offer help, once all the resources had been assembled and the first definite success had been achieved, and with aid from an unexpected quarter, blandly attempted to hijack the whole as a going concern of their own. This seems to happen often with successful treasure-hunting expeditions, but I had never thought to see it in archaeology. The lure, of course, was not gold but fame and reputation. These attempts to turn a scientific investigation into a species of "power game" soured a considerable part of the season, and the bitterness was not entirely one-sided, for most of the rival

group did not really understand what was going on and had,
I think, offered their services with the intention of giving
genuine assistance. Certainly most of the other newcomers
that season were offering disinterested help, and we could not
have done without them. We had discovered that there was a
fine dividing line between the two types, because naturally no
one will give freely of his time to a project which is either
unimportant or notably unsuccessful. Initially, it is hard to
tell the difference.

However, before there was a band-wagon to jump on or
hijack, it had first to be constructed; and this had taken up
a good deal of our time during the winter. One of its principal architects was Stan Googe, a technician with Thames
Television, who used to go out fishing in Tony Glover's boat
on Sundays and heard about us from Tony. That year we were
confined to Saturdays, for it was only then that Tony could
afford to drop his charge to the pittance we could pay. Like
Tony, Stan had become interested in his turn, and it was
due to his efforts that we had been able to finance the last
half-dozen or so operations in 1970. Given a gun to fire, he
had been even more successful in arousing interest in the *Mary
Rose* and a good deal of our now considerable resources were
the results of his work. But in 1971, the only ammunition we
could supply him with was hot air. We deliberately avoided
any chance of making exciting finds, and set out to obtain
structural information only. The theme of the season's work
was to be: how much of the *Mary Rose* still remains below
the seabed? Day by day, the information was to be built up,
but on a day-by-day basis, the results were hardly "news";
certainly, they were not news of the sort to which the media
had become accustomed, even when dealing with land archaeology, yet alone the submarine plundering which all too
often passed for underwater archaeology. So we promised
them all a conference at the end of the year, when we would
announce the year's results. Whether that would be "news"
or not would depend on how much—or how little—of the
Mary Rose really did remain.

Perhaps the most important result of obtaining definite
site identification in 1970 was that Lord Mountbatten of
Burma began to take a great and informed interest in the
project, similar in so many ways to the *Vasa* restoration

scheme in Stockholm, which was sponsored by one of his relatives, King Gustaf of Sweden. Lord Mountbatten had done a good deal of aqualung diving in his time, and was able to appreciate very well the real possibilities of the *Mary Rose*. He mentioned the matter to the Duke of Edinburgh (who had been trained in the aqualung by the B.S.-A.C.) and also recommended the project for consideration to Admiral Sir Horace Law, the Commander-in-Chief, Naval Home Command, who is a distant relative of Lord Nelson. It was perhaps no coincidence that Portsmouth Local Notice to Mariners No. 24 of 16 April 1971, declared a certain area of Spithead "prohibited" and allowed us to lay full-size moorings buoys there, ending for good the menace to the *Mary Rose* of anchors and trawls, as well as easing our operations considerably. As it happened, this protection was to be critical in 1971. Without those buoys, immense damage might have been caused.

Another development came about from the initiative of Ben Dunk, a local businessman who ran a chain of woolshops under the name of "Mary Rose". The name was a coincidence, but Ben's big idea sprang from my original demand for excavation to be carried out in a "swimming bath" at Spithead. Captain Martin's suggestion had been for a large, concrete caisson, but as this would have to be a "one-off" job it would be expensive, probably costing more than half a million pounds. Ben's suggestion was to use what we all then referred to as an "oil rig" to do the same job, because there were numbers of them about. He and I met his "contact" in one of those immense new tower blocks by the Thames and secured an introduction to British Petroleum, who kindly carried out a feasibility study for us. We had already learned what we wanted was a "self-elevating platform", the largest of which can be used for mounting "oil rigs". With "skirts" fitted, this would do the trick, and in additon could carry out the actual "lift" of the hull. Quite small "jack-up platforms" could manage 3,000 tons or so without trouble. Unlike the Stockholm salvage, we did not intend the *Mary Rose* to break surface until some years after the "lift"; we wanted to keep her underwater in a controlled environment, either in a floating dock or a graving dock, while the interior was excavated and the mud and clay removed (along with the ballast). The future situation regarding availability of docks in the

Portsmouth area had also to be investigated, and there was a preliminary meeting with officials of Portsmouth Corporation, who were very keen, as we were, to see the *Mary Rose* come to Portsmouth.

But in addition to thinking years ahead, to the ultimate consequences of our acts, there was the 1971 season to be planned. It was based on an uncompleted sailing catamaran 40 feet long, designed for shark fishing, with a roomy cabin forward and a large working platform aft. John Barber, another local businessman, purchased this for us and had it completed and launched. We decided to call it the *Roger Grenville*, after the captain of the *Mary Rose*, and it was eventually christened by Mrs. Gwen Holder, who was a direct descendant of the Grenvilles and lived at nearby Petersfield. This enabled us to mount a very large compressor, capable of powering two or three air-lifts simultaneously, plus submersible pumps and lamps. A suitable machine was offered by the British subsidiary of Atlas Copco, a Swedish company which had assisted with the salvage of the *Vasa*, and so were well able to assess the practicalities as well as the potentialities of what seemed to many people mere midsummer madness.

But, provided the hull was sound, and provided that we could find a solution to the difficult archaeological problem represented by the scattered wreckage surrounding the hull (*this* was the one that worried me), then there was only a financial problem. Power to lift was no problem, as the Industrial Revolution had occurred quite some time ago. When we set off each time from Flathouse Quay the first thing we passed on our left-hand side was a small floating dock, often with a 1,500-ton submarine inside, which it had lifted without even noticing it. A "big" ship at Spithead in the 1970s could not be less than 100,000 tons and to be really large she had to be a quarter of a million tons. In these terms, the *Mary Rose* was a toy: nearer to the tiny blue yacht, *Lively Lady*, which was moored opposite the floating dock. We always pointed this out to our visitors, as the craft in which a Southsea greengrocer, Alec Rose, had made a single-handed voyage round the world. Knighted on his return, Sir Alec had kindly consented to become a patron of the *Mary Rose* Association.

I suppose I should have been worried that I might be leading all these people astray, as I certainly should be if I were wrong and there was little or nothing left of the hull for us to raise. But I had gone over all the evidence many years ago, and I was sure. So sure, that there was quite an angry scene in Bristol on 5 April, after my lecture, which was part of a four-day Symposium on Marine Archaeology, when one of the leading London academics suggested that the *Mary Rose* had been blown up like the *Royal George,* the *Boyne* and the *Edgar,* and that the gun I had raised was probably ballast. I replied that many nautical historians did not know what they were talking about, for a start, and that, anyway, the gun was loaded. So was the *Mary Rose* gun he had in his museum, was the academic's reply. At this, Margaret Rule, who normally never speaks, got up and said that she felt compelled to state that the gun we had recovered last year was not only loaded but also primed and ready to fire. This illuminating passage of arms was recorded in shorthand, for publication, but what was not taken down were the whispered comments in the audience.

While there, I compared notes with Peter Throckmorton, on the results of his sonar surveys on Mediterranean wrecks, and then with Peter Marsden, who had lately used an Edgerton pinger on the Dutch East Indiaman *Amsterdam,* wrecked off Hastings and deeply sunk into soft sand, so that the hull was preserved very high up. I had a close look at some of the graphs, which tended to reflect, not the hull at all, but unknown objects inside the hull. There were one or two, however, where it seemed as if the sound waves had been reflected by the side to a considerable depth. There was no trouble in tying in the pinger graphs with the actual wreck, because the upper frames of the *Amsterdam* protruded above the seabed; indeed, on low water of big spring tides, the whole wreck site was exposed to view on the beach. When I got home I took out my album of *Mary Rose* graphs—and nearly kicked myself. On a single graph of a run on the JM4 line, a narrow vertical band going down to 25 feet on the Southsea side of the "W" feature was perfectly obvious. Most of the other graphs had it, but vague and diffuse, easy to confuse with geological features. I could now read this vertical band as the port side, with another, less definite, but very probable, for the starboard side; one at each end of the "W" feature. The *Amsterdam* had reflected on one side only—occasionally; the *Mary*

Rose had reflected on both sides—on one definite occasion; or so I thought, for this was still conjecture. When, recently, an oilman had heard out my original reasons for regarding the "W" feature as being in some way the *Mary Rose*, I had glowed with pleasure when he had referred to my deductions as "bold". Now I knew they were not. I had been slack and slovenly; I had missed perfectly obvious evidence, because it occurred once only in definite form, unlike the "W" feature, which endlessly repeated itself on line after line, and continued to repeat itself when each line was re-run. It would have taken a blind man to miss that.

Oddly, of all that gathering of underwater archaeologists, many of them from warm climes, our outfit was scheduled to go into operation first, on 17 April, ten days later. April is not a very good month, but we hoped to re-mark the JM3 trench. The first shock came as we crossed over Spit Bank—we could look straight down through the water and see the weed on the bottom below! I had heard from an American visitor how his group habitually found their way to a Plate Fleet wreck six miles off the coast of Florida, navigating by landmarks on the seabed below, which could be seen clearly all the way out; but to see Spit Bank in April was fantastic. Even at 50 feet on site, visibility was still 20 feet and by 3 p.m. we had worked ourselves out of a job. Last year's markers were still in place, but we doubled them up in any case, and cleaned up the trench of some of the dangerous debris which had collected in it during the winter. There had been only a light fill of sediment, but the number of odd ropes, tarpaulins, tin cans and plastic containers was beyond computation. Had visibility been two feet, we could still have worked, but everything would have taken much longer and we might have achieved only 40 per cent of the day's programme instead of 110 per cent. We could not dig, because we still had to arrange for mooring buoys to be laid and obtain moorings in Portsmouth Harbour for the catamaran.

We went out again on 1 May with a smaller compressor to start the season's excavation, mark out a base-line, and so on. The boat was very crowded this time and things started to go very slightly wrong. The anchor went down with the Southsea "marks" a bit off, putting us to the south-east of the trench. On his first mark-up dive, Percy Ackland found poor visibility and a very strong current, and came back without being able to find the stake marking Deep Contact "A" in the trench. He did not tell us, but he was not feeling very well. However, he made a second dive and we watched his surface buoy move away from the anchor, as directed, towards Fort Monckton on the Gosport shore to the N.W. That should have taken him directly in to the western end of the JM3 trench where Deep "A" was. But he came back again very quickly, half-climbed the ladder, and hung on there, breathing hard and apparently worried. I moved over and heard him whisper something about "I've seen wood", and, forgetting there were press in the boat, promptly blew it by questioning him openly as to whether it was loose or *in situ*.

Margaret Rule, who was doing her usual job as recorder, noted down what he said: "On first dive, current was strong, towing buoy was murder. So I came back for tape and reel. Second dive, ran out tape westerly 15 to 20 feet headed as Mac instructed (from anchor line). Came across planking and ribs sticking up through bottom of seabed. Carried on following the planking to the South, now 60 feet from anchor. Tape attached to this by looping it round 0 or 9 pieces." When I heard this, my brain started working so fast, steam must have been coming out of my ears. But before reorganising everything. I thought I had better take a quick look myself. What I saw had some very odd aspects indeed. I noted:

A tangle of timbers forming a rough triangle in a gulley cut through the seabed and about 4–6 ft. wide. Timbers exposed to max. depth of 1 foot. Gulley running v. approx. East–West, line of timbers v. approx. North–South.

The current was really pouring down the gulley and visibility was below 4 feet, but eventually the timbers began to make sense.

A row of frames rather less than 12" x 6", with smaller frames between, attached to side-planking on the Southsea side. Conclusion: this is bow castling *in situ*. I had not expected so much of the hull to remain. To check, I went up the gulley for 40 ft. or so to a high mound, which I did not cross. On the way, I came across at intervals three large timbers sticking up slightly and obviously part of the internal structure of the bow castle, possibly fallen deck beams or central supports. Without the gulley, nothing whatever would have been visible of the wreck, which might well have been 4 feet down at its highest parts and, in between, very much deeper. A wreck is rarely a flat surface. A distinct anchor drag mark, large, ran across the gulley at right-angles about halfway along it.

Later dives showed that a group of our mooring blocks lay at the far end of the gulley beyond the mound. The implication was, that a trawl or anchor had fouled them and that the vessel had dragged them right across the wreck, creating the gulley, and so exposing to view the timbers previously lying buried. But we did not know this for some weeks, and at first tended to assign the cause solely to a widespread scouring of the seabed that winter, following a great southerly gale and big spring tides, which had exposed another wooden wreck off Southsea beach.

Both factors had probably played a part in exposing some of the forward portion of the wreck, but on the morning of the initial discovery we had only scraps of information at our disposal. In order to find out more, we had to reorganise on the spot. A team trained and equipped to excavate "overburden" had suddenly to carry out a rapid survey. Were the frames and planking found by Percy Ackland, plus the further timbers I had seen in the gulley beyond, the only portions of the wreck exposed—or were there more? In a sweeping tide and in visibility conditions similar to searching a large field at night with a hand-torch, this was no small order. Fortunately, I had asked along as a visitor, Commander Alan Baldwin, R.N., whom I had met at the Bristol symposium a few weeks before, and he had underwater surveying experience of the type now required. For my third and final dive of the day I went down with Barry Ballard to inspect what had been found away from the wreckage in the gulley, which had not yet been tied in. Alan had reported: "Confirmed compass bearing 195° of timbers and outer planking. A 66-ft.-long run of main planking with timbers on one side."

This sounds impressive, as though the timbers were sticking up obviously, like those exposed in the gulley. But it was not so. The tops of the frames (I had the impression I saw about forty) were almost flush with the bottom. They were not continuous, for in places the "run" disappeared under the seabed only to reappear a little further on. This must have been the *Mary Rose* much as John Deane had first seen her. Apart from those in the gulley, there certainly was "nothing to which the diver could attach a rope". Barry and I dug around one heavy frame experimentally. The top was eroded, but as we dug down we found smooth timber under our hands, "very hard, no trace of gribble or Teredo, only a trace of unevenness from shipwrights' tools. Edges hard, sharp, perfect". It was not upright, but slanted into the ground at a considerable angle. I now suspect it was a collapsed deck beam, but that was not at all clear at the time. I had a real clue in the notes I jotted down, but missed the significance of it. I wrote: "At one point, I identified a portion of double-skin. Otherwise, the skin faced towards Southsea." Quite wrongly. I concluded that because there was continuous planking all along the Southsea side of the heavy frames and, except at one point, no planking on the Isle of Wight side, then the continuous planking must be the outer skin and that the "run" must therefore represent the port side of the wreck. It was less than logical, but Alan fell into the same trap and reported the Southsea side as "outer planking", as later did Morrie Young and Margaret Rule. We were all judging by the initial appearance of what little we could see of a ship whose method of construction was unknown. For several months we might as well have been excavating a Martian Flying Saucer, so little could we assume in advance about the structure. Looking back on that one great error, I can now see that the basis of my mistake was the belief that the wreck was still heeled 40° towards Southsea, and that of the "high side", little could remain above the turn of the bilge. I simply could not believe that I was looking at the "high side". There just could not be that much left of it.

Now quite a number of things became "utmost priority". Somehow or other, cost what it may, mooring buoys had to be laid quickly, as effective protection against further anchoring and trawling. That was defensive. But there was also an urgent demand for offensive action. We had been presented with an astounding opportunity to map a large part of one side of the ship rapidly and easily, with the absolute minimum of digging. What the sea had uncovered the next storm or big spring tide might deeply hide again. But it was not sufficient just to count ribs or measure the length of their "run". They had to be surveyed with fair accuracy. That meant nailing a numbered tag to the centre of each frame-top, then measuring all four sides and two diagonals, then taking an offset to indicate the position of this frame relative to the others; and also measuring distances from the frame to the nearest planking. This procedure was worked out by Margaret Rule and Alan Baldwin, who could bring in a team of amateur divers from the Naval Air Command Sub-Aqua Club. They had their own boat and could send out small survey teams in the evenings two or three times a week at next to no cost. The large, mainly civilian teams already trained in excavation were available at weekends only (apart from the firemen), but required big boats with powerful machinery. The trick was to try to fit the two together, so that although working usually on separate days from different boats and not even knowing each other, their efforts would be integrated. Basically, the N.A.C.S.-A.C. teams would have the task of putting the frame tops and plank-tops on paper, which required minimal removal of soil, while the civilian and Fire Brigade teams would carry out deeper excavation down the sides of the wreck and then draw the curves, thus putting the profiles on paper. The latter was the more critical task, in that, unless properly controlled, it could cause damage; and also possessed a considerable element of risk for the excavators. For this reason, I wanted to reserve the bulk of the experienced civilian team for digging, and to train others.

From the standpoint of organisation, they were difficult days. What we required was a fairly rapid, controlled expansion. Instead, the Technical Sub-Committee which I had formed earlier to handle the machinery and organise the deep excavation teams virtually fell apart. George Clark, who had been the mainspring for years, was promoted to Assistant Divisional Officer in the Fire Brigade and was so tied down by work that he could not undertake any large commitments at Spithead. Sub-Lieutenant Bob Lusty, diving officer of H.M.S. *Reclaim,* and our only professional diver, was going to be away with the ship for long periods on trials. Peter Aitcheson, who had built our air-lift, was about to move to Scotland. I

had absolutely none of their talents for practical engineering
and the handling of work teams, and, besides, I was beginning
to feel my years and could not lead in the sense of doing more
diving and bustling around than anyone else, let alone take
on physically demanding and dangerous tasks. This was true
of some other key people as well, all middle-aged now. The
younger generation were about a year away from archaeological supervisor status, because it takes a long time to learn
a task for which the manuals have yet to be written. And it
took several months before the pressure of events pushed some
of the existing team towards the discovery that they, too, could
design and construct air-lifts, and organise their operation.

There was one other development, the result of devoted
work by Morrie Young and some of the Southampton team
during the winter following the recovery of the gun, which
amazed me. They had taught Margaret Rule to dive. She had
also proved a model pupil, they said. In the long term, this
was a tremendous gain. In the first year or two of the project,
I had learnt a lot from Margaret, but the help a land archaeologist can give, merely by looking at the waves and debriefing divers, is extremely limited. Indeed, after a time,
their efforts become counter-productive, because they do not
understand either the site or the forces at work on it. But,
occurring at this time, the new development was momentarily
embarrassing. Margaret was tough and determined, but nearly
forty. Her aqualung training had been carried out in a swimming pool. Her experience of snorkel diving had been mostly
on brief holidays in the Mediterranean. In the normal way,
I would never consider letting a novice carry out a first sea
dive at Spithead, and especially not in low visibilities among
ropes and lines. But Morrie had perfect confidence in his
pupil and on 15 May down she went. To her surprise, she
loved it!

The log kept by Percy Ackland faithfully recorded the
personal reactions of a land archaeologist to a first sea dive,
compared to the objective reports of divers who really knew
the site and also appreciated the very powerful forces at work
underwater. We were using a light jet with a special semi-
feathered nozzle to examine frame "48", a very large offset
timber. Fireman Mick Russell did the work, while I watched
him and noted what was exposed and how it was exposed and

whether or not this type of jet was a suitable tool for the job. It was designed to work like a soft brush, but even so Mick was using it to dig small holes around the timber and was not actually directing it at the wood. But I didn't like it, because we could find no way of curing the bad visibility problem it created. You dug first, and only after a wait did you see what you had exposed.

The three contrasting dive reports read as follows:

1308:   MRS. RULE claims she will have no sympathy with divers complaining about bad vis. Bottom was just as she imagined it. It was super. (Turning to Morrie.) What did you bring me up for?

1325:   ALEX McKEE reports concern over fact site still appears to be scouring and state of fragile timbers. Recommended air-lift.

1413:   DICK MILLERCHIP reports we are fairly well down now and light airlift would be ideal. We must be 18 inches from Frame 48 and 3 feet deep. Stacks of loose timber. It worries one for fear it will be washed away.

The central fact noted by Millerchip and myself, even in the restricted visibility, was that there had been further scour and that this had exposed to view much loose timber over the site generally. There was little current now, but we could well visualise what would happen on the next big spring tide, due in ten days' time. All that timber, irreplaceable evidence from the wreck, would be dispersed all over the Solent by what would be, in effect, a fast-moving wall of water 50 feet high. I therefore decided to declare a state of emergency and mount operations to remove all loose wood, while noting positions as accurately as possible.

I made a final dive late in the day to inspect the result of the tiny, exploratory dig we had begun around No. 48. Being offset, Morrie considered it an important anomaly, possibly part of a chain plate for the rigging of the foremast or perhaps a vertical wale of typical carrack type. My log report read:

As I came down towards the wreck, it was almost dark and for the very first time I was very conscious of the hundreds of bodies lying literally only a few feet down among those timbers. On the bottom it was nearly night, but visibility was much better. What I saw, I saw clearly. The side of the ship was exposed for about 20 ft. or so; at what height not at all obvious. The jetting run by Russell and Millerchip had been done perfectly. The outside [*sic*] planking of ship was still clay-covered, with a hole about 14 inches deep ringing No. 48. Probably an instant partial fill. As planned, I now carried out the final stage of the dig. I hand-dug around No. 48 on the one side and hand-dug the sideplanks on the other. The clay/mud was almost flush with the top of the sideplank; as I cut it away, so I came on nothing, about 4–6 inches down. This suggested a gunport, so I dug inwards and again came on sideplanking set about an inch or so back. I exposed a foot or so of the sideplanking in this very restricted area. A strange sensation, after all these years, clinging to the side of the *Mary Rose* with one hand, and digging down her side with the other. I had imagined the wreck many times, as it lay under the mud, while working out collapse stages, etc., but it was astonishing to see it so intact, solid proof of how wrong the sceptics can be!

When "rescue" had been completed, and excavation restarted, it was carried out largely by hand, with air-lifts being used merely to transport the sediments away from the diggings. By this means, the excavator could at all times see what he was doing. Because even the softest jet obscured visibility, their use was discontinued. The whole of the season's excavation could have been done in one day by a professional salvage team using really powerful tools; but that would have been salvage, not archaeology. We had to work even more cautiously than usual, at least until some clear picture emerged, and all timber and artefacts removed had to have their original position and depth noted; then receive a number and be entered in the book. All meant *all*. Obviously recent anchorage "gash" was treated in exactly the same way as items obviously from the *Mary Rose*, partly because their stratification was interesting and informative in itself, partly because there were many indeterminate items, partly because we did not want to leave the decision—to record or not to record—to the diver actually doing the work. "Record everything" was a simple formula not to be misunderstood. Initial results, judging purely by pottery taken at face value, indicated that the wreck was that of a British Railways steamer sunk in the early 1970s. Then it became nineteenth century. And finally, there was a possibly significant grouping of sherds dating to the early seventeenth century. Now, that could mean that the accepted dates were incorrect. But not necessarily so. It might mean merely that the wreck had continued to be a substantial obstruction on the seabed until the early 1600s, which meant that it would have been a haven for fish, which in turn meant that it would have been a local fishing "mark" until that time, with the result that debris from the fishing boats above would automatically have been deposited on it and in due course covered over by sinkage and fresh sedimentation. If this was so, then the information was both interesting and relevant. But information could be built up only by recording everything objectively, even if it looked irrelevant and uninteresting.

On these matters Margaret and I were of course completely agreed and all the experienced divers understood them; but the newcomers had to be supervised until it was sure that they also understood. We had to check any tendency to be "helpful"; initiative was positively discouraged. A newcomer, unless strictly warned in advance, might see some old ox-bone lying about on the surface, think it was human, and attempt to "save" it by bringing it to the surface clutched to his bosom. These were the exceptions, and it was gratifying to see how most divers concentrated on the job they were given and, if anything unexpected appeared, immediately stopped digging and reported it. That meant a lot of diving for the supervisors, particularly Morrie Young, the shipwright, and myself, for I had a fund of knowledge concerning the stratification of the site, the result partly of the sonar surveys and partly from years of digging into it.

What was to become the "Deep Excavation Outboard" started as a limited excavation "Both Sides of 48". Morrie Young and I had decided that the thing to do was to go down both sides of the ship at this point, equally. The practical reason was, that a ship's hull is designed to withstand pressure from outside to in, but not from inside to out. By going down both sides, we would keep the pressure equal. The theoretical reason was that in this way we might find a fitting which would give a rapid answer to the question: How high up the

hull are the tops of the frames and planking so far exposed?
If a rapid answer was not achieved, then we would have to
dig deeper to obtain a profile of the hull curves at this point,
which should answer the question. And this question was the
whole point of the season's work.

These were tiny, tentative digs because I was still afraid
of touching off further scouring of the wreck by uncontrollable natural forces. But with the end of the big 16 ft. spring
tides, this soon tapered off. By degrees, a picture began to
emerge. East of "48" the soil was fine, soft mud all the way
down, containing much loose or immediately disconnected
wreckage, much of it extremely fragile. Automatically, the
dig this side of the "run" of frames and planking slowed, and
we kept having to cover in for fear of the effect of tide-scour.
West of "48", however, the soft soil soon gave way to much
harder material, basically clay, but containing a fine scattering
of "grit" which was composed of very small shingle plus tiny
sea shells; similar to the layer found six feet down during
George Clark's first dig into the port mound on the JM3
line. The line we were now on was about JM4½ and further
over the the west. There was also a notable lack of the complicated and delicate ship wreckage found east of "48". By
5 June we had gone down four feet this side, exposing mag-
nificent blackened oak framing, planked only on the other
side, east of the ribs. With my head down at the bottom of
the excavation, my knees were about level with the top plank.
This was not the original upper plank, which had been
removed because it was displaced and loose. Its displacement
had at first given us the impression that it was the top of a
bulwark, but excavation enabled Morrie to read the picture
correctly. Recording the position of anything removed employed the simplest method, that of reading off against the
nearest frame, which had a numbered tag nailed to its centre.
Measurement from frame centres had been advised by Morrie,
because this was standard shipbuilding practice. Hammering
in the nails showed how good the ship was. The nail went in
easily for the first inch or two, after which the blows of the
hammer produced a distinctly healthy "Thonk! Thonk!"

Three small featureless pieces of wood recovered from
the excavation at the 1½-ft. level, which had been very badly
attacked by gribble and Teredo, were selected for a test by

Morrie as examples of the worst timber from the *Mary Rose*.
Two were oak, one was elm. After 48 hours' drying in saw-
dust, they were machine-sawn along the grain, then redried.
Finally, the sawn surfaces were planed, and Morrie reported:

> As the shavings were removed from the samples they curled
> in exactly the same manner as those taken from newly-
> seasoned timber. This, I believe, gives a fairly good idea as
> to its structural strength. Apart from a general darkening
> of the oak samples, visually there appears to be little to
> suggest that the timber has suffered significantly from
> having been submerged for over 425 years, although a
> microscopic examination and pressure tests may give a
> different result. The shavings taken from the elm sample
> appeared to have lost very little of the original colour,
> although they appear to have become a little more brittle
> than those taken from normal seasoned elm. I would stress
> that they were particularly poor specimens and in the worst
> possible condition, from which I would draw the conclusion
> that timber samples taken from farther down in the ship's
> structure would be almost perfect.

Meanwhile, the survey teams were digging and tagging along
the "run" to the north and also to the south. They were uncovering more than they surveyed, so that the plan tended to
lag well behind their digging, because Margaret Rule rightly
insisted that, until a timber had been properly surveyed in,
it did not exist. Consequently, part of the civilian team,
including a group of students from Bishop Otter College,
Brighton, were put in to help. This slow progress south was
awkward for some weeks, because the survey was close to
the excavation around "48", and until it moved away two
quite different teams would be working in the same area.
Then a naval survey team, probing along their line for more
buried timbers below the level of their hand-dug trench, came
upon an obstruction which was not wood. It was another
enormous grey concretion, like a great fat sausage, but
indented at one end, clearly the muzzle. The breech-end, if
there was a breech, lay between two frames of the ship's side.
This gun did have a context and was therefore very important,
but it slowed the survey while the N.A.C.S.-A.C. team dug a
coffin-shaped pit around it. Only with reluctance could they

be persuaded to leave it and continue digging forward for further frames. And here they drew blank. The frames just seemed to stop beyond the gun, and they now had ample cause to curse me, for I had not yet abandoned the thought that the "run" was the port side of a ship headed south. The alignment of the concretion indicated that it was a starboard side gun, pointing south-west towards the Isle of Wight. But as the ship heeled over, it could have become displaced and hurtled down to the port side. It was another indication that I was wrong, but faint and inconclusive. From now on, however, the evidence built up to suggest that the "run" was the starboard side and not the port side after all.

Firstly, as scouring seemed to have stopped, I risked a much more ambitious excavation west of "48". I laid out four 12-ft. metal rods to form a square, stretching from Frame 1 to Frame 9. Frame 1 represented merely the most southerly exposed frame to be tagged originally. The new frames trending south, as they were exposed, were being allotted by Margaret numbers in the 60s. For substantial timbers in the deep excavation, I was about to allot letters, to avoid confusion. The weekend of mid-July gave us visibility up to 20 feet and two air-lifts working perfectly from two separate boats. Margaret directed the use of a new 4-inch air-lift built by Pete Powell on the gun site, while I directed the work of the 6-inch air-lift within the square, intending to take it down evenly to four feet all over. Pete Powell and Alan Kingwell had completely stripped the 6-inch, cleared it, and given us a really efficient tool to remove the sediments raised by the hand-digging. The divers stopped each time they came to significant timber and I went down to inspect and photograph it *in situ*. Where a timber protruded into the square from undug seabed, they did not try to move the timber, but simply dug around it. We got a very neat square, with flat surfaces.

As they went down, Frame 5 began to move. It proved to be broken about four feet down, so it was removed. At the far side of the square, a long, thin piece of wood was uncovered, one end lying much lower than the other. Then, about $2\frac{1}{2}$ feet below this, the excavators found a plank aligned directly towards the hull; and in the very bottom of the excavation, 4 feet down, two overlapping planks, not completely cleared but lying at only a slight angle to the hull. Ninety per cent of the evidence was there, and another foot or so further down was to give us the full story. But for that we had to wait two whole weeks, until we could get out there again.

Then the excavation was taken down a further 4 feet, to a total depth of 8 feet, close to the frames. At 5 feet down, the frames started to curve outwards towards the Isle of Wight, and just below this, they *were* planked. Further, it was now obvious that the frames had originally been planked all the way up, on the west side as well as the east. There were trenails sticking out from the frames, which matched the holes in the planks now lying loose and exposed beside them. The *Mary Rose* was definitely carvel built with planking both inside and out. But which was inside and which was out? It was a momentous question, now.

The distinct curve which was now appearing could be only one of two things. The bottom of the hold on the "low side" or the "tumblehome" of the upper gundeck on the "high side". Very little of the ship—or almost all of it! One or the other, and nothing in between.

If this was the hold, then, considering the original heel of the ship (which certainly took place, although it may have been corrected or corrected itself later), one would have expected piles of ballast stones and much miscellaneous wreckage of great complexity. But there was nothing of that sort. Instead, it was all very simple and uncomplicated. The bare frames with the planks stripped off—and beside them the planks which had been stripped off. Taken with the broken Frame 5, the picture, I concluded, was that of "many planks and one frame displaced violently westwards by grapnels or anchors". This could have been the result of Tudor salvage efforts, or accidental damage incurred later. Now the gun began to fall into its proper place, which was that its original position in the ship was much the same as it was now. Seeking further evidence, I had probes carried out just east of the ribs and planking, and this produced quite a number of shallow contacts, many more than would have been obtained on the Isle of Wight side. But considering what hung on the verdict, I felt I needed more evidence and planned to restart the excavation on the east side. Partly, this was to ease the strain on the side of the ship, partly because I wanted to find an actual deck, as this would enable us to calculate approximately the angle of heel still remaining.

At this stage the excavations and the tagged run of framing were inspected by Ken Barton, the Curator of Portsmouth City Museums. It was his first dive for ten years, his last one having been during his caving career. The interesting thing was, that he saw what we no longer noticed. He came up lyrical with descriptions of the marine life on the wreck, and had even been tempted to pick up an edible crab. What he had seen were dense masses of the beautiful black-and-silver striped whiting pout, and possibly the larger greenish pollack which often accompanied them. They had been resident since 1969, when we had dug the first trench on the JM3, and although the pollack were a trifle shy I could almost summon the pout at will for a photograph. I usually contrived to get them into a picture when I wanted to, and I had got into the habit of beckoning crabs to pose in exactly the right place on this or that piece of wood. The trick was absurdly simple: if you wanted him to move to the right, you threatened him with a finger from the left. When Ken had finished giving a very accurate account of the zoology, botany and biology of the site, I managed to ask him what he thought of the *Mary Rose*. He pondered a moment. "You have a ship there," he grunted. Pause. "A big ship."

A few days later the N.A.C.S-A.C. teams, who were operating two or three evenings a week as well as putting in some time on weekends, made their decisive discovery forward. As their trench produced negative results ahead and probing obtained no contacts on the right, they swung the trench to the left; that is, eastwards, to Southsea. And here, they again came on timber, but more deeply buried. Their trench now swung in a curve and after about 20 feet the timber they were finding was extremely massive and quite different to ordinary framing. They thought this might be the long-sought stem of the ship, the ultimate objective of the survey forward, which would give us the centre-line (although not the extremity of the ship, because the bow castle projected forward of the stem and the bowsprit extended far beyond that). Among these heavy timbers they found a miscellaneous collection of small items, some quite definitely of the right sort and from the right period. There was a pair of stone shot, about 7 inches in diameter, one brown pottery sherd which Ken Barton identified as mid-to-late sixteenth century, a whetstone of the type carried on the belt at that time to keep iron implements sharp, and parts of the skull of an old man, very worn. This was quite a different picture to that revealed by the dig west of 48, where even at eight feet there were no artefacts; nothing at all except broken structure. Now, I was really beginning to believe that west was "outboard", east was "inboard".

When I examined their work a few days later I found that they had not had time to tag the timbers before going on leave, but that they were indeed much heavier and quite differently angled. Many were deeply scored, one had a scarf-joint quite plain; most were lying at a slight incline up to the south. One really formidable piece had what looked like part of a slightly heeled deck attached; but I am not a shipwright and could not be sure. All I could feel certain of was that, while the actual stem was not visible, this most probably was the area of the stem, the massive timbers in the bow. But how high up the bow? What could have been a deck slightly heeled to port looked to me frighteningly like the ceiling-boards in the hold of the *Victory*, which we had toured very recently under Morrie Young's guidance. I succumbed to stage fright. The results of a careful hand-dig "inboard" (i.e. east) of 48 on the same day, only helped it along. After digging, I myself put a probe vertically down the face of the inboard planking, and it went to the full extent—7 feet—without touching anything. At the end of the day I got John Elkins to repeat the gambit and he touched 9 feet without getting a deck. Surely this must be the hold, I thought. In all the seven years I had never felt so depressed, for if it was true, I had led everyone on a wild goose chase.

I telephoned Morrie and explained how the N.A.C.S.-A.C. trench did not incline left but swung round sharply in a bold curve. And I quoted Margaret Rule, who had compared swimming along it to going round a roundabout in a car. That was enough for Morrie. He did not believe that the *Mary Rose* was bluff-bowed right down to near the keel. On the contrary, he thought she probably had fine lines down there. The broad sweeping half-circle could mean only one thing. "We're way up topsides," he said.

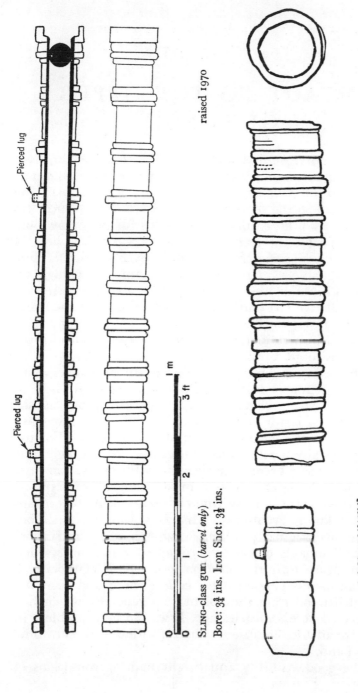

raised 1970

SLING-class gun (*barrel only*)
Bore: 3¾ ins. Iron Shot: 3½ ins.

raised 1971

PORT PIECE with GUNPOWDER CHAMBER
Bore: 8 ins. approx. Stone Shot: 6½ ins.

CHAPTER SEVENTEEN

INTACT TO THE UPPER GUNDECK

Looked at coldly, we had still rather less than certain proof that the stem area really was what it appeared to be. To start with, we did not have continuous framing and side-planking all the way along the semi-circular N.A.C.S.-A.C. trench; far from it. That would require "proving" by further excavation. Nor did we have the stem post, merely a confused area of heavy timbers. Nor was the semi-circle, even if proved, absolutely unarguable evidence for the remains being high up the hull. Bill Majer was able to produce a counter-assertion of the speculative sort one might well meet outside the team. But by now it was the end of August, we had too many valid objectives still unattained and we were running out of time. Two months to go. Could we manage?

We tried first to mount a number of three-day operations to map the stem area inside a grid and to a plan devised by Margaret. It was archaeologically impeccable, but as she reported: "The result of all this hard work is that we have a detailed plan of a meaningless jumble of frames and planking—superficially it all seems a bit of a waste of time." The jumble would only become meaningful as the excavation went on and, layer by layer, the area inside the grid was exposed and recorded, and the loose timbers removed. By this means we should know, eventually, what was *Mary Rose* timber exactly in its original position, what was collapsed timber, what was remnants of castling collapsed from above, what was loose *Mary Rose* timber from other parts of the wreck which had merely happened to "collect" here, and what was merely driftwood from the Solent area generally which had also collected here, centuries ago. It was no light problem in the time available, because all the recording work had to be done by hand.

In the good visibility and bright lighting conditions of

July, I had tried out a small photogrammetric grid experimentally. George Bass, who began with heavy grids in the Mediterranean, had switched over to this method in the end, because it was much, much faster and I daresay more accurate. But because his visibilities were in excess of 100 feet, he could take his photographs from 15 to 20 feet above the wreck, so that a very large area was mapped on a single negative with one click of the camera button. Our best visibility was 15 to 20 feet and I found I could manage the technique by taking photos four feet away from the wreckage, over which, for scaling purposes, I placed a light white-painted wire frame made up of six-inch squares. This was non-operational, because we were surveying in metres, but could be bought off the shelf and was good enough for the experiments. The method did not work at all in average to poor visibility; so it was virtually confined to June and July, and not always then.

Taking measurements by hand was so slow that I began to doubt that we should be able to find and identify the stem itself in the time available. Further, the digging here had to be carried out with extreme care, which again meant slow progress, although I obtained from Atlas Copco a DOP 10 submersible pump driven by compressed air. This employed the principle of sediment removal by very gentle water suction, and proved a first-rate tool for the work. It "proved" part of the framing and planking curving round towards the stem, revealing some startlingly perfect timbers at this point. Even so, although Margaret was extremely keen to see the methods of land archaeology work underwater at Spithead, I faintly distrusted the context in which they were being employed. Inside a big swimming pool enclosing the site, they would be fine; but exposing delicate wreckage to strong tidal currents and gales made me nervous. There was no reason why we should not be driven off site by long-lasting storms in the middle of a delicate piece of work, and then be unable to get back and cover in before the next big spring tide was due. In the event, we compromised. Margaret proved that the method could work; but we stopped before committing ourselves irrevocably. That, of course, was to accept failure in our attempt to identify the stem and so establish the centre-line of the wreck.

Alan Baldwin's N.A.C.S.-A.C. team had now transferred their efforts to the presumed position of the "low" (or South-sea) side in an attempt to find frames and planking which would positively identify it as such. This would be vital—if they succeeded. We already had something like 130 feet of "high side" framing and planking shallowly exposed, of which 23 metres was now on paper and therefore "discovered", with a further four or five metres still to map, before the frames went deep under a high mound. If Alan could expose even a small stretch of framing on the other side, the resulting site plan would look very much better and more convincing. At the moment, if one wanted to be cruel, it was still possible to say that we had only a one-sided ship; and with so many people having staked their historical reputations on the totally imaginary complete destruction of the *Mary Rose* by Colonel Pasley, the residue of their grumbling could adversely affect our chances of support for 1972. Alan was a very determined driving little man and might manage to do it. But again I had doubts. This time they were based on the awkward arithmetic of deep excavation; the deeper you go, the wider must your excavation be, to avoid a fatal cave-in, and the difference between a 4-ft.-deep excavation and 6-ft.-deep excavation is much, much greater than it seems. I had worked all this out some years back, for depths down to 15 feet, and been much depressed by the implications. Alan's lads set to with determination, building an air-lift of their own which was fed not by a compressor but by large compressed-air cylinders. They did hit timber about five feet down, but just exposing a bit of wood at the bottom of a narrow shaft was far from proving side framing even if it was. They kept on trying, not only throughout the rest of the season but right through the winter well into 1972; and the mathematics of the matter defeated them utterly. "Proving" that side of the wreck had to be a task for the main effort next year. It was not to be achieved in 1971.

No one sponsored the continuation of the survey to the north, because a decisive result was not possible there and it was always a second priority task, but both Margaret and I were keen to link the last exposed timber with various points in the JM3 trench, so that everything might be surveyed in on the ground. At present, it was related only by the transit lines formed by geographical landmarks ashore. Now much more experienced under water, Margaret dived twice with Percy Ackland and had laid out ground lines as the start of this work, when the Spithead "ghost" appeared and cut them. The ghost was normally blamed for the appearance of tangled pieces of rope in various unauthorised places, and was a most convenient personage, for at first, with different teams working on different days, each team tended to blame the other. But they tended *not* to cut or remove lines they themselves did not recognise, in case these had a meaning for the other team. Only by comparing notes at length could we decide which lines to remove. In most cases, I think the "ghost" was really the tidal stream bringing along its quota of old rope, which tangled in the wreck and around our buoylines; although it was possible that somebody was diving the site at night; somebody not authorised, that is. But the cutting of a line freshly laid in the last half-hour was something quite different, particularly as it was cut in an area where no one else ought to have been, for all the teams were being directed to work at definite tasks in closely defined areas. We suspected an undisciplined diver from another boat there that day, who had gone for some unauthorised sight-seeing, got himself tangled, and cut himself free. Sometimes, Margaret sighed for a land site, where she could sit at the door of a hut and take in the whole scene at a glance. After that total waste of two dives by two of our best people, we abandoned for the moment the idea of surveying in the "contacts" in the JM3 trench. Time really was running out, the bad weather was due, and we were all set to fail everywhere from having tried to do too many things at once.

Meanwhile, intermittently, interrupted by these other demands, I was still carrying on the outboard/inboard excavation by 48, and making very little progress, even when I put almost the whole effort on to it. Inboard, cautious excavation by hand at selected points in a narrow trench flanking the inner side-planking had to be stopped time after time, just when it was getting interesting, because the uncovered wreckage was too complicated and fragile to leave uncovered. Outboard, the much deeper excavation filled up nearly to the top after only a short time with weed which after a week or so became compacted and was the very devil to remove. On

12 September one of our toughest airlifters, Dave Felton, had the initial task of removing this compacted fill. He certainly shifted it, but what came to the surface was a great mass of interlocked laminaria weed and roots, together with a large expanse of untreated sewage, the stench from which nearly made us all sick. A large conger eel, which had apparently been living in the outboard excavation, and loving it, shot past Felton's face, narrowly escaping going up the air-lift with the effluent. This compacted fill always took hours to remove, and on another occasion the scene was further polluted, apparently by an upstream oil-tanker, and the air-lifters had first to plunge through surface water contaminated by several inches of reeking crude oil before descending to the sewage-impregnated seaweed. There was very little of the "romance of underwater archaeology" for them that year.

However, the inboard excavation had produced more important results than at first appeared. It had shown that there were two distinct types of heavy offset framing. The angled beam "48" was duplicated by other equally angled beams at regular intervals; and they were associated with an elmwood lining and fragile, ruined deck planking. Originally, Morrie had thought that they might be internal heavy framing angled to support a gundeck; but it was now clear that his alternative theory, that they were collapsed horizontal deck beams which had originally supported a deck just above the eroded tops of the visible side frames and planking, was the correct appreciation. A foot or two above the main "run" there had been a deck, which had fallen down inside the hull. But which deck?

The other heavy frames really were frames, not fallen deck beams. Technically, one might call them "cant" frames, for they were inclined forward at a slight angle, as with normal bow framing. But their purpose was different. They were not part of the side, but served to stiffen it internally in a way not found, for instance, in the *Victory*. This was something new, possibly a very old reflection of the Tudor ramming tactics, for the side at this point was given a most unusual strength by them. This appreciation made possible the critical decision: to abandon the "inboard" excavation until, preferably, the *Mary Rose* was safely inside a dock at Portsmouth, and to excavate down one side only—the "outboard" side—to a depth of 12 feet in order to obtain at least a convincing profile of its curve, and at best the discovery of the three "wales" shown on the hull by the Anthony Anthony drawing. The latter would give us identifiable points on the actual hull which could be co-related with the Tudor picture of the ship.

Of course, there was a risk that the hull, unsupported to a depth of 12 feet along a length which must exceed 20 feet, might distort; but it was small. And we now had two shipwrights to check its strength as we went down foot by foot, for Hilton Matthews from the Isle of Wight had now joined us. I felt that a minor disaster which had occurred during the trial excavation of the East Indiaman *Amsterdam* at Hastings would not be repeated by us on the *Mary Rose*. Directed by the Committee for Nautical Archaeology, the excavators had used a mechanical excavator to dig a large hole in the sand beside the ship during the brief time it was uncovered by the sea and lay open to the air. With mud and water inside the ship, and only air outside, and with all the iron bolts rusted away, the *Amsterdam*, like the *Vasa*, was held together by nothing in particular, and one after another, with a remarkable noise, plank after plank "sprung" and water gushed out of the ship. The *Vasa* excavators had foreseen this with their ship and every empty bolt-hole had been refastened underwater by the Swedish divers before the hull was raised. Our situation was quite different, firstly because the *Mary Rose* was underwater, so that the pressure of the water outside was only slightly less than that of the pressure of the soft mud inside; and secondly, because, although her planks had been "hung" in position by small iron nails, the main fastenings consisted of $1\frac{1}{2}$-inch-diameter wooden trenails. Not only was she solidly pegged together but she was still caulked, and the caulking was sound, as we soon found out.

In five working days, unfortunately spaced out between 18 September and 14 November, we did it. This was remarkable, because compacted weed had time to gather, and had to be removed each time before further excavation could begin and, at this depth, there was a considerable amount of light "fill". Also, the days were growing very much shorter, the water very much colder and the bulk of the digging was still done by hand. But the original "hard core" of civilians

and firemen had been almost doubled in number by the best
of the season's new volunteers, drawn from Brighton, Southsea, Southampton and the Isle of Wight. One Isle of Wight
team, which came out in their small inflatable, usually consisted of a farmer and a hovercraft pilot, who took to the
hazardous business as though born to it. In addition, a new
navy team came out in a *Vernon* boat, led by Ian Inskip, first
lieutenant of H.M. Submarine *Odin*; and they too learned the
work almost instantly. We were also much better organised,
with air-lifts left on the bottom so as to cut time in starting
work, and with more than a dozen divers really experienced
in deep excavation. Two of them, George Dart and Adrian
Barak, were also skilled surveyors; and they built a measuring
machine to help them draw the profile of the hull as, foot by
foot, it was revealed.

Already, on 18 September, the excavation was deep
enough for them to draw profiles of Frame 4 to 2.10 metres
and of Frame 7 to 2.15 metres; these showing convincing
"tumblehome". Going down to the bottom of the excavation,
which was deeper than the height of a tall man, I was
entranced, and noted in my log, "BEAUTIFUL BROWN
SHIP". At this depth, the *Mary Rose* was not a wreck any
more, she was a real ship, the planking apparently as sound
and the trenails as smoothly flush as on the day she sank
before the eyes of King Henry VIII.

It was infuriating to see the next weekend almost totally
wasted in obtaining inconclusive results from the stem area
survey; but in October I got the main force back to work on
the deep excavation, with only a token effort for the stem
curve, using the DOP 10. On the first working day, nothing
was to be discovered; the effort was devoted solely to widening the excavation so as to produce an even floor about seven
feet down, from Frame 1 to Frame 15, and outwards for at
least a dozen feet. For a time, I watched Percy Ackland doing
a shift with a 4-inch air-lift built by Pete Powell. He was
digging by hand and using the tube to remove the sediment
and maintain visibility. The upper end of the tube showed
the rhythm of it, with bursts of 'smoke" interspersed with
gushing water, and only tiny fragments of light shell trickling
downwards. Avoiding the tremendous pour of water from
the mouth of the tube, I swam down it to find Percy digging

like some precisely set machine, producing an absolutely vertical wall in an absolutely straight line at the Isle of Wight face of the excavation. Later, we went down together with the compressed-air lamp to inspect and take photographs. The powerful light illuminated only a few feet of the ship's side at a time, so it took a sequence of seven overlapping pictures to photograph some seven feet of exposed side—first, the bare frames, then the intact planking lower down. It was late in an autumn day and without the light the hull appeared black, so black that it seemed as if the timber had been burnt; but when the lamp was played slowly down the side a rich texture, seen in a rosy glow, was immediately apparent.

A week later, on 10 October, we virtually completed the process. With orders to alternately widen and deepen, the pairs of divers dug smoothly to a depth of between 11 and 12 feet, in an excavation now 22 feet long and 18 feet across. In spite of some rapid bottom fill, this enabled Dart and Barak to profile Frame 7 down to 3 metres; that is, to measure and draw the curve of the hull opposite this frame for a total depth (or height) of approximately 10 feet. It showed the most convincing "tumblehome" one could wish; indeed, I christened the marked outward curve of the hull planking the "Mermaid's Sunbathing Deck", because you could actually lie on it. And at the bottom of the excavation the hull was still curving outwards towards the Isle of Wight, even when one slid one's fingers down the planks under the mud. The significance of this is difficult to explain in modern terms, because modern ships do not have this feature; they are either slab-sided or curve the other way. The purpose of it is to decrease the beam, the higher up the ship one goes, so that the guns on the upper gundecks are much closer to the centre-line than the guns on the lower gundeck, thus giving stability. It can only really be appreciated by walking up the gangway of the *Victory*, stopping at the top, and looking at the marked curve of the side at the upper gundeck. The *upper* gundeck. And this most certainly was what we had with the *Mary Rose*, the better part of the upper gundeck, and most of it in far better condition than those parts on the *Victory* which actually date back to Trafalgar, for much of that ship is a replica, not the original. Morrie was to draw this curve full size, and it gave a minimum depth of hull remaining to the *Mary Rose* of 30 feet. That is, a *Vasa*. Condition, just as good. Age, much older. Importance, far greater. And with her contents largely intact, her historical interest far exceeded that of the *Victory*.

But we were puzzled, frustrated even. From a large "blow-up" of the Anthony Roll picture I had drawn the side of the *Mary Rose* at this point in as much detail as could be managed, as a guide to the excavators. Apart from the "tumble-home", it did not match. The Roll showed three "wales"—heavy, longitudinal strengthening timbers—running the full length of the ship's side. There was no sign of them. We thought we had found one earlier, but it proved to be only an ordinary plank which had become partly unfastened and slipped outwards, thus producing a projection like a wale. What we had found instead were four "chafing pieces". These were like small wales, but with rounded instead of rectangular surfaces. To our shipwrights, they were evidence that we were approaching the greatest beam of the hull, but that point had not been reached yet; the *Mary Rose* was still expanding below us.

At this point of puzzlement, everything stopped. Five operations in a row were rendered abortive by bad weather or hopeless visibility. Now, we would have to go on into November, with its shorter days and colder water. The delay brought back the compacted weed problem with even greater force, and although more profiles were drawn the excavation was not made appreciably deeper in the restricted times available. On 27 November we went out for the last time with a Fire Brigade team and pump to carry out the "backfill" of the "inboard/outboard" excavation. This was necessary, not merely to preserve the wreck from scour effect during the winter tides and gales but also to kill off all the marine life which had "colonised" the excavation. The hull was in such good condition that it might still be edible! A row of rods was set up as a start-line and then relays of divers worked the water-jet shallowly on virgin seabed off the wreck and drove the sediments towards the wreck. When they had finished, the deep excavation was full to within a few feet of the top, all the really sound structure was covered, and we could leave nature to do the rest.

We had already lifted the major items which really had to be raised. Apart from the "slipped plank", there was a deck carling exposed by the inboard dig. It was $9\frac{1}{2}$ feet long and although out of position probably indicated the existence of a nearby hatchway in the broken down deck. Almost the first person to inspect it after it had been fully uncovered was Morrie Young and he nearly died, laughing, when he saw it. One of the rebates had been incorrectly cut and a small piece of wood inserted to reduce it to the right size. Morrie could well imagine his Tudor predecessor taking a quick look round the shipyard in Portsmouth, to see if the foreman was about, before he "botched" that piece to make it fit. Bad workmanship or not, the "botch" had lasted more than four centuries under the sea. When we lowered the carling to the deck of Tony's trawler, it was quite impossible to tell the difference betwen the Tudor decking and the trawler's planks, except for erosion on one side and at one end of the *Mary Rose* piece.

The drill for raising the gun was much the same as before, except that N.A.C.S.-A.C. made the initial lift to the surface with a helicopter-lifting-bag attached to a shackled girder from which the gun was suspended in a cradle of ropes. This was a slick job, largely due to Artie Shaw. Then the ship we had used before appeared dead on the appointed time and picked up the gun; berthed alongside another ship in the Dockyard; transferred the gun to Dockyard crane, and deposited it on the vehicle where, in white coat, Chris O'Shea was waiting to receive his "patient". We had, of course, been the recipients of various suggestions as to how to do it, none of them foolproof or having any margin at all for accident or bad weather. But these guns were so important that I was impatient with ideas which risked dropping the things in the entrance to Portsmouth Harbour.

This gun was particularly important because of the height up the ship at which it had been found. And even that was not its true level, for the deck on which it had been originally had disappeared. It was a short, heavy piece of orthodox "built-up" construction with a bore of 8 inches firing stone shot of about $6\frac{1}{2}$-inch diameter. The powder chamber, $18\frac{1}{2}$ inches long, was still in place, the open end being sealed by a slice of circular wood cut from a sapling. Parts of the carriage still existed inside the concretion, as did much of the breeching ropes, and, inexplicably, the barrel appeared to have lain on a bag of shavings. At any rate, there were shavings underneath it. The barrel was quite clear of mud right up to the shot, which fitted a gun from the "high side" of a ship which had heeled right over as she went down. A good deal of the wrought-iron was intact to the outer surface, so that an inscription of a kind could be seen on the blue-grey muzzle. This consisted simply of two parallel diagonal lines. Oysters were in direct contact with the metal under the concretion, confirming that the gun had not been buried originally, but had been exposed to the sea long enough for spat to settle and grow. In 1545 it would have been an easy salvage proposition to anyone equipped with diving apparatus of almost any type.

Reference to the Anthony Roll list of ordnance and ammunition carried by the *Mary Rose* showed that this could only be a port piece or a fowler, and as a document of about 1555 (Cecil's *Memorandum Book*) indicated that port pieces then ranged from $5\frac{1}{2}$ inches to 12 inches in bore diameter, it appeared to be an example of a medium-sized port piece. This weapon may have been similar in principle to the heavy carronades of H.M.S. *Victory*. Short-ranged, lightly constructed, but firing a large projectile, these pieces probably let fly their heavy stone shot at point-blank range just before ramming and boarding. The stones would, of course, break into scores of deadly, whirring splinters on impact.

In due course the entire hull of the ship, complete with its contents, would illuminate the whole Tudor period and not just some technical aspects of it. And that day had been brought appreciably nearer by the events of the 1971 season.

CHAPTER EIGHTEEN

THE STERN QUESTION

Reg Cloudsdale surfaced in the swirling eddies of the air-lift and held up a dark, curved object like a lobster claw. It was the blackened top of a human skull complete to the eye sockets. He had been excavating in the North Trench, exposing strangely splintered side-framing about four or five feet below the seabed, when his digging hand had touched a curved object in the mud; he had thought it was a round shot until his fingers told him that it was hollow and must be a skull.

We gazed at the find with melancholy disinterest. *Annie Moore* pitched and rolled, as she had been pitching and rolling for four hours; and would continue to pitch and roll for another four. Damp and dismal grey clouds raced overhead and now and then the rigging would emit a brief howling to warn us that although the wind was blowing at only Force 5, it was gusting 6 or 7.

Our suits stank from the clouds of macerated sewage which had swept across the site all week, looking, as Margaret said, like revolting shreds of old sponge. Our muscles ached from holding on, especially when shouldering our heavy gear, to prevent ourselves from being hurled from one side of the boat to the other. Holding on, that is, every second of eight hours. With two hours on both sides of that spent each day travelling and in the work of loading and unloading heavy equipment at high quaysides designed for ships, not motor boats. The hours spent underwater might have been luxurious relaxation in comparison, had it not been for the bitter cold sea below and the chilling wind above. There was no way to rest or get warm this side of bed. And it would be the same again tomorrow, for this was the eighth day of a nine-day operation carried out in the wind and water conditions of a particular poor December. But it was not December, it was the first half of July.

Everything which could go wrong, had gone wrong, in-

cluding the circulation pattern of the Atlantic ocean. The
newspapers were saying that drifting ice had pushed the Gulf
Stream south of its normal course, bringing cold water to
Britain and altering the entire pattern of the weather. We
could well believe it. Even the large, spiny spider crabs from
colder West Country waters had moved in on us, the first
time they had been seen in the Solent since a brief foray in
1963, following an "Ice Age" winter of frozen harbours and
sheet ice as big as football pitches circling round Spithead.
Out of the first 50 operations we had so carefully planned,
31 were to be cancelled or prove abortive, and of the remaining 19, many were to be ineffective. Weather was the primary
cause, coupled with the failure of promises designed to give
us a Force 6 capability by cutting out the need to tow a
compressor barge. The winds ranged from Force 5 to Force
9 much of the time, and this stirred up the sediments so
much that a brief calm spell could not disperse the murk and
darkness shrouding the *Mary Rose*.

But now that we had at last got things moving for more
than just a few days at a time, the excavations were going
well, so well, that they provided us with continual surprises.
As I came down on the North Trench, where Cloudsdale had
been digging, I saw that it was being driven forward in a dead
straight line, as ordered, correctly ignoring a chaos of timbers
which abruptly replaced the simple pattern of a "run" of side-
frames and planking, and correctly ignoring also a trench
which N.A.C.S.-A.C. had dug on an eastward curve earlier in
the year. The new excavation was a "copybook" affair, ruler-
straight with strictly-parallel, absolutely vertical sides—no
gang of council workmen digging a road could have done
better. The tides soon altered this, eroding the sides to a slope
and filling the bottom of the excavation with drifted seaweed
and much junk. But its ruthless accuracy exposed the truth.
The frames did not deviate to the east, as had been reported;
what had been dug there were internal timbers. The "run"
of the ship's side carried on due north, but at a lower level,
overlaid by much scattered timber, and disappeared about 5
feet below the seabed into an overhanging bank. Not only
that, but the frames were actually somewhat lower here, their
tops jagged and splintered as if by a minor explosion. The
fibres were distorted rather than eroded. We were all pretty

sure that we were looking at the results of one of John Deane's gunpowder charges. But with so much time lost already, we did not continue this trench much further. It was clear that what had been reported by navy divers as a rudder could be no such thing (although it might be a capstan), and that the extremity of the ship in this direction lay an unknown distance further north. We still thought of this end as being the stern.

Similarly, a "Port Side" Trench quickly dug to verify the naval divers' claim to have uncovered the top of a main frame on that side revealed only a chaos of angled timbers suggesting collapsed castling with a marked slant towards Southsea. This was no surprise because N.A.C.S.-A.C. had lacked the power to remove overburden rapidly and so reach a firm conclusion. The heavens reeled only when we set out, next, to prove the "bow curve". Last year's shallow trench had exposed only a few eroded frame tops which appeared to trend round to the east, with the sausage-shaped concretion containing the port piece lying at the start of the turn on top of two frames. We now dug this line more deeply, so that the nature of the frames would become clearer, and we insisted on the exposure of inner skin planking. With so many heavy internal timbers about, this was the only sure way to follow the actual side of the ship. And every day the picture changed as eroded tops gave way to a well-preserved wooden structure. Last year's two frames (on which the gun had lain) became the Double Frame, when it was clear that they were connected, and finally the Giant Frame, when it was seen that they were two parts of a massive composite timber which, moreover, sloped outboard for some distance under the mud. The original 1971 report (by students from Bishop Otter College) had been perfectly correct, as far as the dig had then gone. But what was now revealed lower down reinforced doubts about the "bow" which Morrie Young had voiced towards the end of that year. The composite timber looked remarkably like a transom fashion piece; that is, the point of transition between a ship's side and its stern.

Summing up what was a necessarily slow and careful excavation, with each item revealed only at time spaced intervals as a result of digging a trench some 20 feet long and 5 feet deep around the "bow curve", we learnt a number of

facts. The basic fact was that we were dealing with an angle
of about 45 degrees, not a curve; this suggested a stern shaped
like a blunt triangle. The inner skin planking butted up
against the composite timber to form this angle but was not
continued; neither of our two shipwrights could suggest why
this was. Outer skin planking over a marked "tumblehome"
was exposed only a few feet lower than the inner skin level,
and the suggestive point about this was that while most of
it consisted of the horizontal strakes we had encountered in
the deep dig the final few planks by the composite timber
were laid vertically; and this change of structure also indicated that we were dealing with a stern and not a bow.

But it was still true that we were uncovering a ship of
unknown build characterised by one very odd structure for
which there were no later parallels at all: a four-storey fighting castle carried well forward of the stem, actually overhanging the sea, which must have required elaborate support
of a highly conjectural nature.

The historical evidence was indicative merely, not conclusive. The battle course of the English ships in their
counter-attack on the French galleys was definitely to the
south and the Cowdray engraving showed this. It also showed
the *Mary Rose* sunk on an identical alignment, with every
suggestion that south or thereabouts was the heading. Only
the two tallest masts were shown rearing out of the water and
the most northerly of these appeared to be the mainmast, not
the foremast, because it wore a flag and was shown higher,
with part of the yard and sail visible. As the two small mizzen-
masts which would have settled the matter were not shown
it was still possible to argue that the hull had come to rest
in a stern down position, thus altering the apparent height
relationship of the fore and main masts. If so, it meant that
the wretched ship had been in such dire trouble that she had
swung right round from her attack course. Or, perhaps, as
Morrie Young suggested, being in trouble, she had tried to
return to the safety of the harbour.

Against this was the evidence of the Anthony Roll picture
of the *Mary Rose* as compared to the results of last year's deep
dig which had exposed to a depth of more than 10 feet and
for a length of about 20 feet an almost completely featureless
expanse of hull. According to Anthony, only at the bow,

where the anchor was catted, was there such a marked absence of gun-ports, and the anchor might easily have been removed by the Venetian salvagers. But Margaret Rule was worried by the nature of the Tudor artefacts we were getting from this area, which we were now beginning to call the South Trench. These were still comparatively few in number, the majority of finds consisting of broken seventeenth century glass bottles, eighteenth and nineteenth century pottery sherds, machine-stitched leather shoes, miscellaneous bones, mostly animal, twentieth century plastic cups, and the prize discovery, an electric light plug. But what Tudor finds there were suggested stern castle and not bow castle. That is, a living area, not a fighting area.

The direction of the work was more complex and critical than in 1971, with a good many options open. The chosen one had to be the right one, there was no time left for mistakes. And a mistake could be defined as pursuing a valid objective which consumed more time than the knowledge gained was worth at that stage. To start with, I marked out the angled corner outboard of the composite frame for widening and deepening. There was a peculiar arch on its south side which could be a hawsehole for an anchor and there were outboard probe contacts which were strange. We went down six feet and all was clear. Both features were the result of outer cladding which had "sprung". And on the actual south end of the ship this deeper excavation revealed outer skin planking which was nearly vertical instead of horizontal and with a slight rake (or overhang) to the south. This did indeed look like a stern, but to prove it, in Morrie's opinion, would mean digging three feet deeper still around the corner. Which would mean widening by another nine feet or so for a fair distance—a major excavation. I decided against that.

Instead, we carried on outlining the "stern" to the east, hoping to find a definite "corner" which would mean that we were on main framing at the opposite side of the ship. We might even find a sternpost and rudder somewhere along the way, although they could lie too deep to be practical this year. The immediate result was a continuing pattern of ammunition finds: stone shot of two basic sizes—approximately $6\frac{1}{2}$-inch and 4-inch—for port pieces and fowlers respectively; lead shot of three basic sizes—$1\frac{3}{4}$-inch, $1\frac{1}{2}$-inch and $1\frac{1}{4}$-inch—pos-

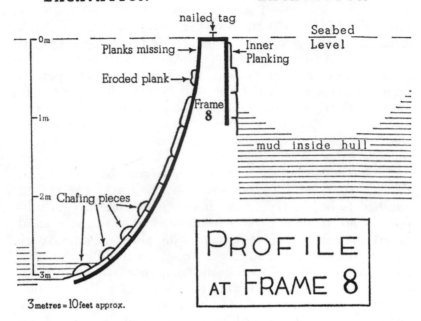

OUTBOARD EXCAVATION   INBOARD EXCAVATION

nailed tag

Planks missing →

Eroded plank →

Frame 8

Inner Planking

Seabed Level

0m

1m

mud inside hull

2m Chafing pieces

3m

3 metres = 10 feet approx.

PROFILE AT FRAME 8

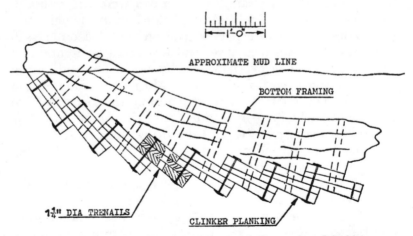

APPROXIMATE MUD LINE

BOTTOM FRAMING

1¼" DIA TRENAILS

CLINKER PLANKING

For comparison with the profile of the *Mary Rose* hull, a section of the highest part of the wreck of King Henry V's carrack *Grace Dieu*. The curve of the frames shows that only the bottom of the hull is left. The frames are planked only on the outside and in clinker fashion. LINE DRAWING: *Maurice Young* sibly for bases of three different kinds; and stone moulds for making lead shot on board, which produced $1\frac{3}{4}$-inch and $1\frac{1}{4}$-inch missiles. The lead-firing guns, as well as the fowlers, were still missing from the historical record, and are almost entirely conjectural. There were also parts of what might have been small powder kegs and two handles for "kidney" daggers, both of wood. A nice base-metal alloy jug, almost intact, provided yet another strong pointer to the stern and together with other fragile materials, such as rope and leather, justified our decision to dig slowly and cautiously.

But even when we had exposed the first ten feet of the south end of the ship to a depth of five or six feet there was still no recognisable feature of the *Mary Rose* exposed to view —no stern gunports, nor any of the other apertures shown by Anthony; just a blank wall of near-vertical planking topped by eroded frames. It was undoubtedly impressive in its massive solidity, and something like awe possessed us as we looked at this evidence of a mighty hull buried since Tudor times.

Beyond this expanse, which was marked by a large concretion, the actual framing of the ship changed utterly; no longer were we uncovering more or less vertical ribs. Instead, we seemed at first to be dealing with fore-and-aft beams projecting into the South Trench; but as the trench went deeper, their true nature became apparent. They were the flatly eroded tops of frames which angled down sharply into the mud, suggesting the raked stern of a wreck heeled over to Southsea, thus preserving part of a stern gallery on the heeled side. In turn, this implied that the surviving outline of the hull, seen in plan from above, would look most odd; and that it would be hard to identify the centre-line if the preserved height was above the level of the sternpost and rudder (or, for that matter, of the stem). This end of the ship did indeed have a prominent point to it, so prominent that Ray McLaren called it the "nose", and for a long time we thought this might be the centre-line, with the sternpost (or just possibly the stempost) lying directly below it. But as the *Mary Rose* had a number of superimposed stern galleries, the rudder might be buried at an impossible distance down (or it could be only two or three feet away from us). Reluctantly, I decided not to get involved in what could be a long, complicated and dangerous excavation, and instead we carried on outlining the hull with the intention of locating a definite "corner" and finding a matching composite timber to the "transom fashion piece" on the other side.

Even this was moderately dangerous because of the generally low visibilities, particularly when clouds of sediment and loose weed and old rope came bowling along with the tide and tended to remain in the South Trench. Visibility of perhaps four or five feet on the seabed could abruptly reduce without warning to only an inch or two in the trench where the anchor rope and airline of the digging machinery represented hazards in themselves. Four times that season I got entangled, as compared to once only in the seven years which had gone before. And Margaret Rule became so completely trapped that her only way of escape was to take off her aqualung, then free the rope from it, and finally surface with the cylinder under her arm, and so coolly that we thought at first that her harness had just come adrift accidentally.

Excavation was slowed not merely by poor visibility and the masses of dead weed which could collect many feet deep in the bottom of the trench within ten minutes or so, but from the surprising fact that, after we had dug round the "nose", the spacings between the timbers to be uncovered increased quite remarkably from a few inches to three feet or more. As we were still looking for a "corner" and a matching composite frame to mark it, the line to be followed was often unclear to us from the misleading clutter of collapsed wreckage which had to be systematically recorded and then cleared away. On average, for one day's work we were uncovering only one new main structural timber.

Often the visibility was poor on the seabed, let alone in the trench. On one occasion when I had invited Maurice Harknett out to see our progress and had rather unkindly roped him in as my partner, the visibility was quite horrible. I had to keep my face mask pressed close to the side framing of the ship in order to read the numbered tags and follow them round the "stern" from 162 to 183, the last exposed timber. Here, there was confusion enough anyway, because the South Trench had broken into the earlier "Port Side" Trench. After locating the air-lift tube, I then had to find the last tagged timber, No. 183, which was at a lower level in the blackness, and then decide where to dig to find the next timber in line. Having decided on the place and line of attack, I then had to position Harknett just to one side of me, with the air-lift, a 4-inch tube some 40 feet long.

Harknett had the hard work of moving the tube to the exact position I needed, while I lay down and dug with my right hand, sifting the soil and letting it be removed by the powerful suction of the tube about a foot away. The "Port Side" Trench at this point gave a false apparent line, but I managed to see just enough to ignore this and actually dig back into the side to where I judged the next timber in line should be. This meant, of course, starting work about three or four feet below the level of the seabed, which cut off much of what little light there was.

In my log I noted: "In the first five minutes visibility was so bad and light so poor that I was only finding where Harknett had put the lower end of the tube by nearly getting my fingernails sucked off; but we soon settled to a useful partnership." The many years we had spent diving together meant that we could communicate, after a fashion, in these conditions. Two divers who did not know each other well, or were not used to air-lift operations, would have faced an impossible task.

Harknett opened up the tap, which caused air to rush into the bottom of the tube with a subdued, bubbling roar; and that also made the tube buoyant, so that it rose almost vertically in the water and became easier to handle and position. Each time my fingers dug out a section of soil, the low visibility became no visibility; but with the end of the tube held close the disturbed sediments made a smooth beeline for it and vanished, to appear at the top, 40 feet above, like thick, swirling smoke emerging from a tall factory chimney and agitating the entire surface of the water. As soon as I could see again, just in front of my nose for a few inches, I would make another hand-cut in the clay and mud, feeling for any object which might be buried there, and releasing another gout of grey-black sediment which left me (and Harknett) in total darkness. As we picked up the rhythm and established optimum distance, rubbing shoulders, so the times of total blackout became shorter; then the scene lightened as the sun came out and visibility improved, and we could see almost all of the

time, the air-lift whisking away the clouds of swirling sediments and sucking in fresh, clear water just in front of our
faces. Apart from any number of sharp-edged old oyster shells,
which had grown on, and died on, the wreck many centuries
ago when it was above seabed level, there were only two finds
during our 26-minute shift—one small bone and one tiny
sliver of wood.

Three shifts later on in the day a new timber duly
appeared in the now much deeper gulley, and I went down to
inspect and tag it as No. 184. It was on the same line as its
predecessors, but two feet lower down; and it had planking
attached which plainly continued the line. The next two
shifts uncovered 18 inches of this planking, and then we were
through for the day. The "finds" totalled twelve, including
items as small as the stems of clay pipes and covering a time
span of four centuries, from the $6\frac{1}{2}$-inch *Mary Rose* stone shot
to a small lump of clinker from a much later vessel's boiler
clean. All, without exception, were recorded, photographed
and the wooden items kept damp until the collection could
be handed over to Margaret Rule for allocation of numbers
in the "Finds" book. It was a typical day's excavation, by
"treasure ship" standards depressing, by our standards highly
successful because we had uncovered one more main timber
and continued outlining structure (as opposed to dislocated
or collapsed wreckage) for nearly $4\frac{1}{2}$ feet.

In 1971 it had been possible to do more work by increasing
the numbers, particularly where survey was concerned, because the divers' tasks consisted mainly of measuring timbers.
If they made a mistake, it could be rectified; and no damage
had been done. Even so, the N.A.C.S.-A.C. team had never
completed their survey, so that this part of the task had lagged
behind excavation until well into the following season. We
saw little of them in the first half of 1972 and nothing at all
in the second half. At their last appearance, they were given
a digging job in the North Trench, but we repeatedly found
them turning up in the South Trench, 130 feet away, having
abandoned their own work in order to go sight-seeing. There
was no guarantee that other clubs which also offered their
services would be any different, and the policy we now adopted
was to feed in newcomers as individuals, in ones and twos. This
worked well and was to lead to the formation of a *Mary Rose*

Special Branch of the B.S.-A.C., composed of divers whose primary interest underwater was the *Mary Rose*. This was necessary, partly because much of the work was now so intricate that it demanded considerable familiarity with the site and its problems and partly because the casual club diver would find it extremely tedious. There was nothing in it for him.

For instance, I once completed a brief log entry with the comment: "The green crab by frame 48, last seen alive yesterday, was dead this morning, lying on his back. Nothing else of note." On another occasion I was worried by signs of minor digging around in the wreck in unauthorised areas, but the proven culprits turned out to be edible crabs, several of which were cooked for it, because occasionally I could pass that way again on my way back to the ascent point. It was an unwritten rule not to take livestock during worktime and Margaret Rule and Percy Ackland went so far as to ignore a lobster three feet long, a real monster. In August I was actually attacked by one of the weird-looking giant spider crabs which had begun to move in on us from the West Country. Instead of the bright pink colour exhibited in the normal habitat, this specimen was dulled all over, possibly with some kind of algae, and far from being frightened it became irritated when I began to record its presence photographically. To start with, the creature had its long stilt-like legs folded under it and its long, thin claws at the mouth-ready position. With everything fully extended, it probably had a total reach of about $2\frac{1}{2}$ feet. I was breathing gently four feet above its back, at correct minimum focussing distance, when suddenly the great clumsy monstrosity took a vertical leap up at me, failed to make the full distance by about six inches and flopped back again into the dust like a 1911 Farman "boxkite" performing an ungainly crack-up. I did not know whether to laugh or applaud.

We did have sharks, the standby of most diving books, but in theory only. The usual porbeagles of around 300 lb. were being taken off the Isle of Wight and out at the Nab Tower, but we never saw any. Excitement, for us, was of a quite different order. And most of that was packed into the month of September, when suddenly discovery followed discovery and everything began to make sense at last.

CHAPTER NINETEEN

THE THIRD MAN

It was not until mid-September that we realised that the wreck had a false "nose". Because the run of good weather which allowed us to tow out the compressor barge put a premium on digging, survey had fallen days behind excavation. But already we were beginning to suspect the truth—that the "nose" was not the apex of a triangular stern but the far corner of the hull. There was still no sign of a companion piece to the giant composite frame on the western side, which should mark the far side of the ship, and the lack of such a frame had also helped to mislead us. We had continued to outline the wreckage without finding it for a quite impossible distance; unless the remains were those of a structure similar to Southend Pier. The eroded frame tops themselves presented a puzzle; not all were at the same level, but this level did not incline either up or down but went up *and* down for no apparent reason, like a fever chart. The structure seemed to defy all logic, even granted that the *Mary Rose* was an unknown ship. But selective re-digging to a lower level of key parts of the now extremely long trench soon made me suspect the incredible truth.

The first clue was the change in the angle of rake which was now revealed as most marked, once we were round the "nose". Up to and actually at the "nose" the angle was acceptable as the stern rake shown in many pictures of carracks and galleons and consistent with part of a stern gallery on a heeled hull which would necessarily give a false impression when seen in plan. But beyond the "nose", not only were the frames much more widely spaced but it was soon revealed that both these and the planking between lay at an impossibly flat angle; it simply could not be rake. And as soon as part of this was revealed I made a note in red: "183–184 looks like fallen castling, NOT STERN". If a long stretch of castling had fallen intact, it would have obscured the matching composite timber which just had to be there, somewhere. The "nose" was false; we were well round on the far side of the ship, but on wreckage which did not match the western side because it was from much, much higher up the hull.

The whole picture gradually fell into place during the four-day work period 16 to 19 September. First, came my suspicion that we were dealing with intact castling, not main hull at all. Then Hilton Matthews surfaced with the surprising report: "The planking between 182 and 183 is clinker". This had not been immediately obvious, because the overlapping clinker construction was partly concealed by lining timbers which presented a flat surface.

Our plans to work nine-day periods at a time, for which people had arranged their holidays in advance, had been ruined by the bad weather in the first half of the year; and now it was difficult to find workers able to come out on weekdays. So on the fourth and final day we were in desperate straits, down to three men—Percy Ackland, Ray McLaren and myself, and both Percy and I felt chesty, probably from cold and exhaustion. We had been driving ourselves hard in a battle with the months, moving inexorably towards winter, and with the sun, which was arcing lower and lower in the sky at midday. Only McLaren was fit enough for the physically tough task of air-lifting; but he had just come off a night-shift at Southampton Docks and should have been sleeping. Instead, he dived until he was quivering with cold, and by then he had completed 80 minutes underwater and was within four minutes of the maximum permitted time anyway. Percy insisted on diving, so I gave him a survey job and forbade him to use the air-lift. Unheroically, I chose not to dive at all, because if I got into trouble there would be no one left in a fit state to rescue me.

In spite of this, and without any dramatic developments at all, the results of that last day's work clicked everything neatly into place. Ray's digging, directed to the extreme end of the trench, had uncovered yet another wide-spaced frame, which would be tagged as 186 when we had enough energy to do that. Percy took many more measurements than I had asked him to, and established that we were indeed well round on the Southsea side of the ship and that we had a minimum of 20 feet of continuous castle structure lying in the mud; a distance which, when corrected back to the "nose", gave a figure of nearer 30 feet. And then he went on to make the key observation of the structure at 182–183, which my as yet undeveloped film confirmed. He coined the term "clinker sandwich" to describe a feature which perfectly explained that inexplicable zig-zigzagging of frame levels.

The construction was almost the exact opposite of the main hull structure which consisted of a single row of massive frames boxed between heavy carvel planking inside and outside the hull. We had been looking at the inside, and with some of the paired frames missing; sometimes this would be an inner (now higher) frame, sometimes an outer (now lower) frame. When this difference was understood, one could readily distinguish between inner and outer, because they were recessed to take the overlapping clinker planks.

I now turned back to my picture collection of authentic medieval and post-medieval ships and thought I recognised on almost all of them something like this structure, depicted (on the outside only, of course) as a series of parallel vertical wales; occasionally the hull proper appeared to be built like this, but more often it was the castling only. Perhaps we had uncovered a key to understanding what the old artists had been trying to represent.

As usual, the Anthony Roll picture of the *Mary Rose* herself was less than helpful. True, the artist had shown just such a series of vertical wales, apparently at the right spacing of between three and four feet, on the stern castle only. However, this was at a great height—the sixth deck up, assuming the hull had both a hold and an orlop deck—and between the outer wales were rectangular black apertures enclosed within an arch of some sort. On the starboard side shown in the picture there were 13 of these, making a total of 26, and I had always assumed that they were firing ports for swivel-guns which I provisionally identified as being some of the 30 "bases" firing lead shot which Anthony put at the lower end of his gun list. Now, from our ammunition discoveries, I connected the base with the lead shot of roughly one pound weight which we had been finding. This was fine, except that no aperture had yet appeared between frames 182 and 183 and there was no sign of an arch.

The good weather looked as if it would go on for ever, but we had to act on the opposite assumption, that it might break at any time, and that we might not get out to the site again until the following year. This thinking ruled out any further outlining of the castling let alone any extension of the North Trench. Instead, we took the course of reinforcing unexpected success. That is, the surprising discovery of actual castle structure which had been the main result of the original decision to opt for outlining. At the time, that too had been only one of a number of possible actions, all valid, but none of them certain of success. By mid-October we had in fact just two weekends work left to us on neap tides before November brought down on the south coast an appalling series of gales and storms, some gusting to hurricane force, which turned the sea yellow for months.

I decided to work backwards from the now well exposed "clinker sandwich" at 182–183 towards the "nose" at 173–175, examining selected areas for the junction between the two types of structure and, in particular, for the still obscure transom fashion piece on the Southsea side of the wreck. For the weekend of 14 and 15 October, I had marked out with red rods a limited area between and behind frames 180–182. We had eight divers on the Saturday, ample for a short winter day. But Margaret Rule was ill, although she hoped to be better by Sunday, and this became my first overload, giving me the additional task of listing and bagging the finds. Then the weather turned out workable but uncomfortable, and poor Alison, our logkeeper, became too seasick to continue. And so I collected a second overload, on top of my primary tasks of direction, briefing, debriefing and dive inspections (which this day required me to dive three times between noon and half-past two, when matters were becoming critical).

There had been only one day this season when matters had gone really wrong, but none of the odd mistakes had been archaeological and none had concerned the main task of the day, which had proceeded quietly and smoothly. I had known from the beginning, and had impressed upon everyone else, the truism that everything movable in the ship would have crashed down from the high side to the low side as she heeled over, and that this side would require therefore great caution in excavation. Margaret had stressed time and again that objects must not be lifted until they had been cleared completely of soil—there must be no grabbing at a half-buried object. And we had both stressed the necessity of stopping work and surfacing to report any unusual or difficult problems. Indeed, Margaret was fond of saying that our work had been immaculate by any standards, let alone those customarily applied to underwater work. By now, I think, we were getting a little over-confident.

The first two shifts, Geoffrey Morgan and Guy Martin, Adrian Barak and Albert Kirby, married one site-experienced diver with one new recruit, whose first *Mary Rose* dive this was; and they were without incident, although the debriefing reports were exceptionally difficult for me to follow. They were clearly into a complicated area and had been unable to find more than one of the red rods with which to mark it out. It is hard to describe an underwater situation exactly, even to another diver who knows the site, which is why hopeful archaeologists and maritime experts who sincerely believe that they can conduct a dig entirely from the surface frequently commit such sorry atrocities. Clearly it was time for me to go and check.

I found that the correct area had been dug and that a false tag had been removed on the divers' own initiative. Having laid all the red rods originally, for a widening of the South Trench months ago, I knew exactly where they were, collected two of them, and marked precisely a small area for excavation. I noted that it was "confused at present with loose timber and timber which might be loose"; but that there seemed to be a possible composite timber part-revealed between 180 and 181. This was one of those typical stages when a pattern has yet to appear and one had to wait patiently for more patient work to be done.

The experienced leader of the next pair met a totally unexpected situation after he had been digging for some time between 180 and 181. First, a near vertical timber with a slot in it appeared, obviously a displaced piece. Correctly, he did not move it. Then, just the far side of it, bones began to appear in some sort of pattern. (Scattered bones had been a commonplace find from 1965 on, and almost all had been animal remains, except in the South Trench, where a proportion of them were parts of totally dislocated human beings. All such remains, human and animal, were noted, removed and listed in the "Finds" book. Indeed, most of us are poor judges of bones and only Margaret Rule, who had dealt with hundreds of bodies in a single land excavation, could tell with any certainty which were animal and which were human.)

What was now beginning to appear was quite different. There were two parallel rows of ribs, somewhat scattered, but nevertheless forming a pattern on either side of what seemed to be the remains of a spine. And to the right were parts of a pelvis and two leg bones lying among planks. To the dive leader, they appeared to be "related"; that is, belonging to one man and not just a haphazard collection. Up to now he had made no mistake. He had not moved the bones as they appeared, but used the air-lift to carefully expose them all as they lay there. He was a very intelligent man, and this was our undoing, for he thought he knew enough to be sure of his diagnosis and able to act on it.

The first thing I knew of this fairly shattering discovery —totally unexpected because so high up the ship and in an area of collapse—was the dive leader arriving at the ladder with half a dismantled Tudor seaman or soldier under his arm. He at once drew from memory the main wreckage and the layout of the bones as he had first seen them, but the damage was done. There was no possibility of waiting for an expert like Margaret Rule to check if they really were related bones *in situ*.

Geoffrey Morgan had already gone down to take over, so I had to contain myself until the end of his shift before diving and without waiting the customary 5 or 10 minutes for the visibility to clear. General visibility was between 6 and 8 feet but in the dig area it did not exist at all; the trench was totally black; so I surfaced, waited six minutes and then dived again. Now all was quite clear, but I could see nothing useful, for the bulk of the evidence had been removed. What I did observe, however, was that apart from the frames 180 and 181 there was still no structure. All we had seen so far had proved to be merely closely packed wreckage. This made the presence of "related" bones even more extraordinary. It was much more likely that the fallen castling was a catchment area and I was able to establish that the remains so far brought up had come from at least two different individuals, being mixed with some animal bones and an eight-sided wooden handle from a dagger. But if there was even the faintest chance of related human remains being found at this amazingly high level, we should have to be scrupulously cautious.

Next day the seas were not quite so unpleasant but still bad enough to part one of the four tow ropes connecting the trawler to the compressor barge. Normally, only one tow rope was used, but this weekend Phil Hammond thought four were necessary, as indeed they proved to be. Alison had decided not to come at all. A seasick person is useless and simply had to sit there, suffering, for six to eight hours without any hope of release short of death. Margaret Rule had not recovered from her illness and so did not turn up. Once again, I had to try to cope with three people's jobs simultaneously; not merely the diving but the paperwork. Including Dick Millerchip, who joined us on site in his own boat, there were seven divers in all, one of whom was slightly seasick.

Direction was critical. Instead of waiting patiently all day for the diggers to uncover something for me to think about, the pattern was changing every thirty minutes or so with each debriefing, with fresh instructions having to be given on the basis of the latest report. In general, what I did was to move the dig slowly along the castling from 181 to 180 to 179, neglecting 181 to 182 as I thought it likely to be the same "clinker sandwich" as between 182 and 183. What I was slowly searching for was the junction between the end of the side castling and the beginning of the stern and also, further back, the point where the side castling had broken away from the main hull. The attempt to clear back foundered almost immediately behind 181 and 180, on the actual start line. Eric Sivyer reported finding "masses of bone".

He had neither moved nor removed any of this, but had cleared a little space and revealed a large bone plus ribs and spine with a fragment of leather which suggested part of a jerkin. At this point, correctly, he had stopped and moved a little distance from the delicate area to continue excavating structure. Millerchip followed him, and when he in turn had reported, I went down.

Visibility was of the peculiar sort we were getting a lot of this year. Six to eight feet at maximum, it was "unfocused". There were so many particles in the water, and the light was so poor, that one could see sharply and clearly what was in front only when the object was less than two feet distant. No overall picture was possible. I swam along the frames and then turned in slowly between 180 and 181, moving only inches at a time and looking carefully. No real structure had yet been exposed, only apparent structure which later that day turned out to be parts of 2-inch-thick planks 15 inches wide, and of beautiful quality but not oak. I could not see any bones at all let alone what, for a rapid distinction, I was calling the "Third Man". I found that Sivyer had exposed no more of these remains than was absolutely necessary, which was very little.

"I only saw him when I had my nose 9 inches away from his thighs, looking at the ends of both thigh bones," I wrote in my report. "He was on a thick plank now angled up, far end disappearing into side of trench. Pelvic girdle in position. Felt very carefully for base of spine, vertebrae, ribs. Above is a smaller plank, trapping him. And further above, left, other items sticking out, possibly fourth man, but did not feel any of this should be touched further. Plank, which has a raised part, may be plank of deck on which he was when he died, before outward collapse of the whole affair." I was certain that this was basically the remains of one man and had the impression that the spine was still articulated, with the head lying inboard. But the thigh bones were an unnaturally wide distance apart and there was no sign of the lower legs or feet. When Margaret inspected a few days later she saw at once that the bones were not articulated, nor were they in any meaningful anatomical position; and that the angled timbers here might form a linear catchment area which "would trap bones in a seemingly meaningful arrangement". In short, the "third man" was probably an illusion. An unresolved oddity was the lack of skulls. For some reason, heads do tend to move long distances or vanish. Some weeks previously Sivyer had uncovered a jawbone about five feet away, between 182 and 183; but this was the only remnant of a head from an area which had now produced bones from at least three individuals.

A careful excavation of the remains from above was out of the question this year, so I simply declared this part of the wreck a "No Go Area", leaving the problems unsolved. There are few hard facts, but many myths, concerning the behaviour of corpses in wrecks. The Royal Navy have in modern times placed nets round the hulls of warships sunk in harbour to prevent the bodies floating out after ten days or so, when they have become sufficiently bloated to rise. Many bodies did rise

to the surface from the *Royal George*, sunk in similar circumstances to the *Mary Rose* in 1782. The nineteenth century
did produce some helmet divers' stories of recently sunken
ships full of drowned people, but cold water was thrown on
these tales by Jacques Cousteau in his book on the pioneer
days of aqualung diving, *The Silent World*.

Recalling that people always asked him what happened
when he had first found human remains in a wreck, he wrote:

"We have learned to be patient with the question, which
arises from myth, because we would like to restore the truth
about the sea and sunken ships. We have dived more than five
hundred times in about twenty-five sunken ships, been into
every cranny accessible to a man with three metal bottles on
his back, and never found a trace of human remains. Very
few victims drown inside sinking ships. They get off beforehand and drown in the sea. But suppose a person has been
unlucky enough to go down inside a ship. One would have to
penetrate the vessel within the first few weeks to find any
trace of the body. The flesh is eaten in a period of days, not
only by fish and crustaceans but by such unsuspected creatures
as the starfish, which is actually a voracious individual. The
bones will then be efficiently consumed, mainly by worms and
bacteria."

With the *Mary Rose* I had always made the opposite assumption and based my claims for support on a minimum number
of 200 corpses available for examination in context, with a
maximum figure of double that. But I envisaged these men
as having been trapped below decks in the main hull where
they would very quickly have been covered by the preserving
mud and clay, together with parts of their clothing, personal
equipment and possessions. In a sense I was making a case for
bringing Tudor times back to life in the twentieth century
through the medium of men who had been dead for over four
hundred years. If trapped in the upperworks, however, I
thought they would lie on the heeled side for a week or so
until the processes of decay inflated the bodies with gas to
give them a buoyancy which would take them up against the
deckhead. Hungry fish could well interfere with this process
and result in immediate scattering of the remains. By the time
the upperworks collapsed outboard, causing further chaos, one

would expect any human remains to be completely dislocated. Yet the bones of the "Third Man" might be related, and possibly those of the first collection also represented mainly one individual. I wondered if, in trying to get at the upper and maindeck guns, the Tudor salvagers had deliberately pulled the side castling away in one piece, thus preserving it for us under an almost instant coating of mud. Quite a lot of the timber we were finding here, including the planks immediately above and below two of the bone collections, was so perfect that one could not believe that it had been exposed to the sea for more than five years or so.

The removal of the first collection of remains did at least mean that the dig between 180 and 181 could be pressed to an immediate conclusion; and what was revealed was a regular rectangular aperture of the right size to be a port. There were no finds at all between 179 and 180, the next area to be cleared down to castle structure, but between 179 and 178 Geoffrey Morgan found many more bones, not apparently related and certainly lying in no particular order. I made my last dive that weekend fairly late, not finishing until 4.30 p.m. Visibility was now exceptionally good and clear, some eight or ten feet, but with the sun low in the sky there was too little light for photography, so instead I sketched the results of the dig, which were considerable. The area between 180 and 181 had been so neatly cleared that one could almost swim underneath the castling and pop up through the port. I could see fish actually doing this, but the cylinder on my back prevented me from following suit. Without disturbing the "Third Man", the trench had been cleared back to a vertical solid which seemed like a large concretion but might be that elusive main hull; and between 179 and 180 a key structural point had been exposed. 179 was now revealed internally as a four-piece composite frame marking the point where the wide frame spacings ended and, at 178, the close spacings began.

In the first week of November the weather was still workable for excavation. I laid down two primary targets for the weekend of the 3rd and 4th: examine, firstly, the "vertical solid" and secondly the "nose" itself from 172 to 175, where the frames were closely spaced. We clearly did not have much time left and were racing winter to the finishing line and the whole "stern question" was still unresolved. The underwater conditions proved to be far too dangerous even to use pairs on one air-lift, let alone run two air-lifts simultaneously, which I had planned. The comments of the diggers were terse. Barak of Brighton: "London peasoup." Dwyer of Philadelphia: "Water doesn't taste too damn good." Young of Southampton: "Black as hell." They went on to success regardless.

The vertical solid was a large, oddly lumpy concretion with a $6\frac{1}{2}$-inch shot embedded; it was not main hull. But nearby the mud concealed the most delicate collections of grouped objects we had yet met. The area they occupied was 9 inches square and no more than 2 or 3 inches deep, and it took two divers an hour and ten minutes to excavate. The group consisted of: 1 circular box base, 1 fine comb, 1 coarse comb, 1 thimble, 1 awl, 1 small knife and 2 spinning bobbins. Clearly one man's personal kit of a similar nature to the modern army issue "housewife" contained in a canvas hold-all. Another delicate find was a rope which had to be lifted in one piece on a polythene carpet and one of the smaller finds was a copper coin not earlier than 1620—probably lost by a boatman fishing the wreck and therefore evidence towards working out how long it had remained as a substantial obstruction above seabed level.

The last day, 4 November, showed the same pattern of hazardously low light and visibility on the fast-water run, improving as the current flow eased off. It was springs, not neaps, but time was so short that we had to accept that. Now the dig began around the "nose" to clear frames 172 to 175 and try to establish if it really was the corner of the stern and not the centre-line. Rapidly, the divers found themselves working down the outside of an inward incline which led in under the wreck; it certainly looked like a raked stern. The usual stone and lead shot were found, but only a single bone and no delicate collections at all. Soon the divers were reporting that frames 172 and 173 made a "V", actually joining a few feet down. When I made my inspection visibility had increased to 5 or 6 feet and I was able to hover over the "nose" and note that 173 was the centre-piece of a three-frame structure, being joined at an angle by both 172 and 174. The effect was that of splayed struts designed to support a platform, possibly the stern quarter gallery; but more work was required before we could be certain. There was also about half a morning's work on measurements to complete certain survey drawings.

With a reasonable forecast of Force 4 to 5, west to north-west, we were all set to clear up the matter on the neap tides of 11 and 12 November. But when we arrived at Flathouse Quay on the bitterly cold Saturday morning, Phil Hammond shook his head. Gusts were screaming down the harbour and he said it was unwise to go out at all. So we cancelled for that day, a great disappointment for those who had driven over a hundred miles to be there. That evening, I cancelled the next day's operation as well. I could hear the wind howling and the sea pounding and roaring on Hayling beach, and feel all too easily the deathly cold. Hammond decided to risk a quick fishing trip on the Sunday, and was caught. *Julie Anne* came back with part of her steel stern stove in and in company with another commercial fishing boat which was limping home with its cabin gone. In Portsmouth Harbour, empty inflatable boats were flying like kites, airborne on the end of their anchor ropes. As I sat at my desk that evening, shingle blown from the beach 100 feet away was rattling continuously on my windows 20 feet above the ground. Local barographs showed an exceptional fall of pressure and the coastguard station at the Needles reported wind speeds of up to 75 m.p.h.; that is, gusts of hurricane force. The local newspaper headline next day was "Gale rips the South apart".

I cancelled the next two operations but risked a quick trip on 18 November, mainly to repair damage to our harbour moorings. It was a breathlessly calm day, hardly a ripple on the mud-coloured sea, the sky along the entire western horizon warningly beautiful, the clearest possible indication that another "front" was less than six hours away. The moorings looked very odd, for one chain had parted completely and the whole affair was hanging by a single link. In four inches visibility, reducing to nil, Percy Ackland surveyed and sorted out the tangle, and we were safe again. Then we ran quickly out of harbour intent on completing the survey at least. We needed to see no more than 18 inches on the bottom. Morrie Young made the first check and reported visibility almost zero. I made the second check an hour later and found myself lying on the seabed but unable to see any of it; the trouble was sediment in suspension. We stayed at home until after Christmas, while storm after storm in succession pounded the South Coast and stirred up the Channel seas to a colour state ranging from soiled marmalade to dirty chocolate. A brief calm improved visibility in the harbours so we made one last try on 6 January; but as soon as we cleared the harbour entrance the colour of the water became downright filthy. I made the first check and this time did not even bother to go to the bottom; halfway down the buoy-chain visibility downwards was nil. I could not even see my hand against my mask.

It had been the worst year for weather since I had started skin diving in 1958; two-thirds of our planned operations had been cancelled or proved abortive—59 out of 97. The programme of long work periods from May to July, the normally good months, had been literally blown to pieces. The excavation and survey problems had been unusually intricate, the most difficult yet. But in 38 operations we had obtained the maximum of vital information. We knew a great deal more about how much was left of the *Mary Rose* and the facts were astounding, particularly when one considered how much other people had got.

Important sites like those of the Armada galleasse *Girona* and unimportant ones like the *Association* had rewarded the finders with brass guns and real treasure—but no wreck as such. Of the hulls, only a few fittings were left. The bulk of the discoveries represented some of the contents of these ships, but not the ships themselves. Strictly speaking, they were not even wrecks. It was very rare even to find bottom timbers preserved under the ballast, and this occurred only on soft seabeds. Even my own early appreciation for the *Mary Rose* had been no more hopeful than a chance that the best side might perhaps be intact "to the level of the lower gunports".

And now I was wondering just which one of her high galleries was represented by the timbers in the South Trench and trying to work out what the original level of the fallen stretch of side castle had been. Where other explorers could count themselves lucky to have only the floor timbers in the hold we actually had intact castling from a point high above the water-line. And with a ship which really was one of the

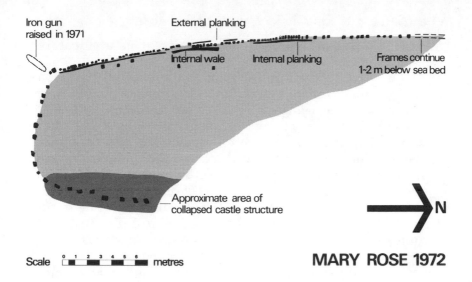

Iron gun
raised in 1971

External planking

Internal wale

Internal planking

Frames continue
1–2 m below sea bed

Approximate area of
collapsed castle structure

N

Scale 0 1 2 3 4 5 6 metres

MARY ROSE 1972

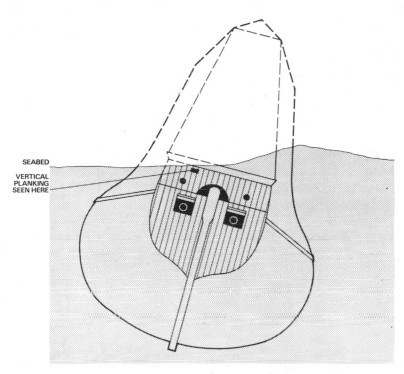

SEABED

VERTICAL
PLANKING
SEEN HERE

CONJECTURAL DRAWING OF MARY ROSE AS SHE
APPEARS TO LIE PRESERVED IN THE SOLENT MUD
BASED ON 1972 SURVEY

"key" vessels of history. It was a miraculous accident of preservation.

The damage from anchors and explosions did not seem very great. The *Vasa*'s stern had been torn right off by a modern ship anchoring on her after her discovery but before she could be raised. The protection given by the Royal Navy to our site, coupled with our own decision not to expose shallowly buried remains until we had such protection, had prevented that. The slight localised damage to frame tops in the North Trench was much the sort of result we had expected from the means and methods at Deane's disposal, while in the South Trench we had found two sections of distorted lead tubing of the type used to ignite gunpowder underwater but no recognisable signs of damage to the ship.

The scare stories put about by the London academics, successively, that we were in the wrong place, that we had only the bottom timbers if anything, but probably not even that because of giant gunpowder explosions detonated by Colonel Pasley, all these were now exposed as undocumented imagination. They had managed to be wrong all the time, on every point regarding the *Mary Rose* and their own record in this field convinced us that it was the brilliantly successful example of the *Vasa* project which we should follow.

In March 1972 we were hosts to the Director of the Wasavaret, who visited Portsmouth and offered the Stockholm Museum's vast experience when we needed it. And in July I was invited to lunch with Her Majesty the Queen and the Duke of Edinburgh at Buckingham Palace. The *Mary Rose* project, begun with five men and a boat, had acquired national status.

CHAPTER TWENTY

THE FUTURE

On 15 March 1973 I was in an S.A.S. jet coming in to a night landing at Stockholm. I had been attending a maritime archaeology conference at Stavanger in Norway, where I had lectured on the *Mary Rose*, and was with two of the Swedish delegates who were returning home—Lars Barkman, head of the *Vasa* conservation department, and Carl Cederlund, an underwater archaeologist from Vasavaret. On my right was a Norwegian who did not know who we were. He spent the last five minutes before touchdown telling me what a wonderful job the Swedes had done with the *Vasa*. In effect, he was serving as an unpaid propagandist for Sweden. The value of this kind of "spin-off" is difficult to calculate when balancing the costs of such projects against the earnings which only begin when temporary museum stage has been reached.

First, the designated ship has to be found on demand. With the *Vasa*, this took three years. We found the site of the *Mary Rose* within one year, but were faced with the peculiar problem of complete burial, so identifying the wreck was a much longer process than with the *Vasa* which, buried only to about her original waterline, was also much easier to measure, evaluate and inspect for possible damage and weaknesses. We had to spend a year or so trying to obtain electronic equipment for a sonar survey of our "invisible wreck" and in organising legal protection for a site that had not even been proved. It then took us four years to acquire the excavation capability even to establish identity beyond doubt and a further two years to uncover and survey the upper part only of what may be less than half of the still-buried and invisible hull. There had been no problems like these with the *Vasa*, which had been treated necessarily as a salvage problem, the only archaeological excavation being a long search for scattered and buried timbers on the site after the ship had been raised (which resulted in 90 per cent of the *Vasa's* timbers being found). We will have to carry out this procedure also, after salvage, but it is a simple matter compared to the intricate excavation and recording of a complex and partly collapsed structure of unknown nature *in situ*.

On the other hand, for technical reasons the *Mary Rose* will probably be able to avoid that long process involving eighteen different lifts which were needed to actually raise the *Vasa* and took from 1959 to 1961. The lift of the hull and its transfer to a dock might well be done in one operation and take a matter of days only, once the lifting cables are in place. One very good reason is, that we do not plan to float her, but to bring her in submerged and keep her submerged, possibly for years, while the interior of the hull is excavated in a controlled underwater environment.

This is a policy decision designed to avoid any damaging haste due to salvage necessities clashing with archaeological requirements and also to ensure that conservation facilities adequate to such an enormous task are in fact deployed in time. The basis of the present thinking is bitter experience of two uncontrollable elements—the weather, with its effect on excavation and salvage, and human delays of all kinds, including financial, which could make nonsense of any plan which was tied critically to particular dates. The overall requirement is that there should be no hurry.

At this stage there must be not only an available dock but a temporary museum structure to cover it and adjacent conservation laboratories. This, possibly the most interesting time of all, is when at least part of the work can be witnessed by the public; and if the project is properly planned to include them, the ship begins to earn money in her own right. The one really costly item comes only at the end—the construction of a suitable museum building to display the conserved ship permanently. After twenty years the *Vasa* has not yet quite reached this final stage, because to preserve forever a hull of this size, solidity and complexity is a mighty undertaking.

The *Victory* is not comparable because her frames, planking, decking, masts, spars, blocks and rigging are continually being renewed and much of the vessel is a modern replica, not the original. This is the penalty for keeping her in the open, in varying temperatures and humidities, and for an initial failure to protect her against the ordinary agents of decay in time to be effective. At least the replica is believed to be accurate, which is more than can be said for so-called "authentic reconstructions" of completely unknown vessels, for which hundreds of thousands of pounds have been paid to modern shipyards. The Tudors did try to preserve Drake's *Golden Hind*, but their technology was not adequate to the task and the real vessel fell to pieces in less than one hundred years.

My visit to Stockholm was not just to see the *Vasa*, although I spent two hours inside the hull and one hour outside, but to compare our project with their immensely successful one item by technical item in order to assess the varying difficulties.

Nevertheless, to my surprise, I found my first view of the *Vasa* actually exciting. I had not expected to feel emotion, because I had studied the Swedish project with admiration for many years, was thoroughly used to dealing with the remains of a yet older warship, and more or less grew up with H.M.S. *Victory*. I suppose, subconsciously, I had expected a slightly smaller *Victory*. Instead, what loomed before me was an immense structure of blackened oak, still damp and glistening from the overnight spraying required to prevent the timbers from drying out too soon, seen in the dim, rather underwater lighting of the temporary *Vasa* "house". Unmistakably, this ship had come from under the sea. This might well be the point we should make with the presentation of the *Mary Rose*, which will probably be housed not far from the *Victory* and must complement, rather than be in competition with, the eighteenth-century three-decker.

However, this was looking far ahead; our problems were more immediate. Few people realised where our real difficulties lay and, ignorant of the actual nature of things, they often raised non-existent objections in all seriousness. One which had some popular reflection was the idea that old ships could not be raised because they were too heavy. So I was amused to find that Gosta Bothén (who now lives in retirement in England but had been the director of the Neptune salvage company who was actually responsible for planning the raising of the *Vasa*), dismissing this part of the operation in one sentence. "The *Vasa* was not a big lift, but a small one." Per Edvin Fälting, the chief Navy diver on the project, similarly passed with brevity over this aspect: 'The actual lift was just a technical and financial problem."

In the early part of this book I have cheated a little. Because I was there dealing with the *Mary Rose* as a unit of Henry VIII's navy, I treated her as such—as a great battleship. And so she was in the context of Spithead in 1545. But not now. Now, the size of many ships going up to Southampton is around 100,000 tons and no ship seen there counts as really large unless it tops 250,000 tons. In that context, and in terms of the twentieth-century technology which can build and handle such vessels, the *Mary Rose* is a toy for children to play with in the bath. A brute reminder was the way a modern dockyard crane had dealt with Tudor guns as if they were no heavier than cigarettes.

Another popular view is that a wooden ship which has been under the sea for many centuries must always be in a greatly decayed state and is therefore too weak to be lifted. In the context of the Baltic environment the Scandinavians have found many exceptions to this rule, of which the *Vasa* is just one (and not even the best preserved). We started from the opposite premise, that any old wooden ship entombed in mud and clay was going to be much, much better preserved than many a comparable structure on land. We regard our immediate task as merely to check results of explosion damage, pin-point areas in need of strengthening (likely to be the bow and stern), check that no great distortion of the hull has taken place, and establish the nature of the underlying strata as a check on the sub-mud sonar surveys which show no jagged rock pinnacles likely to cause a hull to break. Given a clean bill of health on these points (which may take two or three years more exploration) we see no valid reason why the *Mary Rose* should not come up intact. Being largely wood-fastened, the hull is extremely strong.

The *Vasa*, however, was largely fastened with iron bolts, which had rusted away, so that although an immensely strong ship originally, the wreck after 330 years was theoretically very weak, held together by nothing in particular. Later, some 6,000 of these rotted fastenings were replaced underwater, but the first lift was made with an unstrengthened *Vasa* and there were many fears for her hull. But in fact, said Gosta Bothén, "the *Vasa* was much stronger than anybody thought; there was no tendency to give". The *Mary Rose* must have been at least as strong as the *Vasa* originally, because of the ramming-and-boarding tactics for which she was designed; and she is largely wood-fastened, with iron playing only a minor part. And as the 1971 deep excavation showed, the wooden trenails are still in excellent condition, although the small iron nails with which the planks were "hung" have disappeared like the much more important ironwork of the *Vasa*. It is highly probable that the main hull of the *Mary Rose* is stronger even than that of the *Vasa*.

Other popular misconceptions relate to depths and tides. We regarded the *Vasa* salvage as a great achievement because of the great depth, as much as 105 feet to seabed level, and therefore difficult; but we regard the Dutch East Indiaman *Amsterdam* wrecked on an open beach near Hastings as even more difficult, because it is so shallow. Whereas the *Mary Rose*, lying at an average 40 to 45 feet, is just about nice in our estimation: not so deep as to require long periods of decompression by the divers, not so shallow and open as to be critically exposed to wave action. The *Vasa* experts agreed entirely. Forced to deal with a wreck at 105 feet, they had moved her as soon as possible to what they regarded as optimum depth for working in the context of Stockholm Harbour obstructions, which was 17 metres or just over 50 feet. We already had optimum depth to begin with.

This is largely a matter of cost-efficiency. For safety we assume a working depth of 50 feet which gives all of us 84 minutes on the bottom without the necessity for any tedious decompression "stops" on the way up. Taking the comparable assumption for the *Vasa* as a safe 110 feet, the same dive tables give 150 minutes of decompression on the ascent for a bottom time of 90 minutes. Of course, this was out of the question and the Swedish divers usually did 30 minutes' work on the bottom and took a lesser time over the ascent. What it boils down to is that a diver's working day at *Mary Rose* depth is about four times as long as his working day would have been on the *Vasa*.

Even experts worry about the Spithead tides, which do not worry us, because fortituously the *Mary Rose* lies between but safely distant from the two main fast current runs; and we regard this as giving a great advantage over anyone working in the non-tidal Baltic. Visibility at the bottom of Stockholm Harbour did not exceed 5 feet potentially, but was in practice totally black without artificial light. However, once the divers started to dig, they disturbed the sediments and the artificial lights were useless. Fälting told me, with feeling, how the start of work resulted automatically in "a black curtain being drawn down on the diver". This happens to us only when the current is slack and the air-lift has not had its five minutes or so to remove sediment from the trenches. Our currents are actually an advantage, in that they serve to restore visibility rapidly but, except on very high spring tides, are not so strong as to prevent divers working. Having now seen Stockholm Harbour. I regard Spithead as a comparatively unpolluted underwater paradise.

Contrarily, two quite critical salvage aspects are almost invariably overlooked by the layman. The most vital is the question of the site being protected or open. We regard Spithead as being reasonably well protected from wind and weather by land masses and also submerged features such as the Owers Bank and the Bembridge Ledge extension to the Nab Tower which break the force of the seas from those directions. The site is seriously exposed only to the south-east and this arc could be blocked if necessary by floating breakwaters of the type invented by Colonel Hasler and tested recently off Gosport. Gosta Bothén found a study of Spithead charts reassuring, the site was better protected than he had thought and salvage was a reasonable proposition. As far as logistics were concerned, the fact of the site lying within a few miles of a naval dockyard was "marvellous; as good as can be". The position was similar to that of the *Vasa* site, but we did have an edge in that our area is comparatively unused by shipping, whereas the *Vasa* lay originally just outside a busy modern dock and every time a ship went in or came out, all salvage work had to stop.

With equal contrariness, popular opinion ignores what Fälting described as the most difficult and dangerous stage of all in the *Vasa* project: the digging of many tunnels under the wreck at great depth and in total darkness so that lifting cables could be passed through them under the keel. Although mud and clay strata enabled good tunnels to be dug, several divers were temporarily entombed by a collapse of the tunnel behind them. If this method is used for the *Mary Rose,* as it may well be, the dangers will be similar (although the difficulties are not so great) and would require, as did the *Vasa,* the services of a large and experienced salvage organisation.

Both Gosta Bothén and Fälting warned us against the use of air balloons at any stage because, as we would know, this meant that the whole operation was bound to go out of control. The *Vasa* had been estimated as of about 1,300 tons by modern displacement measurement, with an actual weight in water of 750 tons as she lay, filled to above her original water-line with mud. Two pontoons with a total lifting power of 2,400 tons were used on a wreck which proved in fact to weigh 700 tons in water; some of the surplus power was necessary in order to break suction, the effect of which can sometimes almost double the weight of the wreck in water. The sudden release of suction would send a wreck bounding to the surface, and they stressed that it was necessary to apply a direct lift and apply it very slowly over a long period of time, so that the suction effect was broken by degrees and the sunken hull gently lifted from its bed. Neither would now use the old-fashioned and cumbersome pontoons to produce this effect, because the Dutch were making mobile floating cranes of 500 tons capacity which were much more suitable. Two of these, one on either side of the wreck, would be ideal for the raising of a ship similar to *Vasa.* Their lifting capacity could be stepped up by 30 per cent if necessary.

The *Vasa* experts saw no objections to our tentative plan where it differed profoundly from the outwardly similar *Vasa* lift. After the original lift in deep water but before the final lift and flotation of the hull, the weight of the wreck had been reduced to about 400 tons by the removal of "one gun, some tons of stone, many cubic yards of ooze and slime, slag and ashes, plus a number of loose bits of waterlogged oak". For archaeological reasons sound in the context of the *Mary Rose,* we do not want to excavate the interior at all (although we are compelled to do so in the area of the castling, which must be lifted prior to the main salvage effort). Therefore our almost completely mud-filled hull would be heavier than the *Vasa* and certainly could not be pumped out and floated on its own keel. But, again for sound archaeological reasons, we do not want the *Mary Rose* to be floated into dock but to be moved there completely underwater, where the extra weight is of little consequence. Indeed, Fälting thought that her wooden fastenings would make her so strong that she could be raised to the surface by cranes, if necessary, in order to get her over the sill of the dock.

The point here is that a ship hull is designed to resist pressure from without, but not from within; but as long as a mud-filled hull lies underwater there is little pressure difference, because the weight of mud in air and the weight of mud in water are two different things. As I find that even highly-educated and intelligent people often fail completely to grasp this point, which a diver realises every time he gets into the water, it is perhaps necessary to indicate that anyone who possesses a bathroom with a bath in it can undertake a simple, satisfactory experiment. First, weigh yourself on the scales. Then fill the bath with water. Then get into it. Result: you float. You may have weighed 12 stones on the scales in air, but in water you weigh rather less than nothing at all, as proved by the flotation. Similarly with mud and clay. Filling the inside of a submerged ship, the material weighs only slightly more than the water outside. As long as the hull is kept underwater, the latent force remains small. But not so, if the hull is raised high into air.

The Swedes knew this and therefore strengthened the *Vasa* before floating her, particularly by replacing with wooden pegs 6,000 of the iron bolts which had corroded. Thus they avoided the unfortunate experiences of a group of London academics later, when these carried out a "deep dig" in air outside the largely buried hull of the *Amsterdam*. As the pressure was reduced outside by removal of the soil, force built up from within the hull and one after another the unfastened side planks "sprung", with mud and water spurting out of the ship into the excavation. The phenomenon did not even begin to occur with our own "deep dig" outside the *Mary Rose*, largely because of the minor pressure differences underwater but partly because of the great strength of the hull, which we kept under close observation all the time.

Nor are the experiences of the same group of academics with timber objects from the *Amsterdam* any reliable guide to the possibilities of conserving wooden hulls. After the excavations a group of wooden objects, including large blocks and gun-carriage wheels were left unconserved (and not even polythene-bagged) in the dry at Hastings. Only some nine months later, when they had begun to dry out and split, did Margaret Rule learn what was happening and remove them to her laboratory for treatment. It is necessary to say this, because among the many cooks who prepared this particular broth a rumour was circulated some years ago that the conservation of the *Vasa* had failed. If this was so, the implications for the *Mary Rose* would be serious indeed and during her visit to Stockholm in 1971 with Dr. D. Faulkner, a senior chemist for a leading oil company, Margaret Rule was given full facilities by the *Vasa* conservation department. She came away from Stockholm, as I did later, with immense admiration for the thoroughly scientific and successful conservation of the *Vasa*.

The two final and most popular questions regarding the *Mary Rose* are: how long will it take and how much will it cost? I used to say five years to raise her and five million pounds in all over perhaps twenty years, but these were simply a rough riposte to questions which cannot be answered because too many factors are unknown. If a structure is buried, its size and complexity is unknown; and if it is under the sea, the weather during the working periods is critical and cannot be predicted; so far, finance has always come in, but it has tended to come in late, thus causing delay; and the one really costly item, the permanent museum, involves both land and bricks and mortar, the prices of which have been subjected recently to roaring inflation. A further unknown factor is the number of paying visitors over an unspecified period of time, which brings in money to offset the costs.

One can answer only in general terms. Up to 1970 the *Vasa* project had cost 27 million Kroner and had earned 11 million Kroner. Break-even point in terms of paper money was far away, but the value of the *Vasa* to the national image, to business generally, and to education can never be costed. As far as costs go, these are no real guide to the *Mary Rose* possibilities. To start with, Sweden is a small nation of seven million people (fewer than the inhabitants of London), and even including foreign visitors the potential earnings of the *Vasa* can never match those of the *Mary Rose*, situated $1\frac{1}{2}$

hours by train from London and next door to H.M.S. *Victory* which already attracts nearly half a million visitors a year. The two ships together, Nelson's preserved flagship and Henry VIII's flagship from under the sea, might prove such an attraction in combination as to double the number of visitors to a million annually, particularly if the modern shipping background was stressed. Both the *Vasa* and the new maritime museum at Oslo have good waterfront sites, but they cannot begin to compare in modern interest to the spectacle presented by the variety and multitude of ships using Portsmouth. An imaginative use of this free and mobile background could enable the project to be self-supporting over a period of time.

The most cheerful aspect of my visit to Stockholm was that the *Vasa* people had already thought out what they would do if the *Mary Rose* was raised and became in effect a rival to the *Vasa*. We would have the older ship with an immensely important collection of artefacts, but we could not match the unique wood carving, typical of the later period, which had decorated the *Vasa*; and they would stress these. Their attitude was utterly without jealousy and it was heartening to discover that the only real experts in the world considered that there was a strong possibility that we should be able to lift and display the *Mary Rose*.

APPENDIX

Comparative Gun Lists—Henry VII and Henry VIII
(original spellings)

Sovereign 1495 (as in original, listed by decks)		*Sovereign* 1514 (as in original, listed by weight?)	
Forecastell above in the Dekke:		*Curtalles of Brasse,*	
Serpentynes of Yron	16	stocked upon trotill wheles	3
Somercastell alawe:		*De Curtalles of Brasse,*	
Serpentynes of Yron	24	stocked upon trotill wheles	1
Wast:		*Half Curtalles of Brasse,*	
Stone Gonnes of Yron	20	upon wheles shod with yron	2
Somercastell:		*Grete Yron Gonnes*	
Serpentynes of Yron	20	(chambered)	7
Somercastell:		*Culvryns of Brasse,*	
Serpentynes of Brasse	1	without stock	1
Somercastell:		*Slyngs of Yron,*	
Stone Gonnes	11	stocked (& chambered)	4
Stern:		*Serpentynes of Yron*	
Serpentynes of Yron	4	(chambered)	62
Dekke over Somercastell:		*Culvryns of Brasse,*	
Serpentynes of Yron	25	stocked upon wheles shod with yron	2
Poppe:		*Ffalcons of Brasse,*	
Serpentynes of Yron	20	upon shodd wheles	2

TOTALS:		TOTALS:	
Brass Serpentines (chambered)	1	Battery Guns (brass & iron)	13
Iron Serpentines (chambered)	109	Heavy Long-range Guns (brass, iron)	7
Iron Stone Guns (chambered)	31	Light Long-range Guns (brass)	2
		Iron Serpentines, heavy & light	62
Total	141	Total	84

Note:
The upper decks on same level as the waist probably considered as belonging to the castle above them.

Note.
Three types of gun carriage are listed. Possibly fixed beds without wheels, beds with four small wheels, field mountings with two large wheels.

TABLE 2
Comparative Gun Lists for the Flagships
(modernised spellings)

Mary Rose	1514	*Mary Rose*	1545
Brass Guns (7 heavy, 6 light)		*Brass Guns* (14 heavy, 1 light)	
Great Curtalls	5	Cannons	2
Murderers (chambered)	2	Demi-Cannons	2
Falcons	2	Culverins	2
Falconettes	3	Demi-Culverins	6
Little Gun (chambered)	1	Sakers	2
		Falcons	1
Iron Guns (34 heavy, 31 light?)		*Iron Guns* (24 heavy, 52 light)	
Great Murderers (chambered)	1	Port Pieces (chambered)	12
Murderers (chambered)	1	Slings (chambered?)	2
Cast Pieces (chambered)	2	Demi-Slings (chambered?)	3
Murderers (chambered)	1	Quarter-Slings (chambered?)	1
Slings (chambered)	2	Fowlers (chambered?)	6
Stone Guns (chambered?)	26	Bases (chambered?)	30
Top Guns (chambered)	3	Top Pieces (chambered?)	2
Serpentines (chambered)	28	Hailshot Pieces (chambered?)	20
		Handguns—50	
Total	78	Total	91

Great Harry	1514	*Great Harry*	1545
Brass Guns (13 heavy, 6 light)		*Brass Guns* (19 heavy, 3 light)	
Great Bombardes	1	Cannons	4
Great Curtalls	1	Demi-Cannons	3
Great Culverins	2	Culverins	4
Fair Aragonese Pieces	1	Demi-Culverins	2
Long Vice-Pieces	3	Sakers	4
Small Vice-Pieces	1	Cannon Periers	2
Serpentines	4	Falcons	3
Falcons	6		
Iron Guns (42 heavy, 122 light?)		*Iron Guns* (28 heavy, 102 light)	
Great Pieces (chambered)	12	Port Pieces (chambered)	14
Great Flemish Guns (chambered)	4	Slings (chambered?)	4
Great Spanish Guns (chambered)	2	Demi-Slings (chambered?)	2
Great Stone Guns (chambered)	2	Fowlers (chambered?)	8
Stone Guns (chambered)	22	Bases (chambered?)	60
Slings (chambered)	1	Top Pieces (chambered?)	2
Serpentines (chambered)	122	Hailshot Pieces (chambered?)	40
		Handguns—100	
Total	183	Total	152

Note:

All inventories (except *Great Harry* 1514) list guns in descending order of weight/size, making easy the necessarily arbitrary distinction between heavy and light. The *Great Harry*'s 1514 list has been altered to follow this principle so far as present evidence allows.

TABLE 3

Mary Rose Ordnance and Ammunition as listed in Anthony's Roll, 1546

Gun Type	No.	Shot Total	Rounds per gun	"Ordinary" Gun of the Period	
				Bore	Shot weight
Brass					
Cannons	2	50 iron	25	8 in.	66 lb.
Demi-Cannons	2	60 iron	30	$6\frac{1}{4}$ in.	$30\frac{1}{2}$ lb.
Culverins	2	60 iron	30	$5\frac{1}{2}$ in.	$17\frac{1}{3}$ lb.
Demi-Culverins	6	150 iron	25	$4\frac{1}{2}$ in.	$9\frac{1}{3}$ lb.
Sakers	2	80 iron	40	$3\frac{1}{3}$ in.	$5\frac{1}{3}$ lb.
Falcons	1	60 iron	60	$2\frac{1}{2}$ in.	$2\frac{1}{4}$ lb.
Iron				Calibres, c.1555	
Port Pieces	12	200 stone	16	Bore: $5\frac{1}{2}$–12 in.	
Slings	2	40 iron	20		
Demi-Slings	3	40 iron	13	}Bore: 2–$4\frac{1}{2}$ in.	
Quarter-Slings	1	50 iron	50		
Fowlers	6	170 stone	28	Bore: 3–$5\frac{1}{2}$ in.	
Bases	30	400 lead	13	Bore: $\frac{1}{2}$–2 in	
Top Pieces	2	20 stone	10		
Hailshot Pieces	20	? iron Dice	?		
Handguns	50	1,000 lead	20		

Bows of Yew:		250
Bowstrings:	6 ×	144
Lynere? Arrows in sheaves:		300
Darts for Tops in dozens:	12 ×	40
Morris Pikes:		150
Bills:		150

TABLE 4

Mary Rose Ordnance Salvaged by John Deane, 1836 and 1840

Bronze Guns

Gun Type		Bore	Length	Manufactured by	
Cannon Royal	1	8.54 in.	8′ 6″	Robart and John Owyn	1535
Demi-Canon	1	6. 4 in.	11′ 0″	Arcano de Arcani	1542
Culverin	1	5.20 in.	10′ 11″	Arcano de Arcani	1542
Culvarin-Bastard	1	4.56 in.	8′ 6″		

Wrought-Iron Guns and Chambers

Item		Bore	Length	Carriage	Contents	Salvaged	
Barrel & chamber	1	8 in.	9′ 5″	12′ 1″	Shotted	Aug.	1836
Barrel, broken	1	6? in.			Shotted	Aug.	1836
	1		8′		Shotted		1840
	1		6′ 10″		Shotted		1840
	1		5′ 6″	6′ 6″			1840
	1		5′ 5″				1840
	1		5′ 0″				1840
	1		4′ 6″				1840
	1		2′ 6″	6′ 6″			1840
Chamber?	1		2′ 6″				1840
Chamber?	1		2′ 4″				1840
Chamber?	2		1′ 11″				1840
Chamber?	2		1′ 9″				1840
Large Guns	2	6 in.	6–8 ft.	? ?	Shotted	Oct.	1840
Parts (chambers?)	2		?			Oct.	1840
Warrior's Bows:	8						

Note: Apparently all guns of the built-up type and all shot stone.

TABLE 5

Deane's Ordnance Recoveries compared to Anthony's Roll

Large Brass Guns	4	salvaged out of	14
Small Brass Guns	0	,, ,, ,,	1
Large Iron Guns	11	,, ,, ,,	24
Small Iron Guns or chambers*	9	,, ,, ,,	52+52
Bows of Yew	8	,, ,, ,,	250

*Descriptions imprecise: some could be broken guns.

INDEX